Pietro Pucci
**The Iliad – The Poem of Zeus**

# Trends in Classics –
# Supplementary Volumes

Edited by
Franco Montanari and Antonios Rengakos

Associate Editors
Evangelos Karakasis · Fausto Montana · Lara Pagani
Serena Perrone · Evina Sistakou · Christos Tsagalis

Scientific Committee
Alberto Bernabé · Margarethe Billerbeck
Claude Calame · Jonas Grethlein · Philip R. Hardie
Stephen J. Harrison · Richard Hunter · Christina Kraus
Giuseppe Mastromarco · Gregory Nagy
Theodore D. Papanghelis · Giusto Picone
Tim Whitmarsh · Bernhard Zimmermann

# Volume 66

Pietro Pucci

# The Iliad – The Poem of Zeus

—

DE GRUYTER

ISBN 978-3-11-071014-4
e-ISBN (PDF) 978-3-11-060245-6
e-ISBN (EPUB) 978-3-11-060154-1
ISSN 1868-4785

Library of Congress Control Number: 2018951309

**Bibliographic information published by the Deutsche Nationalbibliothek**
The Deutsche Nationalbibliothek lists this publication in the Deutsche Nationalbibliografie;
detailed bibliographic data are available on the Internet at http://dnb.dnb.de.

© 2020 Walter de Gruyter GmbH, Berlin/Boston
This volume is text- and page-identical with the hardback published in 2018.
Editorial Office: Alessia Ferreccio and Katerina Zianna
Logo: Christopher Schneider, Laufen
Printing and binding: CPI books GmbH, Leck

www.degruyter.com

To Jeannine, My Wife

# Preface

This book has been nourished by the comments of many colleagues who invited me to speak on various occasions at Cornell University and at the university of La Sapienza in Rome. I also owe a lot to stimulating exchanges with Christos Tsagalis, Pierre Judet de La Combe, Patrice Loraux and Egbert Bakker, to the editorial skill of Alexander Brock, and to the extraordinary editorial care and efficiency of Antonios Rengakos. I thank all of them.

# Contents

Preface —— VII

Introduction —— 1

**Chapter 1**
1.1 The "Disastrous Request" (XV. 597): Zeus and Thetis —— 9
1.2 Divine Farce —— 21

**Chapter 2**
2.1 Zeus pities his son Sarpedon —— 32
2.2 Hector's Deadly Destiny —— 41
2.3 Zeus' Conspiracy —— 68
2.4 The Poetic Voice and Mythical Narrative: The Epic Paradox —— 77

**Chapter 3**
3.1 The End of the Wrath: The Beginning of the End —— 83
3.2 The Fatal Breaking of the Pairing —— 91
3.3 Zeus' and Apollo's Conspiracy against Patroclos —— 103
3.4 Doubles Voices —— 118

**Chapter 4**
4.1 Achilles' Destiny and Zeus —— 124
4.2 Zeus and Achilles' immortal horses —— 134
4.3 The Ruinous Madness of *Atê* —— 138
4.4 The *Odysseys*' Reaction to the Iliadic Zeus —— 147

**Chapter 5**
5.1 Zeus challenges the Divine Assembly —— 153
5.2 The Breaking of Zeus' Ban —— 161
5.3 Sex without Love —— 171
5.4 Zeus Restores the Order of Things: The Credentials of Monarchic Power —— 190

**Chapter 6**
6.1 A Perverse Comedy —— 201
6.2 The Breaking of the Truce —— 222
6.3 Zeus Closes the Poem —— 231
6.4 Closing Remarks —— 249

**Appendix 1. δῖος Ἀχιλλεύς. The Notion of Divine as Applied to the Heroes —— 259**

**Appendix 2. The Muses and the Poet —— 265**

**Bibliography —— 269**

**Index of Rhetorical and Critical Notions —— 277**

**Index Locorum —— 281**

# Introduction

The long and stimulating debate on the relationship between immortal and mortal agents in the *Iliad* has produced various critical solutions. On the one hand, the gods are thought to function mostly as poetic, symbolic, or allegorical presences that enhance epic exploits as they are touched by the sublime. In accordance with this approach, such events have meaningful human motivations and deployments, but the image of a god who shares in the action increases their significance and force. When divine presence does not occur within a traditional mythical scene, as, for instance, in a divine assembly, the gods' actions and decisions are thought to be purely poetic, imaginative touches, not real events.

On the other hand, a large part of the recent critical literature maintains that many or all divine interventions emerge as real events that imprint a truthfully divine nature upon epic action.[1] What remains debatable is the specific contribution and the specific miraculous effects of each divine intervention, and, in a larger critical perspective, how and to what extent a given divine intervention tinges and overshadows the human side of the action. The critical novelty of this book lies in reopening and re-analyzing these questions. Focusing on Zeus, the most central, original, and complex figure in the *Iliad*'s Olympus, my research examines his interactions with both human and divine beings. Toward the *Iliad*'s heroes, Zeus functions as the god of blind fate, and accordingly determines their mortal destiny, while he himself is fully untouched by moral, psychological, or personal feelings. His attitude is utterly non-human as he ensures, even physically, the deaths of various mortal characters at their appointed moments. Within this panorama of Zeus' insensitivity toward mortals, the Iliadic Zeus, as I see him, is the embodiment of the divine "vault" that surrounds human beings, as in Carlo Diano's (1955, p. 258) depiction of Iliadic theology: "Under the vault of the whole, of the divine, the subject feels that he is there, as a gift, attracted, and rejected by the mystery, by the *mysterium tremendum et fascinans*." In its economy and exactness, this definition is breathtaking. The *mysterium tremendum et fascinans* is visible and speaks: it is Zeus selecting and implementing the death of the best heroes, thus preparing the destruction of the pious city of Troy.

---

[1] The bibliography is immense. I select a few works from different periods: Kullmann 1956; Montanari 1992; Piettre 1996; Calame 2015; Pironti/Bonnet 2016; Brouillet 2016; Clauss/Cuypers/Kahane 2016; Judet de la Combe 2017.

Among his polyvalent aspects, Zeus is also the god pleased to be honored and celebrated by men's rituals and prayers. In this function, he harbors human, which is to say anthropomorphic, feelings.[2] He loves Sarpedon, admires Hector, and yet preordains and determines their deaths. The conflicting nature of this paradox is so radical that no word, no argument can resolve it. Aware of this, the Iliadic text, through ingenious and tricky textual devices, leaves this conflict open. In the case of Sarpedon and Hector, the poetic voice makes Zeus oblivious of his fatal responsibility so that the god does not suffer any inner conflict while the Audience (= the Narratees) of the Poem can still appreciate Zeus' sensitive concern for mortals. The poetic voice displays the god's superhuman (Zeus' control of destiny) and anthropomorphic motivations (Zeus' pity and love) as conflicting and yet parallel discourses, separated and yet permeable views of the same might, asymmetric and yet hybrid.[3] The text does not wish to lean toward one side at the expenses of the other: it does not resolve the paradox. The text does not wish to dismantle the myth that treats as permeable divine and human voices and deeds.

Another example of this conflict between human and divine agents, motivations and voices is offered by the death of Patroclos: while heroes and text identify Hector as the killer of Patroclos, two divine beings assert that Apollo "killed Patroclos and gave the triumph to Hector." There is more than one way to make sense of this ambiguous phrase, but the text complicates terribly the exact attribution of this death. Finally, the text adopts a sort of wishful hybridism between mortal and immortal action. Through the rhetorical device —a metaphor?— the text construes the contradiction as a parallelism that leaves open its deployment.

The ambivalence and porosity between conflicting terms creates in the Narratees a constant stimulus to sustain one or the other, and therefore a reading that either grants responsibility to the superhuman, pure, divine term, or to the relative independence of the human, earthly term. The invisible Apollo's man-

---

[2] For a recent, stimulating illustration of the polyvalent aspect of the Greek polytheistic pantheon, see Pironti 2009, 289–304. I occasionally use the word "might" to designate the whole potentiality of a god's powers, something like the French "puissance."

[3] I use the terms "permeability" or even "porousness" to characterize a specific association between human and divine worlds in archaic myth. When a god inspires a hero with an epiphany, or with superhuman force, he takes possession of the hero's mind or body, which evidently are permeable to divine invasion and are consequently changed by divine intervention. To the extent that a mortal can wound a god, the permeability also works in a very limited measure in the reverse order. Scholars use terms such as "association," "hybridism" —for instance Laizé 2000, 41— or "cointentionalité," as in the doctoral thesis of Manon Brouillet 2016, 23.

gling of Patroclos' body and the breaking of his armor surpass all human power and could reveal the vanity of the text's attempt at parallelism and hybridism: Apollo is the might that destroys Patroclos. And yet, certainly every mortal spectator saw Hector fighting and killing Patroclos, and the poet himself in a simile supports this view. The Iliadic textual strategy opens to the readers three straightforward ways of interpreting the ambivalence in these scenes. Either the readers assume that the text depicts the collaboration of gods and men, the permeability of divine myth and heroic myth in accordance with the mythical metaphysics, or they assume that the asymmetric, discordant, and even conflicting representation of events is meant to contest the successful hybridism or even to discredit the mirage of a mythical collaboration between men and gods. I try to assess the pertinence and the consistency of both interpretations in all these episodes, and most often I conclude with a third interpretation: that the text programmatically leaves open the conflict and manages to leave to the reader an access to the idea of the permeability and hybridism of these terms. While the collaboration is real and effective, its paradoxical and conflictual nature requires men's recognition and endurance: men cannot fully count on the stability of that collaboration, nor trust all its promises, but must ultimately live in the uncertainty of the true being and meaning of the events and endure the naked and desolate human condition.

From this reading situation it ensues that most poetic-mythical-religious notions like divine anthropomorphic attitudes, human piety, free will, variety of motivations, etc., are affected by the chosen interpretation.

In the course of this *Introduction* I will illuminate some of these notions and attitudes, but first I want briefly to illustrate the behavior that the text attributes to Zeus in his relation to the gods. In fact, this book is structured by separating episodes in which Zeus deals with the gods from those in which he controls human destiny. The difference between the two orders is essential, for a divine destiny does not exist, since gods are immortal and forever young.

Though Zeus is the mastermind and perpetrator of the basic Iliadic action, he is slow to share his plan (*boulê*) with the other gods, a prerogative he defends with secrecy and the menace of violence when he is contradicted. Such a position is new, almost foreign and exotic, in relation to what we know of him in the hypertext.[4] Even Hera's traditional hostility toward Zeus is no longer grounded

---

4 With "hypertext" the recent Homeric criticism (see for instance Tsagalis 2012) refers to the whole mythical narrative and lore that surrounds the text during its composition. This narrative comprehends poetic compositions, rituals, and other mythical speeches, as well as iconographic representations. This description is in part analogous to the one which, under a differ-

in her jealousy, but is exclusively a political enmity. His resentment is no longer focused on her mistreatment of Heracles, but on her obstruction of his plans.[5] Hera's persecution of Heracles and Zeus' violence against her are abundantly present in the *Iliad*, but as past events, and we gain the impression that the text in these and analogous re-evocations adopts a half-ironic tone, sounding almost like a parody: it felicitously intimates that such erotic quarrels and violence will not be repeated.

In such ironic and amusing instances, the analogy between the Poet's and Zeus' stance toward tradition becomes conspicuous: meta-poetically, the Poet endorses Zeus when, by granting victory to the Trojans, he breaks the hypertextual representation of Zeus sustaining the Achaeans in view of the destruction of Troy. The poet, allied with Zeus, mocks Hera's hatred for Troy and Poseidon's attempt to save the Achaeans.

The text seems to mock the prior Zeus, the one who punishes Troy for the crime of Paris, a god victim of a jealous wife, and threatened by many odd contenders. The Poet has fun in using comic, almost Aristophanic, touches in depicting with amusing contrasts his new Olympian god.

Unfortunately, we cannot compare the Iliadic text with its sources, models, and contemporary versions so as to judge what appears to be the Iliad's parodic intent: only a precise comparison would allow us to define the reflexive intensity and the innovative, even revolutionary force of the Iliadic text.

The Iliadic Zeus' polyvalent might unfolds through special and unique characteristics: since he is identified as the master of human destinies, he both enjoys an exclusive power among the gods, placing himself in a sort of monotheistic position, and hides his final intentions and motivations. These characteristics mark him in a radical way and depict an original and shocking image of

---

ent classification and purpose, Martin (2005, 14–15) upholds when he speaks of the Greek epic works in this way: "the set of allowable intertexts (oral or written), embracing all those compositions that communicate through consistent mutual allusivity. [...] Clearly, generic interplay and expansion, allusion and multiformity, were essential to the art of *epopoiia* in archaic Greek. It does not make sense to isolate only some of the resultant multilayered compositions as 'epic.'"

5 The diachronic analysis of these different versions is the core of Erbse's (1986) research. See also de Romilly 1983, 10–41. The Poet's silence on Zeus' purposes and motivations does not mean that Zeus does not have any, but that they are inscrutable. Elmer (2013, 155 ff.) touches on these differences in an exciting analysis of the Proem. See on p. 158: "By framing the plot in terms of an ambiguous 'will of Zeus' [concerning his promise to Thetis, the war of Troy, the traditional motivations for the destruction of Troy] the *Iliad* proem promotes an initially open-ended and impartial understanding of the story, especially by comparison with the variant known to Aristoxenos."

him. The most problematic and troubling feature of Zeus as master of destinies is his reticence. His silence about the ultimate motivations and aims of his decisions leaves his governance based on no principles or ultimate purposes, so that his decrees – and the actions he takes to implement them – are suspended in an ethical and political void. No notion of justice, convenience, decency, etc. grounds Zeus' operations, with the result that they thus appear intended for immediacy; they are not endorsed by all-embracing values and seem therefore sporadic and, ultimately, incoherent. Zeus imposes his will —his *boulê*— by threatening brutal physical force, which grants him victory, but this victory does not bring any value or meaning to his governance.

The immediate consequence of Zeus' radical reticence affects negatively the human stage: Zeus' lack of transparency turns mortals into the victims of an unmotivated and paradoxical violence; Zeus' holy might unfolds a sort of negative theology. Theologically speaking, Zeus' reticence is a direct function of his role as provider of destiny. It is a lucid decision of the text to avoid inventing what Zeus' superhuman mind would say to legitimize his decisions, his wars, and his massacres. The paradoxical trouble arises because Zeus personifies that blind destiny, while he is simultaneously an anthropomorphic speaking and thinking being, and the divine natural force controlling or impersonating the world of the sky and heaven.

The consequences of Zeus' lack of transparency affect also his relations with his divine peers. At more than halfway through the Poem Zeus finally gives to his peers a very short account of what will follow according to his will. Only then does he assure them that Troy will fall. Had he been ready to tell them that he honors Achilles because he cannot fail to consent to Thetis' request, or for whatever other reasons, he might have avoided a quarrel with his peers. But he could not, at least not until the book eighth when his new posture toward the Trojans promised to Thetis in the first book becomes operative. Even then, he is sparing with information for declaring the motivation of his *boulê* would have caused endless and unnecessary discussion. He is not a politician, but an achiever, not simply one among the Olympians, but a god quite different from them: a solitary monotheist, an immense might, more powerful than he needs to be in order to control the world, and less capable or willing than he should be in order to display meaning and sense to the order of the world he controls.[6]

---

[6] In the *Iliad* there is no space for a separated status that we call "authority," with its own legitimacy on various grounds —historical, moral, practical, etc. In this poem, "authority" is necessarily dependent on brute, physical force. The fact that the divine world's hierarchical

Ultimately, the consequence of Zeus' total reticence will be his failure to constitute himself as the indisputable founder of a religious system, and the *Iliad* will be a theological text constantly open to fundamental revisions and reformulations. The Iliadic Zeus leaves to Greek culture the difficult task of construing and de-constructing, adding and deleting, elevating and marginalizing the figure of Zeus.

Important notions and effects like piety, immortalization of the heroes, and divine epiphanies are marked by the unresolved tensions that the superhuman will and the divine myth create when meeting the human will and the heroic myth. Mortal beings are unable to share in anything immortal within a real and lasting exchange. The *Iliad*, more decidedly than the *Odyssey*,[7] denies any immortalization of mortals after their death.

The anthropomorphic aspects of gods that open some permeability between them and men are, however, simultaneously inscribed in the gods' immortal and miraculous valence. The divine epiphany, for instance, reaches mortals as a miraculous event, the nature of which mortals cannot explain and the supernatural sense of which they cannot preserve after it touches them. At one point, Zeus, with his divine hand, pushes Hector forward, but neither Hector nor the narrative can explain what it meant for him to lose the familiar sense of space and time and to feel moved, not simply forward, but also outside his own human, mortal, and limited capabilities.

As I have indicated, the language of the Poem leaves open and unlimited interpretations in crucial passages. The language of the *Iliad* is itself prisoner of the conflicting tension between its superhuman source and its mortal and human deployment. The Poet of the *Iliad* invites the Muses, the daughters of Zeus, to inspire him: "Tell me now, Muses, who inhabit the houses of Olympus, for you are goddesses, you are present [to the events] and you know all things…" (*Il.* II. 484 ff.).[8] With such a request, the Poet's voice implies that he needs the help of the divine voice for the creation of his work: he opens a communication with the divine world, trusting its permeability and counting on hybrid cooperation.

---

structure depends on mere physical force, analogously to what happens in the world of men or animals, is a curious and embarrassing feature.

7 Tsagalis 2016, 116 shows how frequently the immortalization of the hero occurs in the Cyclic epic in sharp contrast with Homer, and quotes Zeus' inability to prevent the death of Hector.

8 How the Poet perceives and can record the inspirational process remains for us a problematic and difficult work of imagination and speculation: the Iliadic Poet does not record the sort of personal vision of the Muses that, for instance, Hesiod narrates in *Th.* 26–29. See some remarks on these questions on p. 178 ff. and Appendix 2.

Although the poetic voice intervenes with personal inflections. human versions of the events and comments, using specifically epic utterances such as similes, apostrophes, soliloquies, commentaries,[9] etc., it explicitly aims at reporting appropriately the Muses' narrative, which is to say the divine view of the events.

Contrary to the trust the Poet places in a felicitous hybridism between his and the divine Muses' voices, the epic events that this voice narrates unfold in such a way that the collaboration between mortals and immortals turns out to be problematic, paradoxical, and often disastrous.

Since the Muses' narrative contests or suspends the felicitous permeability and hybridism between gods and men in the heroic age, the Poet of the *Iliad* must think himself to be blessed by the gods just like the Iliadic character Calchas, or like a modern prophet in the time of the Poet's life. Epic poetry presented itself as a felicitous channel for the communication between men and gods. Through this divine, open channel we learn, however, about the inconsistency and rarity, even in the heroic age, of a providential, porous, and hybrid cooperation between mortals and immortals. This paradox is inscribed in, and composes, the Poem.

While the human characters of the Poem are prisoners of the heroic paradox,[10] the Narratees receive, however, a favor from the Poem: they learn about the *Mysterium* and about the human condition from the divine chair of the Muses. The Narratees contemplate the complex knot of the relationships between men and gods from the perspective of the gods themselves. The Poem, as a theological and metaphysical text, teaches the Narratees the harsh rules of that *Mysterium*.[11]

Most of the human characters of the Poem believe in the fair and appropriate help of Zeus, but the narrative has the extraordinary lucidity and audacity to show to the Narratees that Zeus does not correspond to the characters' beliefs, and that, therefore, the characters are often deceived and wronged. It is an incredibly violent and radical lesson.

This negative theology, exemplified by Zeus and his terrible reticence, depicts for the Narratees the nonsense of the events. Even for modern reader, the Iliadic figure of Zeus describes the unintelligible course of human history. It

---

9 See Tsagalis' brilliant pages (2006, 87 ff.) on the Poet's "commentaries" in Homer and Hesiod.
10 Perhaps only Achilles, the son of the goddess, escapes at least partially the ignorance of the rules whereby Zeus brings the heroes to death.
11 For the relationship between language, myth, and poetry, see Ernest Cassirer *Zur Metaphysik der symbolischen Formen*.

teaches men facing action that the gesture of choosing with care and scruple from a chaotic or contradictory horizon of alternatives does not ensure any winning consequence: it may grant only the advantage of recognizing one's right and noble consciousness.

# Chapter 1

## 1.1 The "disastrous request" (XV. 597): Zeus and Thetis

> "Les dieux helléniques sont des Puissances, non des personnes."
> Vernant 1965, 274

In the first book[1] Zeus leads the gods as they all go together to Olympus (πρὸς Ὄλυμπον ἴσαν θεοὶ αἰὲν ἐόντες[2] / πάντες ἅμα, Ζεὺς δ' ἦρχε· I. 494–5[3]): they are returning from the land of the Aethiopians[4] (where they enjoyed a feast). Zeus appears here as a *primus inter pares*, but when Thetis reaches him she finds him sitting apart from the others (I. 498–99):

> she found the deep thunder-voicing son of Kronos sitting
> apart from the others upon the highest peak of rugged Olympus.[5]

Confronted with Zeus' leadership of the gods in the previous passage, his isolation on the highest peak of Olympus, where he sits apart from the other gods, is emphatically stressed. The geographical emphasis, "on the highest peak of Olympus," designates figuratively not only Zeus' uniquely preeminent position of authority among the gods, but also his clear separation from all the other gods[6] and his privacy, expressed by that detail "sitting" which in Homer often

---

[1] Tsagalis (2008, 209–238) has written a splendid and creative analysis of the supplication scene (I. 493–530), providing illuminating remarks on its style and its composition in the network of hypertextual versions. I quote from it what I find relevant to my themes.
[2] "The gods who live forever" (four times in the *Iliad*). Either as an epithet or as a noun, the word *athanatos* ("deathless," "immortal") qualifies the gods more than one hundred times in the *Iliad*.
[3] Syntactically and rhetorically (by chiasmus) the text singles out Zeus from the other gods.
[4] Tsagalis (2008, 214 ff.) finely describes the solemnity the text exudes in referring to this return.
[5] "In the late Hellenistic treaty *Peri kosmou* where a pseudo-Aristotelian author summarizes the cosmology of Aristotle, the narrative traverses the universe from its center (the earth) to the outermost sphere (the celestial vault of the fixed stars). The upper region is the abode of the deity, who is supreme, dwelling, in the words of Homer, 'on the loftiest crest of the heaven'" (I. 499). Wildberg 1999–2000, 236.
[6] Rousseau ch. 5, p. 9 develops the same argument. Tsagalis (2008, 218, n. 39) writes: "Zeus, the only god mentioned by name, is synchronically presented as a separated and independent agent, whose opposition to the rest of the Olympians will become obvious as the plot unravels." See Tsagalis' comments in his next work (2012, 141 ff.) where he derives precious psychological, symbolic and poetic insights (a sort of "theography") from the geographical features of the gods' mountain.

denotes metaphorically the individual's separation from others' activities (see for instance I. 421, 488, etc.).[7]

The *diêgêsis* (the Muses' narrative in the hands of the Iliadic Narrator) at 498 defines Zeus as εὐρύοπα Κρονίδην, "son of Kronos with deep thundering voice":[8] both epithets deserve our attention, since this selection is the Narrator's authorial choice in a non-epiphanic address line.

This epithet recalls Zeus' control of the sky and specifically both the thunder by which Zeus often communicates his will to mortals, and the lightning by which he often terrorizes mortals. The text figuratively combines Zeus' mastery in the sky with his monarchic power over gods and mortals: his descent from Kronos, the monarch of the Titans, qualifies him to hold such power. Finally, his uniqueness and isolation characterizes his function as master of destinies, since he will decide, in secret and apart from the other gods, the victory of the Trojans. All three functions of Zeus' polyvalent Might are here recalled.

The Narrator selects here *Kronides* and, immediately after, with the same freedom of choice, Δία Κρονίωνα ἄνακτα ("Zeus, lord, son of Kronos")[9] on line 502, and Κρονίων, "son of Kronos," on line 528. Though these epithets are frequent in the *Iliad*, the emphatic repetition of Kronos' paternity of Zeus in so few lines could be significant. As this paternity designates primarily not a biological relationship, but rather carries a social and religious connotation, these epithets celebrate Zeus as the supreme might among the gods, as Kronos once was. *Kronides* and *Kroniôn* are never used for any other gods, but only for Zeus,

---

[7] This private and supreme position does not only qualify Zeus' monarchic role among the gods, but is also needed for the meeting with Thetis: in order to obtain its calculated effect, the provisional nature of the Trojan victory must remain unknown to the other gods, and accordingly also to the human characters.

[8] The word εὐρύοπα can have a different meaning, "with a large sight," but the frequent connection of Zeus with thunder as his medium of communication with mortals induces me to prefer what could be also the older meaning of the expression that Chantraine *DELG* and Kirk 1985 assume. The whole noun-epithet phrase is used two other times (XV. 152 and XXIV. 98), always by the *diêgêsis* when some god (Iris, Thetis again) reaches him, obeying his summons, while he is making substantial decisions. It is a noun-epithet that characterizes him for his political and universal power. It could also be the choice of the Narrator for its strong assonance, εὗρεν δ' εὐρύοπα Κρονίδην.

[9] This whole noun-epithet phrase is a *hapax* in Homer in the accusative, but occurs four times in the *Iliad* in the dative, of which two occur in *diêgêsis* (II. 102 and VII. 200), always on solemn occasions. Here the situation is extremely grave and ceremonial: a goddess (!) is accomplishing the ritual of supplication to Zeus, who, like Kronos, his father, is the mighty lord of the gods.

though of course some of the other Olympian gods (Hades, Poseidon, Hera, Demeter) are also sons and daughters of Kronos.[10]

In Hesiod, Zeus is *basileus* (king) and in the *Iliad*, Zeus is *anax* (king, savior, protector),[11] never *basileus*. Wackernagel (see *DELG* s.v. *basileus*) assumed that *basileus* is a more recent word than *anax*.

Kronos' insistently and almost uniquely declared paternity of Zeus must also suggest Zeus' stronger force and his greater religious and political dominance. Zeus defeated Kronos and keeps him prisoner (VIII. 478–81): accordingly, the insistent mention of Kronos functions also as an insistent assertion of Zeus' unmatchable power.

The combination of Zeus' "deep-thundering voice" with his unique religious and political dominance, both of which separate him from his brothers and sisters, decreases the anthropomorphic and familial features of Zeus. It projects his image up high as a natural phenomenon of the sky and simultaneously as the absolute holder of political and fatal power. The context, however, preserves some anthropomorphic color, since the ritual of supplication is essentially a human ritual, and Thetis' request of honoring her son steeps her demand in a family-related context.[12] The text keeps silent on the menace that Thetis could have been for Zeus, had he generated a child with her. This silence is preserved during the whole supplication scene.

With these remarks on the anthropomorphic features of the two gods in this scene, I intend to recall Detienne's arguments about the impropriety and incorrectness of some of our understanding of the anthropomorphism of the Greek gods.[13] Some of their typical behavior and characteristics contest what we understand about their human-likeness: the fact that the god was thought of as inhabiting his/her own statue or image should create some caution in using that

---

**10** A few times Hera is called "daughter of great Kronos" in the form: Ἥρη πρέσβα θεὰ θυγάτηρ μεγάλοιο Κρόνοιο, V. 721=VIII. 383, XIV. 194, 243. Poseidon once is identified with Zeus, in a dual form, as the son of Kronos: δύω Κρόνου υἷε κραταιώ, XIII. 345, and he himself once boasts of being the son of Kronos (XV. 187–88). See Higbie 1995, 53. On p. 23 she writes: "By not using the proper patronymic for Poseidon, Homer might intentionally reduce Poseidon's power in order to maintain a certain focus to his story, a focus which he moves out of only twice in the two mentioned passages." See also Pirenne-Delforge and Pironti 2016, 30.
**11** In the *Iliad*, *anax* occurs eight times for Zeus, and the vocative *ana* is used only for him. In the article on *anax*, Chantraine (*DELG*) emphasizes the connotation of "protector and savior" implicit in the word.
**12** Both a goddess's supplication to the main god and her prayer in favor of a third person are amply present in the Ancient Eastern tradition: see West 1997, 353.
**13** On the signification of "anthropomorphism" in respect to the gods, on its limits, and in its function in the *Iliad*, see also Appendix 2.

definition. In the *Iliad* we see Thetis emerging from the sea "as mist": this is probably not a metaphor, but a form she takes to emerge from the waves. Athena descends from Olympus as a meteor and as such she reaches the ground. Accordingly, the epithets that describe Zeus as a sky and storm god, while he acts and speaks as a person, do not sound simply "traditional" and passively employed: they attach to him a larger dimension that is not anthropomorphic. This larger dimension is present even if it is obscured or ignored in the necessary dramatization of family relationships, dialogues, and actions.[14] I am aware of the complexity of the problem that I am here simply touching upon.

As Thetis, a sea goddess, suddenly reaches Zeus, the god of thunder, she crouches beside him and accomplishes ritual supplication by embracing his knees with her left hand and by grasping his chin from below with her right hand (I. 500–03).[15]

If Thetis displays such a dramatic and self-humiliating gesture, she must realize that she is going to require from Zeus an almost impossible decision, a crazy one, which will create troubles for him. Indeed, it implies the breaking of the traditional alliance of Zeus with the Achaeans. She has no powerful arguments to persuade him: she apparently knows of no ethical principle, justice for instance, into which she may inscribe the fact that Agamemnon has dishonored Achilles by stealing his prize.[16] She only demands reparation, an action that may re-establish Achilles' honor.[17] Her arguments are emotionally grounded on this point (I. 503–510):

---

[14] See on this topic Lloyd 1996, 200: "... in a certain context, the conception of the society of the gods may be said to have a certain quasi cosmological significance..., at least in so far as some of the gods are connected or even identified with world-areas or even with what we should call natural phenomena."

[15] Kelly 2007, 250, n.1 favors the idea that Thetis' utterance has the characteristics of a prayer and argues, "If this were to be interpreted as a prayer by the audience, they would intuit the success of Thetis' supplication, as its substance is not traditionally impossible."

[16] Achilles himself and Athena in their dialogue at I. 202–18 define Agamemnon's offence as a matter of *hubris* (203, 214): "insolence," "arrogance."

[17] Tsagalis 2008, 211: "Thetis' supplication unravels the first thread of the poem, i.e. the fulfillment of Achilles' will, which is how the *Iliad* translates his wrath (*mênis*) against Agamemnon."

Zeus father,[18] if ever before in word or action
I did you favor among the immortals, now grant me this wish:
honor my son, who has the shortest life among all.[19]
Agamemnon has dishonored him, has taken and holds his prize.[20]
Come! Do him honor, Olympian clever and efficient Zeus,[21]
grant victory to the Trojans[22] until the Achaeans
give my son compensation and increase him in honor.[23]

Thetis' first argument refers, very discreetly, to the favor that Thetis, as Achilles has recalled (I. 396–406), did to Zeus when she helped to save him from the plot

---

**18** The appellative Ζεῦ πάτερ has a religious connotation, which is difficult to render in modern languages. Zeus is conceived of as ruler of men and gods (many times in the *Iliad* and in the *Odyssey*); he is lord over all gods and all men (II. 669, XII. 241–42); he is the dispenser of good and bad things to men (XXIV. 527–33), of war to men (XIX. 224), as the anonymous voice repeats at IV. 84: "Zeus ... dispenser of wars to mortals." And see II. 118–19 where Agamemnon says of Zeus: "...before now he has broken the crowns of many cities / and will break them again, since his power is beyond all others." The passage is repeated at IX. 25:

ὅς δὴ πολλάων πολίων κατέλυσε κάρηνα
ἠδ' ἔτι καὶ λύσει· τοῦ γὰρ κράτος ἐστὶ μέγιστον.

The verb λύσει repeats the composite verb κατέλυσε, and, as often in poetry, in a sequence of repeated verbs, the simple form acquires force for it brings out the immediacy of the verb's meaning. Here it gains supplementary force by closing the clause.

**19** 505: τίμησόν μοι υἱὸν ὅς ὠκυμορώτατος ἄλλων. The long superlative takes up a large part of the line, and constitutes an insistent characterization of Achilles, granting him a strong pathetic appeal for the audience (I. 352, XVIII. 95, etc.). The subtext would have evoked, for the ancient Narratees, the story of the divine decision to have Thetis marry a mortal, since her son from a divine father would have been stronger than his father. See note 25 and Ch. 5.3, p.176.

**20** ἠτίμησεν· ἑλὼν γὰρ ἔχει γέρας αὐτὸς ἀπούρας. The notion of honor is central in Thetis' words.

**21** 508: ἀλλὰ σύ πέρ μιν τῖσον Ὀλύμπιε μητίετα Ζεῦ. For the rare and specific position of Zeus' proper name in the vocative at the end of the verse, see Kahane 1994, 104: "It is interesting that Zeus' only 3 times terminal PNVs appear as Thetis, Achilleus, and Athene make their respective requests of him, requests which will determine virtually the whole plots of the Homeric epics. Terminal position is thus linked not so much with the epic protagonists [for whom, as Kahane shows, such terminal PNVs are common] as with their 'narrative destinies.' Setting such destinies is precisely Zeus' role in Homer." The half-verse expression Ὀλύμπιε μητίετα Ζεῦ is found only here.

**22** Achilles at I. 408–9 had asked for a more precise and determined form of punishment: "to pin the Achaeans back against the ships and the sea, dying, so that thus they may all have profit of their own king." His sarcasm implies the desire for revenge not only against the king but also against his comrades who have left him alone facing the violence of Agamemnon. He had cried (I. 231–32) that Agamemnon was ruling "nonentities," otherwise his outrage against Achilles would have been Agamemnon's last. Thetis singles out Agamemnon's outrage and requests a generic dominance of the Trojans over the Achaeans.

**23** Or "improve his honor by compensation."

organized by Hera, Athena, and Poseidon.[24] She does not mention it explicitly, and thus Zeus can impute whatever value he will to her past assistance. She must conclude that the argument, grounded on the reciprocity of favors (*do ut des*), does not have great force, since when she repeats her supplication she alludes to it only very indirectly. She has no other explicit arguments with which to persuade Zeus, but the audience does, and the reader may detect some implicit innuendos. First, Thetis' hint that Achilles has the shortest life among all may silently allude to the myth according to which Zeus saves himself by not marrying Thetis, as he was ready to do, and from whom he would have generated an immortal son stronger than himself.[25] It is, however, important to notice that this allusion, if it is there, is remote: mentions or recalls of Zeus' amorous life are almost completely nonexistent in the *Iliad*: the large exception, in book XIV, is caused by Aphrodite's magic erotic band and is intended to show its exceptionality (see Ch. 5.3). In the *Iliad*, Zeus' concerns are fully addressed to his fatal and monarchic roles.

Such an allusive hint would have no persuasive power, but rather would cause an emotional response by the audience, since they see Thetis as a pathetic and marginal goddess, mother of a mortal son, instead of the glorious one that she could have had.

Thetis' strongest persuasive argument is that Agamemnon has dishonored Achilles and that therefore Zeus should help to re-establish Achilles' honor. For Zeus *can* help, and his help would efficiently change the situation: "Come! Do him honor, Olympian clever and efficient Zeus!" (ἀλλὰ σύ πέρ μιν τῖσον Ὀλύμπιε μητίετα Ζεῦ). Out of the sixteen occurrences of the noun-epithet μητίετα Ζεύς, the epithet enhances sometimes the intellectual value of *metis*, sometimes its connotation of efficiency. At I. 175 Agamemnon shouts to Achilles to leave the war, as he has threatened to do: I, he says, will not remain alone since there are other leaders with me "who will honor me and above all clever and efficient Zeus":

---

[24] For some critics, this is an archaic-sounding myth, probably invented by Homer to sustain, at least indirectly, Thetis' request to honor Achilles and to crush the Achaeans (see Griffin 1978, 7). It is no coincidence that the three conspirators are Zeus' brother and sister, and Athena, his daughter. Poseidon could be fighting to conquer the royal position of Zeus, with the help of his sister and Athena: a new reconstituted family.

[25] This myth is the basis of the pseudo-Aeschylean *Prometheus Bound*. Tsagalis (2008, 232 ff.) elaborates a strong argument on the importance of this theme. On this subtext, see also Slatkin 1991, 101. As she puts rather dramatically: "The price of Zeus' hegemony is Achilleus' death." In fact, there are no succession crises for Zeus in the *Iliad*, no menacing Titans, no Prometheus. See also Wilson 2002, 64–70.

πάρ' ἔμοιγε καὶ ἄλλοι
οἵ κέ με τιμήσουσι, μάλιστα δὲ μητίετα Ζεύς.

Agamemnon, aware of Achilles' possible desertion, imagines that his peers and especially Zeus, will cleverly, miraculously help him —to win the war, of course —, and honor him. At II. 197 in a similarly conflicting and passionate context, Odysseus shouts to one of the fleeing leaders that "the wrath of the kings nursed by the gods is violent: honor comes to them from Zeus and they are dear to clever and efficient Zeus":

θυμὸς δὲ μέγας ἐστὶ διοτρεφέων βασιλήων,
— τιμὴ δ' ἐκ Διός ἐστι, φιλεῖ δέ ἑ μητίετα Ζεύς.

At XVI. 349, a "clever and efficient Zeus" who already honored Achilles (237) is begged by Achilles to give triumph and safe return to Patroclos; at XII. 292 the same Zeus drives "divine Sarpedon" like a lion to break apart the battlements (308). It is a dramatic moment of reversing the fighting situation. Sarpedon will then describe the honor of the king in a most famous passage, XII. 310 ff.[26]

In many cases, as also in the passages we have mentioned, the context evokes Zeus as a provider of something that will efficiently change a situation and reverse it (as in I. 508).[27] In our passage (I. 508), Thetis begs Zeus to create the situation whereby the dishonored Achilles will recover his honor: the clever and efficient means to accomplish this is to reverse the course of events and to give victory to the Trojans. It is a hard path, requiring efficient, masterful actions.

Thetis' appeal to honor also constitutes the persuasive argument in her second supplication. She admonishes Zeus that his refusal would make her a most dishonored (ἀτιμοτάτη) goddess among all the gods.[28] All this does not create a

---

**26** On this famous passage, see Pucci 1998. The meaning of the epithet has permitted all sorts of renderings: "wise," "Zeus of the counsels" (Latimore), "sapiente" (Cerri), "prudent" (Lasserre), "who rules the world" (Fagles).
**27** The person or the text evoking μητίετα Ζεύς has confidence in his skill and masterful power to obtain the reversal (I. 508, VIII. 170, XII. 292, XV. 377, XVI. 249, XXIV. 314). Zeus possesses the means to effect a new situation by giving honor, victory, help, or the exact opposite. In some of these cases, Zeus reacts or answers with thunder (VII. 478, VIII. 170, XV. 377). In some cases he is preparing or considering evils (X. 104, XI. 278) that reverse a situation and force the hero to abandon the fight, thus losing honor and glory. It is not therefore "wisdom" or "counsel" that the epithet attributes to Zeus in these contexts, but what is specific of *metis*, skill, efficiency, craft, mastery: in a word, "practical intelligence," as Chantraine defines it in *DELG*.
**28** Because of Thetis' presentation of herself as "the most dishonored of all gods" (I. 515–16), if Zeus rejects her plea, he would realize that he is behaving toward her as Agamemnon behaves toward Achilles (I. 171, 244, 505–06). Zeus cannot stand this implicit comparison.

strong argument in favor of a decision that, as Zeus knows, will be opposed by some of his peers. In fact, the *diêgêsis* at XV. 597 defines Thetis' request as "a prayer overstepping destiny," or "disastrous," as it is often interpreted (ἐξαίσιον ἀρὴν).[29] Indeed, by accepting Thetis' request, Zeus will find the accomplishment of his original plans complicated, and will be forced to hold to a doubly contradictory policy.[30]

It is therefore not surprising that Zeus remains silent a long time (I. 511–12),[31] as if he were unable to agree, and at the same time unable to refuse. His silence constitutes a dramatic discourse to himself. During this long moment, Thetis does not relax her hold upon his knees, and once more raises her request (I. 512–16):[32]

---

[29] The word literally means "beyond what is ordained or fated" (Liddle-Scott) and is understood metaphorically as "immoderate," and therefore" "wrong." See Janko 1992 at XV. 598–99. In this context the Poet reminds his audience that Thetis' request was overstepping the traditional destiny concerning Zeus' attitude towards Troy (XV. 598–99: Θέτιδος δ' ἐξαίσιον ἀρὴν / πᾶσαν ἐπικρήνειε· τὸ γὰρ μένε μητίετα Ζεὺς, "[Zeus wished] to accomplish entirely the prayer of Thetis, that was behind the established destiny. Clever-efficient Zeus was waiting for this [i.e. the burning of one Achaean ship]"). For Zeus to give victory to the Trojans means to overstep the pro-Achaean stance that the tradition attributed to him. Since Zeus' decision implies enormous losses of men and the killing of some of the best heroes, it is also a disastrous decision. For Zeus the first implication of the word is the preoccupying feature of his decision; for the Poet and his audience, it is the double implication that is troubling.

[30] Elmer 2013, 159 ff. illustrates perfectly this situation by analyzing it as "Zeus' politics of exceptionalism." Some critics try to give some substance to Zeus' decision to champion Achilles' honor. Whitman 1958, 225 ff. implies that there is a sort of identification between Achilles and Zeus when the god promises to honor Achilles: "from this time on Zeus slowly acquires the characteristics which have made him appear violent and irresponsible. The so-called 'plan of Zeus' is the immediate offspring of the Wrath of Achilles" (p. 226). On the troubles that Zeus' *boulê* creates for Zeus' larger and traditional plan, the destruction of Troy, see Scodel 2017, 83 ff.

[31] In line 511: ὣς φάτο· τὴν δ' οὔ τι προσέφη νεφεληγερέτα Ζεύς, "So she spoke: but Zeus gatherer of clouds answered her nothing." The negative οὔ shockingly breaks, for the only time, the regularity of the formula. In the dialogue between Thetis and Zeus, the *diêgêsis* introduces Zeus' speech only with the verse (511 and 517) that closes with νεφεληγερέτα Ζεύς. This line often contains an indication of Zeus' mode of being: angry (I. 517, IV. 30, VII. 454), looking darkly (V. 588), or smiling (VIII. 38). The "naturalistic" force of the epithet combines with the anthropomorphic features of silence: Zeus gathers the clouds in order to prepare a tempest, to send warning thunderclaps as messages of his mindset; his silence is his message: terribly dissappointing message for Thetis, and an equivocal one for the Audience.

[32] "The poet, in a unique instance of repetition of this part of the type-scene, has Thetis timidly renew her request." (Edwards 1987, 185).

> Unfailingly give me the promise and nod in agreement[33]
> or refuse it – you have nothing to fear – so that I may learn
> to what extent I am the most dishonored of all gods.[34]

Zeus cannot dishonor her and yields (517–25). The text first depicts "cloud-gathering Zeus" as "deeply disturbed" or "troubled" (517: Τὴν δὲ μέγ' ὀχθήσας προσέφη νεφεληγερέτα Ζεύς),[35] and then it records his worrying message:

> A disastrous affair! For you will set me in conflict
> with Hera, whenever she will irritate me with insulting words.[36]
> For, even as things are, forever among the immortals
> she chides me and maintains that I support the Trojans in battle.
> But now go back again, lest Hera may see us.[37]
> I will take care of these things that they be accomplished.[38]

Instead of asserting that Thetis' request is troubling or impertinent because it is contrary to (or overstepping) destiny (ἐξαίσιον ἀρήν, XV. 597), of which he is guarantor, Zeus turns his eyes to the gods of whom he is the monarch and laments that accomplishing Thetis request would mean quarreling with Hera, his sister and wife. She has no legitimate authority in any of his roles – storm and sky god, monarch and lord of fate – except, as she claims and as is indeed the case, she is a god just like he is and she is his wife (see IV. 57–61, XVIII. 364–66).

The Poet places his Zeus in another context of the god's traditional figure — Zeus' quarrels with Hera— that immediately decreases his majesty as in line 522: "But now go back again, lest Hera may see us." The fear of being spied by his wife is slightly comic for the great Zeus.

---

**33** νημερτὲς μὲν δή μοι ὑπόσχεο καὶ κατάνευσον: the second part of the line ὑπόσχεο καὶ κατάνευσον is a variously inflected phrase in Homer (in the *Iliad* see II. 112, IX. 19, XII. 236, XIII. 362, XV. 374), but only in our passage (I. 512) are the promise and the nodding qualified by νημερτές ("unfailing, sure, truthful"), which powerfully initiates the line and gives new energy to the expression.
**34** She might mean that her own specific help and her general value are not recognized.
**35** Zeus gives an answer that reveals his mode of being and his difficult solution. Not a storm, but almost. Notice again the PNN.
**36** For the syntax of the text, see Kirk 1985 and Chantraine 1953, 2. 258, who confers a future meaning to the expression.
**37** He thinks that he is not observed in the isolated place where he sits, but Hera is presently spying on them: see I. 555 ff. His shaking of Olympos tells the gods that he is taking an important decision, but he does not know that he is actually being spied upon.
**38** For an analysis of the rhetorical force of the passage, see Kirk 1985, 108.

It is typical of the Iliadic Narrator to avoid psychological arguments to explain his characters' decisions: here once more the text has him evoking the structure or game of forces in which he is involved and by which he might be troubled: the text sees Zeus' real conditions of power rather than his supposed mental operations.

However, the evocation of Zeus' traditional brawls with Hera is marked by a textual touch different from that of the hypertext: the *Iliad* never attributes Hera's hostility against Zeus to her jealousy, and here the text makes clear that she keeps on fighting against Zeus' support of the Trojans. The narrative, from the beginning, announces the importance of Hera's political action. She and Athena in several decisive moments seem to represent the only voices of the divine assembly. While it is striking that Zeus mentions here the name of Hera as the main hindrance and source of hostility to his agreement with Thetis, this choice serves also a dramatic and political purpose. For the name and the authority of Hera reduce a potential revolt of Zeus' brothers to a narrower context, that of a domestic and private relationship. A real quarrel with a great god, such as Poseidon, would be painful and challenging, as we will see.

Due to her intimate relationship with Zeus, Hera is always able to attack him in all his functions since she feels entitled to share his decisions and power—a privilege he denies her (see chapter I, 2). Her domestic condition complicates and transforms the 'anthropological' structure of the "enemy brothers": it sustains her ambition to share his powers, but determines also her failure.[39]

Zeus closes his promise by producing the gesture and using the words that bend the events of the world and human destiny to his decision (524–27):

> Come on, I will nod assent with my head, that you may believe me:
> for this, among the immortal gods, is my mightiest sign
> since it[40] cannot cheat, nor is it revocable,
> nor remains unfulfilled whatever I assent to by nodding my head.[41]

---

**39** Hera will fight against Zeus' will to honor Achilles in the scene following immediately after (I. 533–569, and in others later, e.g. VIII. 1–40, 438–83, etc.).
**40** The text has the possessive *emon* followed by no noun: interpreters supply either "word" or "sign." Probably it is the nodding sign since assenting with his head, or denying by throwing back his head, are the signs – visible only to the gods – of Zeus' irrevocable decisions.
**41** (I. 524–27):

εἰ δ' ἄγε τοι κεφαλῇ κατανεύσομαι ὄφρα πεποίθῃς·
τοῦτο γὰρ ἐξ ἐμέθεν γε μετ' ἀθανάτοισι μέγιστον
τέκμωρ· οὐ γὰρ ἐμὸν παλινάγρετον οὐδ' ἀπατηλὸν
οὐδ' ἀτελεύτητον ὅ τί κεν κεφαλῇ κατανεύσω.

Such words can only be the words of fate, and the gesture of nodding is a sort of signature that endorses the breadth of a universal decision. Zeus' words become events.[42] A new analogy between Zeus' and the Poet's words emerges here: both are performative since the Poet's words meta-poetically acquire the same power of reality as Zeus' words. The *Iliad* is truly the Poem of Zeus.

As West (1997, 354) remarks, "The idea that a god's decision is irrevocable is a commonplace of Mesopotamian literature," and he quotes several passages relating the decisions of Marduk and others. He goes on: "Similarly in the Old Testament: 'I will not profane my covenant, and what went forth from my lips I will not alter' (Ps. 89. 35 [34])."

Through words that can never be unfulfilled, the Iliadic Zeus provides a unified control of the order of things and reverses the Olympian order that is divided, discontinuous, contradictory, and chaotic due to each god's having his or her own limited power. Greek tragedy will derive abundant, distressing themes from these fragmented powers. Zeus' mastery of human destinies is not dependent on private and anthropomorphic passions, but on universal, impersonal, and unknown motivations. Most importantly, it departs from the poetic and mythical imagination that stages the plots and characterizations of the gods: the image of Zeus as the Golden Scales is almost not representable as an anthropomorphic dramatic entity; it belongs to the things of the world and to their mysterious and tremendous necessity. The Iliadic Zeus becomes the firm link between divine power and the order of the world: as such, he almost moves outside Olympus and its tight cluster of gods.

The text, then, provides a physical portrait of Zeus that seems to allegorize the effective force of his word through images that recall his rule over storm and sky (I. 528–30):

> He spoke and with his dark brows the son of Kronos nodded,
> and the lord's divine locks [ἀμβρόσιαι δ' ἄρα χαῖται][43] swept forward
> from his immortal head [κρατὸς ἀπ' ἀθανάτοιο]: he shook great Olympus.[44]

The passage stages a grandiose image of Zeus: each line adds a trait to his physical stature and increases his authority and greatness. The graphic movement of

---

**42** Zeus remains forever loyal to his signature: for instance, in book XV. 75 Zeus recalls that assent ("and I nodded assent with my head," ἐμῷ δ' ἐπένευσα κάρητι), and his irrevocable word solemnly given to Thetis.
**43** The text employs two different words for the immortal head of Zeus: ἀμβρόσιαι δ' ἄρα χαῖται and, in the next line, κρατὸς ἀπ' ἀθανάτοιο. They are at the beginning of the lines 529 and 530, and the order of the words is chiastic: adj. + noun and noun + adj. The immortal locks are selected as the moving and somehow flowing and airy part of his immortal head.
**44** "These verses inspired Pheidias in the design of the great statue of Zeus at Olympia," cf. Kirk 1985, 109 on lines 529–30.

his brows and locks makes no sense unless it evokes allusively the specific context of Zeus as ruler, master of the sky, cloud-gatherer.

Notwithstanding Kirk's skepticism,[45] I think that the terms of the description sound allusive or allegorical of Zeus' function as *nephelêgereta* ("gatherer of the clouds," as Zeus is called at 511 and 517). The physical identification or connection of Zeus with the sky elements is surprisingly frequent: at XV. 153, two gods reach "Zeus with deep-thundering voice" and find him "sitting and he was crowned by a fragrant cloud."[46] The "gatherer of clouds, really creates and gathers them and they stand as a crown upon his head": because of him they are even fragrant. It is impossible for us to decide whether in images like these the Narrator and his audience felt the identification of Zeus with the clouds and thunder, or imagined him as creator and master of these: as Parker 2011, 77 writes: "The line between the god as the cause of a natural phenomenon and the natural phenomenon itself is a fine one doubtless not worth agonizing over."

Concerning this situation, it appears to be too cautious for the interpreter to refuse to connect Zeus' nodding of his dark brows with the gesture with which he can be imagined to gather the clouds and with the common epithet for Zeus, κελαινεφής ("black with clouds," "surrounded by black clouds") which occurs eight times in the poem. It appears at I. 397 —one hundred lines before our passage: κελαινεφέϊ Κρονίωνι, in Achilles' words.

The sweeping of Zeus' locks suggests the sweeping of clouds and winds (see XIII. 796–7, XXIII. 367),[47] and the shaking of Olympus invites one to think of his thundering messages.[48]

As the thunder and dark clouds become blended with Zeus' purposes and will, nature too acquires specific personal purposes and ends: when lightning

---

[45] "It seems to me unlikely that, as Willock suggests [...] the description here is based on thunder-cloud imagery." Kirk 1985, 109.

[46] XV. 152–53:

εὗρον δ' εὐρύοπα Κρονίδην ἀνὰ Γαργάρῳ ἄκρῳ

ἥμενον· ἀμφὶ δέ μιν θυόεν νέφος ἐστεφάνωτο.

See Janko 1992, 244: "Zeus, still sitting in the clouds he created at 14. 350, is aptly called 'cloud gatherer'!"

[47] Willcock 1978, 195 thinks that the flowing hair represents "the 'anvil' of cirrus which commonly spreads from the top of the cloud."

[48] West 1997, 354: "This striking detail [the shaking of Olympus] which was much admired in antiquity, stands almost alone in classical literature. It is repeated in the *Homeric Hymn to Dionysus*, 13–150. It seems to reflect the Mesopotamian idea that when the god utters his decisive word, the heaven and/or the earth quakes." By shaking the Olympos, Zeus makes manifest to the gods that he is taking a very serious decision: this very sign creates in Hera the deep fear that Zeus is taking a very serious commitment with Thetis.

sweeps the sky and thunder breaks, these phenomena are a sign and a message of Zeus or even, more directly, the actual forms of his physical presence. He is an immense manifestation of violence, light and sound, and a human-like conscious figure ruling the world of Being: a phenomenon of nature, a speaking being, and a universal principle, all at once.

## 1.2 Divine Farce

> "Positivement un dieu [grec] est un système de notions."
>
> Gernet 1932, 222

After Zeus' solemn promise to Thetis, they both depart from the high spot on Olympus (531–35):

> The two made these plans and separated: she
> lept down to the deep sea, leaving shining Olympus.[49]
> Zeus reached his own house, and all the gods rose up at once
> from their seats facing their father (σφοῦ πατρὸς ἐναντίον),[50]
> none dared remain at rest as he advanced, but all stood up and faced him.

Through the use of a polar expression, the text underscores the absolute respect and deference of all the gods for Zeus: <u>all of them</u> rose up, <u>none</u> dared to remain sitting and <u>stood up and faced him</u> (I. 533–35; cfr. *HIGK*). They know his force and his past readiness to use it if they do not obey his orders (see VIII. 5–27 and below, Ch. 5.1 "Zeus Challenges the Divine Assembly").

Zeus rules the divine assembly (533–604),[51] acting before an effectively virtual presence of the other gods: at least until the intervention of Hephaistos, the

---

**49** Through the chiasmus, the text contrasts the depth (and obscurity) of the bottom of the sea with the luminous Olympus: the described places suggest, for the two characters, figurative connotations that are so profound and as vast and diverse as are those of the sea and the sky. The chiasmus is also emphasized by the sounds: *al-, al-, le-, ol-*: εἰς ἅλα ἆλτο βαθεῖαν ἀπ' αἰγλήεντος Ὀλύμπου. Two different and distant worlds have agreed on something that will happen in another world, on the earth: the agreement ὣς βουλεύσαντε "made these plans") occurs in horizons that have no human presence, yet it decides the trajectory of human lives. See below (Ch. 6.3 "Zeus Closes the Poem") the marked difference between the two horizons.
**50** The iconographic mention of Zeus as "their father" should be read as something that contains also the connotation of "their ruler," as we have seen.
**51** In seventy-one lines, the gods are presented for the first time to the audience in a council that mirrors that of the heroes: the critical literature has shown that both assemblies produce a conflict, both stage a sort of autocratic figure conflicting with a special target before a group of

assembly attaches a solely political color to what could have been be a conjugal brawl. The poet attributes to the gods social gatherings analogous to those that heroes have, but whereas human assemblies are places of real encounters and political and military disputes, the divine assemblies are, with a few serious exceptions, virtual gatherings and mute décor for the private political quarrels between Zeus and his wife, or sometimes, and more realistically, the edifying occasion for a joyful party.[52]

Hera did not fail to perceive that Thetis was imparting her counsels to Zeus (536–37) and "suddenly" she turns to him with "provoking words" (κερτομίοισι Δία Κρονίωνα) (540–43):

> Who among the gods, again, my treacherous one,[53] made plans with you?
> It is always your pleasure to make decisions while holding aloof
> from me and plotting in secrecy.
> You never deign to share openly with me what you think.

She sneers at Zeus with the rhetorical question, "Who among the gods...," since in fact she has seen Thetis counseling with Zeus (555–57). The question is therefore a provocation: if Zeus denies he has been planning with another god, he is a liar, if he admits it, he must explain.

Hera depicts Zeus as a perverse husband and collaborator: he always (!) loves (αἰεί τοι φίλον ἐστίν) to plot and decide in secrecy, and he does not deign to share his views with her.

Zeus answers (I. 545–50):

---

indifferent peers. Elmer 2013, 146–47 underscores a parallel between Agamemnon's and Zeus' autocratic positions. Yet Zeus' open declaration before the gods that he conceives plans privately, apart from the others (549–50), is unique and characterizes his consciousness of having exclusive power among the immortals, obviously as god of Fate.

**52** The Iliadic images of the divine assemblies "unmistakably resemble the divine gatherings of Hittite and Babylonian and Canaanite literature." Griffin 1995, 2.

**53** The amusing detail is that Hera herself is four times called "treacherously (or deceptively) thinking" in the *diêgêsis* addressing line (δολοφρονέουσα προσηύδα πότνια Ἥρη) as she turns to Zeus or another god (XIV. 197, 300, 329, XIX. 106). She is reproached for her treacherousness also at XIX. 97, etc.

> Then to her the father of men and gods answered:[54]
> "Hera, stop hoping to know all my thoughts (μύθους):
> they will be hard for you, though you are my wife.[55]
> But whatever is fitting for you to hear, no one, neither
> god nor man, will know before you.
> Yet, whatever I may choose to plan apart from the gods (ἀπάνευθε θεῶν ἐθέλωμι νοῆσαι),
> do not keep on questioning each thing and probing me.

Zeus offers a partial concession to his wife by granting her a relative privilege. It is clear that the information he covers with his silence —"whatever I may choose to plan apart from the gods"— refers to his promise to Thetis. The monarch Zeus announces in full assembly before all the gods that he can plan events without any consultation with them. No god protests: only Hera continues the quarrel and communicates her fear (I. 555–59):

> ...and now I am terribly afraid at heart lest Thetis, the silver-footed,
> the daughter of the old sea god, has won you over:
> for at early dawn she sat by you and clasped your knees;
> to her, I believe, you gave the certain sign that you will
> honor Achilles and slaughter many Achaeans[56] beside their ships.

Hera's revelation that she knows about Zeus' and Thetis' encounter and knows even what he decided, contradicts the assertion that Zeus has just made before the whole assembly about the secrecy of his plans. She scores a point over him. At the same time, the revelation reduces Hera's political stature: just like a meddlesome wife, she peeked at Zeus and Thetis and interpreted Zeus' sign as he nodded. Then in the assembly she created a troublesome scene by protesting about Zeus' secrecy, pretending not to know what she in fact knew very well.

---

**54** Zeus' epithet, "father of men and gods," celebrates his universal power, since "father" in this expression means "ruler" and the polar expression embraces all living, rational beings. As Chantraine writes (*REG* 59–60 (1946–47), pp. 234–36), this religious connotation is extended, and we find an example of it in lines 503, 540. "The line introducing Zeus' speech is a variant — instead of a more common line— emphasizing Zeus' outstanding authority." The formula is well analyzed by De Jong (1987) 2004, 198 and West 2007, 170. The same commentary remarks on the three negative imperatives Zeus addresses to Hera.
**55** It is difficult to gauge the irony or the seriousness of the line: on the serious side, Zeus denies equality and transparency with his wife: "some of my plans and decisions," he seems to imply, "are too hard for anybody —even for you, my wife— to accept and approve of."
**56** The text contains a powerful chiasmus ὡς Ἀχιλῆα τιμήσῃς, ὀλέσῃς δὲ πολέας ἐπὶ νηυσὶν Ἀχαιῶν. The honor for one contrasts with the death of many: an awful contiguity that the chiasmus reproduces graphically —so to speak— by the position and the sound of the words.

The father of gods and men cannot avoid becoming angered by her skillful manipulation; he turns impatient and cuts off the discussion (I. 561–67):

> "Damn you! Always a suspicion, I can keep no secret from you.
> Yet you will not be able to accomplish anything,
> but will be more estranged from my heart. And that will be worse for you.
> If what you say is true, it must be my pleasure.[57]
> Now go, sit down, be quiet and obey my orders
> lest all the gods who are in Olympus be unable to protect you,
> when I should come against you and lay my invincible hands on you."[58]
> He spoke and the ox-eyed lady Hera was frightened...[59]

With his angry response, Zeus, first of all, flatly refuses to say anything about his promise to Thetis and lets Hera and the assembly invent the precise terms of his promise. Furthermore, he threatens Hera with physical violence lest she

---

[57] The comment is particularly sarcastic (see Latacz 2000 *HIGK* Band 1, Gesang 1, 564). Zeus mockingly confirms Hera's accusation of perversity: "If I love to be silent, as you say, things cannot change."

[58] What characterizes Zeus' "invincible hands" in the two unique passages (I. 567 and VIII. 530) where the hands are Zeus', is that he himself proclaims their insuperable power: when the expression is applied to heroes, the "invincible hands" are attributed to them by other heroes or by the poet, since the human characters do not boast of them. Only Ajax in XIII. 77 extolls his own invincible hands: he has been inspired by Poseidon and the poet intends to show, through his personal claim, the divine power that Ajax now feels in himself. To feel and proclaim the invincible power of one's own hands is perhaps a divine prerogative and it is twice Zeus'.

[59] Here and at 551 (a formulaic introductive verse) Hera's epithet "the ox-eyed lady Hera" (βοῶπις πότνια Ἥρη) appears for the first time in the poem: its perfect metric equivalent "white-armed goddess Hera" (θεὰ λευκώλενος Ἥρη) has been employed already three times (55, 195, 208) when she is mentioned in relation to her positive participation in stopping Achilles' murder of Agamemnon. It will appear again at 572 where Hephaistos is said to bring comfort to Hera and at 595 as Hera smiles. On another occasion (see XIV. 159, 222, 263 and below in Ch. 5.3), the theriomorphic epithet is used prevalently, as here, during Hera's hostile action against Zeus. The poet could choose the one or the other epithet and perhaps he meant to send an eloquent message when he employed the epithet that brought light and white splendor to her beauty during her positive action, but the theriomorphic epithet during her hostile behavior against Zeus. This seems especially eloquent during the first episodes of the first book of the poem. Of course, this distinction is lost if we exclude the animal reference or attach an aesthetic connotation to the epithet that would celebrate the "large" or "beautiful" eyes of Hera. Delforge/Pironti 2016, 25 do not exclude the animal reference, but make "the hypothesis of an aesthetic code the most part of which we do not know," according to which it would be correct to attribute that aesthetic connotation to the epithet. Then both epithets would celebrate the beauty of Hera. Yet the choice of the epithet in accordance with different contexts could trouble that hypothesis. See other comments on Ch. 5.3, p. 176–78.

continue to raise questions. He repeats the same boast of the superiority of his physical force to the divine assembly in book VIII (see Ch. 5.1). As I will elaborate concerning that passage, Zeus' brutal menace serves as a deterrent: it scares Hera and induces her, though irate, to silence herself and creates tension in the assembly.

It is relevant to notice that as a monarch, as the *primus inter pares*, Zeus has no established pact or recognized credentials that legitimize his power save for his greater physical force. The "divine" nature of the god is his force. It is by threatening violence that he deters the rebellion against his secret decisions, against his power as a god impersonating Fate. There cannot be any politicking or negotiating for the master of destiny, when his "not unfulfilled word" is pronounced. This feature confirms, though indirectly, that Zeus, in his roles both as monarch and ruler of destinies, does not represent, in the eyes of his peers, the ethical and political principles the defense and support of which would grant him authority and grounds for being obeyed and respected. Viewed from the perspective of the Iliadic composition, such situation may depend on the newness of Zeus' role as protector of the Trojans, a role that has no earlier tradition and is grounded on his fully unmotivated agreement to Thetis' supplication. Accordingly, Zeus needs the deterrence embodied in the menacing violence of his hands to insure his authority as lord of destiny.

In the eyes of the audiences and readers of the poem, Zeus' brutal threats constitute a complex and troubling scene: as a figure of Fate, he necessarily has no ethical code, and this indifference is expected; because he is a monarch, some violence could be expected (since in the past he fought against the Titans, Prometheus, Typhoeus etc., according to what the succession myth narrates). In the *Iliad*, however, his violence always appears only in the form of a successful deterrent and is never carried out.

This sort of literary provocation is especially relevant in view of what follows in this episode, where the mention of Zeus' past violence merges into a comic scene. A question ensues, whether Hephaistos' comic performance could be read also as an amusing and polemical reference to a scene that, in the hypertext, was thoroughly serious and dramatic.[60]

Hephaistos recalls Zeus' past violence, when Zeus threw Hephaistos off of Olympus; through a humorous recollection, Hephaistos removes the characters' and the Narratees' fear that this gesture may be repeated now. He begins talking

---

[60] This comic strategy of replaying traditional themes and motifs – which sound distant or out of place within the new Iliadic Zeus and his cultural horizon – is used other times, e.g., at IV. 1–72 (see Ch. 6.1), or at XV. 16–32 (see Ch. 5.4), with different textual strategies.

from his position among the gods who are "troubled" (ὄχθησαν)⁶¹ by the quarrel that is unraveling (I. 570–76):

> the Uranian gods in the house of Zeus were troubled:
> and among them Hephaistos, the famous craftsman, began to speak,
> bringing to his dear mother, white-armed Hera,⁶² a little comfort (ἐπίηρα φέρων):
> "A disastrous affair! And an unbearable one
> if the two of you will quarrel in this way for mortals' sake
> and set the gods in tumult:⁶³ not even the splendid banquet
> will give us joy, since evil prevails."

The awful threat of divine internecine battle is evoked by Hephaistos with a parodic overtone, amusingly alluding to scenes of wrangling and hostility among the gods. The exaggerated language: λοίγια ἔργα τάδ' ἔσσεται οὐδ' ἔτ' ἀνεκτά, makes reference to the seriousness of the "plague" (*loigós*, see I. 67) and especially to Zeus' comment when he, after a long silence, agreed to Thetis' request (I. 518). With that expression, Zeus was precisely foretelling the quarrels Hera would raise against his decision to honor Achilles. The prophecy was correct and the narrative confirms it with an eloquent repetition of "A disastrous affair!" The familiar context evoked by Zeus reduced the majesty of his power (Ch. 1.1), but it also channeled the future hostility into a manageable situation as it is now confirmed by the comic repetition of "A disastrous affair?": what "the disastrous affair" threatens is the pleasure of the party. When food and song are the core desire, comedy, even farce, is not far away. Even the cause of the turmoil is without any real gravity: "for mortals' sake!" Think of the silly scandal: to spoil a great banquet, accompanied by Apollo's playing and the Muses' singing, because of mortals' affairs!

Hephaistos then advises his dear mother (578) to be kind (ἐπίηρα φέρειν) so

> that father Zeus
> may not upbraid her again, and disturb our feasting.
> For if Olympios,⁶⁴ the lord of lightning,⁶⁵ should ever be minded

---

61 It is not certain whether one should understand "troubled" or "angry," and what their motivations are: troubled by fear, or troubled/angry due to the quarrel that would destroy the pleasure of the banquet, or angry with she who contested Zeus, etc.

62 This epiphanic presentation of Hera as λευκωλένῳ Ἥρῃ, and later (595) as θεὰ λευκώλενος Ἥρῃ, ceases to define her when the theriomorphic epithet βοῶπις πότνια Ἥρῃ (I. 551, 568) appears during the quarrel with Zeus. In the *Iliad* the "white-armed" epithet occurs twenty-four times for Hera out of twenty-eight instances of the epithet.

63 Notice the rhetorical contrast between "for mortals' sake" and "gods in tumult." Apollo too, in another context, refuses to fight for the sake of mortals.

to dash us from our seats...⁶⁶ For he is, by far, the strongest.
Come on, speak to him with soft words,
then the Olympios in turn will be gracious to us." (578–83)

Hera refuses to follow her son's advice —to speak a soft word to Father Zeus. The Narrator does not provide any psychological explanation: probably she still cares for her mortals, the Achaeans, and certainly the narrative cares for more farce from Hephaistos. The text constellates a political quarrel with the flashes of lightnings —dashings from Olympus to the earth or even below— and the love of an immense father/ruler who is menacing to disturb a party. The domestic narrowness of the fight is overcome by celestial vastness and cosmic phenomena that enlarge and make sublime the mocking representation of what a human family quarrel would be.

Hephaistos, then, leaps up and, as an affectionate cup-bearer, places a cup of nectar in his mother's hand, beginning in this way the party or symposium: a good party also needs a good story with a moral lesson. He tells her to be patient and endure it: τέτλαθι μῆτερ ἐμή ("endure it, my mother," 586). We learn that gods too have to endure unpleasant and unwanted circumstances. "Endurance" is a mode of being that is opposite to the heroic one, even for mortals (see Ch. 4.1), and here of course it underlines the comic tone of the scene. "Yes, be patient," says Hephaistos (I. 587–94),

> "for fear lest, dear as you are, I see you before my eyes
> struck down, and then, sorry though I be, I will not be able
> to give you aid: it is hard to fight against Olympios.
> Already another time when I was resolved to protect you,
> he caught me by the foot and threw me from the divine threshold
> and the whole day long I was carried down; and at sunset
> I fell in Lemnos and little breath was left in me:
> there the Sintian men received me as soon as I touched the ground."

---

**64** This name "Olympios" (sometimes an epithet) occurs six times in the first book out of its nineteen appearances in the *Iliad*. See I. 353, 508, 580, 583, 589, 609, all of them in dialogue, except 609 (*diêgêsis*). The "Olympios" epithet occurs in a context in which Zeus' actions concern the destiny of men, therefore when he is a fatal god, or monarch of the gods as in this passage I. 580. Here, as in I. 609 and XII. 275, the noun-epithet Ὀλύμπιος ἀστεροπητής also adds the evocation of Zeus' personal power over the sky, and in particular over lightning — about which Hephaistos is thinking, given the context—, and the connotation of punishment that the lightning contains might be revitalized.
**65** See 570: νεφεληγερέτα Ζεύς with its possible revitalization of the reference to lightning.
**66** Perhaps the conditional sentence is left to be mentally closed by something like "he could do it, since he is by far the strongest." The sentence prepares the audience for an account of a similar gesture enacted by Zeus, which occurs at 590–94.

Hephaistos did not become lame because of this long tumble, for, as he says in *Od.* viii. 314–18, he was born lame. In *Iliad* XVIII. 394–405, the same Hephaistos tells the story of how once his mother Hera – the bitch, as he says – threw him off of Olympus with the purpose of hiding him "because I am lame."[67] This story is connected with the quarrel between Hera and Zeus concerning Heracles.

This saga is a frequent source in the *Iliad* of Hera's and Zeus' quarrels and conflicts: if we knew exactly the texts of the saga we would be able to measure the distance between the Iliadic narrative and the possible source of this specific episode. We may assume, however, that the original narrative, whether or not pronounced by Hephaistos, could hardly have been so comically self-aware as it is here in the *Iliad*. Here it is narrated a long time after the event, and it is quoted as an example not to be repeated, and its violence is therefore halfway eliminated.

This reminiscence is a masterpiece of Homeric visual, pregnant representation: the rhythm of the description is rapid, built on short, factual sentences — times, places— with quick changes of subjects, and a tense rhythm with frequent enjambments: it expresses no pathos but gives an economic account of bare gestures and movements, as on a puppet stage.[68] Hephaistos' fear that Zeus might now strike Hera sounds implausible, especially since it is attached to a comic image of Hephaistos as an inane savior and to the obviously comic recognition that it is hard and painful to fight against Olympios. Viewed from the angle of an allusion to another text, the episode could almost look parodic and be, not a frivolous representation of the gods, but an amusing reference to traditional scenes about Zeus' violence, as he throws gods off of Olympus. As the audience certainly caught the parodic reference, they understood that the *Iliad* was in this way dismissing that sort of insolent image of Zeus from its own Zeus.

As Hephaistos ends the story of his long tumbling —yet another comic touch—, Hera begins to smile; the story gives her pleasure and frees her from the memory of her past unpleasant experience:

---

**67** In this version Hephaistos, after his fall, is received by Eurynome and Thetis: this version may be an adapation of the story made for the occasion of Thetis' visit to Hephaistos. The version with Hephaistos' fall onto Lemnos has some internal coherence: Lemnos is characterized by volcanic activity and it was considered sacred to Hephaistos, god of fire.

**68** There is only one epic epithet in the whole narrative of the tumble: the epithet θεσπεσίοιο, for the threshold, the "divine" place from which Hephaistos is thrown. As Chantraine, *DELG* remarks, the Narrator dismissed or did not recognize the etymological meaning of the word.

> So he spoke and the white-armed goddess Hera[69]
> smiling accepted the cup out of her son's hand.
> And then, moving toward the right, he poured to all the other gods
> sweet nectar, dipping from the crater:
> and uncontrollable laughter arose among the blessed gods as they
> saw Hephaistos hobbling[70] about the palace."[71] (I. 596–600)

Zeus' menace that pervades Hephaistos' self-ironic recollection provokes, finally, the expected laughter. The scene needs only the addition of a ridiculous detail in order to explode: Hephaistos' funny hobbling. His serving the gods while moving with his ridiculous gait points to a parodic image of Ganymedes.

It is a sort of aristocratic attitude to laugh at the sudden discovery of some unexpected oddity in another person.[72] Here "the blessed gods" (599) laugh at Hephaistos' disablement and the curious exception he provides in the perfect Olympus. It is most improbable, therefore, that the gods laugh because they see in Hephaistos a ridiculous imitation of Ganymedes. Hephaistos has no reason to pose himself as a ridiculous image of Ganymedes: he really is crippled and he really limps. As I suggest, the gods follow their aristocratic and blessed nature by being pleasantly surprised by Hephaistos' disablement. A parody hardly raises an "uncontrollable laughter." On the contrary, it is certain that the Narratees recognize and appreciate that the text suggests an actual parody of Ganymedes' mythical figure. There is an Aristophanic freedom and malice in this comic creation. The Poet makes his audience and readers smile with his parodic skill: he looks upon the figure of Hephaistos not as the actual being at whom the gods laugh for the reasons I suggested, but rather appropriates him, identifies him through parody with a ridiculous Ganymedes. By making Hephaistos what we would call a literary figure, the Poet ridicules him in order to achieve the successful performance of the text.

This distinction is paramount: the gods cannot laugh in response to the comic effects that the text produces on its audience and readers, for the gods are

---

[69] It is probably an eloquent indication that here the Poet has chosen the "white arm" epithet for Hera: she is smiling and softening her resentment against Zeus. Compare line 568 and my n. 59 on that line.

[70] The verb ποιπνύοντα, a present with reduplication, reveals *pneô* as its root, and therefore the notion of "getting out of breath" is not absent from it. See Chantraine, *DELG*.

[71] The motivation for this laughter is not clear for us modern readers: Kirk 1985 explains that Hephaistos' hobbling may have appeared as a parody of Hebe and Ganymedes, the regular wine-pourers among the gods.

[72] Thus the soldiers laugh when Odysseus beats up Thersites and makes manifest his weakness and the pompous vanity of his words (II. 265–75).

neither. They react to what they see and experience. Many comments and similes invented by the Poet presume this distinction. When in the fourth book (127–31) Athena deviates Pandaros' arrow from the body of Menelaus, she is compared by the Poet to a mother who flicks a fly from her sleeping baby: it is improbable that Athena felt like a mother and the *diêgêsis*, by calling her "the spoiler," confirms her warlike attitude and actions. The text, however, aims at removing the heroic impact of the whole action and the simile serves just this purpose (see below, Ch. 5.2).

As Hephaistos goes around pouring nectar, the party develops into an entertainment that goes on until the coming of night (601–604):

> Thus, all day long until sunset, they enjoyed
> the banquet; they did not miss, in their heart, the equally allotted food,[73]
> nor the most beautiful lyra in the hands of Apollo,
> nor the beautiful voice of the Muses who sang in alternation.[74]

Hephaistos' amusing intervention and the pleasant, musical end of the quarrel creates a strong contrast with the dramatic seriousness with which the human assembly ends in the same first book. This contrast suggests that Zeus' power does not produce an immediate and lasting split among the gods, as Agamemnon's offense to Achilles produces among the mortal Achaeans. Zeus' plan still bothers Hera and remains a partially secret fate, yet merriment follows nonetheless. Furthermore, the contrast sheds light on the irreconcilable differences between human and divine beings, and accordingly between the earthly life of men and the mythical-Olympian world of the gods.

It is extraordinary that the poetic text closes its first song with a divine song: it mirrors its own singing and stages the goddesses' song as its poetic double in Heaven.

The Muses are a very important poetic presence. For Barmeyer 1968, 67 the lines, οὐδέ τι θυμὸς ἐδεύετο… δαιτὸς ἐΐσης… οὐ μὲν φόρμιγγος περικαλλέος… Μουσάων θ'…, imply that the gods would have felt the absence of the Muses as

---

[73] While lines 601–02 are fully repeated (e.g. 602 = I. 468, II. 431, VII. 320, XXIII. 56; *Od.* xvi. 479, xix. 427), lines 603–04 are unique. The presence of the divine song in Olympus closes the first book and will never be repeated: it shines as an exceptional event. It is a possible model, but unrepeatable, for human banquets. When mortals sing to celebrate a god, as for instance at I. 469–474, the ceremonial sequence follows the cessation of the desire for food and drink: "But when they had put away the desire for eating and drinking, the young men filled the mixing bowls…All day long, they propitiated the god with singing…"

[74] The verb ἀμειβόμεναι is variously interpreted: either each Muse sings in alternation or Apollo sings and the Muses' chorus responds each time to his song.

an essential deficiency. This recalls the Pindaric myth of the birth of the Muses according to which after the creation of the world, "Zeus asked the gods whether they felt a want of anything [*ei tou deointo*], and the gods demanded that he create for himself some gods, who by means of words would set in order [*katakosmesousi*][75] this great work,"[76] and Zeus created the Muses.

It would be exciting to know the theme of the Muses' song on the occasion of the celestial party: they do not sing epic songs, but lyric poems, and I am tempted to speculate that poet and audience imagined that the Muses, daughters of Zeus, are celebrating, in a hymn, the power and glory of their father Zeus. This assumption could be sustained by the parallel examples the text offers in this first book (469–74), where the young men celebrate Apollo, and by Hesiod's *Theogony*, where the Muses are singing for Zeus and celebrate him, his victory, and his power (*Theog.* 36 ff., and especially 69–74).

This assumption allows us to see better the poetic purpose of the divine symposium: the episode began with Zeus' thoughtful and painful acceptance of Thetis' request; it continued with Hera's provocations —a reenactment of a traditional theme that looms large in Heracles' saga—; it turns into an amusing scene with Hephaistos bustling about the palace; and finally the episode unfurls as a hymnic celebration of Zeus, performed by Apollo and the Muses. Homer may hint that what is sung by Zeus' son and daughters cannot be but the praise of their father, yet he avoids saying that this is the case: perhaps he prefers to have us imagine that there is no song so vast and beautiful, as the song whose theme is Zeus himself.

As we speculate on the theme that the Muses and Apollo chose to sing at the divine banquet, we imagine, also, that the Muses did not tell the Poet about their own singing with Apollo on that specific occasion. It seems indeed improbable: they sing to the Poet —and without Apollo— only epic stories.

---

[75] Many scholars interpret the verb as meaning "praise, celebrate". See Pucci 1998, 31–33.
[76] Pindar narrated this myth in his *Hymn to Zeus*, which we know through the summary provided by Aristides (ed. W. Dindorf 1964, 2.142).

# Chapter 2

## 2.1 Zeus pities his son Sarpedon

> "The *Iliad's* compound of caring and uncaring gods does justice to the problem of the meaning of an often contradictory existence, when contradiction itself is the only satisfactory explanation."
>
> Murray 1924, 265

In this chapter I begin to analyze the episodes that showcase Zeus' interventions as the ruler of heroes' destinies and as the embodiment of the Golden Scales. I first examine Zeus' vain attempt to save his son Sarpedon, and then the analogous endeavor in favor of Hector.

In a passage in book XVI, Zeus longs to save Sarpedon, his son,[1] in another (book XXII), Hector, and in a third (book IV) the city of Troy. All three passages are marked by insistent repetitions of roles and phrases, in order to strongly persuade the audience that the topic, "Zeus facing a dear hero's death," may simultaneously include Zeus' pity and concern, as well as the impossibility of satisfying his desire.

As Zeus glances at Sarpedon and Patroclos who are beginning to fight, he feels pity for them both (431, τοὺς δὲ ἰδὼν ἐλέησε Κρόνου πάϊς ἀγκυλομήτεω)[2] and breaks into a passionate appeal to his wife (Ἥρην δὲ προσέειπε κασιγνήτην ἄλοχόν τε),[3] debating within himself and asking of her whether he should save his son Sarpedon from death or let him die (XVI. 433–38):

> Ah me! Sarpedon, my most beloved of men,
> is destined to die under the hands of Patroclos, son of Menoitios.
> My heart in my breast debates and ponders in two different ways,
> whether I should snatch him alive out from the tearful battle

---

1 On the authenticity of this episode, see Nagy 1990, 130–31.
2 The seven examples of this epithet "devious-devising son of Kronos" for Zeus show that it occurs especially when Zeus accomplishes something miraculous (e.g. II. 319, XII. 450) or accomplishes something with an ambiguous intention (e.g. IX. 37, II. 205, XVIII. 293): it is tempting to deduce some ambiguity here too, if not explicitly in his mind, at least in his different roles and images.
3 "... at the sight of Patroclos about to kill Sarpedon, Zeus appears suddenly in a staging noun epithet formula (XVI. 431–32). The staging formula reports an act of commiseration: it stages an important character vis-a-vis what is already in the scene, and thus it effects a shift of scene that is crucial for the reality of the epic tradition: Zeus lets himself be persuaded not to allow the anti-fact of the fated Sarpedon staying alive" (Bakker 1997, 192).

and set him down in the rich country of Lycia,⁴
or now I kill him under the hands of Menoitios' son.⁵

ὤ μοι ἐγών, ὅ τέ μοι Σαρπηδόνα φίλτατον ἀνδρῶν
μοῖρ' ὑπὸ Πατρόκλοιο Μενοιτιάδαο δαμῆναι.⁶
διχθὰ δέ μοι κραδίη μέμονε φρεσὶν ὁρμαίνοντι,
ἤ μιν ζωὸν ἐόντα μάχης ἄπο δακρυοέσσης
θείω ἀναρπάξας Λυκίης ἐν πίονι δήμῳ,
ἤ ἤδη ὑπὸ χερσὶ Μενοιτιάδαο δαμάσσω.

The text brings to light an alternative for Sarpedon's destiny: though Zeus leaves open the possibility of abandoning Sarpedon to his *moira* ("destiny"), it is clear that he would like to save his son: he would not suggest to Hera the option of rescuing him, if this were not one dear to his heart. Yet, as we will see, the alternative he announces stands upon ambiguous intentions.

The second option, according to which Zeus may say, "or now I kill him under the hands of Menoitios' son," is a typical example of the mythical permeability or porousness between human and immortal terms. Since Zeus is the master of Sarpedon's and Patroclos' destinies, by allowing Patroclos to kill Sarpedon, Zeus is actually killing Sarpedon through the hand of Patroclos. Zeus considers Patroclos an instrument of his will. This logic shows that, within this mythical permeability, another structure emerges, that of instrumentality: the human being becomes a sort of tool for the god. The notion and the effect of permeability constitute a perfectly mythical mirage and utopia, which assumes that a sort of perfect mingling may emerge between the two terms. But, in fact, what really functions in a divinely permeated action is the abuse that the god inflicts on a mortal by treating him as an instrument of the god's will. Athena uses Pandaros (in book IV) and Achilles (in book XXII) in this supplemental way.

Zeus' first option, on its surface, reveals the edifying strategy of the narrative: it extols Zeus' sorrow for his son's imminent death and invokes a chance of

---

4 Both phrases, μάχης ἄπο δακρυοέσσης and ἐν πίονι δήμῳ, are repeated expressions, but the contrast of the two epithets is eloquent: the battle as *lacrimabile bellum* and the rich and prosperous Lycia graphically offer two opposite human destinies.
5 By twice defining Patroclos as the son of Menoitios, the text creates a paradoxical contrast by which the son of Zeus may be killed by the son of Menoitios: the absurdity explodes on line 438. In fact, as Chiara Aceti remarks (2008, 95 n. 204), in accordance with the Iliadic rule, the man of higher birth should overcome the man of lower birth. This infringement of the rule is somehow compensated by the dialogue among the gods, in which, as Letoublon 1983, 34 n. 2 writes, Zeus confirms the greatness of Sarpedon and his destiny of death.
6 For Dietrich 1967, 212 this μοῖρ(α) is an impersonal might, but it is still the destiny decreed by Zeus. See n. 7 on next page, and below on XVI. 849, Ch. 3.3.

saving him. It showcases a merciful and affectionate god, while silencing the fact that Zeus himself has established Sarpedon's fate, when he made public his plan to honor Achilles (XV. 64–67):[7]

> ...Achilles shall rouse up Patroclos
> his companion. And shining Hector shall cut down Patroclos
> ... after he has killed many others of the young men,
> and among them my own son, divine Sarpedon.[8]

The Narrator manages to bury away this decision of Zeus. By having Zeus evoke an anonymous, fatal *moira* of Sarpedon at XVI. 434, the text cleverly avoids making Zeus the master of Sarpedon's destiny (*moira*). The narrative displays Zeus' pity and love for his son: for a short and intense moment, the text combines Zeus as lord of human destinies with Father Zeus, the loving genitor, oblivious of his past condemnation of his son.

The epithet "divine Sarpedon" (υἱὸν ἐμὸν Σαρπηδόνα δῖον, XV. 67) is applied to Sarpedon by his father as he announces and decrees the death of his son: "my son, born of Zeus, Sarpedon." The daring of the text is endless. Zeus

---

[7] For the authenticity of Zeus' "forecast," see Janko 1992, 234 ff. n. 56–77. The forecast commits the god to ensure that the events happen as he predicts. Yet here the "forecast" stands, in fact, for Zeus' predetermination of how the events will follow. From 69 on, Zeus abandons his enunciation forecasting the future events and introduces the events as results of his own will and ordinance. By having Zeus relate the future deaths of Sarpedon, Patroclos, and Hector as mere forecasts, the text, through this rhetorical device, avoids denying the heroes' free will. Of course, their destiny is also inscribed in their traditional stories, but by using this sort of anonymous expression, *moira*, that both fails to engage specifically Zeus –since his earlier decision is buried– and evokes no absolute tradition —as Zeus appeals to the heroes' survival–, the text leaves some textual space and chance to human free will. Indeed, the three heroes are represented as masters of their own decisions and actions ("Achilles shall rouse..." "Hector shall cut down," etc.), and during the dramatic action they will be shown to decide autonomously, yet in agreement with Zeus' will and plan (XV. 69–77). As Bruce Heiden (1997, 226) writes, with a metaphor that I sometimes use, "Zeus proclaims his authority to Hera, and once again pronounces the script that events will follow" (XV. 4–77). Zeus forecasts some of the same events at VIII. 470–77, where he announces that he himself will cause many deaths among the Achaeans and that the events which will follow are *thesphaton* (by divine ordinance, 477), i.e. ordained by him.

[8] υἱὸν ἐμὸν Σαρπηδόνα δῖον. For the qualifying function of the epithet δῖον: "depending on Zeus" or "son of Zeus," see Appendix 1. The expression introduces a strong personal touch in the otherwise objective series of "many other young men" killed by Patroclos, and perhaps betrays Zeus' "anguish," as Janko (1992, 375) writes. In the passages XVI. 638, 678 where this epithet returns, Sarpedon is the conqueror. There is no reason to exclude the argument of metric convenience: it is the context that brings back to the epithet its proper functional meaning.

with this epithet confirms the terrible destiny that he bestows on his own son.⁹ The text reports no tragic conflict in Zeus: he grieves because he is the father of a son who is going to die, and not because he is aware that he is at once the father and the murderer of his son – which would be an extremely tragic contradiction to bear. The text, however, cannot prevent the Narratees from being aware of Zeus' responsibility and accordingly the Narratees feel sympathy for Zeus' grief, but also disconcertment at his lack of awareness, and finally embarrassment at the strategy of the text. Zeus' feelings and the feelings that the narrative, through Zeus' words, instills in the audience are distinct and different emotions.

Returning to the scene of Zeus' desire to save his child, the text shows that Zeus and Hera admit without hesitation his capability of saving a man already under the hold of his appointed destiny.¹⁰ The *Iliad* wants to show that a positive mythical deployment is possible and that Zeus can save his son in the same way as he saved Heracles many times, for instance. Yet this admission is real only in principle, for as a matter of fact Zeus cannot suspend Sarpedon's death that he himself has announced and decreed. The text faces therefore the impossible task of harmonizing Zeus' irreconcilable images, that of the pitiful father and that of the master of human destinies.¹¹ If Zeus saved Sarpedon, "the world order" would be threatened,¹² since he rules the events of the world in an irrevocable manner (I. 526–27):

[...] since it cannot cheat, nor is it revocable,
nor remains unfulfilled whatever I assent to by nodding my head.¹³

---

9 For the double etymological force of the adjective, see Appendix.
10 There are five examples of a god whisking away a warrior in danger of being killed: III. 379–80, V. 445, XX. 321 ff., XX. 443, XXI. 597; but in none of these examples is the snatching of the warrior accomplished contrary to the destiny (*moira*) that has been appointed, as in this case. Zeus saved Sarpedon in two earlier occasions (V. 662 and XII. 402–03), but, in those passages, there was no mention of destiny. It is not clear what sort of rescue Zeus intends to grant to Sarpedon by sending him alive to Lycia: being mortal, Sarpedon would then die there at a later time.
11 Feeney 1993, 47 quotes and translates a scholiast who remarks: "The poet is not to be reprehended, for he must either drop the kinship between men and gods or else speak consistently with it (T 16, 433–8)."
12 See, for instance, Burkert 1985, 82: Zeus' pity "suggests an irresponsible act to the father of the gods, the desire to save Sarpedon: and Hera must remind him of *die Notwendigkeit der Weltordnung*."
13 See Ch. 1.

After Zeus' confession of his painful alternative to presumably friendly ears, Hera reminds him that Sarpedon is a mortal and doomed by his mortal fate (XVI. 440–44):

> Terrible son of Kronos, what sort of word you have spoken![14]
> A man, born mortal, since long ago doomed to his sort
> You want to save back from cruel death?
> Do it, but not all of us other gods approve you.[15]

> αἰνότατε Κρονίδη ποῖον τὸν μῦθον ἔειπες.
> ἄνδρα θνητὸν ἐόντα πάλαι πεπρωμένον αἴσῃ[16]
> ἂψ ἐθέλεις θανάτοιο δυσηχέος ἐξαναλῦσαι;
> ἔρδ'· ἀτὰρ οὔ τοι πάντες ἐπαινέομεν θεοὶ ἄλλοι.

Lloyd Jones 1971, 5 persuasively writes: "When Hera reminds Zeus that he cannot save Sarpedon, she is only warning him that he cannot sacrifice to a sudden whim his own settled policy."

Hera's warning, "do it, but not all of us other gods approve you," constitutes the declared obstacle that saves Zeus' role as guardian of destinies and therefore of the order of things. The text cannot have Hera providing, as the motivation for her hindrance, Zeus' role as the god of fate. Hera simply mentions the fact that since many sons of gods are fighting, Zeus would produce a bad example (445–49). She has heard from Zeus the announcement of the events to follow (XV. 64–77), among which that Troy will fall through the plans of Athena (71), and she has offered him her collaboration. In her present role, she appears sensitive to Zeus' feelings and responsibilities and even suggests to him how he might celebrate the death of his son, so the assumption that she is here protective of Zeus' role as master of fate must be accepted. In a change

---

14 Rousseau 1995, Chap. 5 and 8 shows that the phrase is found six times in the *Iliad* (IV. 25, VIII. 462, XIV. 330, XVI. 440, XVIII. 361, always spoken by Hera, the only god who calls Zeus Kronides in the vocative. The line brings forth the speaker's strong indignation: Chantraine 1953, 2.162 shows that the article in the phrase ποῖον τὸν μῦθον gives relevance to the noun: "what sort of idea is this word you have spoken?" Hera's line initiates in all six passages her indignant reaction to Zeus, and this is the only passage in which, as the context shows, she obtains Zeus' consent. The devious strategy of the text becomes evident also from this detail.
15 Lines 440–44 open up an etymological contradiction: how is it possible or thinkable to free from death (*thanatos*) someone who is *thnetos*? Of course, mythology overcomes this *adunaton*, but the *Iliad*'s ontological principle denies it. The adjective δυσηχέος has been interpreted in different ways since antiquity, as being either from ἠχέω or from ἄχος.
16 Hera defines Sarpedon's mortal condition: Zeus decreed the specific occasion in which Sarpedon is destined to die; this occasion has arrived.

from her last humiliation in Book XV, she is now collaborating with Zeus. However, Hera's tone, when she dismisses Zeus' appeal, is unpleasant and reproachful (see line 440) as often in her insolent interventions, and the text does not avoid using for her the occasionally combined theriomorphic epithet in 439: see I. 551–52; XVIII. 360–61.

Zeus truly often does disregard the general disapproval of the gods and acts just as he likes,[17] so that the narrative leaves to its audience and readers to evaluate the nature of the obstacle that prevents Zeus from saving Sarpedon.[18]

At this point, the Narratees are uncertain how to read the exchange between Zeus and Hera. Zeus' power to save Sarpedon is questionable: Hera tells him "Do it," but the gods and the Narratees know that he cannot: Zeus alone seems to have forgotten his fatal role. He feels sorry for Sarpedon's destiny and tortures himself wondering whether to save his son or not. He loves the man but does not act. What are Zeus' final intentions? Why does he eventually consent to the death of his son?

The rhetoric of the whole scene exudes a deep ambivalence that seems purposefully intended to integrate both Zeus' edifying feeling of love for his son and his impassionate acceptance of Sarpedon's death. Zeus' love for his son does not instigate him to rise up and effect the rescue of Sarpedon. On another occasion, as Zeus feels pity for the Immortal Horses (XVII. 441), he rushes to do something for them: he prevents Hector from getting them and pushes them

---

**17** For instance, in Book I. 560 ff., Zeus, reacting to Hera's suspicions and fears, commands her to be silent and to accept what he is doing and threatens her that all the gods will not be able to come to her defense, "if I lay my unconquerable hands on you." At IV. 56 Hera agrees that she cannot prevent Zeus (from doing something he wants) since he is much stronger (ἐπεὶ ἦ πολὺ φέρτερός ἐσσι). At VIII. 5–27 Zeus forbids the other gods to meddle; at 477 ff., Zeus tells Hera, "for you and your anger I do not care;" in Book XV (16 ff.), after Hera's trick, he reminds her of how, in relation to Heracles, he punished her publicly, how the gods were angry and wanted to set her free, but he prevented it. In the line, "do it, but all we gods shall not approve it," Chantraine 1953, 1.231 remarks the "tone ironique" of this form of imperative, "do it, but...".
**18** Janko 1992 *ad loc.* writes: "Homer neatly evades a dilemma: if Zeus saves Sarpedon, the story fails, for Thetis could save Achilles, as Hera hints, but if Zeus does nothing, he looks implausibly weak, so he must yield to a higher power." Yet, though Thetis might desire Achilles' rescue, she could not decide what Achilles wants: immortal glory (*kleos*) or return (*nostos*). Besides, it was she herself, as she says, who sent Achilles to Troy (XVIII. 58–59). Zeus could choose the alternative of making Sarpedon immortal, as Eos makes Memnon in the *Aithiopis* (see Nagy 1979, 204–08). But the immortality of the heroes is rigorously excluded by the text of the *Iliad*, which considers itself the unique agent of immortality for the heroes, an immortality the text accomplishes by granting the heroes immortal fame (*kleos*) through the narrative of their heroic deaths (see Nagy 1979, 172–73, etc.). Zeus, however, grants Sarpedon a cult hero status and, as Nagy puts it, "a sort of immortality" (Nagy 1990, 132 ff.).

back to the battle. The fact that Zeus feels pity for Sarpedon, and yet is also ready to kill him, as he says, "under the hand of Patroclos," suggests that his son's death has been already internalized by him.

The Narrator displays Zeus' grief and pity as a mere linguistic gesture, as the only possible spectacle his text can provide for Zeus' feelings. For the alternatively-facing Zeus, "do I save him or do I kill him," does not respond to a feeling of love and grief: pity and love would induce him to rush and save his son and to prevent him from formulating such an absurd alternative. The alternative that the Narrator places before Zeus presumably entails Zeus' question of whether he has the power to save his son or not. However, if the text intends to intimate this sort of question and meaning when Zeus announces his alternative, it plunges its Narratees into a confusing ambiguity. For if Zeus, when he places the alternative before Hera, means to question his own legitimacy or power to save Sarpedon, he must really have lost his mind. Who else but himself could have the answer? Only because the Narratees respond to the serious and pathetic force of Zeus' appeal to Hera are they induced to think that Zeus has forgotten his role as lord of the destiny.

As they are induced to imagine that Zeus failed to remember that he preordained Sarpedon's death, the god will be affected by embarrassment and lose some of the edifying purpose at which the text has aimed through the scene. The felicitous, or at least silent, coexistence of Zeus' cruel indifference for the death of his son and his grief for this death is the source and the effect of a wishful, mythical metaphysics.

Thus the voice of Zeus and his cry of love, though caught in a paradox, produce a mimetic effect on the audience. Considering the negative aspect of Zeus' position, the Narratees are induced to take that confession of love as what they themselves may feel, and Zeus' desire to save his son as what they deem Zeus ought to have done.

The text offers to its Narratees another help in order to understand Zeus' lament, desire, and final acquiescence: that is, Hera's friendly and correct advice. As I have suggested, she offers a form of solution, a funeral celebration that would in some fashion impute heroic status to Zeus' son.

The contradiction between the merciful god and the soulless impersonation of Fate or of the Golden Scales[19] displays the lack of any sensible and describable motivation which would induce Zeus to kill his son; nothing in Sarpedon's life deserves what he is to suffer, no justice demands his death. He defends Troy

---

**19** The golden scales are mentioned four times in the *Iliad* (VIII. 69, XVI. 658, XIX. 223, XXII. 208–13. See my reading of the passage at XXII. 208–13, on Ch. 2.2.

and Troy is pious and very dear to Zeus. His reticence at the moment of his decision is repeated now at the moment of his pity and affection. Both moments of reticence leave space for the only cause of Sarpedon's death that is not debated: man is mortal and doomed to his fate, as Hera explains. The two moments of reticence and Zeus' inability to act differently from what he decreed and about which he now complains, also illustrates the distance and isolation that characterize Zeus and his role.

This singular posture of the god makes him unique, almost a stranger among the Olympian gods. Had the Poet dared to have Zeus experience both his responsibility for and his pain at Sarpedon's death, he would have thereby created a new god and a new religion. This solution saves Zeus from a crisis, but must also be conceptually upsetting and emotionally dismaying for the Narratees. How can it be that Zeus decrees the death of his son, forgetting that he loves him?

Not being able to save his son, Zeus begins to celebrate Sarpedon's death with a miraculous portent: he pours drops of blood to the ground (XVI. 459–60).[20]

After Sarpedon's death, Zeus asks Apollo to remove and wash Sarpedon's body, to anoint it with ambrosia (XVI. 670 and 680) and to cover it with clothes that are ambrosia, i.e. immortalizing.

It is difficult to measure the boldness of the text when it represents Apollo washing the black blood and wounds from the dead body of Sarpedon in the streams of the river. As the mythical principle still active in Greek tragedy shows, the gods cannot face death, even the death of the mortals they love. Here Apollo takes up the dead body of Sarpedon and becomes the divine example of celebrating the funeral rituals due to the dead.

---

**20** On this symbolic portent (XVI. 459–60: αἱματοέσσας δὲ ψιάδας κατέχευεν ἔραζε / παῖδα φίλον τιμῶν) Reinhardt 1961, 342 writes: "Never is Zeus so deeply torn by pain as ruler and father. The marvelous feature of bloody tears that he pours to honor his dear son harmonizes heavenly pain to flowing earthly blood." This harmony, however, is bitter and unmerciful for the two armies: Zeus' bloody drops for Sarpedon must be connected to his analogous symbolic act at XI. 52–55, where Zeus, so to speak, initiates the vast bloodshed among Trojans and Achaeans by this same portent: "And the son of Kronos turned the evil turmoil upon them and from aloft cast down dew dripping blood from the sky, since he was minded to throw many strong heads to the house of Hades." This same symbolic portent forecasts in book XVI the carnage around Sarpedon's corpse. While this carnage is a sign of the importance and distinction of the fallen hero and gives him honor (XVI. 492–501), it is also what characterizes the murderous economy of war established by Zeus and according to which Sarpedon is destined to die. In this act of celebrating his son's death, Zeus restores his fatal role.

The twins Death and Sleep shall convey Sarpedon's body to Lycia (XVI. 454–55, 671–73), where, Zeus says, "his relatives and comrades will give him a funeral with a tomb and a stele" (454–55= 674–75). The Greek expression suggests granting his body a heroic cult and some sort of immortalizing status.[21] Explicitly, however, the *Iliad* and, less rigorously, the *Odyssey* refuse to grant post mortem physical immortality to their heroes.

Only the Narratees know Zeus' contradictory position: the characters of the poem know nothing of this. Glaukos, the first interpreter of Zeus' action, deeply saddened by the loss of his cousin and companion, finds it scandalous that Zeus did not save his own son (XVI. 521–22): "the best hero perished, Sarpedon, the son of Zeus, who does not even stand by his own child" (ἀνὴρ δ' ὤριστος ὄλωλε / Σαρπηδὼν Διὸς υἱός· ὃ δ' οὐδ' οὗ παιδὸς ἀμύνει). He has to accept that it is so and fight in order to snatch the body of his dead companion from the hands of the Achaeans.[22]

Glaukos' accusation of Zeus' failure to save his son is correct, for Zeus did not save Sarpedon, but also ideologically typical. Glaukos sees his cousin through the eyes of Zeus and as dependent for his life on Zeus' will. Though Glaukos defines Sarpedon as the best warrior, still he attributes the responsibility of his death to Zeus. Patroclos and even Hector will do the same, attributing their deaths to Zeus. But Hector will, at the last moment, acquires consciousness of his personal autonomy, his value as a warrior, and his separation from the divine destiny, and will die as if he were choosing his death by a free and noble gesture. Glaukos and the other heroes have a more dismal image of themselves than that which the Narratees have. For the heroes, their lives are determined by the insensitive will of the Olympians. The goal of the text is therefore to tell the Narratees that Glaukos' ignorance should not remain the Narratees' ignorance. It is impossible to resolve the knot of Zeus' irreconcilable attitudes: but

---

[21] Analyzing the word *tarkhuô*, of Anatolian origin, Nagy 1990, 132 ff. agrees with Chantraine that there Sarpedon will "be treated like a god" and demonstrates, through a magisterial scrutiny of archaeological and linguistic data, that this treatment means that he will receive a heroic cult and achieve a sort of immortalization: "... the verb *tarkhuô* indicates not only that the relatives and comrades of Sarpedon will treat him like a cult figure but also that he will thereby attain some form of immortalization after death" (138).

[22] Glaukos is the champion who looks like an immortal when he meets Diomedes in VI. 128 ff.; he belongs to the race of Bellerophon, most handsome and of lovable manhood (VI. 156): Glaukos does not fight against Diomedes, but exchanges a gift of friendship with him: Zeus blinds Glaukos as he exchanges bronze for gold. "The impossibility for mortals of making confident statements about the intentions or nature of the gods is a commonplace in Greek texts..." (Parker 2011, 33).

the difficult religious and conceptual problem grants audiences and readers a liberating awareness. Human misery is inscribed in the divine, Zeus murders his son through his emotional void, and the text invites the Narratees to endure it. Divine pity is not in vain: by its mimetic power, the text invites the Narratees to understand the value of funeral rites. By celebrating impressive rites, as Zeus does, mortals should express their deepest pity and their love for the dead person in order to internalize their sorrow and to create a long-lasting memory, a story and a monument of this sorrow. It is in this context that the poem inscribes its purpose.

## 2.2 Hector's Deadly Destiny

> "The recurrent scene-shapes are as characteristic a product of oral poetry as the stock epithets. And, like the epithets, they provide artistic opportunities for difference —within similarity— which would be difficult, if not impossible, for a writing poet."
> 
> Taplin 1992, 10

Zeus' conspiracy against Hector begins at the first lines of book XXII when the narrative tells us that Hector remains in front of Ilion, outside the protection of the walls (XXII. 5–6):

> The deadly destiny shackled Hector, forcing him to stand fast
> in front of Ilion and the Scaean gates.
> 
> Ἕκτορα δ' αὐτοῦ μεῖναι ὀλοιὴ μοῖρα πέδησεν
> Ἰλίου προπάροιθε πυλάων τε Σκαιάων.[23]

With the definition of "destiny" as "deadly," the Narrator tells us —almost as a confidential piece of information— that this destiny is inscribed in the will of Zeus. We learn as much since this epithetical unit has been used by characters to indicate the will of Zeus.[24] Zeus is present as the destiny that shackles Hector

---

[23] In line 5, almost every word covers its own metrical foot, thus often combining musical and intensity accents.
[24] ὀλο(ι)ὴ μοῖρα with inverted sequence is found three times in the *Iliad*: XVI. 849 (Patroclos speaking of his death), XXI. 83 (Lycaon speaking of his ruinous destiny), and in our passage XXII. 5, where the poet is speaking. In XXI. 83–84 Lycaon identifies the μοῖρ' ὀλοή with Zeus: "now again deadly destiny has put me in your [Achilles'] hands: surely I must be hated by Zeus who has delivered me to you, again." In XVI. 849, the identification with Zeus is certain (see Janko, "the ring formed by 845 and 849 confirms that Zeus and Fate are equated," though Janko leaves open an alternative: see below Ch. 3.3). Indeed, this equation is suggested by

and prevents him from entering the gates under the protection of the walls. This prevention is the sign of Hector's death sentence: by remaining outside the walls, alone, waiting for Achilles, Hector offers himself to his preordained death.[25] Hector's death will make Troy the defenseless victim of Athena's will (XV. 71), according to Zeus' long-term resolution (*boulê*). The restoration of Achilles' honor has already been attained when Achilles sent Patroclos to fight, and the provisional victory of the Trojans essentially ended with the burning of an Achaean ship.

It is unclear in what way "the deadly destiny <u>shackles</u> Hector": the binding is certainly a metaphor, but a metaphor for what? Does it paralyze his mind or inspire a sort of madness, as *atê*, for instance, would do?[26] Or did it even suggest to him the argument of what sounds like Hector's own resolve, as again *atê* could do? We are left to assume that in some way the deadly destiny may have subliminally affected Hector's decision, but an assumption cannot be proved and must remain a hypothesis. The indefinite connotation of the metaphor is therefore tricky: it allows the Narratees to assume that Zeus' will acts subliminally, binding Hector's mind, but it does not assert nor clearly intimate it. The metaphor only tells us that the "deadly destiny" acted as the power that "shackled" Hector, and does not exclude that Hector made a free and autonomous decision –though fatal– when, as he argues, he considered it his best option to remain outside.

---

Patroclos, through a compositional strategy, and not by the narrative or by Zeus himself. As Patroclos is dying, he has prophetic power and correctly knows Zeus' responsibility. We too know the active role of Zeus in Hector's death. The equation between Zeus and the "deadly destiny" is therefore implicit in our passage. The synonymity of Zeus and human destinies is sustained by Eustathius (ad *Od*. 11, 297) and therefore it has a long history. Some forms of synonymity between human destinies and the gods are asserted by some modern authors: Chantraine 1952, 71 takes the gods as executors of human destinies; Lloyd-Jones 1971, 3 interprets the gods and Zeus as expressions of destinies; and analogously Rousseau 1995, 428, n. 33: "la destinée est l'expression de l'ordre qu'ils [les dieux] instaurent et font regner..."

**25** Zeus preordained that "divine Achilles, in anger at the death of Patroclos, shall then kill Hector (XV. 68: κτενεῖ Ἕκτορα δῖος Ἀχιλλεύς). It could be that the epithetic unit δῖος Ἀχιλλεύς is used for contextual and functional meaning aside from its mere metrical convenience: Achilles, the killer of Hector —who has no epithet— is defined by his "divine" label, with all the evocations that this earmark implies: his divine birth, his superior might, his tight relation to Zeus, etc.

**26** Durante 1976, 111 thinks that the reference of the metaphor is to the "magic binding" of which there are a few concrete examples in the *Iliad*, for instance through the verb *thelgein*.

At line 99 ff. Hector imagines entering the city, and he argues on subjective grounds why he should reject that idea. As is shown by Hector's soliloquy,[27] the narrative produces a convergence between Zeus' deadly *moîra* and Hector's free will.[28]

Hector feels shame and remorse for the orders that, against the better advice of Polydamas, he gave to the army: his orders caused a terrible and bloody loss of men (XXII. 99–110):

> Oh me, wretched! If I go now inside the gates and the wall [πύλας καὶ τείχεα],
> Polydamas will be the first to lay reproach on me
> since he tried to make me lead the Trojans inside the city
> on that baneful night when divine Achilles [δῖος Ἀχιλλεύς][29] rose up
> and yet I would not obey him, though that would have been far better.
> Now[30] since by my own recklessness I have ruined my people,
> I feel shame before the Trojans and the Trojan women with trailing robes[31]
> lest somebody else, lesser than I, will say of me:
> "Hector believed in his own might and ruined his people."[32]

---

**27** The text says, literally, that Hector "spoke to his great-hearted heart" (99). On the soliloquy and its organic construction, see Pelliccia 1995, 121–22, 136 ff., and on this monologue see 198–99. One wonders how the Muses can see or even know and therefore report the true words of a soliloquy, i.e. of a speech that a subject elaborates inside himself. It is not clear whether the text is aware of this dilemma: the soliloquy, by escaping those terms, would explicitly manifest itself as a creation of the Poet's work.

**28** See the theory of "double motivation" in Lesky 1961, and for this case of "overdetermination" see also Janko 1992, 3.

**29** It is the epiphany, the apocalypse of Achilles, appearing with all the earmarks of his "divine" nature: his military superiority, his divine birth, his shining like a star (XXII. 26–31): the word "divine" that evokes all these characteristics could be the Narrator's way of interpreting Hector's fear and despair as it intimates the unbearable menace arising in that fatal night. It could be Hector's positive evaluation of his opponent and therefore a sign of his "heroic chivalry" as De Jong 2012, 85 tends to interpret it. For the meaning and import of this epithet, see Appendix 1.

**30** "Now" comes after the reproach that Polydamas will throw against Hector, since Hector refused to follow Polydamas' advice (XVIII. 254–83). Furthermore, an insignificant Trojan warrior —who stands for the whole army— will shame him for his presumption and his failure to save his army. This reproach will be spread on the whole city.

**31** This epithet occurs three times in the *Iliad*, exclusively for the Trojan women, and is used only by Hector. It is a touch of his style. He often identifies the defeat of Troy with the enslaving of the women, the loss of their free and civilized life.

**32** See the good commentary of De Jong (2012, 86–7, n. 106–108): "It is clear that as always, the speech of the anonymous person in fact externalizes the inner thoughts of the speaker himself: thus the *tis* virtually repeats what Hector earlier said himself (Hector ruined his peo-

> Thus they will say; and as for me it would be much better
> to face Achilles, slay him, and come back,
> or else to be killed by him in glory in front of the city.[33]

Hector is remorseful both for the ruin he has brought upon his army, and for the ruin of his reputation; he feels both guilt and shame.[34] This coupling of the two different feelings eliminates the neat anthropological distinction between shame and guilt cultures that became popular in the sixties. As we see in this case, both forms of cultural response are simultaneously present in Hector: the one and the other reinforce each other, creating a strong emotional field that prevents Hector from thinking seriously about Achilles' stronger ability and the safety of his own fatherland.

Gill (1996, 84 ff.) explains the ethical position of the hero and offers a non-Cartesian definition of the "self-consciousness" that Hector displays in his monologue: "a psychological state in which the person internalizes the kind of dialogue (including the dialogue of ethical persuasion) that is normally conducted with others."

Accordingly, the monologue, though addressed by Hector to his magnanimous heart (or mind, 98), does not dig into the conscious or unconscious layers of man deeper than a normal dialogue would do.

Gill does not take into account Hector's destiny brought to accomplishment by the will and action of Zeus; yet he recognizes that Hector "is trapped," and explains that "his decision to fight is forced on him by the logic of events rather than by the logic of his own goal-directed reasoning" (p. 89).[35] Indeed, the nar-

---

ple) replacing 'through his reckless behavior' by 'trusting on his own strength.'" See, for the same line of thinking, Gill (1996, 84 ff.).

33 ἠέ κεν αὐτῷ ὀλέσθαι ἐϋκλειῶς πρὸ πόληος. The word ἐϋκλειῶς is found only here in the *Iliad*. Richardson 1993 translates πρὸ πόληος "in defense of the city," and of course both translations are correct. See Chantraine 1953, 2. 311: Hector means dying gloriously before and in defense of the city.

34 Redfield 1975, 157–58: "The same inner force that sent him to battle —his *aidôs* ["reverence"] before the men and the women of Troy— prevents him from returning home." Gill 1996, 83 correctly distinguishes Hector's recognition that "he was wrong to reject Polydamas' advice" and that because of his recklessness he destroyed his army, from the loss of his reputation that intensifies the shame that he has already internalized as a feeling of failure.

35 Hector uses the conditional mode, "it would have been much better" (103) (namely if he had obeyed Polydamas), and it would be much better (107–8) to fight than to face social reproach. But if he should be killed, would the result of this decision be a much better solution? The conditional clause seems to respond positively to this question, but for himself and for the defense of Troy and of the women of the city, his retreat to the city would have been much better. This is also what Hector's father suggests to him (56–57). Therefore, two factors – one

rator, in order to display the two converging and independent motivations for Hector's fight, needs both Hector's reasoning justifying his decision and the divine intervention that must accomplish Zeus' *boulê*.

Both motivations sound textually unsatisfactory to the Narratees: the divine *moira* leaves unexplained the way it shackles Hector's mind, and Hector's resolve is grounded on a weak line of reasoning. The miraculous convergence of divine and human motivations appears therefore instrumentally constructed by the text to avoid conflict. It succeeds through the trick of the metaphor in the phrase: "the deadly destiny shackled Hector" that does not explain how it shackled him and leaves room to any imaginary ways.

It is during this illogical moment of resolution that Hector reveals an image of himself that is independent from that which he had when he felt certain that Zeus would fully support him in the task of destroying the Achaean fleet. It is the image that he displayed to Polydamas at XVIII. 293–5 and that led Hector to reject Polydamas' correct proposal. Now, on the contrary, Hector sees himself lacking any assurance of Zeus' support and turns to an image of warlike fervor, to win or to die gloriously. The contrast between Hector's two images of himself deserves critical comment on two accounts. First, the contrast is stressed by the two different signs of victory that he receives. When Hector boasts to Polydamas that Zeus "has given me to gain shining triumph (*kudos*) at the ships, and to pin the Achaeans on the sea" (XVIII. 293–4), Hector evokes the distinctive sign of victory, *kudos*, with which Zeus marks him and thus removes from him the danger of dying; when now in his soliloquy he sees himself dying with glory (*eukleiôs* XXII. 110), he appeals to "*kleos*" which is provided to heroes by poetry that celebrates their heroic death. The contrast between the two signs and their providers shows two different ways in which the *Iliad* evokes heroic comportment: one through the name and assistance of Zeus, and the other through the immortal force of poetry. Zeus will abandon Hector and the poem will save his glory.

Secondly, as I insist on defining Hector's two different attitudes as images of himself already inscribed outside himself, I intend to call attention to the fact that the victorious image that Hector attributes to himself through divine *kudos* and the glorious image he will receive from poetry, both precede his view of himself and establish two epic ways of inscribing the hero into poetic patterns. In other words, the "double motivation" begins by giving the hero divine and human images of himself, i.e. by splitting his human awareness, and makes this split awareness the production of the Poet's and the god's interventions.

---

internal and the other external – shackle Hector, his inconsequential reasoning and the deadly destiny, and keep him outside the protection of the city's wall.

If Hector's reasoning is inconsequential, his emotion is strikingly powerful: the monologue carries the intensity of despair and, in its deepest significance, it points to Hector's readiness for suicide. Hector's diction has impressive touches: the redundant and emotional mention of "the gates and the wall";[36] the evocation of the "deadly night" in which menacing, "divine" Achilles moves (νύχθ' ὕπο τήνδ' ὀλοήν, 102), which reminds the audience of Hector's "deadly destiny" (ὀλοιὴ μοῖρα) in line 5; Hector's admiration for the people of his city and their civilized life that he wants to preserve at the cost of his life; the vision of the whole city seeing him fighting and eventually dying gloriously for her and before her. The deployment of his heroic death is already present in his soliloquy.

Through the effect of the divine decree, the Narrator induces his audience to realize from the beginning of Hector's action the desperate inconsistency of human decisions.[37] At each step of Hector's action, his presumptions, hopes, and wishes are wrong. The events appear to him with aspects that he misinterprets. This happens also in this dramatic moment: his decision to face Achilles, which Hector determines to be the most advantageous resolution (*polu kerdion* 107), is not only grounded on weak logic, but is also an impossible one for him to follow. As Achilles reaches him, Hector is taken by a mad panic and flees in desperation.

The long footrace allows the Poet to amplify and intensify the pathos through which Hector descends to hell. The running itself on the edge of the walls evokes a terribly pathetic contrast: Hector runs around and close to the walls that he defends simply by being there and which, at the same time, keep him from safety.

---

**36** Pelliccia 1995, 140 describes eloquently how the text focuses on Hector's isolation: "Hektor's isolation outside the gates of Troy at the beginning of book 22 is established with elaborate care: at the end of 21 we learn that ἄλλοι Τρῶες ['the other Trojans'] (606) have fled into the city; at the beginning of 22 (5f.) that while they flee, a baneful fate has bound Hector to stay there before the gates; at 38 Priam addresses Hector from the walls: μή μοι μίμνε ...οἶος ἄνευθ' ἄλλων ['do not await alone, away from the others']." Insightfully, Pelliccia sees the isolation as one of the specific features determining and accompanying Hector's speech to his heart (see 198 ff.). No one can be the witness of this inner talk, so as to report it, not even the Muses.
**37** Heiden 1997, 227 says it eloquently: "The Muse of Homer accords mortals psychological autonomy precisely in order to caution them as to its use." Yet mortals cannot "take their decisions in careful dialogue with Olympus," as Heiden goes on, for Olympus does not open this dialogue with the mortals of Iliadic times, only in exceptional circumstances and with exceptional people. Mortals have no privileged access to the Muses, unless they are poets, and even so only to learn about mortals' deeds in the past. The present is excluded from the Muses' inspiration.

The narrative can use three different focalizers to describe Hector's racing around Troy: Hector himself, the gods, and the Poet himself. At one point of Hector's running, the text nostalgically describes the washing pools where "the wives and the beautiful daughters of the Trojans" were accustomed to wash their shining robes in the old days, the days of peace before the Achaeans came (XXII. 147–156).[38] The poetic language imagines with anguish —almost speaking in the place of Hector— the lovable scene of the beautiful women, their shining robes (154), their elegance, which Hector evokes when he describes them as "with trailing robes" (105), and for whose freedom Hector fights and risks his life.

As Hector runs, pursued by Achilles, the narrative develops two different similes to describe this desperate race. The first is a description with the support of a simile and seems to focalize the Poet's point of view (XXII. 158–60):

> In front, a brave man fled, but a far better one pursued him
> rapidly, since both men were not trying to win a sacrificial beast
> or oxhide trophy, —for these are prizes given to runners—,
> no, they raced for the life of Hector, breaker of horses.[39]

Similes are a creation of the Poet: here it is particularly elaborated by the chiasmus and the balance of expressions in 157–58. Hector's epithet "breaker of horses" is chosen purposely: it is used five times in the *Iliad* and does not carry any victorious connotation; on the contrary, it occurs at VII. 38, at what will be the inception of a duel that Hector will not win; at XVI. 717 as he desists from the battle; at the moment in which the Golden Scales announce Hector's death (XXII. 211); and as the last word of the poem which closes the description of his funeral (XXIV. 804).

The force of the passage derives initially from the contrasting content: the nostalgia for the serene aura of peace ("before the Achaeans came," 156) gives

---

**38** Tsagalis 2012, 8 shows how the topographical washing pools "are turned into a cultural space, standing for the peaceful years enjoyed before the outbreak of the war."
**39** πρόσθε μὲν ἐσθλὸς ἔφευγε, δίωκε δέ μιν μέγ' ἀμείνων
καρπαλίμως, ἐπεὶ οὐχ ἱερήϊον οὐδὲ βοείην
ἀρνύσθην, ἅ τε ποσσὶν ἀέθλια γίγνεται ἀνδρῶν,
ἀλλὰ περὶ ψυχῆς θέον Ἕκτορος ἱπποδάμοιο.
The chiasmus on line 158 graphically emphasizes the contrast of the fighters' actions and value. Notice the enjambments of καρπαλίμως and ἀρνύσθην that prolong in some way their preceding lines, mostly dactylic, and therefore "running" fast. The poet has chosen the epithet ἱπποδάμοιο instead of the metrically equivalent ἀνδροφόνοιο ("killer of men"): of course, Hector here will be killed and will not be the killer. The mention of "breaker of horses" anticipates also the next simile.

place to Hector's deadly flight as Achilles pursues him. Hector desperately runs in a race that he has already lost, since "a far better man pursued him": the force of the priamel, "not for this prize...but for," ends upon the tremendous paradox that the prize of the race is Hector's life. The voice of the Poet describes Achilles' pursuit of Hector as if he saw it unfurling before his eyes and captures the paradoxical mechanics of the footrace: if they were running for a prize, Hector would be running to reach the finish line first, yet Hector does not run for a prize, since the prize is his own life. Hector is at once one of the competitors and the prize of the competition, the runner and the (passive) object, the prize (to be claimed) for the winner.

The simile illustrates the poetic voice's tragic vision and emphasizes the epic paradox of this footrace.

The Poet surprisingly contrasts his strong assertion that Hector races for his life with a new simile (XXII. 162–166):

> As when prize-winning, single-foot horses
> [ἀεθλοφόροι περὶ τέρματα μώνυχες ἵπποι][40]
> run at full speed
> around turnposts and a great prize is laid up,
> a tripod or a woman, in honor of a dead man,
> so these two swept three times around the city of Priam
> [ὣς τὼ τρὶς Πριάμοιο πόλιν πέρι δινηθήτην]
> with rapid feet and all the gods were looking upon them.

Most surprisingly, this simile transforms the death-seeking pursuit of the previous image into a prize-winning horserace. It shockingly contradicts the previous statement and even mentions the objects offered for a splendid prize, a tripod or a woman. In this new simile the racing is not by foot, but by horse: it removes the desperate effort of the running fighters by evoking – inconsistently enough – the footrace only at the end of the simile (166); and, in contrast, it emphasizes speed (163, 166) and athletic conventions ("circling around the turnposts" 162, "three times" 165).

The simile ends with the remark that "all the gods were looking upon them" and, by this remark, the simile delivers to the Narratees the identity of its focalizers: the gods. For certainly the narrative focalizes at this point the views of the gods, as also De Jong notices. The gods see the pursuit of Achilles and the flee-

---

**40** The contrast with the previous passage is insisted upon by the mention of the prizes: 160, "the life of Hector," and 162, the "prize-winning horses" running for the splendid prizes of ritual races. Notice also the mention of the turnposts.

ing of Hector as an elegant and rich athletic competition, with horses, splendid prizes for the winner, and perceive the dramatic pursuit as a pleasant spectacle for their eyes. It is a shock: they do not see either the heroic or the tragic aspects of the fighters' race. They cannot, for they do not know and do not understand death: accordingly, they do not understand what heroism is, since heroism is constituted by a fighter's readiness to risk his life. They do not see the paradoxical trait that the epic simile has emphasized, that Hector is both a runner competing in this race and the prize.[41]

The explicit and disturbing contrast of feeling and vision that emerges from the two similes raises questions about the Poet's intentions, since the similes are the Poet's free creation. The purpose of showing in such a dramatic way the incomprehension of the gods witnessing a heroic situation could be simply that of asserting a matter of fact: the gods are blind to the reality of human feelings and experiences connected with death. This explicit and banal assertion might, however, also intimate a dissatisfaction with such divine incomprehension and suggest how the gods' attitude at the sight of Achilles' deadly pursuit of Hector is, in human eyes, unwittingly cruel and even ridiculous.

At any rate, whatever shade of interpretation we give to the contrast between the two similes, an important theological principle emerges: an equal and hybrid evaluation of serious matters among men and gods is impossible, since death preordains human views of important phenomena – yet this precondition is completely absent from the divine mind.

With the divine focalization of the race, the text moves its stage among the gods ("all the gods were looking upon them," 166) and assumes also a temporal scansion of the events in agreement with the gods' interventions.

Through the simile, the Poet prepares the audience for the epic device of "three times … at the fourth time" (see below p. 55).[42] This module scans time in

---

**41** In the third book of the *Iliad* we will see the gods feasting and drinking nectar while attending to the duel between Paris and Menelaos. The ancient Greek commentators show surprise and indignation at this divine behavior. Yet this sort of moral reaction is illegitimate because the gods cannot be sensitive to human behavior that ensues from mortals' consciousness and the reality of death.

**42** The force of this module is that of creating a dimension of time and space that serves exclusively narrative conventions and scans time in accordance with a divine final act at the fourth moment. Here the third time occurs as Zeus debates whether to save Hector and the hero runs for the third time around the city to save his life; the fourth event is kept in suspense until 208 when the 'Golden Scales' decide and ratify Hector's death. This module is applied to a situation in which a hero's thrice-repeated assault is stopped at the fourth charge by a god. In Patroclos' and Apollo's confrontation (XVI. 702–09 and 784–92), Apollo, after Patroclos' three charges,

accordance with the divine presence: it measures time in four phases whose last one is determined by the intervention of the god. We have here a new intimation of a divine plot that unfolds around Hector's and Achilles' fight: even the time of their running is measured through time measurements that are significant in a divine context. At the end of their third circling of the city, Zeus intervenes.[43] He has observed the scene with the other gods and unexpectedly he breaks forth with an appeal to them, as to whether they should save Hector or let him die (XXII. 167–87). The *diêgêsis* reports his lament (167–76):

> and the father of men and gods[44] broke forth among them:
> "Ah me! It is a beloved man the one whom I see before my eyes
> hunted around the walls.[45] My heart grieves
> for Hector[46] who in my honor burned many thighs of oxen
> on the crests of Ida's many valleys,
> and again on Ilium's heights;[47] but now divine Achilles[48]

---

stops him and, as the fourth act, disarms Patroclos, confirming the fatal meaning of the module. Other applications of this module occur at XX. 445–54 and XXI. 176–79.

**43** De Jong 2012, 100 thinks that "It is perhaps not far-fetched to read the fact that the race in the simile forms part of the funeral game as an ominous sign and to take it as an anticipation of Hector's death." The ominous allusion is there, but it hardly explains the addition of the problematic and surprising second simile, since the suggestion of Hector's death is made explicit in the first description and short simile at 158–60.

**44** The epithet acquires a contextual connotation, as Zeus, ruler of men and gods, feels pity for a man, and, wishing to save him, proposes to the gods his rescue.

**45** Zeus has watched the thrice-repeated racing of the two heroes around the walls. The emphasis on his subjective stance as a viewer prepares us for his exceptional and isolated feeling about Hector's predicament. Given the stress on the "walls" in this scene and elsewhere in the Poem (see Tsagalis 2012, 130 ff.) the description, "around the walls," is not idle: the walls should defend and not expose Hector. At XXII. 3 the men who have escaped the tremendous fury of Achilles are leaning along the "ramparts" and the text calls them "beautiful," almost as if the men were the focalizers of the epithet, since the ramparts are ensuring the men's safety.

**46** In the parallel scene at XVI. 431, the Narrator attributes to Zeus "pity" for Sarpedon, which Hera, at 450, describes as Zeus' "grief." About Zeus' grief for the death of the dear man, De Romilly 1997, 151 writes: "On ne saurait mieux préparer notre pitié." Notice the transfer from the subject "I," who sees —and may turn the eyes elsewhere— to the subject "my heart," which feels pain and grieves independently of any will.

**47** By praising Hector's and Troy's piety, here and at IV. 44–49, XXIV. 66–70, Zeus implicitly questions the common Achaean stigmatization of Troy due to Paris' abduction of Helen. The text mentions two of the various places where Hector sacrificed on Zeus' altars: indeed Zeus, in reality, is the god who has altars everywhere.

**48** δῖος Ἀχιλλεύς: this standard noun-epithet phrase is not otiose here: with the mention of Achilles' "quick feet" in the next line, it performs the full epiphanic entrance of Achilles. Furthermore, by evoking all that is actually divine in Achilles (from his divine birth, to his superi-

pursues him around the city of Priam, running with quick feet.⁴⁹
Come, you gods, think and consider
whether we save him from death, or now, for all his virtue,
we strike him down at the hands of Achilles, son of Peleus."

We, Narratees, enter the divine stage and attend to the scene already played out (in Book XVI. 421 ff.) between Zeus and Hera concerning Sarpedon. In both scenes, a goddess domestically related to Zeus raises the same hindrance to his wish and he consents to the death both of Sarpedon and of Hector. The differences between the two versions are, however, remarkable. The most significant one is that here Zeus opens a sort of consultation with the gods and asks them to consider the possibility of saving Hector, as he grieves for the pious man. Zeus does not speak privately to his wife as in the previous version, but, in his role as chief of Olympus, he addresses the entire divine gathering that happens to be watching the race.

The result is astonishing: no god answers Zeus' appeal. Only Athena, his "dear daughter," answers and produces the objection that Hera raised in the earlier scene (179–81):

a man born mortal, since long ago doomed to his destiny
you want to save back from cruel death?
Do it, but not all of us other gods approve you.

With these three simple repeated lines, Athena undermines Zeus' three roles: by mentioning man's mortal destiny appointed from long ago, Athena refers intentionally or casually to Zeus' breaking of his own decree, that Hector should die on this specific occasion; by stating that the gods will not approve of his proposal, she undermines his authority as leader of the Olympian gods; and by questioning the motivation of his grief ("save him back from <u>cruel</u> death") for the most pious hero, she proves that Zeus' grief cannot have serious grounds: he attaches his affection and grief to a man whose death is inevitable, for whom Zeus cannot and should not do anything.

---

ority, to his shining like Sirius, etc.), it separates him from Hector's diligent and constant ritual piety. Still, though Zeus recognizes Achilles' Zeus-like divine traits, he seems ready to frustrate Achilles' attack and deprive him of his victory by saving the pious man.

**49** The standard expression "with quick feet" is repeated three times in the course of this event (8, 172, 230) and shows how the context revitalizes what seems dead or conventional in the epithetic expression "quick-footed Achilles." The expression, as a sort of synecdoche, denotes Achilles' warlike aggressiveness.

Another striking difference is that, in the corresponding episode with Hera, Hera proposes an immortalizing ceremony for Sarpedon's funeral, whereas here, Zeus surprisingly reacts to Athena's utter denial in a sweet and consenting tone (XXII. 182–85):

> Then, answering, cloud-gatherer Zeus told her:
> "Take heart, Tritogeneia, dear child! I am not saying this
> with zealous heart, and with you I want to be kind.
> Do as your mind bids you and hold back no longer"

Athena does not need another word, and rushes from Olympus to meet Achilles. Zeus answers in this surprising way for at least two major reasons. First, the text, without giving any account of its strategy, has transferred Zeus' public appeal into a private and domestic dialogue: the text blurs public and private spaces. Athena speaks to Zeus simply as to her father, in what we could call his fourth role and function in the *Iliad*, that of his fatherly relation to her. Zeus does not answer to the gathered Olympians but to his "dear child," the one who habitually fulfills his plans, satisfies his concerns, and dons his armor. Zeus has even appointed her as the one who will accomplish the destruction of Troy, "in accordance with the plan [and will] of Athena" (XV. 71: Ἀθηναίης διὰ βουλάς).[50]

Athena's rejection of her father's appeal cannot really stand in for the assembly's answer. This is the textual trick that allows the narrative to stage Zeus' appeal to the assembly and his complicity with his daughter: in this way, the text prevents the contradiction or the paradox in Zeus' mind from exploding and produces a false impression of coherence: how can he not accept his dear daughter's arguments?

This blurring of roles also causes a psychological blur. The text forces Zeus to move straight from his pathetic appeal to his peers to his smiling approval of Athena's denial: the text dismisses all coherence and consequentiality in order to insure, at the structural level, Zeus' fundamental responsibility: the death of Hector.

The second reason for which Zeus answers Athena sweetly is that, by encouraging her, "Do as your mind bids you and hold back no longer," he seems to have understood that his wish delays or even suspends her own violent, irre-

---

[50] Athena receives from Zeus an exceptional favor on another occasion and through an unexpected and analogous solution to the dispute between the two (VIII. 30–40): the same surprising transfer from a public to a private and domestic context occurs. Some of the same lines are repeated: see below, Ch. 5.1.

pressible desire, her *boulê*, the destruction of Troy. She immediately rushes to reach Achilles in order to kill the unique and indispensable defender of Troy.

The text must navigate with some difficulty between psychological and structural pressures.

The end of the divine scene, leaves unexplained Zeus' initial words —"a beloved man whom I see... My heart grieves for Hector who in my honor burned many thighs of oxen..."— and his public gesture: "Come, you gods, think and consider whether we save him from death." Why does Zeus react with grief to Hector's death on the grounds of the hero's piety, and why does Zeus propose an alternative that is objectively impossible and that he himself has made unfulfillable?[51] The text could not omit this expected reaction to Hector's punctilious practice of sacrifice. This emotional, merciful, and exceptional attitude harmonizes with Zeus' ritual and cult function: his affectionate tone and his grief shape therefore a theologically positive figure of Zeus.[52]

Yet this figure conflicts with the other function of Zeus, as hypostasis and embodiment of Hector's destiny, a function in which Zeus is actively promoting Hector's death.

The myth, or pious people's expectation, represents Zeus as a god with anthropomorphic, compassionate, and fatherly feelings, while Zeus as master of human destinies is a divine might in the sense of a "superhuman," "infinite"[53] character. The two functions are not permeable or compatible even though they belong to the same being: the conflict between divine and human natures lies in

---

[51] He himself, as god of Fate, has decreed Hector's death on this specific occasion (XV. 68); he has adapted Hector's armor in view of his death (XVII. 210: see Ch. 2.3), and he has shackled him before the walls (XXII. 5), forcing him to remain outside.

[52] Zeus responds to Hector's devotion with pain and with a sort of dutiful sympathy. The *Iliad* avoids giving Zeus that appreciation and admiration for the character's personal qualities that we see in other poems, as, for instance, when Zeus speaks of Odysseus' superior intelligence at *Od.* i. 65–67, or when Athena, revealing herself to Odysseus in Ithaca (xiii. 291 ff.), glorifies Odysseus' cunning and deceits in the deployment of which he is by far the best man, and comparable to what she is among the gods. In the *Iliad*, the text limits the positive porousness between the man and Zeus to a ritual connection. Oddly it is Iris who, bringing a message from Zeus to Hector, addresses him with this invocation: "Hector, son of Priam, equal to Zeus in intelligence" (XI. 200: Ἕκτορ υἱὲ Πριάμοιο Διὶ μῆτιν ἀτάλαντε). She adds this compliment by her own will, and of course this is the decision of the Poet. Did the Poet feel an excessive severity or sparingness in Zeus' appreciation of Hector and other mortals?

[53] I use "infinite" in the sense of "*apeiron*" ("limitless") as it is used for instance by Anaximander and in the phrase "*apeiron periekhon*" (the *surrounding limitlessness*) as illustrated by Diano 1970, 52–58. With this anachronistic definition I intend to qualify Zeus' non-anthropomorphic aspects, his endless power over human destinies, and his celestial vastness.

Zeus. The narrative deals with the conflict by keeping the two figures of Zeus separated and by making the pitying Zeus unaware at this point of being responsible for Hector's deadly destiny. We have underlined the textual blurring as the trick through which the two facets of Zeus' polyvalence are not allowed to communicate with each other.

The dramatic figure of a Zeus overtaken by mercy and yet aware of the impossibility of this feeling would have created a revolutionary, new religious figure, but the text cannot or dares not fully fashion this figure and stages via textual devices a positive anthropomorphic god.

Since only the Muses know what Zeus said and did on that occasion, the religious and poetic dramatization of this scene mirrors the concern and the purposes of the human Poet. In the useful but fictional distinction that I draw between the Muses' narrative and the poetic voice, some effects of the dramatization belong to the poetic voice.

In the episode of Sarpedon's death, Zeus' anthropomorphic feelings —his grief and pity as a father— are easier for us to understand than Zeus' anthropomorphic feelings that have their source in Hector's deep and punctilious piety. Zeus appears to grieve for the loss of honor that will occur with the death of such a great sacrificer as Hector, but if this source of pain were serious, he should not let Athena decide about the loss of his honor.

The narrative, however, manages to impress its audience with the mimetic force of Zeus' cry of sorrow and gains an enormous poetic power by having Zeus' voice resonate alone on the theatrical scene. His appeal to the whole assembly of the gods resounds through the vastness of Olympus and of the world;[54] the whole city of Troy, standing on the walls, attends mute and desolate to Hector's death, the whole Achaean army watches immobile, and the whole gathering of the gods avoids answering Zeus' grieving appeal. In this cosmic silence, only the word of Zeus spectacularly resonates with grief and affection to deplore the death of the pious and beloved hero. The Poet's voice seems to resonate strongly due to the dramatic inflection in this theatrical context. However inconceivable, superfluous, and ineffective it may be, Zeus' pity induces the pitying reaction of the Narratees, the only ones capable and ready to respond to that theatrical appeal. The theatrical dramatization turns into a metapoetic device by which only the Narratees fill the silent theatrical scene with their own pain. Through them, the metapoetic resource stages the lament of humanity answering to Zeus' appeal and to the misery of the human condition.

---

54 On the marvelous, illogical staging of the spectacular scene, see Aristotle *Poetics* 1460a 11–17.

This extraordinary effect allays, of course, the Narratees' disappointment at Zeus' inability to save Hector, but does not preclude their realizing the disconcerting, asymmetric, and incompatible relation between Zeus' anthropomorphic and superhuman facets and in general between the divine and the human worlds.

Returning to the action on the Iliadic stage —the race of the two heroes— Hector and Achilles are running for the fourth and last phase of the 3+1 divine temporal module. Zeus is watching and, according to the divine module, at the fourth moment a god ought to intervene.

Here the expected event is produced by the surprising appearance of the Golden Scales (209–13):

> But once they reached the springs for the fourth time,
> then the father stretched out the Golden Scales, and in them
> he placed the two destinies of sorrowful death,
> the one of Achilles and the other of Hector, breaker of horses,[55]
> and balanced them by the middle: Hector's fatal day went down
> and reached the house of Hades[56] and Phoebus Apollo left him.[57]

The Golden Scales are not a metaphor or an allegory, but a real instrument of measurement that tells the will of Zeus in an impassive and visible form and sign.[58]

Through this agreement of the Scales with Zeus' *boulê*, Zeus' grief for Hector and its anthropomorphic nature vanish. Nothing like this divine instrument bespeaks the impassive and inalterable force of Zeus as dispenser of destinies. It is under that divine and surrounding might, that the heroes suffer their death.[59]

---

[55] The Poet chooses to emphasize the mention of Hector by the epithet that evokes his infelicitous lot.

[56] It is a real instrument, since, as soon as it has measured the weight of destinies, it is perceived by the gods, and Apollo, seeing it, abandons Hector. The instrument must have a cosmic dimension if it can reach Hades. The scene has abandoned the earthly ground and is occurring on the divine stage.

[57] καὶ τότε δὴ χρύσεια πατὴρ ἐτίταινε τάλαντα (209). Notice the impressive temporal markers that resume the module and have the effect of bringing the attention of the audience to a specific "now, finally." "Father" abbreviates the formula, "the father of men and gods," and leaves the graphic stress to "the golden scales," with which πατὴρ ἐτίταινε τάλαντα, by assonance, forms a strong association. The "father" and his dealing with the Scales are of course anthropomorphic details, but they are projected into a non-human vastness.

[58] At XVI. 658 the Golden Scales are called "sacred" and are equated to Zeus' decision.

[59] The fact of not fully appreciating the divine significance of the "fourth moment" in the module of 3+1, has prevented some critics from seeing or appraising the metaphysical force of

Now Zeus' implicit identification with the Golden Scales redeems him from the humiliation of his previous ambiguous behavior: as Zeus' splendid appeal to pity proved unheard and inefficient, Zeus' stature had accordingly shrunken.

Thus, as Reinhardt[60] saw, through the Scales we have an image of the Zeus of the first book, the one who, with the movement of his head (another sign-image!), declares to Thetis the irrevocable power of his decision.

Athena,[61] in the manner of a ritual patron god[62] – suddenly and unexpectedly for Achilles, though not for us readers – stands beside him (XXII. 215, ἀγχοῦ δ' ἱσταμένη).

Athena tells Achilles (XXII. 216–223):

> Shining Achilles, dear to Zeus,[63] now[64] I expect that the two of us[65]
> will bring to the ships of the Achaeans [the prize of] our great triumph
> [οἴσεσθαι μέγα κῦδος][66]
> after we have killed[67] Hector, though he is insatiate of battle;

---

the Golden Scales: see, for instance De Romilly 1997, 118–19, who emphasizes the literary and dramatic role ("la solemnité du moment") of the theme, or De Jong 2012, 103, for whom "*the fourth time*" simply increases the temporal force of the adverbial expression.
**60** Reinhardt 1961, 166–67.
**61** In the *Iliad* Athena is no longer the consistent ally of the gods connected with the Succession Myth, as she seems to have been. See for instance *Il.* I. 399–406. Kelly 2007, 423 concludes his analysis by writing that, in the *Iliad*, "Athena is the embodiment of Zeus' success and power."
**62** See Nagy's (1979, 144) definition and description of the two "ritual antagonists" of Achilles and Hector and his lucid and contextually impressive description of the battle: "...just as Paris and Apollo are named by the *Iliad* as the killers of Achilles (XIX. 416–17, XXII. 359–60), so also the death of Hector is described as being actually caused by Athena, albeit with Achilles and his spear serving as her instrument (XXII. 270–71, 445–446). Athena not only intervenes overtly in the final duel between Hector and Achilles (see especially XXII. 222–23, 255–277, 298–299); she even says that she and Achilles are the ones who vanquish Hector (XXII. 216–218)." My comments adhere to these critical statements.
**63** As Richardson notes, the epithet "dear to Zeus" "has point here, since Akhilleus' success must depend ultimately on Zeus' favor, and perhaps the poet also felt θεοῖς ἐπιείκελε to be inappropriate in Athena's mouth." The combination of Διὶ φίλε and φαίδιμ' Ἀχιλλεῦ is unique in the *Iliad*. The vocative Διὶ φίλε is used only for Achilles and Patroclos, emphasizing the heroic identity of their pairing (I. 74, XI. 611, and XXII. 216.) The combination of the two epithets in line 216 distinguishes Achilles from the regular φαίδιμος Ἕκτωρ.
**64** De Jong 2012, 215 comments on this "now": "The thrice repeated *nun* (216, 219, 222 and cf. 235, 253, 250, 268, 300, 303) marks – to Achilles and Narratees alike – that the moment of revenge has *now* come after all the delays and retardations."
**65** Most Mss. read νῶι γ' where the γ' emphasizes the dual.
**66** For this interpretation of the phrase see Pucci 2010, 205–06. One can add that on lines 245–46 Athena – though speaking as Deiphobus – seems to confirm and expand the meaning I impute to the phrase.

no way for him to escape us two now,
not even if far-darting Apollo should take many troubles,
groveling over and over before father Zeus, bearer of the aegis.
Now stand you here, and catch your breath while I go
and persuade the man to fight you, face to face.

Zeus is the supreme supervisor of the event: if Apollo wanted to save Hector, he would have to supplicate Zeus.[68] Athena signifies, with her sarcastic representation of Apollo, that Hector's destiny is sealed, and that Apollo will not intervene as he did before at XXII. 7–20, nor save Hector as he did at XX. 443–44 (Achilles had recognized the god, 449–51).

Achilles has nothing to answer: the ritual patron assumes the direction of the strategy and the development of the fight and tells him what to do: Achilles may well have forgotten his hatred for Hector, his destiny of dying after killing Hector. Athena permeates him and, to some extent, replaces him. This is another result of the epic paradox: the divine association elevates the heroic deed to an exalted height, but, since the divine nature intrinsically does not need heroism and accordingly fails to take heroism seriously, it empties the human fight of heroism and transforms the fight into a magic game and the human hero into a mere instrument: Athena uses Achilles' spear as her own weapon.

We face here a structural issue. On the one hand the battle between Achilles and Hector is unique and specific due to the heroic stature and function of its fighters, due to the episode's position as the last and decisive act of war in the *Iliad*, and due to its detailed differences with similar episodes; on the other, the battle mirrors other similar battles in the Poem and specifically the battle between Menelaos and Paris, and the aggression in which Athena cooperates with Pandaros, etc.[69] The individual features of the duel between Hector and Achilles offer therefore a unique occasion and an original narrative; but structural devices that place these episodes within a common type tend to attenuate their originality and to depreciate the unique function of each element. To give only

---

**67** The verb δηώσαντε is a dual form and implies that Athena participates in the action of cutting down Hector. The verb has a violent connotation meaning *to tear, cleave, rent* and it is used for savage beasts (e.g. XVII. 65).
**68** We have seen Thetis, among the gods, supplicating Zeus (I. 500–01, 557, XXII. 20). Athena's sarcasm is a sign of the festive and mocking tone of her behavior during the action. The drama of the last confrontation, played on the human stage, but with a divine conspirator, glorifies the joy of victory, the jubilation at the end of the gods' support for Troy, and the exaltation at the near destruction of the city.
**69** Bakker 2017 has traced the structural and schematic echoes in these episodes, underlining the intended allusive force of the line repetitions and of characters' roles.

one example, the specific presence of Athena and her shrewd contributions in this last duel identify, through her function, the other occasions when she contributes, such as when she directs Pandaros' arrow. The structural function evokes the very complex architecture of the Poem and directs critical investigation toward this aspect rather than taking the readers toward an appreciation of the individual force of each event. At any rate, it invites the reader to be aware of this double function of the repetitions. The architectural structure should not prevent the appreciation of the individual scene, since any semantic element, even when repeated in a similar context, receives a slightly diverse meaning. The "air de famillle" of similar poetic texts opens a complex game of allusions, echoes, variations and differences: it is not a quotation.

This principle is certainly also valid for the structurally repeated features of this great Iliadic episode: I have underlined the differences between the similar features in Sarpedon and Hector episodes, and I will trace the specific traits of Zeus' and Athena's conspiracy against Hector. The provocative force of details emphasize the univocal poetic tone and meaning of similar architectural contexts.

The epic narrative knows well the effects produced by the divine intervention, namely the displacement and confusion of the human quality of heroes' actions and intentions. Athena (220–21) mocks the ritual antagonist god, comforting Achilles and promising him victory through their joint work ("we will bring the prize of our great triumph"). Athena has no respect for Hector or the Trojans, as she is the eager planner of their destruction. She has no respect for heroic performance, or for its formality, seriousness, and fatal end.

This situation teaches us that in the *Iliad* "the heroic" is submitted to the purview of the divine and the miraculous and that, therefore, it carries a metaphysical breadth, and necessarily the suspicion of some textual cunning. The Narrator preferred to risk this suspicion rather than subtract this battle from the gods' control and participation.

A miraculous scene follows: Achilles stops in the middle of the field, catches his breath, and Athena, disguising herself as Hector's brother Deiphobos, encourages Hector to fight against Achilles ("let us stand fast against him," 231) and to use unsparingly the spear ("let there be no sparing of the spear," 243–44). The last piece of advice is particularly nasty and ungodly.

Athena's trick contravenes the theme of solidarity between champions and produces a violation of all the expected modes of fighting between two champions (Tsagalis 2012, 43 and 48 ff.).

The dialogue between Hector and his brother is an exchange of repartees in the middle of what is a no-place in a no-time. It is a miraculous parenthesis that suspends reality on the human stage, on which Hector knows that he operates.

Hector falls victim to the divine deception: he stops running, forgets his panic, and faces Achilles. He knows that he can count on the help of his brother.

Hector, facing Achilles, endeavors to reach an agreement about the respect of the corpses; Achilles answers with the ostentatious confidence of a winner (XXII. 261–72): he rejects all agreement.

The presence of Athena and her words assure him that he and she will kill Hector who no longer has any chance (268–72). He forecasts an open and harshly fought battle, full of skill and force:

> Have recourse to all your valor. Now hard need
> comes to you to be a spearman and a bold fighter.[70]

Achilles addresses this harsh encouragement to Hector in order to intimidate him, and the Narratees may be induced to expect a real battle without any magic tricks.

The text suddenly topples the expectation built by Achilles' self-confident words: the great hero throws his spear and misses Hector.[71] It becomes uncertain whether Achilles at this point can really beat Hector. As Richardson writes, "Hector's escape from being hit has momentarily raised the tension as if this were really an open fight and Hector had a chance (so bT 274)." The Narrator is too skilled a poet to avoid at least a potential exchange of blows: Athena directed Diomedes' spear against Ares (IV), the arrow of Pandaros against Menelaus (IV), and she could have prevented Achilles' failure. But Homer, as a virtuoso artist, follows the usual fighting scheme, prolongs the audience's suspense, and gives Hector his virtual chance. The pathos increases.[72]

Athena, invisibly for Hector and for the rest of the actual viewers, brings back the spear to Achilles, as the text indicates in one and half lines (276–7):

---

70 παντοίης ἀρετῆς μιμνήσκεο· νῦν σε μάλα χρὴ
αἰχμητήν τ' ἔμεναι καὶ θαρσαλέον πολεμιστήν.
Ameis & Hentze see the asyndeta of this and the next two sentences as a sign of passionate speech. Each of the three sentences is short and delivers strong and menacing words.
71 The missed throw is unexpected from such an exceptional warrior but not in principle, for this process of the exchange of blows is traditional (see Fenik 1968, 6).
72 The text presents this detail in two different stages. Achilles' missed throw occurs on what I call the earthly stage: Athena does not help Achilles, and the unimaginable happens: the greatest fighter misses his throw. The Narrator draws the poetic advantages I noticed. But then Athena has to fix the situation and on the divine stage she recovers Achilles' spear.

but Pallas Athena snatched it up
and gave it back to Achilles, unnoticed by Hector, the shepherd of the people.⁷³

Hector does not see this trick, which suppresses empirical vision and place – yet this trick really happens, and Achilles will have a spear for his second attack.

Hector exults over Achilles' failure: he can assume that Achilles was only bragging about Athena's presence. He does not see her. A new vain hope! Hector addresses Achilles: "You failed... Achilles, equal to the gods (XXII. 279: θεοῖς ἐπιείκελ' Ἀχιλλεῦ) and in no way you knew from Zeus my destiny." We do not know whether it is by chance or by intention that the epithet sounds ironic, even sarcastic. For, in this moment, Achilles is objectively similar to a god, even if he missed the throw on the earthly stage. The text now places Hector in the wretched mindset in which it places him so often throughout the Poem, that of being confident, even optimistic, about himself and his goals, even when the objective situation does not justify these feelings.⁷⁴ The *Iliad* showcases Hector in all his frail, hopeful, pathetic human nature.

Yet Hector's blindness this time is short. As he throws his spear, he hits Achilles' shield, but, as the audiences know well from XX. 261–72, the shield, being manufactured by Hephaistos, is impenetrable. The spear rebounds from the shield. As Hector does not wound his enemy, he calls Deiphobus for another spear: quickly Hector realizes that Deiphobos is not there and concludes that Athena has cheated him.⁷⁵ He understands that his death is near⁷⁶ and he turns to himself in a soliloquy (297–305):⁷⁷

---

73 The text presents a parataxis ἂψ δ' Ἀχιλῆϊ δίδου, λάθε δ' Ἕκτορα ποιμένα λαῶν that places the two actions in a parallel order, "to Achilles she gave it and was unnoticed by Hector," and with a beautiful chiasmus that graphically contrasts the parallel terms.
74 See VI. 476–81, 526–9, XVIII. 305–9, XXII. 129–30, etc.
75 See the dramatic line XXII. 295: "he called for a heavy spear: but the man was not near to him"; and the felicitous comment by Taplin 1992, 242 who stresses the force of the pause or division in the middle of the line. This division "marks the moment when he [Hector] joins Achilleus in the certainty that death is imminent. Just as Achilleus was told by Thetis (18. 133) and by his horse (19. 409) that his death is *eggúthen* [near] so Hector realizes that it is his death, not Deiphobos, who is *eggúthen* [near]." Louden 2005, 96 interprets Athena's deception as a "parody" of her function of working in tandem with Achilles.
76 He imagines correctly that the false Deiphobus was a disguise created by the patron goddess of Achilles, Athena whose presence Achilles mentioned on lines 270–71. He sees in the divine epiphany only its cheating purpose and effect. We readers know that Zeus sanctioned her (XXII. 183), and Hector knows that if Athena did what she did, Zeus was in collusion with her, or at least not forbidding her. Hector acquires the knowledge of Zeus' divine will.
77 Pelliccia 1995, 198–99 remarks that the monologue is not addressed to the *thumos* and produces "a temporary break in the action"; it is "spoken with null addressee/audience" and

> Ah me! It is certain: the gods have summoned me to die.
> I thought that the strong Deiphobos was here beside me
> but he is inside the walls: Athena cheated me blind.
> And now, I see, evil death is close to me, and no longer far away,[78]
> no longer escapable: for truly since long ago this was the pleasure
> of Zeus and his son who strikes from afar, though, before this, they
> gladly defended me: but now fate is upon me. [νῦν αὖτέ με μοῖρα κιχάνει.]
> Well, may I not die without a struggle and without glory,
> [μὴ μὰν ἀσπουδί γε καὶ ἀκλειῶς ἀπολοίμην,][79]
> but in accomplishing a great deed, to be known by men to come.
> [ἀλλὰ μέγα ῥέξας τι καὶ ἐσσομένοισι πυθέσθαι.]

This noble speech does not need to have its source in the Muses' *diêgêsis*, but may appear to the Narratees as an invention of the Poet. There is indeed a difference in tone between the *diêgêsis* and the private voice of Hector: in the narrative, Athena's cheating is called *kerdosunê* (247: "skill," "shrewdness"), while Hector accuses the goddess of "total deceit," "total mockery" (*exapatêsen*, 299). The gods' summons to death implies a pitiless, authorial decision (300–01): "Ah me! It is certain: the gods have summoned me to die" (ὢ πόποι, ἦ μάλα δή με θεοὶ θανατόνδε κάλεσσαν). He discovers that he was part of the divine *boulê* that prescribed his death,[80] even when he did not suspect it. This discovery suggests him that Athena's act of deception was not the only one he suffered from the gods who, until now, had gladly protected him.

Hector addresses to himself the phrase that the Narrator addressed in apostrophe to Patroclos (XVI. 693). Through this repeated line, Hector is made to speak with a knowledge equal to that which the Narrator has of the gods' deci-

---

without any isolation, since Hector is in front of Achilles and "a direct speech contact is possible." With these remarks, the author emphasizes what I would call the mere metapoetic function and legitimacy of the monologue: the poetic voice enacts Hector's own voice, uttering despair for the deception that the goddess and the text have planned against him. He, indeed, uses the language normally at the disposal of the Narrator (see n. 81).

**78** νῦν δὲ δὴ ἐγγύθι μοι θάνατος κακός, οὐδ' ἔτ' ἄνευθεν. In this fully dactylic rhythm, the negative polar expression unfurls itself clearly, with the sound of theta embracing the most important words, and an almost rhyme in θάνατος κακός.

**79** The negative force of the expression is remarkable: through the figure of litotes, the expression replaces the positive form that would make a much weaker utterance: "May I die with glory." Through the litotes, the utterance, "May I not die without glory," seems almost to deny death, as if in the absence of glory Hector would not die. The force of the expression is increased by the fact that the verb is desiderative, and the line is emphasized by the frequent alpha privative.

**80** The text makes a distinction between the gods summoning Hector to death and his *moîra*: the purpose of this distinction is to intimate, for Hector, some autonomy within the divine plan.

sions and to employ the same language, as if Hector knew he was the Narrator of his own story.[81]

Hector assumes a decisive and autonomous authority in the most significant part of his speech, as he turns his attention to the mode and the scope of his death: "may I not die without a struggle and without glory." He makes himself master of his own death, so that he does not die by obeying Zeus' summons, but, so to speak, by his own decision. He entrusts his immortality —that the gods deny him— to the epic poem, to "accomplishing a great deed, to be known by men to come."

His authorial gesture is invented and produced by the poetic voice that severs him from the divine summons and makes him speak as a hero who finds a resource and an escape in the epic narrative. The epic narrative, on the other hand, needs a death like this one to become itself immortal.

The poetic voice steals the character from Zeus' summons and inserts Hector's gesture into its own text: without Hector's final gesture and words, Hector would meet his death simply as an absurd victim of Zeus' whim, and not as a hero.[82]

The "heroic death" is the great invention of the *Iliad*. From Socrates to the Romantics, the heroic death has depicted a tragic and sublime experience.[83] With his words, Hector implies that, though he knows a superior force is crushing him, he will rush against it, as by his own will, ready to accomplish a great deed. In this way, Hector faces his death by a free and noble decision.

Different cultures have depicted wise, religious, and patriotic people who, looking at the survival of their ideas through different media, were ready to die "a heroic death" by challenging oppressive powers. The media have been diverse: philosophy, the arts, chronicles; and they have appropriated, as their own voice, the voice of the heroic victims.

---

**81** No messenger or voice has ever summoned Hector; the metaphorical "call" stands for the message that Hector reads in Athena's deception. Taplin 1992, 242: "Now Hector is able to use language which is normally only at the disposal of the Narrator."

**82** In Hector's eyes, Zeus' and Apollo's sudden change of attitude has no explanation. In the Narratee's eyes, since Zeus treasures Hector's piety and since Zeus wishes to (at least on the level of his ritual role) save him, Hector's death is senseless. The notion of the "sublime" is well chosen in this context, since the poem here sees the immense, even infinite continuity of its own song. In my 2002 analysis of Hector's speech I made a too simple contrast between the poem and the will of the gods.

**83** Plato *Apology* 28: Socrates chooses the heroic example of Achilles and quotes his words from *Il*. XVIII. 98: "Let me die forthwith since I was not defending my friend from his death." Though he is under the threat of being killed if he continues to teach philosophy, Socrates dismisses the fear of dying in order to be faithful to his philosophical mission. Plato immortalizes Socrates' heroic death.

By recording Hector's aristocratic gesture, the text composes a challenge to an apophatic theology. Against the blind suppression of the hero through divine despise and deception, the poetic voice celebrates Hector's rush to struggle and his accomplishment of a glorious deed. Hector's death is a "belle mort"[84] within these edifying registers.

In the aristocratic context, Hector's heroic death tinges with metaphysical and ideal value the proud choice he made when he found it much more advantageous to fight rather than to enter the city walls and be exposed to Polydamas' reproaches. His argument was objectively weak, of course, and the fact that it was paralleled by the "deadly destiny" that bound him outside the walls (XXII. 5) suggests to the Narratees that Zeus' will and Hector's decision have an unsolvable, mysterious, and frightful imbrication. When one considers Hector's death, and the destruction of the city, all the males —even Hector's small child— killed, all the women dragged to slavery, and the whole city given to flames, one wonders how "advantageous" Hector's choice was. The perception of Zeus' personal, but external, parallel induction makes the Narratees aware of the enigmatic nature that the *Iliad* confers on human destiny. The Poem does not deny what we would call Hector's "free will"; on the contrary, the text sustains it, and, by making it parallel to the inescapable will of Zeus, in this and in other similar cases, the text implies that the two convergent motivations —Zeus' will and Hector's passions, his pride and shame— are equally binding and interwoven.

The Narratees of the *Iliad* know Zeus' will and how it is deployed, but Hector makes his decision while unaware of Zeus' will and its binding nature. Therefore he acts, as men generally do, while hoping for the gods' help: "We shall see," Hector almost paradoxically concludes, "to which one the Olympian grants glory" (XXII. 130). The silence of destiny for all human beings makes Hector's condition a model for the whole humanity.

This text invites us modern Narratees to meditate on the meaning of "free will" in the various and complex contexts in which this concept has been discussed and elaborated in our long religious and secular culture. I am thinking of the aporia that the notion of divine "grace" and its relation to free will has created in Catholic and Protestant discussions. That a loving god may leave men free to do evil is a difficult and debatable principle.

---

**84** Vernant 1979 has eloquently defined Hector's death as "la belle mort." Within Hector's own knowledge of Zeus's control over his fate, this definition is correct: he is young, beautiful, his corpse will be protected by Apollo and reach his house as immaculate; he will have immortal glory. All these and other features Vernant lists for the definition of the "belle mort" are indeed there.

Even in a secular debate, the notion of free will has become questionable after Freud: it remains highly debatable what free will may imply in the context of our "ego," our "unconscious," and the historical destiny that hangs over us.

That the Iliadic text conceives of both the human act of will and the divine plan as autonomous acts, and that it depicts their relationship as a mysterious and frightful convergence, proves the Poet's high sensibility and pessimistic knowledge of the human condition.

The fight between the two champions begins and is played out on the human stage with almost no divine intervention. The text creates a rich crown of similes to ennoble the heroes during the last phase of the greatest duel in the Poem. The simile for Hector reads (XXII. 308–311):

> gathering himself together, he swept like a high-flying eagle
> that launches itself through black clouds to the land
> to catch away a tender lamb or a fearful hare;[85]
> so Hector made his swoop, swinging his sharp sword.

The detail of the "black clouds" that the eagle crosses evokes the presence of Zeus, for these black clouds conjure up Zeus' epithet: *kelainephês* ("Zeus in the black clouds") —eight times in the *Iliad*—, and his other epithet: *Zeus nephelêgereta* ("Zeus gatherer of clouds") —twenty-eight times in the *Iliad*.

The simile linking Hector to an eagle, the bird of Zeus,[86] occurs another time in the *Iliad*, at XV. 690–95,[87] where the poet, through this image, gives dramatic presence to the help of Zeus who with his large hand pushes Hector on toward the Achaean ships. It is an exceptional occasion: never again does Zeus help any champion in any physical way. The poet, accordingly, equates Hector's swoop to that of the eagle, making the god and his animal both symbolically present. There is no mention of storm and Zeus is present with his physical force, "strongly pushing him [Hector] onward, / with his big hand" (XV. 694–

---

**85** There is an illogical detail in the textual emphasis on the undefended prey upon which the eagle swoops: whether an eagle is the sign of Zeus or not, it always plunges on weaker animals, but here Hector, the eagle, attacks Achilles. The Poet signifies here that Hector assails his adversary with the pride and the aggression of an eagle, unconcerned, like the hero he is, about the force of its prey.

**86** The simile of a hero with the eagle is rare; more often Zeus sends the eagle as a public or explicit sign of his consent to those who pray to him (e.g. XXIV. 315, VIII. 247). Sometimes the eagle appears as an unfavorable sign for Hector (e.g. XII. 201, XIII. 822).

**87** XV. 690–94: "As a fierce eagle plunges upon a flock/ of winged birds, as they feed by a river,/geese, or cranes or long neck swans, /so Hector struck ahead/ and charged a ship with its black prow, for Zeus/ behind him pushed him on with his great hand/..."

95). The swoop of the eagle makes sense, for it refers to Hector's being pushed onward by the immense power of Zeus.

The polyvalence of the god in this scene is extraordinary: Zeus, master of clouds and storms, lord of human destinies, as a symbolic figure and as an anthropomorphic physical presence, thrusts Hector on. To imagine the hand of that god on the shoulders of Hector evokes another unimaginable world: it is a holy, cosmic event.

Now the Narratees are invited to compare that moment of Zeus' providential presence with Hector's rushing to death under the wings of Zeus' bird: the poetic voice composes a sinister and perverse comparison. The edifying theology of Zeus' earlier epiphany is displaced by the negative theology of Zeus' symbolic presence in Hector's meaningless death. It is significant that Zeus is present only symbolically, through his animal, because though Hector's death is inscribed in Zeus' will, Hector himself rushes forward in order to die for another end, that of asserting his heroic freedom, in this way satisfying the poetic voice of the Epic.

The simile that accompanies Achilles' charge against Hector occurs at the end of a list of the beautiful and shining pieces making up Achilles' armor: the shield is "beautiful" (314–15: σάκος ... καλόν), the helmet is "shining" (315: κόρυθι δ' ἐπένευε φαεινῇ), the fringes are "beautiful and golden" (316–17: καλαὶ δὲ περισσείοντο ἔθειραι χρύσεαι), and, finally, the point of the spear shines like Hesperos, the most beautiful star in the sky[88] (317–20):

---

[88] The superlative form of the epithet of Hesperos, κάλλιστος: "the most beautiful," "the fairest," qualifies human beings, horses, and artifacts, but rarely natural phenomena. In fact, only the waters of the same river are so called at II. 850 and XXI. 158. Beauty is a difficult notion to define: the poetic beauty is limited to the beautiful voice of the Muses, but almost never to the song/poem (*aoidē*) of the poet itself. In the present simile, the adjective suggests itself as a synecdoche for Achilles' divine personality. The heroicization of Achilles is complete here; it occurs two other times in the book (XXII. 25–32; 131–35) with different qualifiers of his status as a divine being. Other passages in which Achilles or his armor are described in terms of fire or light are XVIII. 205–4, XIX. 16–17, 365–83, 398, XX. 371–72, 490–94, XXI. 12–16, 522–25. See Richardson 1993, Nagy 1979 and Kelly 2007, 371, for whom the beauty of the star "points out the terrible nature of heroic beauty and excellence in that it always demands the death or suffering of others." Yet, by making Achilles a part of the divine order of things, the text removes all human experience from the image and creates an "extraordinary distancing from the action," as Moulton (1974, 393–94) writes.

> As a star comes from among the stars in the darkness of the night,[89]
> Hesperos [the evening star] who is the fairest star in heaven,[90]
> so the gleam shone from the point of the sharp spear which Achilles
> was shaking in his right hand, thinking evil thoughts against divine Hector.

Athena is no longer felt as being present. Another divine presence is evoked by the poetic voice, that of a starry night.

As Hesperos "is the fairest star in the sky" (318: ὃς κάλλιστος ἐν οὐρανῷ ἵσταται ἀστήρ, with respect to the other stars), so the point of Achilles' spear is more luminous and more beautiful than the other luminous and beautiful military implements of Achilles. His whole armor looks like a starry night.[91]

The spear's point is singled out because it will be the tool that kills Hector, as Christos Tsagalis has correctly interpreted.[92] The specific nature of the comparandum is remarkable: beauty and light are the earmarks of Achilles' armor and of his assault. The vision of Hesperos in the starry night conjures up the divine order of the world: for the *ouranos asteroeis* is the seat of Zeus, and men pray to Zeus by raising their hands toward the starry sky (XV. 370–71), or by "raising the eyes toward the vast sky" (*idôn eis ouranon eurun*, III. 36, VII. 178, 202, XIX. 257, XXI. 272).

The simile casts a totalizing image on the divine will (the *boulê* and its poetic narrative): This representation of the starry vault can be identified with the imaginary totalization which, beyond death, names the presence of being.[93] This identification is supported by the figure of Zeus as god of the sky and master of the human destiny: his "not revocable, not unfulfilled word", and the bending of his head as sign and cause of an incoming event, his Golden Scales crossing the world from Olympus to Hades and deciding the happening of

---

**89** οἷος δ' ἀστὴρ εἶσι μετ' ἀστράσι νυκτὸς ἀμολγῷ: "as a star comes from among the stars in the darkness of the night," echoes line 309, which describes the eagle in the simile for Hector's swoop: ὅς τ' εἶσιν πεδίον δὲ διὰ νεφέων ἐρεβεννῶν: "that launches itself through black clouds to the land." This initial similarity emphasizes the radical difference between the two similes: shining and darkness.
**90** The three repetitions of the word ἀστήρ and its being the phonetic model in the line: κάλλιστος ... ἵσταται ἀστήρ, show the preeminence of the sound-image of the star and its beauty.
**91** As we will see, the simile also ties Achilles to the heroic action.
**92** The fact that the text has singled out the spear as the leading term in the starry night is remarkable because this weapon is the only one in Achilles' armor that is not divine, but merely human: it has been fabricated from an ash tree from the Pelian mountain (XXII. 133).
**93** I am referring to Paul de Man: "The constellation signifies the most inclusive form of totalization, the recuperation of a language that would be capable of naming the remaining presence of being beyond death and beyond time" (1979, 52).

things are images of his cosmic impersonation, of his infinite greatness as Walter Otto defined it.[94] The *Iliad* (I. 70) describes the world itself, the *kosmos*, through the sign and notion of 'being' when it defines Kalchas as the one "who knew the things that are (*eonta*), the things to come (*essomena*), and the things past *(pro t'eonta)*. Today we could approximate the presence of Zeus' cosmic impersonation to what we may define as the presence of being, of the *Mysterium tremendum et fascinans*.

The Poet steeps the assault and the killing of Hector in the shine of the divine order of the world, but more directly his poetic voice presents and mirrors in itself that order, a glimpse of that beauty, a spark of that light.[95] The poetic voice compensates, through the simile, for both the omission of a real *aristeia* that the Poem ought to have given Achilles and Athena's misappropriation of the hero; and it attributes to Achilles the divine touch that he deserves as the greatest fighter in the *Iliad*, the Poem that gathers together the largest constellation of heroes.

Since Hesperos' appearance may intimate menacing effects, Achilles in that starry image can still be viewed as the actual menace to and the real killer of Hector, "his heart being filled with savage fury" (XXII. 312).[96] The divine order, the *mysterium tremendum et fascinans* just as the divine Poem, is not free from terrible beauty and from sublime violence.

---

**94** Otto 1955, 171 "...this greatness of Zeus which waxes toward infinity and issues in the inconceivable."
**95** Gods do not appreciate and understand heroism, but when they inspire a hero, or grant him a supernatural force, they may surround him with light (*kudos*): often this miraculous sign announces Zeus' presence, luminescence, and order of things. While this epiphanic manifestation intimates the celestial and the supernatural, it does not promise a beneficial result. It is a flash of light that is not lasting and marks the hero for the immediate deed. Zeus grants *kudos* also to Hector with the result that we know. Tsagalis 2008, 281 thinks that the simile is still a sign of disaster as the light of the spear's point foreshadows the fatal blow of the spear (XXII. 319–27). Moulton 1977, 85; Scott 2009, 74 admire, with different emphases, the serene atmosphere, the calm and peaceful view of the night that this simile evokes, in contrast with other similes in which the image of the star conjures up troubles and evils (see for instance XXII. 25–32–27).
**96** See De Jong 2012, 137.

## 2.3 Zeus' Conspiracy

> "A hero's desire to engage in battle is itself an acknowledgement of mortality and death; indeed, conceptually, it might even be regarded as an act of self-destruction."
>
> Kahane 2005, 172

As Achilles and Hector, each introduced by their similes, enter the last phase of their fight, the action unfolds as if Athena were no longer present. The poet's voice interrupts the explicit divine intervention, but, in an unsuspected way, this intervention continues.

An opening in Hector's armor exposes his throat, where the collarbone divides the neck from the shoulder, and Achilles hits there with his spear. Hector is killed. The armor encasing Hector's body is the armor that Hector stripped from Patroclos; it is Achilles' armor and it is the gift that the gods gave to Peleus for his and Thetis' wedding. It certainly had no holes. As it is unthinkable that this gift would have an opening on the neck, someone must have made it. At XVII. 210, Zeus, before Hector puts the armor on, "fitted [it] tightly to Hector's body" (Ἕκτορι δ' ἥρμοσε τεύχε' ἐπὶ χροΐ). Since the armor, being divine, could not be transfixed, it is necessary to assume that Zeus, god of fate, purposely opened that dangerous spot for Achilles to hit while fitting it tightly to Hector's body.[97]

Zeus' shaping of the armor is an exceptional and most surprising gesture. This god, who almost never physically enters into the human world, who only once pushes, with his hands, Hector forward (XV. 694–95), turns, like his lame son Hephaistos, into an artisan and prepares the weapons for Hector's last duel. Foreseeing the difficulty, he shapes the armor in order to grant Achilles access to Hector's body. He creates the conditions to make his own *boulê* come true.

Before shaping the armor for Hector's body (XVII. 201–11), Zeus, shaking his head –perhaps a sign of his fatal role –, holds an odd soliloquy (XVII. 201–10):

> "O poor wretch! Death does not sit heavy in your heart
> and yet death stands close beside you. You don the immortal armor
> of the best fighter:[98] others tremble before him.

---

[97] The text shows that Zeus controls the destination of the armor: at XVI. 793–800 we learn that Apollo struck away from Patroclos' head the helmet and this rolled under the feet of the horses. The poet comments that this helmet "had guarded the head and the handsome brow of a godlike man, of Achilles; but now Zeus gave it over to Hector to wear on his head, as death was close to him" (799–800). It is evident that Zeus, from the moment in which Apollo removes Achilles' helmet and corselet from Patroclos' body, preordains that they shall be worn by Hector.
[98] "The best fighter" alludes to the conventional definition of Achilles, "the best of the Achaeans."

You killed his companion, gentle and strong,
and took his armor from his head and shoulders, improperly.[99]
But now I will grant you great force to compensate you for what
will happen: you will not return home from the battle,
and Andromache will not receive the famous weapons of the son of Peleus."
So the son of Kronos spoke and nodded with his dark brows,[100]
and fitted tightly the armor to Hector's body.[101]

Zeus, as the ruler of human destinies, speaks to his heart (XVII. 200), but mentally addresses the victorious Hector: the hero is victorious because Zeus himself helps him to win. But Zeus is also the god who determines Hector's approaching death and who can measure the absolute nonsense of Hector's heroic behavior, his donning immortal weapons as he nears his immediate fate. The terrible irony is that while Zeus sees the vanity of Hector's donning of Achilles' armor, he is in fact adapting that armor to Hector's body to make his death possible.

He wonders that Hector, being so close to death, has no premonition of it, no feeling of foreboding. Zeus is made to display his inability to understand and appreciate Hector's heroic attitude: for Zeus, this attitude makes no sense, since it necessarily leads Hector to his own destruction. This is a very upsetting version of the epic paradox.

As Zeus explains to himself, though mentally addressing Hector, what he is going to do with Hector,[102] he asserts that he "compensates" Hector for his approaching death by granting him great force (*kratos*).[103] The word "compensa-

---

**99** Probably Zeus considers it presumptuous for Hector to don an immortal set of armor. In fact, it was Apollo who, on the divine stage, threw the helmet down from Patroclos' head (XVI. 793) and "Zeus granted Hector to wear it on his head, since Hector's death was close to him" (XVI. 799–800). For Thetis and the Immortal Horses it was Apollo who really killed Patroclos and gave Hector only the triumphal honor of the killing. See Ch. 3.4.
**100** Zeus' gesture of nodding with his black brows signifies his firm commitment, as god of Fate, to his own plan: it means that his word will be accomplished and become an event (see I. 524–30). Line 209 is identical to I. 528. Notice that at the moment of feeling incomprehension at Hector's attitude and action, Zeus shakes his head (XVII. 200), but as soon as he commits himself to granting Hector victory, he nods with his black brows.
**101** For this *skhetliasmos* and its fictive moment of contact, see Pelliccia 1995, 161–3 and in particular 163: "The sympathetic or pitying apostrophizing of a helpless or weaker figure who is out of contact creates intense *pathos*."
**102** In lines 205–08, Zeus speaks as the one who is responsible for Hector's death.
**103** μέγα κράτος ἐγγυαλίξω,
τῶν ποινὴν ὅ τοι οὔ τι μάχης ἐκ νοστήσαντι
δέξεται Ἀνδρομάχη κλυτὰ τεύχεα Πηλεΐωνος.

tion" triggers a double reading of the paradox that Zeus embodies with his action and words.

Let us first examine how Zeus describes the damage he is going to inflict on Hector. The god uses a pathetic epic expression when he refers to Hector's death as the event whereby Andromache will not receive Hector as he returns home from the battle, and with him the famous armor of Achilles. This description recalls Achilles' own description of the many Trojans he will kill (XVIII. 121–25): he identifies their deaths with the despair of the wives who will not see the return of their men. These cruel expressions create pathos by bringing to light the sharp and long-lasting pain of those who remain, and not the mere departure of the dead. Zeus has no need for compassion: the repetition of that theme, even if less pathetically and less hatefully expressed than in the mouth of Achilles, sounds unfit for his fateful role, and readers wonder at Zeus' anthropomorphic concern for making up for the disadvantages that he himself has brought about.[104] Yet, his real concern is with the famous armor of Peleus that Andromache shall not receive. This stress on the weapons harmonizes with the next gesture Zeus accomplishes as he "nodded with his dark brows, and fitted tightly the armor to Hector's body." Indeed, this armor shall not return to Andromache, just as Hector's body will not —Zeus anticipates Achilles' detention of Hector's corpse. But, after being appropriately modified by Zeus, the armor shall give access to Achilles' shining spear, and shall return to Achilles.

Let us now analyze the troubling notion of the "compensation" that Zeus grants to Hector. This "compensation" is the Greek *poinê*, i.e. the advanced reward or prize that Zeus gives to Hector in payment or compensation for killing him.[105] It is the only case in which a *poinê* (compensation) for the death of the hero is determined and given before the hero's death: in other cases, if I am correct, the *poinê* is the "blood-price" that is exacted by the hero's kinsmen as a compensation for the death inflicted on a member of the kin (XIII. 659, XIV. 483, XVIII. 498, I. 633). It comes after a killing and it is the blood-price that resolves the conflict between the kinsmen and the murderer. Sometimes the *poinê* implies merely "vengeance" (XVI. 398, XXI. 28). In one case (V. 266), the *poinê* is a compensation for a theft: by giving horses to Tros, Zeus compensates him for stealing Ganymedes, Tros' son.

---

**104** Zeus objectively deceives Hector, since Hector takes Zeus' support as a confirmation that the god will help him to burn the ships of the Achaeans —for Hector's trust in Zeus' endorsement, see e.g. VIII. 169–183, XV. 718–25. Of course, believing so, he has no foreboding of his death.
**105** See Rousseau 1995, Ch. 1 and 6.

Only in the present case (XVII. 207) is the *poinê* a price-reward given by Zeus in anticipation of (Hector's) oncoming death: Zeus' reward of greater force for a day is, in human eyes, a senseless reward-compensation.

Used as it is here, the word in human terms would mean "vengeance." This meaning, however, cannot be applied here. If Zeus' principle of compensation is applied to the great battles, it would serve to show the absurd economy presiding over the heroic life. For Hector's victory over Patroclos will be the "advance price" he receives for his death at the hands of Achilles, just as Patroclos' victory over Sarpedon would be the "advanced price" Patroclos would receive in payment or compensation for his death at the hands of Hector, and analogously Achilles' victory over Hector would be the "advanced price" in payment or compensation for his being killed by Paris and Apollo.

This rotten economy of heroic battle in the three quoted examples entails an iron-cast sequence of preordained results, of anticipated payments for succeeding disasters. What is wrong in Zeus' language is the use of the metaphor *poinê*, as we have seen, but not the iron-cast sequence that connects heroic killing and revenge on (compensation for?) the killer. The Narratees know well that this very economy is the composition device of the Iliadic battle: an Achaean hero slays an enemy warrior, and immediately a companion of the slain warrior kills the Achaean hero or one of his friends. This sequence, with alternating Trojan and Achaean fighters, is endlessly and mechanically repeated. The revenge is not defined as a "compensation" or a "reward," but pays the companions of the murdered hero for his death in a bloody way.

The Narratees are therefore aware that the principle that Zeus evokes under the idea of "compensation" is a textual compositional principle that can be completely independent of Zeus' will. It is, however, hard to believe that any human in the battlefield would describe this mechanical sequence with the metaphor of "compensation." No one would define the first killing a *poinê*, a "compensation" for the following death of the killer. For the reverse order, Achilles asserts that Hector, by being killed, will "pay the price/penalty" for killing Patroclos and stripping him (XVIII. 93 Πατρόκλοιο δ' ἕλωρα ... ἀποτίσῃ). There the notions of revenge and compensation are closed, but the word *poinê* is not used.

The metaphor used by Zeus implies a superior and non-human logic of a sequence that is typical of the epic convention. For Zeus is unmoved by human death and therefore not embarrassed by the absurdity of considering Hector's short triumph in the fight as a compensation, even a reward, for Hector's loss of life. The two statuses, short triumph and everlasting death have, in human eyes, not the same weight, but in the mechanically repeated deployment of the Iliadic fights, this absurdity emerges, though not under the notion of "reward".

The same metaphor inscribes the rotten economy that governs epic battles in a non-human logic, but it is contradicted by the epic logic of the "heroic death." To the extent that "heroic death" immortalizes the hero through Iliadic poetry, the hero's glorious behavior in battle is compensated and rewarded by the poetic immortality of his achievement. The reward is provided by the Poem and not by Zeus, for whom the hero's heroic status consists in his splendid victory (see XV. 612), not in his death.

We could even deepen the contrast between Zeus' and the Epic views about the "compensations" and "rewards" of the heroic life. Zeus' plan and conceptual image of the heroic economy endorse the mechanics of endlessly repeated killings and brings them under a higher and sublime light. Humanly speaking it is paradoxical, but it has a divine justification. Zeus' metaphor could even legitimize and validate as "divine" the Epic use and abuse of the mechanical economy of heroic battles.

For the Iliadic conception of the heroic economy, the privileged moment of the heroic life consists in the death of a repeatedly victorious fighter, both as he consciously sees himself deserving the immortal memory of the future generations, and as he serenely accepts that his immense battling success, his unmatchable fighting virtue have produced deep pains all around himself and will not prevent him from dying under the will of the gods. The former case is Hector's, the latter Achilles' (see Ch. 4.1).

Zeus' "compensating calculation and economy" vibrates with terrible eloquence and, for human sensibilities, disgraceful duplicity in the passage in which the Narrator depicts Zeus' responsibility for Hector's double destiny (XV. 610–14):

> Zeus himself from the height of heaven was helping him [Hector]
> and among so numerous of fighters to him alone
> he conferred honor and triumph (τίμα καὶ κύδαινε).
> For Hector's life had to be short
> and already now Pallas Athena was urging against him
> the day of his death through the strength of the son of Peleus."

The premises of Zeus' paradoxical posture and his later conspiracy against Hector are already present in these words. The narrative gives an account of what Zeus defined as his "compensation," i.e. his mastering the dramatic succession: the winner will be the next loser. The narrative states the tragic senselessness of the game that Zeus practices so as to satisfy Thetis' miserable (or "wrong," or "extraordinary") prayer (XV. 598: the meaning of *exaision* is open). In order to honor Achilles, Zeus plays a monstrous game: on the one hand, he cheats Hector, betrays his expectations, and prepares his death; on the other, he makes the Achaeans unable to resist Hector and to protect their ships. The Narratees realize at least the limited purpose of Zeus' game, as the text also confirms when in the same line (XV. 598) it calls him *mêtieta*, "clever and efficient." Yet the characters on the field are unaware of Zeus' intent and are fooled: Hector believes that he is winning, and the others fear that they will be defeated and their ships will be burned. For Zeus, the feelings and lives of mortals are negligible pawns in his game.

Hector is occasionally aware that Troy is condemned and that he himself will be slain, but, as Zeus grants him *kudos* ("triumph"), he falls into the illusory belief that he will win the war and, under that illusion, draws masses of Trojans to their death. Fearing their criticism, as we saw, Hector remains before the wall to lose his life in battle against Achilles.

The text has the difficult task of showing Hector winning, but not winning too much; he should not kill too many Achaean heroes among their great fighters, but only Patroclos.[106] The strategy that Zeus devises from book VIII to book XVI in order to give Hector victory entails a long succession of supporting actions and interruptions: constant delays – Zeus consents to Agamemnon's prayer (VIII. 245 ff.), giving space to Agamemnon's *aristeia* –; absences – Poseidon intervenes when Zeus turns his attention away (XII. 90 ff.) or when Zeus is seduced by Hera and falls asleep (XIV. 352–XV. 5) –; and ambiguous signs (XII. 200 ff.). The text causes its addressees to feel that the decisive moment of Hector's victory will never come to pass.

Zeus needs Hector to believe in his support, since he wants to accomplish his promise to Thetis, and when Polydamas interprets correctly Zeus' ambiguous sign (XII. 200 ff.: Zeus —Polydamas argues— will not consent to burn the ships), Zeus needs Hector to reject that truthful interpretation. The textual strategy is here again appropriate to Zeus' duplicity: Zeus' sign cannot be false, and yet Hector must not believe it. The *diêgêsis* displays the impossible position of having Zeus accomplishing simultaneously his two contradictory plans.

Zeus' plan of honoring Achilles, which determines most of the action of the poem, must, however, be fulfilled. He adapts the armor to Hector's body and leaves the necessary hole, executing such manual or miraculous labor in half a line (XVII. 210), a minimal detail, almost unnoticeable after the powerful meditation, and immediately preceding the figure of Ares surging into Hector's heart

---

[106] At the end of book XV, however, the great Achaean fighters have been wounded, yet not so seriously that they cannot fight, immediately after Patroclos' death, around his corpse.

(XVII. 210 ff.). Indeed, this half line has passed before the eyes of many readers who have missed its exceptional significance: though it does not posit explicitly Zeus' creation of an opening in the armor, it intimates that action and proves the theological intent of the poem. It shows that the will of Zeus has come to its *telos* ("accomplishment," I. 5), and that Zeus was responsible for keeping Hector outside the walls (XXII. 5), though again the god is only alluded to rather than mentioned as the one carrying out the action. It is a nasty trick, unworthy of the great Zeus, whose nodding brows indicate the fulfillment of his universal decisions. He turns here almost into a caricature as he puts his hand on the armor to shape it: the Narrator reduced this gesture to six words.[107]

As Hector falls (XXII. 330), the human stage takes over: Achilles' hatred for Hector emerges with all its pain. Achilles does not recognize any divine help in his victory and proudly tells Hector: "I made your knees slack" (335). Though Hector knows well who gave Achilles victory, he is too noble to waste words in order to correct his enemy.[108]

Only later when Achilles speaks to the Achaeans does he recognize that the gods granted him the slaying of Hector (379: τόνδ' ἄνδρα θεοὶ δαμάσασθαι ἔδωκαν),[109] but he uses a generic expression, even conventional, with no intended reference to the real presence of Athena. Then he invites his comrades to celebrate the shining triumph with a paean (XXII. 391–394):

> But now, young men of the Achaeans, let us sing a paean
> and go back to our hollow ships, and take this with us.
> We have won a great triumph (*kudos*): we have killed divine Hector[110]
> to whom the Trojans prayed in the city as to a god.

The first-person plural is problematic for the audience and the readers: Achilles extends the sharing of the victory to all the Achaeans, but he could also mean: "I, the Achaeans, and the gods have won a luminous triumph." The paean is sung to a deity, probably in thanks (see I. 473): the *scholia* intimate that lines 393–94 relate the content of the paean, and Richardson writes: "the asyndeton after 392 is in favor of this idea, as the asyndetic simplicity, brevity, and balance

---

**107** De Jong 2012 *ad loc.* fails to see the hand of Zeus in the exposed spot of the armor. Louden 2005, 95 observes that Achilles hits Hector in the neck, just where Athena hits Ares (XXI. 406), and adds that Athena has Achillean characteristics in the *Iliad* but Odyssean qualities in the *Odyssey*.
**108** The contrast with Patroclos, who grudgingly throws in his winner's face the help of Zeus and Apollo, is striking (XVI. 844–45).
**109** The plural θεοί (the "gods") generally invites one to think of Zeus.
**110** For the noun-epithet phrase, see Appendix 1.

of the separate hemistichs of 393." Accordingly, the paean begins with this verse: "We have won a great triumph (*kudos*): we have killed divine Hector," and was addressed to the deity who granted them the *kudos*.

The tone is victorious but measured: Achilles' silence on Athena's personal presence and decisive help is expected. Though he had told Hector (XXII. 270–71):

> for you there is no escape: *soon* Pallas Athena
> will crush you with my spear.

he is now silent about her, for the audience of the poem is accustomed to experiencing a character's partial or total silence after he has had full contact with a god. The character seems unable to recall the details of that full contact.

We can assume as an explanation for this behavior the fact that, as the divine presence fully appropriates the human being, the latter loses awareness in some way of his human situation: we do not see Achilles upset by his failure to hit Hector, he does not answer to Hector's provoking words, and he is not surprised by the fact that he has a second spear and that his old armor has an open spot close to the neck. All these events have taken place and therefore Achilles should have experienced and registered them. But he did not.

Achilles' behavior is analogous to his silence to his mother about Athena's epiphany (in the first book), and to Paris', Hector's, and others' silences about having their bodies snatched away by gods who save their lives. This silence is therefore the typical reaction of a character who experiences a full magic touch or possession by the divine. It is another version of the epic paradox in the *Iliad*.

This behavior makes a lot of sense: it explains the inability of the character to put into words the suspension of the whole empirical world: the character is drawn out of human space and time. Thus, for instance, at a certain moment Achilles stops running: he rests and waits, breathing calmly, while Athena reaches running Hector, tricks him, and brings him back to Achilles. All this is surreal: it is enough to say that the human witnesses saw nothing of these events. They simply saw Hector stop and then go to meet Achilles. I will not continue with the other magic events – the invisible recovery of Achilles' spear, etc. It is evident that perhaps not even the poet would have been able to describe in what suspension of consciousness the human character found himself when the magic, divine power obliterated all the coordinates of the human world. The Muses tell the Narratees what lies behind actions that seem simple and univocal: in reality, these actions can be polyvalent, but they may often appear to the characters as carrying no divine imprint. The gods are always there and may add their hand to what appears to be absolutely and exclusively human.

When presenting a miraculous event, the Iliadic practice consists in altering the consciousness of the mortal character as the miracle unfolds: it suspends a human awareness of time and space and makes the character able to comply with divine directives or actions. Once this contact is over, the mortal character loses awareness of what happened. If he could continue to experience that presence and be able to describe it, he would no longer act on the human stage, but would feel he was in another level of the world. He would participate in the divine world. Accordingly, if Achilles were able to recall and describe Athena's presence and actions, he would not feel the victory was his own. That is why Achilles, in the first book, could not tell his mother about Athena's epiphany, and yet Athena had changed his mind: she stopped him from killing Agamemnon and directed him to insult him. She moved him to play the role of the "wrath of Achilles."

The epiphany occurs, the miracle unfolds, and the mortal character is made to retain only what is necessary or useful for the dramatic action. The virtuoso skill of the poet derives dramatic advantages from the miracles, but, as he cannot maintain the permeability of the character's consciousness to the divine presence, he, without any scruples, effaces it.

An enigmatic consequence ensues from the simultaneous reality and invisibility of the gods. It follows that mortal characters in the heroic age had a warped, incomplete vision of what really happened. They failed to realize the real and active permeability between the two worlds, the divine and the human. This failure was unavoidable, since this permeability occurred to individuals and often in private: it is only in these conditions that the characters receive a miraculous intervention and is affected by it.

This permeability continues on the individual level when the Muses inspire each individual poet.

After experiencing the presence of the divine world, Achilles falls again into the consciousness of his mortal condition. As the dying Hector prophecies to Achilles that Paris and Apollo will kill him, Achilles answers with noble reserve (XXII. 365–66):

> I shall accept my death at whatever moment Zeus,
> with the rest of the immortals, wishes to accomplish it.

He directed these same words to his mother when she (XVIII. 115–16) announced that he would die soon after killing of Hector. The text repeats these two lines to make the audience aware that Achilles is conscious that his present victory is the cause of —Zeus would say the "compensation" for— his death. We have another example of a heroic death: Achilles knows that if he follows what he deems to be his duty, he will be crushed by divine destiny, yet he follows his duty and accepts that destiny.

Responding to his mother, Achilles had added (XVIII. 117–121):

> Not even the force of Heracles avoided death,
> though he was most dear to Zeus son of Kronos, and king,
> but death crushed him and the cruel anger of Hera.
> And I too, if the same fate awaits me,
> shall lie dead.

Since part of the hypertext knew of the divinization of Heracles, these lines assert a contrary view: under the regime of the Iliadic Zeus, the heroic death, that of Sarpedon or Achilles, does not lead to any form of immortalization among the gods.[111] It leads only to the Poem granting the death, and receiving from it, an immortal *kleos*. Zeus and his peers, like Athena, ensure the association and permeability between human and divine orders, but only within the limits that we have marked out, and that Achilles' words to his mother (XVIII. 117–21) cruelly expose.

## 2.4 The Poetic Voice and Mythical Narrative: The Epic Paradox

> "L'expérience montre qu'il n'y a pas de tradition en soi, de continuité, de flux, mais une série infinie d'évènements différents, singuliers, plus ou moins réussis qui, par leur singularité, donnent son existence à une tradition."
>
> Judet de La Combe 2017, 55

I will now underline and develop some of my critical remarks, paying special attention to the internal tensions or disjunctions that emerge in the textual attempt to represent an event marked by edifying permeability between the human and divine orders.

The association of the human drama with the divine action is what, on the surface, creates the fascinating appeal of, and the enthusiastic response to, Iliadic poetry. This interrelation is well captured by Whitmann when he writes: "Their [the gods'] appearances, in so far as they can be explained as organic to the human situation, represent as a rule an extended access of power, a dimension momentarily transcendental, reflecting in various contexts and forms the deep-seated Hellenic association of heroic force with absolute being" (Whitman 1958, 221–22).

---

[111] For the divinization of Heracles in the hypertext and the absence of such divinization in the *Iliad*, see Arrighetti 1998, 480–81.

This association is the splendid mirage of Iliadic poetry. In the episode of Hector's death, this association grants "an extended access of power" to Achilles, while the Narrator, through his starry similes, inserts Achilles' warlike figure into the totalizing image of "absolute being." The final combat of the *Iliad* is played on a cosmic and starry horizon.

This could be the edifying reading that the association of myth and human drama suggests. The narrative (*diêgêsis*) catches the charged energy of the action: it is exhilarating when Zeus cannot refrain from appealing his peers, confessing his grief and asking them for the chance to rescue Hector from his imminent death. The voice produces an image of his care for the mortal hero. A flash of edifying, positive theology illuminates the divine stage: the divine pain anticipates and reflects that of the Narratees, as Zeus' mythical mercy and its dramatization appear to be possible and offer the audiences the expectation of a miracle.

Yet the epic permeability between the human and divine orders here breaks quickly, almost at the act of its announcement, as we realize that the lord of human destinies will not rush to accomplish the miracle. Zeus' anthropomorphic pity is easily suppressed by his role as the Golden Scales, just as the anthropomorphic lover of a devoted mortal vanishes before the manipulator of Achilles' armor.

The mere notion of "grief" divides Zeus from the Narratees: the god's grief derives from the death of the great sacrificer, while the grief of the Narratees ensues from the untimely death of a great patriotic fighter, of the only savior of his city. The destiny of the hero is determined by Zeus himself, in his role as master of destinies, when he grants Hector a brief victory as a "compensation" for his death that Zeus himself prepares by perforating Hector's armor.

Zeus' grief is in principle unimaginable because the blessedness of the gods would be troubled by a deep sorrow. Yet in practice this grief speaks and reveals itself: its trouble is that it emerges from an ambiguous and undecided premise so that it is unclear whether it announces Zeus' pain for the valuable nature of the hero or for the cultual loss Zeus receives from the hero's death, whether his control of the heroes' destiny makes him subliminally unable to act so that the alternative he mentions —saving or not saving the hero— is psychologically unreal. Accordingly, Zeus' grief resounds as an empty voice, unfitting to receive answer from its addressees; a rhetorical manifestation of anthropomorphic feelings, quite different than the voice that is "not vain, not revocable, not unfulfilled" (I. 526–27). Zeus' appeal does not manifest the might of Zeus, not even the might of his sorrow —compare it with his violent and graphic utterances when he threatens the gods; it emerges as Zeus' vain regret for the death of a great sacrificer, reflecting therefore religious and poetic concerns, rather than his real distress.

Zeus' final incapability of doing anything for Hector, his negative theocracy, increases our pity for Hector and for the human condition: even a great god's grief and pity —whatever these might mean for the god— cannot save a man deserving of being saved.

The gods' silence before Zeus' appeal is an eloquent sign: it marks the presence of the divine world as a mute body before such an appeal and makes evident the apophatic theology that obscures the light of the permeable divine and human stages.

I have also paid attention to the authorial poetic voice which, through forms of focalization, intervenes in the narrative and confronts it. The gods' incomprehension of human death forbids them from understanding the virtues connected with heroism —courage, nobility, and frankness. The poetic voice shines through Hector's soliloquy, as he becomes aware of Zeus' and Athena's game that has made mockery of his warlike effort and its important purpose. He has a clear image of what they are and what they did to him.[112]

The battle directed by Athena and Zeus unfolds as a divine death dance: its directors are virtuosi masters of music, and yet they do not know and feel what death really means. The dancer, however, knows well what death means and inflects the virtuoso dance with his personal intensity and purposes. The text opens a hard tension between the dance music and dancer, between the narrative (*diêgêsis*) of the Muses and the poetic voice of the poem.

When facing the spirited Athena, Achilles sounds like her helper;[113] as a result, Achilles —despite 261–67— does not seem to fight because of his unappeasable hatred for Hector, but as a sort of divine background actor. Before the final fight, the poetic voice comes to his rescue, removing him from his service to Athena and inserting his image in the metaphysical horizon of a starry sky as a compensation for the misappropriations and mishandlings of his person.[114]

---

**112** Nagy 1979 and elsewhere has illustrated the daring of the poet(s) to attribute to their poem the power of immortalizing the heroes, while denying this power to Zeus in contrast with the hypertext that consents to him this power in specific cases.

**113** Athena does not commit herself to Achilles' heroic life. In the very near future, the divine power will dispose of Achilles just as it has now dispatched Hector through Achilles' spear. On that day, a perverse repetition of the roles, now inverted, will occur. Athena will not stop Apollo and Paris as they kill Achilles.

**114** The poet of course does not enter into an open polemical relationship with Athena: the poetic voice qualifies Athena's cheating and deception by the word, *kerdosunê* (247), which

The divine presence and actions muffle in Achilles the human, the perfect champion, the ambitious *aristos*, and makes Hector —about whose death Athena is concerned— the main actor.[115] There is a serious dramatic disjunction in this inversion of who is playing the lead role. Finally, Achilles wins because of Athena's help, in a battle that brings no humiliation for the defeated hero and only figural superiority for the winner.[116]

The symbolic compensation that the two heroes receive for their respective deeds qualifies the different nature of the providers: Achilles gets *kudos* ("splendid triumph," XXII. 216–17, 392), which is mostly granted by the gods; and Hector, *kleos* ("glory"), which is provided by the poetic production.

The two different compensations have natures and effects that correspond exactly to the definitions that the text grants to Achilles' and Hector's behaviors and deeds in the episode. While the divine gift of *kudos* spreads divine light around the fighter, the poetic —but divinely blessed— compensation of *kleos* spreads the narrative of the *klea* ("the heroic deeds") and transmits the *kleos* to future generations. It is the poetic rhythm and pristine resonance at each performance that repeats Hector's words and grants him reputation and fame. The same voice, however, cannot offer the light of the gods and of Achilles' starlight. As a consequence, the poem produces a different poetic presence: while Achilles' divine light is only imaginable through *kudos* and the simile with Hesperos but does not shine in our eyes, Hector's words ("may I not die...without glory [*akleiôs*]") reach our ears with their poetic rhythm and pristine force at each performance of the poem. Accordingly, Hector's words strike us with truer presence and greater emotional force than the bright light of Achilles' victory.

---

may simply mean "ability," "smartness," but also "cunning," as however some modern translators interpret it. See p. 61.

**115** Another feature reduces the protagonistic role of Achilles as a fighting champion. The text dramatizes his role through the effects that it produces on Hector: Hector's fear, flight etc. As Whitman writes (1958, 212), "In presenting the *aristeia* of Achilles almost wholly through its effects on others, and especially Hector, Homer has done not merely what was most dramatic, but also the only thing he could do. We know the absolute only as it impinges on human life, and the angel of death can be seen only by him who dies." The angel of death here is Athena, and I have purposely emphasized her role.

**116** See how the Iliadic Narrator has Odysseus (XIV. 85–87) define the heroic life:
"...over us, to whom Zeus
has appointed the accomplishing of wars, from our youth
even into our old age, until we are dead, each of us."

There is nothing great but only pathetic resignation in the heroic death when it is viewed as a destiny imposed by the will of Zeus.

The two different compensations of *kleos* and *kudos*, which Hector and Achilles receive in this episode, intimate indirectly their specific and different epic values. Gods do not provide *kleos*, but the heroic assets and virtues that the poem celebrates as glorious earmarks of the fighter. At V. 1–8, Athena to Diomedes

> granted strength and courage in order that he be conspicuous
> among the Argives and gain splendid glory.
> On his helmet and his shield she made vivid fire blaze
> like the star of the waning summer that brightest
> shines among the stars when it emerges from the bath in the Ocean:
> such fire she made to blaze from his head and his shoulders
> and pushed him in the middle where the melee was strongest.[117]

Before gaining admiration and reputation (*kleos*), Diomedes must become visible and distinguishable among his comrades. He gains from Athena the brightest shine, which seems here to be equivalent to the *kudos* that often Zeus, and more rarely Apollo and Athena, grant to a few great fighters. Diomedes' *kleos* ("glorious reputation") among his comrades becomes, by incorporation, the *kleos* that the *Iliad* attributes to him, while his bright appearance momentarily makes him fully visible, even shining like a star.

When the poetic voice announces the brightness of the star shining in Achilles'spear, it stages the favor of the god, the agreement of the mysterious order of things and recalls the *mega kudos* that Athena promises to Achilles (XXII. 217) and that Achilles boasts to have gained through his victory over Hector (XXII. 393).

Achilles' *kleos* need not be mentioned, because in the poem it has been attached to him ever since the prophecy his mother told him (IX. 413–15). Nagy (1979, 102), commenting on this passage, writes: "The choice for him [Achilles] had been clear all along: either a *nóstos* wihout *kléos* (IX. 414–15), or *kléos* without *nóstos* (IX. 412–13). If he gives up a safe homecoming [...] Achilles will die at

---

117 Ἔνθ' αὖ Τυδεΐδῃ Διομήδεϊ Παλλὰς Ἀθήνη
δῶκε μένος καὶ θάρσος, ἵν' ἔκδηλος μετὰ πᾶσιν
Ἀργείοισι γένοιτο ἰδὲ κλέος ἐσθλὸν ἄροιτο·
δαῖέ οἱ ἐκ κόρυθός τε καὶ ἀσπίδος ἀκάματον πῦρ
ἀστέρ' ὀπωρινῷ ἐναλίγκιον, ὅς τε μάλιστα
λαμπρὸν παμφαίνῃσι λελουμένος ὠκεανοῖο·
τοῖόν οἱ πῦρ δαῖεν ἀπὸ κρατός τε καὶ ὤμων,
ὦρσε δέ μιν κατὰ μέσσον ὅθι πλεῖστοι κλονέοντο.

Troy, but will have *kléos* that is *áphthiton* "unfailing" (IX. 413). In other words, he will be the central figure of an epic tradition that will never die out. And the key to the *kléos* of Achilles is the *ákhos-pénthos* over Patroclos."

Indeed, as Achilles, in despair over Patroclos' death, decides to kill Hector, he signs his own death and ensures his "unfailing *kleos*."

My insistence on the divine incomprehension of the values enclosed within human heroism could appear to be contradicted by the generous dispensation of *kudos* that Zeus imparts to important heroes and to the Trojans in particular. Yet *kudos* has two specific aspects that diminish the divine commitment to the heroic fighters. First, it produces only a temporary effect, a spreading of intense brilliance on the image of the fighters before their *aristeia* or during their triumph as a mark of their victory. It does not remain a permanent sign, a distinguishable, continuous privilege. This explains the second problematic effect, that it can be contradicted and whisked away at any moment. In Zeus' dispensation of *kudos*, we realize just this inconsistency, which results from the various phases of Zeus' paradoxical behavior: when, for instance, by helping a hero, he leads him to his end; or when he helps a party and then changes his mind and helps the adversarial party, etc.

*Kudos* is also difficult for us to define precisely: it is unclear how essential and intense the notion of shining is and what is the precise heroic privilege accorded by *kudos*: victory, triumph, or honor. There are passages in which heroic behavior is completely absent: for instance, Zeus compensates Achilles with *kudos* for his friendly reception of Priam and his acceptance of the ransom (XXIV. 210).

For all these reasons, the divine dispensation of *kudos* does not imply a divine appreciation of the meaning and value of the heroic life.

In the final book, Achilles indirectly confirms the idea of the divine discredit of heroism that I have elaborated. Achilles indirectly belittles even the consolation Hector finds in epic glory, and with sharp eyes Achilles gazes at the nonsense of abandoning his father, of Patroclos' death, and of killing Hector, as has been determined by his destiny, according to the dispensation chosen by Zeus (see Ch. 4.1).

# Chapter 3

## 3.1 The End of the Wrath: The Beginning of the End

> "...the evidence of the overall narrative of the *Iliad*, where Patroclos earns the role of a ritual substitute of Achilles. This role makes Patroclos not only a body-double, but even a story-double of the central hero of the *Iliad*, where things happen to Patroclos that would otherwise have happened only to Achillles."
>
> Nagy 2013, 54

We are now going to analyze Zeus' will and plans concerning Patroclos and Achilles, beginning with the first part of Zeus' *boulê* and forecast: "Achilles shall rouse up Patroclos, his companion [ὃ δ' ἀνστήσει ὃν ἑταῖρον / Πάτροκλον] whom shining Hector will kill with his spear before Ilion" (XV. 64–66). Because of his pronouncement, audience and readers know that whatever Achilles may want and decide, he will send Patroclos to fight and die.[1] However, when we audience and readers hear or read the description of Achilles' decision to send Patroclos to fight, we learn that this decision was Achilles' fully voluntary and autonomous act. Achilles' decision unfolds through unreasonable acts that lead him to decide in a way that denotes freedom of volition, but also in mysterious convergence with Zeus' plan. We are reminded of the "inconsequential logic" that persuades Hector to remain outside the walls, in agreement with his "deadly destiny" (XXII. 5) as determined by Zeus. It is impossible to know whether this "deadly destiny" is meant to have subliminally affected Hector's decision.

The scene of the decision begins at XVI. 2 ff. Patroclos, in tears, comes up to Achilles, for he has seen the defeat of the Achaeans.[2] The simile (XVI. 3–4):

> pouring hot tears like a dark-running spring
> that drips dim water from a steep rock,[3]

---

[1] Lowenstam 1981, 32 shows that Patroclos' death is anticipated several times by Zeus and by the Poet (VIII. 475–76, XV. 65, XVI. 259–62; XI. 604, XVI. 46–47 etc.). The author claims that Patroclos' slap on his thigh (XV. 397–402) is an essential device of foreshadowing his death.
[2] In a previous book, Achilles had called Patroclos out of his hut to find out what was happening to the defeated Achaeans. The text describes Patroclos coming out "equal to Ares, and that was the beginning of his doom" (XI. 604). To be "equal to Ares" is a simile already implies that the hero will face defeat, or worse, death.
[3] δάκρυα θερμὰ χέων ὥς τε κρήνη μελάνυδρος,
 ἥ τε κατ' αἰγίλιπος πέτρης δνοφερὸν χέει ὕδωρ (XVI. 3–4).

repeats exactly the one that the poetic voice employs to describe Agamemnon as he weeps for the defeat of the Achaeans (IX. 14–15). The Poet's voice uses this simile only to characterize Agamemnon's and Patroclos' pain. The Narrator has chosen this unique repetition in order to create a reference to a significant context, but not, as Martin (1989, 62) suspects, to characterize a weak rhetorician. Agamemnon is suffering for the disaster that he has provoked by his past insistence on holding Achilles' girl. The dark, unceasing flow from the hard and insensitive rock symbolizes Agamemnon's hard and insensitive vanity that is the source of the disaster for which now he endlessly weeps (cf. IX. 115 ff.).

Patroclos' unceasing tears are caused by Achilles' blind vanity and hard arrogance, which are the source of the disaster afflicting the Achaeans.[4] The simile attributes the affliction for which the two characters abundantly weep to the hard and uncompromising stances of the agents of the lamentable disasters: Agamemnon weeps for his foolishness and Patroclos for Achilles' mindless arrogance that is now ruining his peers.[5] An arrogance that now continues and induces Achilles to deride his tearful companion.

If this interpretation is correct, the poetic voice by the unique repetition of this simile condemns Achilles for his harsh and irresponsible behavior.

It is no wonder that both Achilles and Agamemnon will later (XIX. 85–90 and 270–74)[6] recognize that their uncompromising postures were in effect caused by *Ate*, since Zeus wanted to increase the bloodbath. Achilles' recognition of *Ate*'s intervention is not confirmed by the Muses' narrative, but remains his subjective belief; yet it is true that his wrath was suggested and sustained by a series of gods: Athena induced Achilles to transform his murderous drive into a display of hostility ("Abuse him [Agamemnon] with words," I. 211); Thetis told him, "be angry at the Achaeans and stay away from all fighting" (I. 422); and Zeus took upon himself the task of restoring Achilles' honor. It is this divine support that transforms Achilles' psychodrama into a wordly event, and transfers it into the poetic story of the *Iliad*.

The attempted reconciliation in book IX displays, if nothing else, Achilles' public reputation, the love of his companions, the recognition of his being *aristos* by Agamemnon; so that now Achilles himself agrees that he should forget

---

[4] Tsagalis 2012, 325 n. 127 quotes Dué (2010, 291), who argues that the simile at *Il.* 14–16 "recalls the iconic lamenter of Greek myth, Niobe."
[5] It is probably coherent with my interpretation that, on line 2, Achilles receives the epithetic expression ποιμένι λαῶν, commonly (six times) attributed to Agamemnon. Achilles receives this generic designation a second time, without the name, at XIX. 386.
[6] See below, Ch. 4.3, "The Ruinous Madness of Ate".

his anger: the outrage he received, he says, is a fact of the past, and his anger has relented (60–62). Yet, not sufficiently: Achilles strongly resents Patroclos' devotion to the Achaean cause and his incomprehension of Achilles' refusal to fight. Simultaneously, he also feels pity for Patroclos' uninhibited crying and pain (5: τὸν δὲ ἰδὼν ᾤκτιρε ποδάρκης δῖος Ἀχιλλεύς), so that he subliminally resolves his internal tension by brutally[7] reacting against his own pity: through a sarcastic simile, he mocks Patroclos' tears and sorrow (XVI. 7–19):

> Why are you in tears, Patroclos, like a silly
> little girl who runs after her mother and begs to be picked up,
> and clings to her dress, holding her back as she tries to hurry,
> and keeps on gazing tearfully at her until she is picked up.
> Just like her, Patroclos, you pour soft tears.[8]
> Have you some news to tell me or to the Myrmidons?
> Have you alone[9] received some message from Phthia?
> Yet, they tell me, Aktor's son, Menoitios, still lives,
> and Aiakos' son, Peleus, still lives among the Myrmidons,
> the two people we would be deeply pained for if they were dead.
> Or is it the Argives you are mourning over, seeing how they are dying
> by the curved ships because of their arrogance?
> Tell me, do not hide it in your mind, so that we both know.

By assimilating Patroclos to a silly little girl who insistently pesters her mother until she gets what she wants, Achilles first depersonalizes his friend into a generic "somebody else." The comparison places Patroclos in a humiliating role and transforms the normal relationship of "companions-in-arms" between him and Achilles to that of chief and "squire," of master and subaltern, as the Greek

---

[7] Edwards 1987, 257: Patroclos "is in tears and Achilles instead of waiting for his message, addresses him first showing the same aggressive impatience he did when Athena interrupted him in book I." My psychological interpretation is necessarily hypothetical: the Iliadic *diêgêsis* does not illustrate the inner feelings of characters.

[8] Notice the different connotations of Patroclos' crying in the Poet's and Achilles' simile. The phrasing τέρεν κατὰ δάκρυον εἴβεις (with variation for the verbal form) is used four times in Homer, three times for the crying of a lady (xvi. 332, III. 142, XVI. 11) and once for the old Peleus as he is imagined to weep for the death of his son (XIX. 323). The contrast between "tears like a running spring that drips dark water from a steep rock" and "soft tears" is remarkable: it does not seem to refer to the same crying and therefore characterizes the posture of the focalizer and the function the Poet attributes to his simile.

[9] The designation "alone" is emphatically placed at the end of the line – as often–: ἐξέκλυες οἶος; It is a sort of announcement that Achilles and his *therapôn* have different, even contrasting, experiences, and the fact that Achilles mockingly underlines this point makes its premonitory force more threatening.

*therapôn* —see, for instance, XVI. 246— is variously understood. The military framework is replaced by a domestic and mockingly pathetic one. Achilles' mockery is haughty, since it ridicules Patroclos' distress from a situation of power; and it is irresponsible, since it translates a possibly dangerous situation into a scurrilous domestic attack. This sarcasm nevertheless is made possible by the intimacy that exists between the two men. Without that intimacy and pity, his mockery would be unexplainable.[10] By putting into Achilles' mouth a sarcastic simile that implies a domestic context and the feminization of both characters, the Iliadic Poet underlines the private, marginal aspects of Achilles' and Patroclos' friendship, its sharply felt intimacy, unconcerned with shared social norms.[11] Whether this marginality intimates an erotic, sexual relationship, remains, of course, an untold alternative.

Pursuing the domestic and sarcastic tone, Achilles feigns to think that only serious troubles of his and Patroclos' fathers would be appropriate for Patroclos to weep over.[12] He is, of course, mocking Patroclos and his rhetorical question, "Or is it the Argives you are mourning over...?" ridicules Patroclos and displays his displeasure, for he knows that this is the real answer.

The daughter/mother scene in Achilles' simile explicitly recalls the scene (I. 348 ff.) in which Achilles cried on the beach and called for his mother, Thetis. In that scene, the fictional situation, as represented in the simile, was experienced as a real event. Thetis' deeply affectionate behavior contrasts, however,

---

**10** With great erudition, and authentic vision, Nagy has elaborated a rich interpretation of Achilles' and Patroclos' intimacy and special friendship, as it is illuminated by the term *therapôn* and its possible Hittite connection (1979, 292–3; 1990, 129–30: "In the *Iliad*, Patroclos functions as the ritual surrogate of Achilles"; and 2013, 146–68). See below on Ch. 3.2. For a different reading of the simile, see Ready 2011, 165 ff. He finds that "the simile is meant to offer comfort" in contrast to the Narrator's simile that shows Patroclos as 'desperate'" (p. 166). Reinhardt 1961, 27 notices that Achilles is silent about Zeus' punishment of the Achaeans. Achilles cannot, or forgets to, contextualize his anger within the divine *boulê* for which he himself has begged.

**11** For an accurate analysis of Achilles' simile and its long critical history, and for a sensitive interpretation of it, see Nannini 2003, 72–77. The author realizes that the simile emerges from Achilles' psychological conflict between his *philotes* for Patroclos and his anger, his need of restoring his honor and *kleos*. She is advisedly cautious about the identification —which appears already in some ancient scholia— of Achilles as an internal *aoidos* and spokesman for the Narrator of the *Iliad*.

**12** Edward 1987, 181 describes Achilles' behavior as his "aggressive dissimulation." Janko *ad loc.* comments perceptively: "We may indeed imagine that Achilleus gruffly steels himself to resist by reminding himself that the Greeks are in the wrong and that the only death which should move him is one of his own family."

with Achilles' brutal mockery. As Thetis appears and sits close by her son, she asks him why is he crying and adds: "Tell me, do not hide it in your mind, so that we both know" (I. 363). She encourages her son to release his pain and is ready to listen to him before commenting on his tears. As soon as Thetis understands what Achilles wants, she promises her help. By repeating the line (XVI. 19 = I. 363), the poetic composition obviously intends to display how Achilles' repetition of the phrase that in his mother's mouth is deeply affectionate and helpful, sounds in his mouth parodic and, because of the allusion, doubly brutal and sarcastic. Through this allusion, the Poet takes over the Muses' narrative and displays Achilles' troubled haughtiness.

Patroclos answers with deep groans[13] and disregards the bullying teasing of his friend. As always, the Narrator does not give any psychological motivations for a surprising gesture or attitude. Patroclos is older and wiser than Achilles: he simply ignores Achilles' pride, the continuation of a resentment that, as Achilles himself confesses, no longer has reason to exist. Patroclos is too distressed to question the tone and sense of Achilles' simile: he comes from the shelter of the wounded Eurypylos and has seen the Trojans sweeping over the rampart (XV. 390–96). It is not a surprise therefore that Patroclos addresses his friend coolly and respectfully as a great warrior (21): "Achilles, son of Peleus, far greatest of the Achaeans." This staging epithetic line is used only three times in Homer: once by Odysseus (XIX. 216); once by Patroclos, in our passage (XVI. 21); and once again by Odysseus in his visit to the underworld (*Od.* xi. 478). The address is respectful and appropriately characterizes Odysseus in his deferential ("Achilles... far greatest of the Achaeans") but problematic (and sometimes polemical and paternal) relationship to Achilles.

By this specific contextualization, the poet stages Patroclos who now eschews the private terms of their intimacy, restores full masculinity —even at the expense of Achilles' divine *genos*–, and uplifts Achilles' military and social status.

Following Nestor's recommendation, Patroclos assumes authority over Achilles. At XI. 785–88, Nestor reports what Menoitios, Patroclos' father, told his son before he left for Troy:

---

13 The staging epithetic line (20): Τὸν δὲ βαρὺ στενάχων προσέφης Πατρόκλεες ἱππεῦ, constitutes the Narrator's apostrophe to Patroclos. Perhaps the Poet judges the situation worthy of this pathos, and/or he misses the epithetic form for the nominative of *Patroklos*, *Patroklês*: see Hoekstra 1965, 138. Kahane 1994, 112 considers the Narrator's use of Patroclos' PNV as "sympathetic."

> My child, by right of blood Achilles is higher than you are,
> but you are the elder. Yet in strength he is far the greater.
> You should speak wise words to him and give him good counsel,
> and guide him. He will listen to you for his good.[14]

Patroclos, by answering with the voice of his own father and Nestor,[15] is made to reverse Achilles' mockery and to assume the responsible voice of a father. Through the simile, Achilles took the role of a mother (indeed of his mother) speaking to a child, but now Patroclos speaks to Achilles as a father to a son. He enjoins Achilles "not to be angry" (μὴ νεμέσα, XVI. 22): he correctly interprets Achilles' sarcasm as the expression of an irritation caused by Patroclos' mourning over the Achaeans.[16]

With Nestor's words, Patroclos gives an impressive list of the wounded Achaean heroes (24–27) and describes the doctors who are busy curing their wounds. He ends the catastrophic description with a sudden address to Achilles: "but you, Achilles, are the incurable one" (29).[17] After this pointed reproach that singles out Achilles as being indifferent to the Achaeans' general misery and to the medical concerns of the doctors, Patroclos blames Achilles for foolishness and cruelty (XVI. 31–35):

> What advantage shall any man born hereafter have,
> if you do not avert from the Argives this outrageous destruction?
> (Ἀργείοισιν ἀεικέα λοιγὸν ἀμύνῃς;)[18]

---

[14] At the end, Achilles will listen to Patroclos and consent to his request, but certainly not for Patroclos' good. Nor for Achilles' good. The friendly advice of the enemy is particularly dangerous.

[15] The whole line 22: "do not be angry: such grief has fallen upon the Achaeans," repeats Nestor's line to Odysseus at X. 145. Patroclos is made to use Nestor's words from the very beginning of his answer. Again, lines 24–27 repeat Nestor's lines XI. 659–62 (Eurypylos is made to pick up line 24 at XI. 825); and the whole passage XVI. 36–45 repeats word for word Nestor's advice in XI. 794–803. Patroclos, in the poem, speaks only 102 lines: he is a "listener" and not "a heroic speaker," as Kahane 1994, 139–40 correctly characterizes him. It is symptomatic of his subordinate role that in his longest and most important speech —twenty-four lines— he is made to repeat, literally, so many lines from Nestor's advice. There is almost nothing autonomously Patroclean in all this arguing, unless it be his pathos.

[16] Janko 1992, 318 reads differently: Patroclos "begs indulgence not for his tears but for his request."

[17] Noticing the assonance in line 29, Martin 1983, 19 interprets: "they can be healed; you cannot be healed." The PNV in terminal position signals the character as a "protagonist." This position is almost regular for Achilles in the *Iliad* and for Odysseus in the *Odyssey* (Kahane 1994, 80 ff.).

[18] The phrase is standard for denoting the averting of outrageous disasters and is sometimes applied to Achilles as the only one able to accomplish this task (see I. 341, IX. 495, XVI. 32). By requesting to go and push back the Trojan invasion, Patroclos takes on Achilles' task as the

> Pitiless! It is not true that your father is Peleus the rider,
> and your mother Thetis. No! The blue[19] sea
> and the inaccessible rocks gave you birth,[20] so harsh is your mind.

Patroclos continues to employ the most impersonal language, avoiding intimacy. The accusation of birth from natural elements is a traditional metaphor used to designate inhuman feelings, and Patroclos, by emphasizing the difference between the divine and natural identities of Achilles' two anthropomorphic parents, offers a sort of empirical evidence for Achilles' insensitivity. "Your real mother is the sea, not the anthropomorphic being, Thetis." This curious and clever transposition betrays the Narrator's pleasure in taking advantage of the gods' polyvalence, and in exploiting the difficult nature of the metaphor within this context.[21] For, on the one hand, Achilles is necessarily born from the human-like Thetis and not from the natural element, the sea: accordingly, the attribution of Achilles' birth to the sea is a perfect metaphor – an image in which the vehicle, the sea's insensitivity, resembles the tenor, Achilles' insensitivity. But since the sea is Thetis' natural correlate, Achilles' birth from the sea is hardly a metaphor: he is born from (= son of) the anthropomorphic form and body of Thetis the marine goddess, and his insensitivity is naturally the same as that of the sea.[22] While the poet plays on the polyvalent nature of the goddess and cleverly shows the Narratees his ability to make enigmatic and to disable a

---

averter of the outrageous disaster (see especially I. 341). The theme of warding off disasters (Apollo's plague, the Achaean defeat etc.) is spread throughout the *Iliad*: see Nagy 1979, 76; Nannini 1995, 30; Slatkin 1991, 87.

**19** We do not know the exact color denoted by the adjective *glaukê*. See Bergson 1956, 84 who cites Kober's work that supports the meaning "grey." Gostoli 1999, 862–63 notices the chiasmus that inverses the order of the natural phenomena that are attributable to father and mother: a) father Peleus, b) mother Thetis, b) mother Thetis, the sea, a) father Peleus, the rock. Here the intimated blending of Thetis with the sea is helped by the definition of the sea as *glaukê*: it describes the sea only here in Homer and it is the name of a sea-nymph at XVIII. 39. The attribution of naturalistic features to divine beings is protracted by this epithet.

**20** Patroclos transforms Thetis, the marine goddess, into the physical sea and derives Peleus from the rocky mountain Pelion.

**21** Perhaps the whole language of this dialogue between Achilles and his double denounces the relatively recent arrival of the couple in the tradition (West 2011, 42–7). The unique reference to Agamemnon's crying, Achilles 'simile, his reference to his mother' line, Patroclos quotations from Nestor, and now the play on the metaphorical and non-metaphorical connotation of Achilles' birth from the sea evince a sort of occasional and creative context, circumscribed references, and linguistic novelties.

**22** Thetis emerged from the sea as mist at I. 357–59: "She heard him [Achilles] as she was sitting near her father / the Old Man, in the sea depths: / suddenly up she rose from the grey water like mist." It could be a simile or the marine presence of the goddess.

typical poetic device, Patroclos, on the other hand, must dismiss the ambivalence that his utterance may suggest. The poet can play where his character cannot. Patroclos inscribes the passage in the poetic style in which a regular mortal can metaphorically be as insensitive as a piece of the natural world.

In the case of Peleus ("It is not true that your father is Peleus the rider" but "the inaccessible rocks gave you birth"), Patroclos is made to play on the linguistic similarity between Peleus and the mountain Pelion. Achilles birth from the rocks is metaphorical, since there is no natural identity or connection between Peleus and the mountain: born from rocky Pelion, Achilles is as insensitive as his metaphorical father Pelion.

Patroclos repeats the accusation that many people in the army have addressed to Achilles, using the very word "pitiless." In book nine, Phoenix blames Achilles in this way (496–97), as does Ajax (624–42, a friend who attacks Achilles with the harshest insults); Achilles is begged by Odysseus to pity the afflicted Achaeans (IX. 300–02). He has heard his own soldiers use the same words to blame his withdrawal and cruelty, and when later he harangues the Myrmidons, he shows them that he knows the words they were muttering against him (XVI. 203–04 and 207):

> "Cruel son of Peleus! Your mother nursed you on gall.
> Pitiless, to keep your companions here by the ships unwilling."[…]
> Often you would gather in groups, and mutter in this way against me…

While the soldiers muttered among themselves these imputations against Achilles, Patroclos is now throwing them in Achilles' face. In Patroclos' view, it is indeed Achilles who is behaving like a whimsical child.

After the reproaches, Patroclos must still declare the request that Nestor suggested to him, and, using and adapting Nestor's words (XVI. 36–45 = XI. 794–03), Patroclos asks Achilles to let him go alone, leading the Myrmidons against the Trojans (XVI. 36–43):

> But if you fear the warning of some oracles known
> in your heart, and one that your lady mother told you from Zeus,
> send *at least me* to battle, quickly[23]: let the rest of the Myrmidon army follow me,
> if ever I may become a light for the Danaans (ἤν πού τι φόως Δαναοῖσι γένωμαι).
> Give me also your armor to wear on my shoulders
> to see whether, believing that I am you, the Trojans stop
> their attack, and the fighting sons of the Achaeans,
> worn out, may breathe…

---

23 This sense of urgency is not in Nestor's corresponding line at XI. 796.

The proposal is astounding, since it breaks the pairing of Achilles and his *therapôn*. It implies also that Patroclos will take Achilles' place as commander of the Myrmidons and as the savior of the Achaeans.[24]

Patroclos' assumption (36–38) —which comes from Nestor (XI. 794 ff.)— according to which certain oracles might be preventing Achilles from fighting, singles out the only condition under which this break between the pair should safely and legitimately occur. Yet the assumption looks here like a courteous way to offer a strong pretext for Achilles' refusal to fight, without mentioning his implacable pride, his terrible obstinacy, or other analogous, unkind justifications.

## 3.2 The Fatal Breaking of the Pairing

> "Suppléant et vicaire, le supplément est un adjoint, une instance subalterne *qui tient lieu* [...] Qu'il s'ajoute ou qu'il se substitue, le supplément est *extérieur*, hors de la positivité à laquelle il se surajoute, étranger à ce qui, pour être par lui remplacé, doit être autre que lui."
>
> Derrida 1967, 208

Achilles acceptance of Patroclos' proposal is such an incredible and unexpected event that we hardly understand why he does so. The victory of the Trojans is what he asked Zeus to grant in order to receive honor from the Achaeans. Now he has the chance for this success, as he well knows (83–86): he should either go himself to fight or wait for the Achaeans' request.

Probably the narrative disregards this inconsequential aspect of Achilles' acceptance, because it follows the pattern of a very strong model, the similar story of Meleager, as we will see at the end of this chapter.

Achilles' separation from his *therapôn* in the battlefield breaks the unity that is almost sacred between Achilles and his "ritual substitute," his sort of alter ego and "double-body." I do not need to repeat the by now famous analysis through which Gregory Nagy has illustrated the unique relationship between

---

**24** Even the role of the "savior" is typically Achillean, but here it is realized by a syntactical and metaphorical unit (on line 39) that Kelly 2007, 277 identifies as an expression that "predicts a reversal to be suffered by the hero as he tries to bring that salvation to the Greeks." The text continues to employ expressions that, at the analysis of careful readers, disclose a negative connotation under the cover of a positive one.

Achilles and Patroclos:[25] the intimacy between them is sacred, and, as *therapôn* of Achilles, Patroclos carries also the epic identity of Achilles, a fact made evident by their shared epithets announcing that they live and die in the same way. Their separation in the act of fighting is dangerous.

The Poet at this dramatic point intervenes with a personal comment (46–7):

> So he spoke, supplicating,[26] the great fool: for he was
> entreating for his own grievous death and destruction.

The Poet, knowing Zeus' plan, realizes the double vanity of Patroclos' begging to fight and feels both compassion for the character's irresolvable situation,[27] and bitterness at his choice: "great fool" reveals the Poet's disappointment at Patroclos' proposal to go fighting alone, without Achilles, who remains unaware, as it seems, of the dramatic effects that will result from breaking their pairing. The Poet distances himself from the Muses' narrative of Patroclos' proposal and emotionally rebukes him, as if the Poet did not know that Patroclos could not choose differently.

The Muses' narrative sees Patroclos as condemned to his fatal destiny: the Poet's voice avoids blaming Zeus for his control of Patroclos' fate and absurdly grants Patroclos a chance for minimal autonomy. The impossibility of both gestures —accusing Zeus and granting Patroclos autonomy— reveals the extent of the poetic voice's bewilderment or despair. The text reveals a difficult theological situation: the divine power takes possession of the mortal being, giving him no suspicion of the irresolvable knots in which he is tied up.

It was Nestor who proposed that Patroclos fight alone. Nestor is the mastermind of the rescue of the Achaean ships and of his and the Achaean army's return, and he is concerned for this goal, not for Patroclos' and Achilles' destinies.[28] By his bitter reprimand and by showing that Patroclos not only follows Nestor' proposal, but even borrows Nestor's own words, the Poet invites the Narratees to identify the external source of Patroclos' relative autonomy. Patro-

---

**25** Nagy 1979, 292–3; 1990, 129–30; 2012, 48–57; and 2013, 146–168, his double-body. See also Tarenzi 2005 who examines the role of the "royal substitute" from the Hittite to the Greek *therapôn*.
**26** On the rare use of the verb λισσόμενος in this non-religious context and on the structure of the dialogue, see Beck 2012, 73–74.
**27** Taplin 1992, 177: "It is the current of compassion, set in motion by Nestor, that sends Patroclos to his death. In the *Iliad*, pity advances suffering as well as to some extent redeeming it."
**28** This goal is even inscribed in his name, for "Nestor" etymologically means "qui rentre heureusement" or "qui ramène heureusement son armée." See Chantraine, *DELG*, 745.

clos is obviously influenced by the authority of the great old man and, once again, appears as playing a subaltern role.

Achilles in his answer will not mention Patroclos' accusations: he possibly understands that his own posture appears extravagant and incomprehensible to his friend, just as to his own soldiers. Patroclos' list of wounded heroes, at any rate, does not change Achilles' feelings for the Achaeans.[29]

Achilles takes seriously Patroclos' *pathos* and request: he feels the need to explain to him —though with irritation (48: μέγ' ὀχθήσας)— the reason for his attitude by repeatedly evoking the terrible pain (*deinon akhos*, 52 and 55) that he is still suffering from the Achaean outrage.[30] However, he ends this psychodrama with a sort of imperative addressed to himself (60–3):

> Still, let us leave all this as a thing of the past (ἀλλὰ τὰ μὲν προτετύχθαι ἐάσομεν):
> I see that it was not possible to be forever angry in my heart
> (ἀσπερχὲς κεχολῶσθαι ἐνὶ φρεσί).
> Certainly I thought that I would not stop my anger
> until the clamor of the fight came to my own ship.

He does not elaborate any argument to justify this change of mind and behavior; yet his decision dismisses his contract with Zeus concerning the restoration of his honor. Achilles offers only a motivation that, though realistic, is external to his feelings, a sort of *force majeure*. He certainly does not care about the suffering of the Achaeans, and Patroclos' description of the catastrophic defeat does not move him. The risk that the Trojans may burn the ships strongly suggests the need for an interventional rescue (62–3),[31] but no more than that. Though Patroclos made his appeal on different grounds, Achilles takes the present danger to the ships as the cause of his concession.[32]

---

**29** For a more effective impact of compassion upon Achilles' decision, see Burkert 1955, 94.
**30** τόδ' αἰνὸν ἄχος κραδίην καὶ θυμὸν ἱκάνει, αἰνὸν ἄχος τό μοί ἐστιν, ἐπεὶ πάθον ἄλγεα θυμῷ (52–5). He details the offenses he has received by "a man who robs his equal"; he mentions the girl that the Achaeans had picked out for him and Agamemnon stole from him, treating him as a "dishonored vagabond." He repeats pathetic details that Patroclos knows well, as if he needed to justify a behavior that he himself feels no longer appropriate. Of course, the girl Agamemnon stole from him is here the "sign" of his offended honor. Achilles' love is Patroclos, aside from Briseis.
**31** At IX. 650–5, Achilles had said that he would not end his wrath until the war reached his ships. As Janko shows, Achilles shows here (XVI. 62–3) a "weakening resolve" in comparison with his harder position at IX. 653.
**32** Edwards 1987, 258–9 describes Achilles' confusion and exasperation: he adds a comment on the illogical position of Achilles, "for by allowing to drive back Hector from the ships, he is

The plural in line 60, "Let us leave (ἐάσομεν)…" according to Janko (1992, 323), "associates Achilles with all who feel likewise." I propose that Achilles purposely interacts with Patroclos as if they felt similarly. Achilles, though on a different ground, agrees with his "ritual surrogate" that an intervention is needed. Reciprocally, when Patroclos harangues the soldiers, he shares the feelings of his friend Achilles (273–4):

> …and so the son of Atreus, the great ruler Agamemnon, may know
> his own madness, that he did not honor the best of the Achaeans.

At this point, Achilles and Patroclos seem to be two faces of the same person. But it is a unity undergoing separation.[33] After the momentous declaration, Achilles goes on (XVI. 64–7):

> Come on, put my famous armor on your shoulders,
> lead the Myrmidons who delight in battles,
> since the black cloud of the Trojans
> has mightly surrounded our ships…

Achilles finds unproblematic that Patroclos may substitute him in battle and be taken for Achilles himself; in his prayer to Zeus he even intimates that Patroclos may fight, in the absence of Achilles, like Achilles himself (XVI. 242–5):

> …so that even Hector
> may know whether my therapôn is able to fight
> even alone or his invincible hands rage only
> when I myself go into the struggle of Ares.[34]

---

removing the best chance of fulfillment of the conditions under which he said he himself would return."

**33** As the Narrator explains at XVII. 401–11, Achilles knows from his mother that it is not Zeus' will that Achilles and Patroclos conquer and sack Troy together. He knows that he himself will be killed prior to Troy's fall, but he misconstrues this prediction by imagining that Patroclos will survive him and will be among the conquerors of the city. Yet later, at XIX. 315–37, Achilles "recognizes the error of his previous interpretation as a deluded, optimistic hope, and as such he assigns it to his *thumos* […] His *thumos*, on Achilles' account, has been in effect, the channel for divine *mis*information, or perhaps, more accurately, it has caused (by its hopeful desires) the misinterpretation of a perfectly sound, but ambiguous divine prediction" (Pelliccia 1995, 246–47). Here, in XVI, Achilles still thinks that he and Patroclos will fight together and he even dreams that together they will conquer Troy.

**34** Through this alternative, the unproblematic nature of the substitution becomes questionable: it appears that Achilles' presence is necessary, or at least desirable, in order for Patroclos

Since Achilles insistently details the various dangers that Patroclos should avoid on the battlefield (83 ff.), he seems to feel a premonition of danger. But he shields this premonition by praying to Zeus in a most solemn fashion, asking that Patroclos may return safe to the ships (232 ff.).

Patroclos' and Achilles' "pairing" belongs to a structural type or model, that of the "master and his substitute" (and, analogously, "the original and the copy," "the presence and the appearance," etc.), that is governed by a supplemental relationship. In the pairing of Achilles and Patroclos, the supplement is the *therapôn* and the original entity is the king; yet their love minimizes their different hierarchical powers, ontological natures, and social conditions.

In the abstract model of Patroclos' supplementarity, the *therapôn* (i.e. the "alter ego") doubles and simultaneously defers the master (just as in analogous "pairings," the copy doubles and substitutes the original, the appearance doubles and defers the presence, etc.). By the effect of substitution, deferral, vicariousness, representation, etc., the master (the original, the presence) risks being merely evoked by and being indistinctly glimpsed through the surrogate, the copy, and the appearance. The master and its correlates may even disappear. The supplement, the alter ego stands fast in his stead. In his prayer to Zeus, Achilles implies that Patroclos' "invincible hands rage" not "only when I myself go into the struggle of Ares" (XVI. 244–5). We recognize that Patroclos, capable of fighting just like Achilles even in the absence of Achilles, substitutes the master, the one, however, that, only by his presence and essence, is supposed to communicate to the *therapôn* his force. This vision of equality is Achilles' loving and wishful view of Patroclos; but if the full identity between him and his *therapôn* were real, there would no longer be a pairing, no longer a supplemental relationship, but two individuals with analogous power.

The supplemental connection, true to the meaning of the word, implies that the "substitute" (the valet, the surrogate, etc.) adds itself during the action to the master, and, by this addition, displaces, miscasts, defers —all different forms of supplementation— the master (the original, the presence). This, of course, sounds like an illogical and uncanny result, since common sense and the wishful metaphysical interpretation of these terms assign priority, force, and superiority to the stronger term: master, original, presence. The deconstructive analysis, however, refuses this domesticated view and shows that, though

---

to produce an Achillean performance. The *Iliad* offers no example of the two friends fighting together. Of course, the substitute is always different than the original. On this issue, see Tarenzi's remark (2005, 31–32) that Patroclos does not carry Achilles' spear, since only Achilles can brandish it (XVI. 140–44, XIX. 387–91).

the negative and damaging effects of the supplement may not surface explicitly, nevertheless the supplement hides its own differences from the master and lets only the shadow of the master survive. Indeed, in a supplemental structure, the substitute survives and turns the master into a merely thinkable but not effective entity. In some way, the strong terms are the conceptual instantiations that only emerge from their own supplement. First was the supplement, and then the original.[35]

The narrative structure that Homer produces, through the pairing of Achilles and Patroclos, essentially unfolds as expected: as Achilles sends his *therapôn* to fight and assumes the role of master, Patroclos seems to replace Achilles, but in effect he cannot: the supplement is even taken, at least initially, to be the master, yet he is not, but rather distorts the figure of the master by excess or lack. Patroclos will betray the master by his excess and will be killed and, finally, will indirectly cause the death of the master.

In the pairing of Achilles and Patroclos, the Iliadic Poet raises an edifying homage to the master. This follows the principle of the narrative, which in general extols heroic values as they are embodied by individual fighters in an ascending scale of intensity and sublime force. This ascending scale is artificial and wishful. It is artificial because it determines values a priori: the king is, in principle, the best, and Achilles, as the son of a goddess, is the best, unbeatable, etc. It is wishful because it allows the narrative to create a difference among the individual heroes, when indeed their essential heroic nature and behavior are the same. This explains the constant evaluation of the hierarchical position of the heroes, through a comparison of their same heroic nature: for example, of Diomedes in relation to his father Tydeus, and of Ajax in relation to Achilles, who is "the best of the Achaeans." This explains also the inimitable and special value of a military skill (the archer, for instance) or of a specific function (the irreplaceable defender of the city): these distinctions permit characterizations that are fully external to the fundamental sameness of heroic value. This sameness makes the heroes to some extent indistinguishable.[36]

Achilles himself —as the son of a goddess— is a construct of the mythical imagination: yet in the *Iliad* he is the unhappy result of the permeability between the human and the divine, for he has no immortality. He has a utopian, wishful view of his relationship with Patroclos. Twice he implies the perfect

---

[35] A full "presence" is thinkable only from the many "present instantiations" and remains conceptually dependent on them.
[36] This indistinguishable nature of the Iliadic heroes is one of the strong points of Codino's interpretation.

equality of their powers: in his delirious image at XVI. 97–100 and in his prayer to Zeus (XVI. 242–45); while Patroclos, on the contrary, has a more realistic view of himself (40–41):

> Give me also your armor to wear on my shoulders
> to see whether, believing that I am you, the Trojans stop
> their attack...

The supplement is aware of being a supplement. By inventing an identity of value between himself and his *therapôn*, Achilles is dreaming: if Achilles were on the battlefield in person, Patroclos would not be necessary or even substantial.

This structural model sufficiently illuminates aspects of the Homeric pairing, its internal logic and the necessity of the loss of both terms. The *Iliad* does not, however, deconstruct the supplementary logic and leaves to the master his socially and metaphysically granted privileged role.[37]

I return to Achilles' long response to Patroclos. Giving to Patroclos the unique purpose of saving the ships[38] allows Achilles to be coherent with himself and to reference the similar statement he made at IX. 650–5, though now he omits his former condition that the ships must be ablaze (IX. 653). At that time, he did not think of a later return home, while now he is concerned that the "desired return home" – his and/or that of the whole army – could be jeopardized (XVI. 82: φίλον ... νόστον).[39]

Having arrived at this decision, Achilles enters into a jocular mood: he finds pleasure in emphasizing the seriousness of the defeat that the Achaeans are

---

**37** Derrida describes the logic of such supplements, for instance, in 1967, 207–18. A deconstructive plot about our pairing would imagine that Patroclos fighting alone saves the ships and pushes the Trojans inside their walls as Achilles insured that he would be capable of doing so. When Patroclos comes back, the Achaean elite honor him and realize that they do not need any longer to honor Achilles. The supplement has fully substituted the master. But then Patroclos would demand and become the general of the Mirmidon army —the supplement outdoes and exceeds the master's power— and at this point Agamemnon and his men would realize that through his excess and failures, Patroclos, the supplement, has distorted the real heroism of Achilles. He does not deliver what the aristos (the best) promised to deliver, yet now the Achaeans have only him, the supplement. Of course, this could never happen —nor be thought— in the Homeric heroic age.
**38** He exhorts Patroclos three times to take care of the safety of the ships: XVI. 66–67, 80–82, and 95–6. Even in his prayer to Zeus the safety of the ships remains his main concern: XVI, 246. As this last passage makes evident, by recommending the limited action of pushing back the Trojans from the ships, Achilles is simultaneously thinking of ensuring Patroclos' safe return.
**39** It is not clear of whose return Achilles is speaking, that of the Achaeans or that of Achilles and Patroclos. Rousseau (Ch. 2 and 9) thinks the latter.

suffering because of his absence. He selects the names of Agamemnon and Diomedes, explaining, with a polite smile, that they were unable to stop Hector (XVI. 74–75):

> The spear of Diomedes, the son of Tydeus, does not rage
> in his hands to avert the disaster.

The inactive, personalized spear supplements Diomedes himself and Diomedes supplements Achilles, both failing to achieve what the original would or is expected to achieve. Achilles enjoys displaying this double supplementarity that shows himself to be indeed irreplaceable. He should have believed in his own irreplaceable position when sending Patroclos to fight alone, as he wrongly trusts that his supplement, surrogate, and alter ego is equal to himself on the battlefield. Love blinds him.

In his mocking analysis of the effects of his absence from battle, Achilles claims that he could not hear the voice of Agamemnon "from his hateful head," while "the voice of Hector encouraging the Trojans broke all around" (76–78). The contrast between the silence and the roaring of the two men is exaggerated and sarcastic.

His tone is amused, elated, and impressionistic as he looks with merriment at the past disaster he has caused by merely not being present.[40] His missing presence was, nevertheless, sustained by Zeus, who helped the Trojans gain the upper hand.[41] Achilles misses that he himself is the supplement of Zeus' *boulê*, and that all that Zeus did and does in order to recover Achilles' honor finally brings about Zeus' plan for the final destruction of Troy. The narrative of Achilles' honor is the temporal narrative on the human stage of Zeus' plan to destroy Troy. Zeus displays this program at XV. 64–77:

> Achilles shall rouse up Patroclos
> his companion. And shining Hector shall cut down Patroclos
> ... after he has killed many of the other young men,
> and among them my own son, divine Sarpedon.
> In anger at him, divine Achilles will kill Hector.

---

**40** The metaphor Τρώων δὲ πόλις ἐπὶ πᾶσα βέβηκε ("the whole city of the Trojans descended upon…" 69) is unique in Homer (cf. Hesiod, *Erga*, 240); that at the mere sight of the front of Achilles' helmet the Trojans would rout and fill the water courses with their corpses (70–72) has the touch of a miracle. Achilles' description of Agamemnon's arrogance against him as a lack of "kindly feelings" (72–73) toward him, is sarcastic.

**41** When Achilles later prays to Zeus, he recalls his help and recognizes the honor that Zeus gave him by listening to his prayer (XVI. 236–7).

> From that moment on I will favor the counterattack from the ships
> always and continuously until the Achaeans
> capture headlong Ilion through the will of Athena.
> Before this, I will not stop my anger, and I will not let
> any other of the immortals come here to help the Danaans
> until the desire expressed by the son of Peleus has been satisfied
> as I first promised to him and bent my head in assent to it
> on the day when, embracing my knees, divine Thetis
> begged honor for Achilles, sacker of cities.

Zeus connects his overarching plan for the destruction of Troy with his specific promise to Thetis. As he speaks to the gods, forbidding them from helping the Achaeans, he must emphasize his commitment and his firm decision to respect his promise (72–77). His final and major plan, however, is the destruction of Troy through Athena's *boulai*. Whether the destruction of the major heroes — Achilles included— constitutes a deviation or an implementation of Zeus' major project is impossible to say. To be sure, Hector's death is necessary in order for the Achaeans to capture the city, but Zeus is reticent even on this point.

From this perspective, it ensues that the narrative theme of the death of the major heroes, resulting in the restoration of Achilles' honor, replaces the narrative Zeus had originally conceived for the capture of Troy, but this theme remains subsidiary to and coherent with the principal and final *boulê* of Zeus.

Achilles instructs Patroclos to return as soon as he has driven the Trojans from the ships: his success will cause great honor for Achilles and the restitution of the girl (80–86);[42] but Patroclos should not gain so much glory that Achilles' own glory would be diminished (89–90):

> You must not long for war against the Trojans
> without me, you will make my glory much less.

He does not know the structure of the supplement, but he recognizes its effects. Achilles wants to be considered and treated as the "best of the Achaeans" and suspects the double danger of the substitute: on the one hand, Patroclos can lessen Achilles' glory if he really has the force of the master; on the other, Patroclos can risk being suppressed in the absence of the master.

---

**42** Achilles already obtained —and refused— the restitution of the girl in the ninth book ("The Embassy"): scholars have discussed at length the "contradiction." De Romilly 1983, 30–31 minimizes it by attributing the contradiction to the narrative strategy since, through Achilles' earlier refusal, the text now produces a strong reaction.

In the eyes of the Narratees, who know what will happen, Achilles' misgivings are correct, but not complete and strong enough: they will not lead him to desist from his dangerous decision.

At the end of his strict instructions to Patroclos, Achilles prays to the gods and expresses an extravagant, almost delirious desire (XVI. 97–100):

> O father Zeus, Athena, and Apollo
> may not one of the Trojans escape death, as many as they are,
> and not one of the Argives, but may we [Achilles and Patroclos] emerge from the slaughter
> so that we alone may break Troy's sacred coronal.

Only a man in love can express such a desire.[43] It reveals the subject's longing for his absolute marginality and uniqueness: the world disappears and a blessed, miraculous event emerges that unites the two lovers in a joyful forever. The hallucinatory dream has an inner motivation. Achilles surmounts the terrible tension of his conflicting feelings and closes his dialogue with Patroclos through the loving image of their regained unity in fighting. He prays that his desire be achieved with the support of the gods and uses a strong male language with the sexual metaphor of the rape of Troy. They are no longer a little girl with her mother, nor a father and his son. The city is conquered and the adventure that has until now turned out badly is happily over. The pair wins felicitously together.[44]

After Achilles' prayer, the dialogue between the two characters ends and the narrative turns to Zeus as he accomplishes the last steps of the plan he devised to honor Achilles: by Zeus' help, Hector contrives to throw fire on one ship's stern (XVI. 101–24).

With this last event, a marvelous coincidence emerges. On the one hand, since Zeus has completed his project to honor Achilles, he turns to overseeing his larger plan that will lead to the capture of Troy "through the design of Athena" (XV. 71). On the other, by his autonomous decision —a foolish one, as the poet defines it (XV. 597)— Patroclos will join the fighting line, where Zeus, god of Fate, expects Patroclos to be.

The narrative underscores this marvelous convergence by having Achilles turn to Patroclos as the flame on the ship breaks out (126–9):

---

[43] Zenodotus and Aristarchus considered the passage an interpolation, given that it presupposed an erotic relationship between Achilles and Patroclos.

[44] Tsagalis 2012, 57: Achilles "explicitly tells Patroclos that only together will they be able, if the gods grant them victory, to sack the city of Troy."

Rise up, divine Patroclos,[45] rider of horses:
I see the ravening fire roaring over the ships!
May they not capture the ships and prevent our escape:
quickly get on the armor: I will muster the army."[46]

This burning ship signals a paradoxical contrast and parallel: both the end of Zeus' strategy to honor Achilles and Achilles' decision to stop this strategy. This paradox underlines the discrepancies that may abide in the "double motivation" and reveals the extraordinary theological irony of the Iliadic god (119–25).

I will now summarize the principle points of my analysis. Achilles is responsible for the events that follow this episode to the extent that he sends Patroclos alone to fight in order to protect the ships. The psychological process that leads him to this decision is not described by the text, that, once again, dismisses that sort of soul searching. We, Narratees may try to imagine it: still conflicted about the Achaeans, surprised by Patroclos' determination to help them, and troubled by his love for Patroclos, Achilles is finally persuaded by a *force majeure*, the "fire roaring over the ships." When Iliadic characters decide or act in a surprising fashion, the text suggests that a game or the emergence of specific forces motivate them. Epic does not study the inner movements and agitations of the soul, but the impact of external forces on a character's behavior.

Achilles attributes the failure of his companions to stop Hector to his own absence from the battlefield; he fails to see that his absence means the presence of Zeus on the battlefield and that in truth, by his consent to Patroclos, he inscribes his own death in Zeus' ultimate plan.

Achilles realizes the impossible-to-control oxymoron of the double, substitute, and alter ego: if Patroclos is equal to the master, then he acquires the honors of the master, but if he is a supplement and lacks in various ways the master's power, then Patroclos risks being suppressed. Achilles becomes aware of this structural knot but cannot face it and resolve it: he overcomes it with a

---

**45** The noun-epithet διογενὲς Πατρόκλεες is used four times in the *Iliad* and its meaning "descendant from Zeus," "divine" (instead of the usual "illustrious," "splendid," "Prince," etc.) seems to me to be supported by the text at XVI. 707: as Patroclos "equal to a god" (δαίμονι ἶσος) attacks for the "fourth time" —in the usual role of a god (705)—, Apollo addresses him with the noun-epithet διογενὲς Πατρόκλεες. By effacing and removing the direct or indirect presence of Zeus from the *dio-* epithets, readers and translators dismiss the powerful aura of Zeus that pervades the text and Zeus' ruling authority (Zeus is "father of men and gods").
**46** This passage explains why Zeus says that Achilles will "rouse" or "incite" Patroclos to fight (XV. 64) and why Thetis tells Hephaistos that Achilles "put his armor upon Patroclos and sent him into the fighting" (XVIII. 451–52).

hallucinatory prayer in which he recomposes the unity of the pairing and its final success.

The Narratees may better understand Achilles' extraordinary change of mind by referring to a mythical model that the Poet may have taken as a basic structure of Achilles' situation. It is the story of Meleager that we know through the narrative Phoenix offers in book IX. 524–99. Like Achilles, Meleager is insulted by an unjust and offensive treatment and refuses to fight, but when the Courets are at the point of storming the city of Calydon, authorities, friends, and parents come to Meleager. They promise him a reward and supplicate him to end his boycott and save their and his city. Meleager, still feeling offended, refuses, and it is only his wife, Cleopatra, who, at the last moment of danger, persuades him. Calydon is saved, but, by entering the fight, Meleager, just like Achilles, condemns himself to death.

The wife's name Cleopatra ("*kleos* ['glory'] of the father") is a parallel, though inverted compound, that recalls the name of Patroclos ("*kleos* of the ancestors") and suggests a specific message. In the scale of ascending affections to which Meleager is exposed by the begging people of the city,[47] he responds only to his wife Cleopatra. While Phoenix's story about Meleager has a strong and immediate message for Achilles in book IX, in which Achilles' friends try to persuade him to end his boycott, it is also suggestive at the moment when Achilles, in book XVI, yields to Patroclos. Nagy 1979, 105 has made this connection eloquent: "For Achilles, then, the story of Meleager has a distant message: in his own ascending scale of affections, as dramatized by the entire composition of the *Iliad*, the highest place must be taken by Patroclos whose name has the same meaning as the name of Cleopatra."[48]

Here in book XVI, Patroclos comes as the last person to supplicate Achilles (after Achilles' friends in book IX), at the moment of ultimate danger for the Achaean ships, and persuades Achilles to enter the fight. He does not gain the whole success that Cleopatra achieved in the Meleager story of the hypertext,

---

[47] This scale of ascending affections in analogous situations to those of Meleager has been drawn by Kakrides 1949, 20 ff.

[48] Meleager's story has attracted great critical attention as a paradigmatic story that may have suggested the wrath of Achilles: see Mahaffy 1881, 11; Mülder 1910, 50–56. Andersen 1987, 4 writes: "Meleager's role is a prefiguration of Achilles' and even of the outcome of the story as a whole." The adaptations that Homer made in order to create a closer parallelism between Achilles' and Meleager's situations are analyzed by various scholars. Sacks 1997, 7 has seen in it "an amazing piece of Homeric virtuosity." See also the rich commentary by Griffin 1995, 134 ff. West 2011, 227 is skeptical about Meleager's wrath as a model for Achilles' wrath. On *philotes*, see Sinos 1980, 40 ff.

but he comes close to it, as Achilles does not himself go to fight, but sends and commits his alter ego —his "supplement"— to save the situation.

The echo of Meleager's final yielding to his wife Cleopatra in order to save her, even at the price of his own death, surely resounds in Achilles' yielding to Patroclos. Achilles also yields in a concession inspired by love: though he sends Patroclos alone, and though he obeys a *force majeure,* he dreams that he and Patroclos should conquer Troy together. Achilles' destiny will show an even closer parallel: Achilles will fight to avenge Patroclos, knowing that this fight will be unavoidably followed by his own death.

## 3.3 Zeus' and Apollo's Conspiracy against Patroclos

« Pour jouer tragique, il faut et il suffit de faire comme si les dieux existaient, comme si on les avait vus, comme s'ils avaient parlé : mais alors quelle distance de soi-même à ce qu'on dit ! »

Roland Barthes, "Témoignage sur le théâtre,"
*Œuvres Complètes* II, p. 71,
quoted and commented by Samoyault 2015, 152

Zeus, god of Fate, does not care for Achilles' love for Patroclos, and accordingly he only partially agrees to the ritually elaborated libation and solemn prayer that Achilles addresses to him, begging for rapid success and the safe return of his companion (XVI. 225–48). Achilles specifically asks of Zeus (241–5):

Let shining triumph [*kudos*] go forth with him,
make his heart inside his breast breathe courage so that Hector too
will find out whether our *therapôn* knows how to fight alone
or whether his hands rage invincible
only when I myself enter the struggle of Ares.

Achilles demands *kudos* for Patroclos, i.e. the shining sign of triumph, as he himself would expect to receive from Zeus. He deems that with the help of Zeus Patroclos will win, just as Achilles himself would. Zeus, however, will increase Patroclos' fighting fury in order to lead him to death, and Apollo will give *kudos* to Hector (XVI. 730), who, after Apollo, will kill Patroclos.

The text immediately lets us know Zeus' response (XVI. 249–52):

So he was praying and clever and efficient Zeus listened to him.
Yet of the two requests the father granted one, but denied the other:
[τῷ δ' ἕτερον μὲν ἔδωκε πατήρ, ἕτερον δ' ἀνένευσε]
he granted [δῶκε] that Patroclos should push the battle and onslaught away from the ships, but he denied [ἀνένευσε] Patroclos' safe return from the battle.

The Poet stages Achilles' libation and solemn prayer for specific purposes. First, he allows us to imagine Achilles' misgiving about Patroclos' going to fight alone and, second, he wants to make us aware of a tight dependence between Achilles' ritual and Zeus. The goblet from which he drinks has always an exclusive user, Achilles himself, and an exclusive god, Zeus, to whom the libation has been addressed (XVI. 225–27). The goblet traces a direct connection and an exclusive relationship between the immortal and mortal beings, and points to a ritual aspect of the "double," Zeus and Achilles, that I already mentioned. The "double" is also referred to by the sustained mention that Thetis herself placed this goblet in a chest to be taken to Achilles's ship (XVI. 221–24). By having Thetis placing this goblet among Achilles' most personal objects, tunics, mantels, etc., the text suggests both the unique and familiar ritual relation that Achilles entertains with Zeus, and refers to the mythical references that sustain this double. At this point, when Achilles' prayer for the safe return of Patroclos is denied by Zeus, the mortal destiny of Achilles appears inevitable in the eyes of the Narratees. Achilles replaces the immortal god that Zeus would have begotten had he married Thetis: Achilles' mortality replaces an immortal being that would have been destined to replace Zeus.

During the rite, Achilles cleans the goblet with sulphur and then washes it out in bright-running water. The prayer contains certain details that also imply a geographical, if not a directly personal relationship between Achilles and Zeus. The invocation to Zeus, "lord of Dodona, Pelasgian" (229–30), references Zeus' major cult in northern Greece from where Achilles comes.

The ritual significance and symbolic force of the goblet in this dramatic instance are accompanied by a textual and architectonic function. Achilles' libation in his precious goblet must recall another precious goblet, that of Nestor on XI. 631–37, "which the old man had brought with him from home"—a personal object, therefore— and elaborately and richly wrought. Lovely-haired Hecamedes prepares for Nestor and his companions a restoring potion that Nestor drinks in this personal goblet. There is no mention of a libation to a god, but the libation is implied by the mention of the "holy barley" on 631, for instance. These features are sufficient to make Nestor's goblet noticeable, but what connects it to Achilles' goblet is that Nestor's restoring moment takes place when Patroclos arrives, and then received the instructions from the old king. Patroclos repeats word for word Nestor's advice and, in this way, persuades Achilles. Nestor' goblet is the object that symbolically signals Nestor's relaxed relation with Patroclos and the disastrous results of his advice, while Achilles' goblet, with its textual function, completes the preparation for a disaster and through its ritual significance allows the display of Zeus' endorsement of said disaster.

Returning now to the specific text of 251–52, we might assume that there is a significant lexical distinction between Zeus' "granting" and Zeus' "refusing": his "granting" is expressed by the verb "to give," which is a generic and a normal expression for a god's concession of favors, but Zeus' refusal is identified with his gesture of "throwing his head back," a sign of denial that, either literally or metaphorically, refers to the gesture that characterizes Zeus as god of Fate. For example, when Zeus approves Thetis' request, he makes a gesture with his head, here by dropping down his head (I. 524–5):

> I will nod assent with my head, that you may believe me:
> for this, among the immortal gods, is my mightiest sign...[49]
> τοι κεφαλῇ κατανεύσομαι ὄφρα πεποίθῃς·
> τοῦτο γὰρ ἐξ ἐμέθεν γε μετ'ἀθανάτοισι μέγιστον...

The text may want us to realize that Zeus' denial falls under his role as master of human destinies, while his concession to change the course of the battle concerns a contingent event.[50]

After Sarpedon's death, Zeus intervenes twice in the scene of the battle (XVI. 458–61, 567–8) in order to increase the fury and the flow of blood, and on two other occasions Zeus' intervention targets Patroclos directly. First, at 644–655, Zeus is shown to be uncertain whether he should have Hector kill Patroclos immediately, upon the corpse of Sarpedon, or have Patroclos first push back the Trojans into the city, inflicting larger ruin on them. He decides in favor of the latter. The inconsistency of this decision with Zeus' plan to help the Trojans win may have only one explanation. He desires a bloodbath to honor his son's death, yet he cannot allow the Achaeans to be massacred, since this would make Patroclos' intervention completely useless. Even later (XVI. 779–83), the text characterizes the Achaeans' victory as being "against destiny," since Zeus' plan is to have the Trojans win until Achilles returns to the fight.[51] Yet the *diêgêsis* could not deny a great victory to Patroclos, even if this victory around the body of Sarpedon and then that of Cebrion (779–85) causes the Trojan's defeat. Even Zeus, the greatest god, must follow the rules of epic conventions, even if these rules break the coherence of his plot.

---

**49** See above Ch. 1.1. See also XV. 75.
**50** The verb *neuô* signifies "to incline the head": it is etymologically connected with the Latin *numen*, which evokes "the will of the gods." *DELG*, 748.
**51** Nothing happens against the will of Zeus, but here the text evokes a sort of *adynaton* to magnify the valor of the Achaeans.

The text seems aware of this difficulty. Casually or intentionally, Zeus is made to argue and act as an epic character who is uncertain about his alternatives (652–5):

> As he was thinking in this way, the better path seemed to him
> that the strong henchman of Achilles, son of Peleus,
> again push the Trojans and bronze-helmed Hector
> back on their city and tear the life from many fighters.

The same line 652 – "As he was thinking in this way, the better path seemed to him" (ὧδε δέ οἱ φρονέοντι δοάσσατο κέρδιον εἶναι) is used two other times in the *Iliad* within the *diêgêsis* to indicate a human character's choice of a more profitable alternative. Indeed, a literal translation of κέρδιον is "more profitable." At XIII. 458 the *diêgêsis* introduces what Deiphobos takes to be a more profitable decision: to fight side by side with a companion rather than alone. He chooses Aineas, who becomes the main hero in the ensuing battle; Deiphobos' choice thus initiates a new narrative episode. At XIV. 23, the same line introduces an analogous decision on the part of Nestor, who, by choosing to meet Agamemnon, will give him important advice. There are five other examples of this line in the *Odyssey*.

At XVI. 652, Zeus, by choosing to have Patroclos prolong his victory and magnify the massacre, gains the profit of honoring the death of his son. The epic poet frequently introduces a large bloodbath when he describes a battle around a corpse. This happens, for instance, around the corpse of Patroclos: Zeus (XVII. 401) and then Athena, sent by Zeus (XVII. 545) —without any incertitude or doubt about their choice— increase the bloodbath in honor of Patroclos. Again, Zeus honors Sarpedon by creating a large massacre of fighters around his corpse, even if this means that many Trojans be killed under Patroclos' assault.[52] This bloodbath is also a clever narrative artifice on the part of the Poet and is —so to speak— the Poet's most profitable narrative resource, for it belongs to the conventional theme of "the battle around a corpse." The Poet gains a supplementary profit from Zeus' choice: he suggests that Zeus himself considers the bloodbath to be the more profitable event to honor the corpse of a great

---

**52** Zeus engages in a "*mermerizein* scene" (a scene of introspection) also at II. 3–6, where, however, he is not uncertain about two alternatives, but meditates on the best way he may honor Achilles and kill many Achaeans. The line that describes Zeus' seeking the best way is: ἥδε δέ οἱ κατὰ θυμὸν ἀρίστη φαίνετο βουλή (5), "now in his mind this appeared to be the best counsel, [to send...]"

victim. The poet can silently intimate that there is no arbitrariness in this conventional pattern, but rather it is justified even by the decision of Zeus.

The rain of bloody tears that Zeus sends from the sky to the ground is textually connected to Zeus' *boulê*. A sort of thread connects I. 3, XI. 52 ff., and XVI. 58–61, showing that the image of bloody raindrops characterizes Zeus' prodigious participation in the bloodbath, as the massacre is announced in his *boulê* (I. 3).

The text that connects all three passages is XI. 52–55:

> ...and the son of Kronos
> drove down the evil turmoil upon them and from aloft cast
> down dew dripping blood from the sky, since he was minded
> to hurl down a multitude of strong heads to the house of Hades.

Sending dew dripping blood from the sky signifies Zeus' participation in the bloodbath that he intends to increase. Line 55 picks up line I. 3 and, accordingly, whereas before "the wrath of Achilles was the cause of a fearsome massacre, now Zeus is going to bring it about" (Hainsworth 1993, *ad loc.*).

Compare the passage at XI. 52–55 with I. 3–5:

> [the wrath of Achilles] that hurled to Hades multitudes of strong
> souls of heroes [...]
> and the will [*boulê*] of Zeus was accomplished.

and with XVI. 458–61:

> and he wept tears of blood that fell to the ground, for the sake
> of his beloved son, whom now Patroclos was presently
> to kill in fertile Troy and far from the land of his fathers.

The commentators tend to interpret Zeus' sending of bloody rain and tears in both passages as an "obvious symbolic figure."[53] Yet it could also be interpreted as a magical act performed by Zeus: for instance, the dew is blood or has traces of blood.[54] If this bloody rain has to manifest his deep pain for the death of his son, its magical nature would offer a stronger manifestation. At any rate, symbol or fact, Zeus wants the entire battlefield to be covered with running blood and devastation.

---

53 Hainsworth 1993, *ad loc.*
54 See West 2011, 249: "the morning dew has a bloody tinge."

The second of Zeus' interventions in the conspiracy against Patroclos happens in the course of Patroclos' fight, after the Achaeans succeed in gaining possession of Sarpedon's armor. Patroclos sends it to the ships for his companions.

Until this point, Patroclos has behaved as he had been advised, but now he suddenly seems to begin a new onset. The Narrator describes this and comments (XVI. 684–93):

> Patroclos meanwhile, spurring the horses and Automedon,
> went after the Trojans and the Lycians, completely blinded,[55]
> the fool! If he had obeyed the command of the son of Peleus,
> he would have escaped the dim doom of black death.
> But the mind of Zeus is always stronger than that of men,
> Zeus, who inspires fear in even the bravest man and takes away victory,
> easily, from him, even when Zeus himself excites him to fight.[56]
> Thus he now filled Patroclos' heart with fury.
> Who was then the one you slaughtered first, who the last,[57]
> Patroclos,[58] when the gods called you to your death?"[59]

---

[55] The Narrator addresses Patroclos as *nepios* ("fool") because he seems blind or blinded as he begins a new assault. Perhaps, as I am reading the passage, there is no mechanical double motivation (see Janko 1992, *ad loc.*) in the Poet's recognizing at once both Patroclos' foolishness and Zeus' intervention. In the metaphoric play of "he was completely blinded" (*aasthê*) the double motivation is present and readable.

[56] The two lines 689 and 690 are repeated by Hector at XVII. 177–78 when he speaks to Glaukos, in order to relativize the full autonomy of a fighter, even of a great fighter. The lines seem to have the same function in our passage. The epic paradox emerges vividly from these two lines: Zeus deprives of victory even the fighter whom he himself has driven to fight. This paradox announces the one that will destroy Patroclos: Zeus excites him to fight so that he might be killed.

[57] Perceau 2011, 47 has an ingenious intuition: the list of the names that follow (694 ff.) could sound in some way as Patroclos' answer to the Narrator's apostrophe. Thus Patroclos would compose, through the *androktasia*, the title of his glory and simultaneously the ground of his death.

[58] The name Patroclos is at the beginning of the line, in an emphatic spot, and is a direct address to him by the poetic voice.

[59] 692–3:
  Ἔνθα τίνα πρῶτον τίνα δ' ὕστατον ἐξενάριξας,
  Πατρόκλεις, ὅτε δή σε θεοὶ θανάτονδε κάλεσσαν;
The line, "the gods called you to your death," is uniquely repeated in Hector's episode (XXII. 297) where it is Hector himself who realizes and asserts: "the gods called me to death." Because of this repetition, we surmise that the Poet was comparing the two episodes and bringing to light their profound difference, as we already briefly indicated (Ch. 2). In both cases,

The Poet joins the action and apostrophizes the character, as he already did earlier, and also expresses a note of anxiety and reproach, as he describes Patroclos' new course of action. The Poet has seen him kill Sarpedon in an open battle without any divine intervention and assumes that Patroclos may still be in control of his mind. He calls him "blinded" and "fool!" because now, after having pushed back the Trojans, he should come back, as Achilles ordered him. By so doing he would save his life. On the contrary, Patroclos starts a new and senseless attack.

The reproach that the poetic voice addresses to Patroclos thus makes sense if the Poet considers Patroclos to be still in control of his mind, yet on the verge of losing it. However, the poetic voice's addition, "But the mind of Zeus is always stronger than that of men," could imply that Zeus and Ate may somehow be responsible for Patroclos' forgetting Achilles' orders. In this case, the poetic voice's reproach to Patroclos —"blinded," "fool!"— would make sense only if the human action and the divine intervention are combined.

Apollo implies that initially Patroclos acts autonomously: accordingly, Apollo stops him and orders him to withdraw, explaining to Patroclos that his conquering fury is useless (707–9). Patroclos obeys (710–11). In this passage, Patroclos behaves as one who is master of himself and of his actions, though it is not clear whether he understands the full significance of Apollo's intervention.[60] As Apollo interprets Patroclos' action in this way, he, coherently and correctly, does *not* add: "But the mind of Zeus is always stronger than that of men." Patroclos should be aware of his capabilities, and then realize that he will not conquer Troy. The Poet, on the contrary, presents two contradictory motivations for Patroclos' behavior and lets his Narratees wobble between them. The question about the nature and agency of human action emerges in the heroic age, when gods freely permeate human characters and events. In such a world,

---

however, Zeus is calling them in accordance with his fatal role. Scodel 2017, 79 refuses to see the main responsibility of Zeus in this call:
"when the gods called you to your death." Her reading is too "literal": the collective "the gods" means the "divine will," but it is definitely the will of Zeus as the text repeatedly shows. Zeus causes Patroclos' oblivion of Achilles' warnings, and Patroclos, when he dies, prophetically says (845–46): "... the son of Cronos, Zeus, and Apollo... have subdued me/ easily since they themselves stripped the arms from my shoulders." Patroclos mentions Zeus and Apollo, though only Apollo struck him; yet Patroclos recognizes correctly the will of Zeus in the whole action and names him: a literal reading of Patroclos' words would make no sense.
**60** It is difficult to speak of Patroclos' autonomy: his consciousness remains unfocused. It is only as he dies that he seems to gain full consciousness of being the victim of Zeus' and Apollo's plans (844–50).

human free will can be assumed to operate autonomously and responsibly even if it acts within a mysterious and miraculous convergence with the divine plan. Outside this exceptional condition, that we have seen in a few cases, hybridism cannot be a given condition since the two agents, the human and the divine, are too asymmetrical and too divergent to cooperate in the same measure and fully autonomously. When man is permeated by a divine force, his free will might cease to operate. The text, however, can wishfully represent and stage a hybrid cooperation between man and god, if it cheats and if, through some rhetorical device, it leaves both motivations possible and parallel so that one does not obstruct the other. In our passage, the trick lies in the double connotation — literal and metaphorical— implicit in the verb *aasthê*: "he [Patroclos] was fully blinded." If the verb is heard connected with *nêpios*, "fool," it connotes Patroclos human blindness, his oblivion of Achilles' orders; yet, if the verb is heard and logically coupled with "But the mind of Zeus is always stronger than that of men," Patroclos' blindness is divine, inspired by Zeus/Ate who is the source of his oblivion. There is no reason to be surprised, since always —even in this case, in which we can see Patroclos held responsible for his foolish autonomy— the mind of Zeus is stronger than that of men. Read in this way, the contradiction is somehow turned into a sort of imbrication.

The two orders are somehow coordinated and form a hybridism. Even the slaughter of Patroclos has two different and coordinated agents depending on whether the point of view is human or divine: Apollo and/or Hector, as we will see.

I now return to the action on the battlefield. By inspiring Patroclos with a strong fury, Zeus allows him to obtain an immense success: he could have conquered Troy. Yet the accorded condition of this success is perverse: the capture of Troy would have to happen against the destiny that Zeus himself controls, and thus could not happen. The narrative simply opens the prospect of an impossible action; this prospect designates Patroclos' success as a rhetorical hyperbole meant to justify his death at the hands of Zeus and Apollo as he goes through a sort of murderous *askesis*.

We are reminded of the episode when Zeus grants Hector great force as an advance reward, compensating him for the death that Zeus himself causes (XVII. 206–8, and see also XV. 610–14).

As Patroclos comes close to performing the great deed of capturing Troy (XVI. 698–711), Apollo intervenes and prevents it (XVI. 698–709):[61]

---

[61] Lines 703–711 echo lines V. 437–44, which refer to Diomedes' and Apollo's confrontation. Diomedes stands in a very different relation to the divine than does Patroclos, since Diomedes is inspired and helped by Athena.

> At this point the sons of the Achaeans would have conquered gate-towering Troy
> under Patroclos' hands as he raged with his spear before them,
> had not Phoebus Apollo taken his stand on the powerful tower
> planning death for him and help for the Trojans.[62]
> Three times Patroclos mounted the jut of the high wall,
> three times Apollo battered him backward
> with immortal hands, pushing back Patroclos' gleaming shield;
> but when, at the fourth time, Patroclos, equal to a god,
> (ἀλλ' ὅτε δὴ τὸ τέταρτον ἐπέσσυτο δαίμονι ἶσος)
> attacked, Apollo shouted terribly and spoke winged words:
> "Withdraw, divine Patroclos:[63] it is not destined that
> the proud Trojans' citadel fall before your spear,
> not even before Achilles' —a far greater man than you.

The temporal module within which Patroclos almost captures Troy is the epic device I have illustrated in the previous chapter: it inserts the human action into a divine scansion of time. The order of phases is respected: the god intervenes and stops him at the fourth instance of Patrocolos' repeated assaults. Yet at 704 —"when, at the fourth time, Patroclos, equal to a god, attacked"— the audience is invited to believe that Patroclos, being equal to a god, might succeed in his goal.

The bitter irony of calling Patroclos "equal to a divine being," at the moment when the divine scansion of time foresees the intervention of a real god, proves the Narrator's command and stylistic virtuosity when deploying his mythical and literary devices.[64] The false expectation that this device produces is not simply a formal subtlety; it also carries an emotional connotation: the epithet suggests irony and pity. Patroclos is like a god in respect to the fighting power that he receives from Zeus, but a false one, a phantom, occupying improperly, on the fourth occasion, the position of a true god.[65] He is even here a

---

**62** On the so-called suspense of anticipation, see Tsagalis 2012, 55, n. 81.
**63** The noun-epithet διογενὲς Πατρόκλεες is used four times in the *Iliad* and its meaning "descendant from Zeus," "divine" (instead of the usual "illustrious," "splendid," "Prince" etc.) seems to me to be supported by the text at XVI. 707.
**64** Jedkriewicz 2014 implies that the Narrator exposes the human desires of challenging the gods, and connects this ironic gesture with what he sees as the anti-divine impulse of men in the *Iliad*. Certainly, here the poetic voice is impatient and displeased with Zeus' behavior.
**65** Tsagalis 2012, 55–56 illustrates perfectly how Patroclos transgresses the fixed epic terms of space and identity: "Patroclos extends the limits of the area within which he is supposed to act... and thus violates all the rules of its symbolic function... Patroclos tries to overcome the very boundaries of the plot within which he functions as a heroic figure. Apollo...reminds the audience that the son of Menoitios is just the surrogate of Achilles."

replacement of some greater original: his heroic curriculum constantly underlines his misplacement, his inferior status, and his vain, supplemental role.

The correct god, Apollo, intervenes at the fourth phase of the module and physically and morally stops Patroclos. He pushes Patroclos back and tells him that neither he, nor the much greater Achilles will ever conquer Troy. By comparing Patroclos to Achilles, while denying them both that success, Apollo implicitly intimates that the exploit Patroclos tries to accomplish has a sort of Achillean grandeur. Yet as he belittles Patroclos' greatness in comparison to Achilles' ("far greater than you"), he describes a relation that the Narratees know well as the relation of a master to his surrogate. Apollo's statement minimizes Patroclos' heroic stature in the moment when the hero accomplishes his strongest-yet-self-destructive deed. The text keeps on emphasizing the surrogate and supplemental function of the hero.

Apollo's assertion that Achilles himself is not destined to capture Troy opens the poignant question concerning the purpose of Achilles' fighting at Troy. Shall his glory (*kleos*) ensue from taking revenge upon Hector? It is both bold and embarrassing for the text to have Apollo make such a declaration: the best Achaean hero shall not conquer the city against which he has been fighting for many years, and for whose conquest he has a hallucinatory desire (XVI. 99–100). This announcement of Achilles' failure anticipates Achilles' own recognition of the nonsense of his heroic participation in the war (XXIV 507–55) and points to the moral and religious message the *Iliad* delivers to its Narratees.

As the text ascribes the administration of all these events to the will (*boulê*) of Zeus and its unrecognizable motivations, it sees in him the paradoxical control of the terrible snd fascinating order of things (*mysterium tremendum et fascinans*).

Apollo's destruction of Patroclos unfolds through the repeated "three times...fourth time" module, which, at the fourth moment, brings in the destructive action of Apollo (XVI. 783–93):

> And Patroclos rushed against the Trojans, meditating their ruin:
> three times he charged, similar to quick Ares,
> shouting frightening cries, and killed each time nine men.
> But when, on the fourth time, Patroclos rushed, equal to a god,
> then, Patroclos, the end of your life appeared:
> Phoebus came against you in the violent melee,
> terrible, and he did not notice that the god came through the battle,
> for shrouded in a thick mist the god came in against him,

and stood behind, and struck his back and his broad shoulders
with his flat hand, and Patroclos' his eyes spun.
Phoebus Apollo threw his helmet from his head...[66]

The setting of Patroclos' and the god's action in the repeated three + one temporal and narrative module stages again the essential movements and phases of the previous deployment of the module (XVI. 701 ff.). Though the repetition necessarily has some passive features, this new deployment unleashes an irony more bitter than in the earlier display of the module: the identity of the hero with a divine being (δαίμονι ἶσος) is still merely nominal, and by contrast it flaunts the nothingness of the human hero in comparison with the might that is a real god. Here the bitter use of the epithet is stronger than in the earlier example due to many different details that show how the Poet is embarrassed by the situation he has to describe. First, he repeats line 705 to produce an emphasis on the merely rhetorical equality of the hero with the real god.

Secondly, the Narrator suggests that the god whom Patroclos resembles is Ares (784). As many interpreters recognize, the comparison of a hero with Ares signifies here, and often elsewhere, the defeat or even the death of the hero.[67] Accordingly, while the Narrator celebrates the speed of Patroclos' attack, he simultaneously announces that with this attack Patroclos will meet his death.

Third, in the same line the Narrator reports that Patroclos is meditating or planning the Trojans' ruin, and indeed, in each of his three assaults he slays nine men, i.e. a multiple of three. Notice that the expression, "meditating ruin for the Trojans," picks up the recent description of Apollo, "meditating" or "planning Patroclos' ruin" (701). Once more the Narrator extols the almost superhuman violence of the hero while recalling the impending menace of Apollo.

Fourth, in this event, Patroclos should be aware of the menace Apollo constitutes for him. He, of course, does not know the epic module of 3+1, and merely ignores Apollo's order (707–9). His behavior would be irresponsible, especially in view of the warning that Achilles just gave him concerning Apollo, were he not induced by Zeus to fight, as Zeus "filled with fury Patroclos' heart" (691).

Fifth, here the god does not simply warn Patroclos, but makes him defenseless and a dead victim to be somehow massacred a second time. Among the six

---

66 The arrival of Patroclos' death —ἔνθ' ἄρα τοι Πάτροκλε φάνη βιότοιο τελευτή— in the person of Apollo is the real fourth act in the temporal scansion of events that Apollo controls. The epithet *deinos* is placed in the most effective form of enjambment, with a full pause after it. Patroclos realizes only *après coup* that Apollo has destroyed him (XVI. 845).
67 See Pucci 2010; and see Nagy 1997, p. 295: "Patroclos becomes identified with Ares rather than with Achilles when he fights alone." See also below Ch. 3.1 n. 2.

examples of this 3 + 1 module in Homer, this is the only instance in which the god intervening at the fourth moment acts physically against the agent who three times has pursued his intent.

Finally, the Poet addresses Patroclos directly in a pathetic breaking of the narrative (XVI. 786–9):

> But when, for the fourth time, Patroclos rushed, equal to a god,
> then, Patroclos, the end of your life became visible:
> Phoebus came against you in the violent melee,
> terrible!

The description is, as Homer does best, economic, rapid, and cogent. The instant in which Apollo starts his attack is highly emphasized by the temporal expressions, ἀλλ' ὅτε δή... ἔνθ' ἄρα, creating a strong suspension and expectation for what the next event will be. The Poet's apostrophe announces the completion of the epic module that both inscribes Patroclos' destiny into Zeus' *boulē*[68] and certifies the truth of the module as an epic device. Through the apostrophe, the Poet again becomes present at the scene as a witness of the menace of the god,[69] since he realizes the determining presence of Zeus in Patroclos' ruin.[70]

The god's tremendous violence crushes, pulverizes, piece after piece, Patroclos' armor, the armor of Achilles, showing the devastating physical power that the divine can exhibit and the purpose of this violence.[71]

Apollo emerges visibly for the readers, luminous indeed, as both the verb φάνη (787) and the naming of the god by Φοῖβος (788) strikingly emphasize, but remains shockingly invisible for Patroclos; he comes suddenly ("he stood be-

---

[68] It is perhaps an improper remark to notice that the Poet too, through the apostrophe, makes himself present together with Phoebos, only at the fourth moment of the module (787–88). If, on the contrary, it is a proper remark, this metapoetic use of the module bears witness to the textual sophistication and virtuosity of the Poets.

[69] The apostrophe provides a sort of pause full of emotional power: the sudden change from the third to the second person, the affable address ("Patroclos!"), and the becoming visible of Patroclos' death build up a sort of autonomous and almost lyrical scene. This new presence, however, is not semantically complete: see the distance between the invocation, "you," implying the presence of the speaker-poet at the moment of the event, and the aorist of the verb that relates to the past, i.e. to the action at which the speaker-poet is not present. See the illuminating observations of Bakker 1997, 25; de Jong 2004, 13–14; Dubel 2011, 143–44.

[70] The Narrator now avoids calling Patroclos "foolish" (*nepios*) as he had done twice before (XVI. 686 ff. and XVI. 46): now it is too late to reproach him, since his destiny is accomplished.

[71] Apollo divests Patroclos of Achilles' divine armor, for if he were protected by it he would be invulnerable and Hector would not be able to kill him. See Reinhardt 1961, 319–21.

hind Patroclos") at the conventional fourth moment. He produces a performance of striking horror and beauty, for he debunks and plays in reverse the armor dressing scene that in epic poetry is the sublime 'overture' of the heroic *aristeia*. The symbolic force of the reversal of that scene's sublimeness is enormous and brings to light the perverse and scornful view the god has of the heroic performance. The god reduces to nothing the signs of heroic fighting, even if these signs are divine weapons.

The destruction continues: Patroclos' spear breaks into pieces,[72] shield and corselet fall to the ground, the helmet runs under the feet of the horses. The *diêgêsis* comments (796–799):

> Before this time it had not been permitted
> to defile in the dust this helmet, crested in horse hair,
> no, it protected the head and the handsome brows
> of a godlike man, of Achilles; but in that day Zeus granted Hector
> to wear it on his head, as his death was close.

The narrative invites the audience to measure the difference between Achilles and Patroclos: "before this time" means that the helmet never fell before Patroclos wore it and accordingly —the text suggests— it is not worn properly by Patroclos, a man who is not godlike (*theios anêr*).[73] The Muses' narrative appreciates Achilles' divine birth and emphasizes that the god strips the armor from Patroclos' shoulders.

Lines 799–800 explicitly introduce Zeus collecting the divine pieces of the armor in order for Hector to use them and die inside them. The gods abuse the very weapons with the purpose of destroying the two heroes, while for men the description and the wearing of the armor is a sort of synecdoche that brings to light the entire personality of the hero.[74]

Besides the standard motif of fallen objects rolling onto the battlefield (see Janko 1992, 412), Achilles' helmet on the ground intimates the presence/absence of Achilles in the battle: he is present only in the voided object, in the useless sign of him: and even this immaculate sign has been defiled. The sacred pairing itself of Achilles and his *therapôn* is poignantly defiled. Indeed, as Griffin writes (1980, 136): "the fall of the helmet in the dust is made almost more moving than Patroclos' death itself."

---

[72] "A plethora of stately epithets (the spear has five) slow the narrative further." Janko 1992, 411.
[73] See the analogous interpretation in Rudhardt 1999, 21.
[74] With lines XVI, 799–800, the text prepares the audience for Zeus' mishandling of the armor, as we saw in Ch. 2.3.

The demise of Patroclos goes on until he is practically without a weapon, "naked," as the text concisely and dramatically defines him (815). A Trojan, Euphorbus, hits his back with a spear. Patroclos is wounded and runs, withdrawing to the middle of the crowd. It is at this point that Hector emerges, hits him in the low belly, and Patroclos falls to the ground to finish there his life (818–828).[75]

Patroclos has no weapons with which to fight, and therefore he does not fight —there is no combat. The Narrator, however, celebrates Patroclos' fighting with a simile that describes Patroclos' and Hector's battle as a battle between a lion and a boar (823–28):

> As when a lion overpowers a tireless boar,[76]
> and the two fight in their pride on the summit of a mountain
> over a little spring of water: they both want to drink,
> and the lion overcomes by force the all-panting boar,
> so Hector, Priam's son, with a close spear-stroke[77] stripped the life
> from Menoitios' strong son who had killed so many…"

The simile, when applied to the actual fight described on the divine stage, makes no sense. Patroclos could not defend himself and could hardly raise a hand: he could hardly be compared to a tireless boar killed by a lion. The simile, however, while elevating Hector's murder of a victim to a heroic victory, effaces the divine presence that gave Hector such easy success, and introduces a register of "double truth," of hybridism: the Narratees know that the essential feature of the "event" has been Apollo's intervention, but the characters miss this view of the event and see in Hector the exclusive agent of the victory.[78]

An individual simile should not be judged by itself without referring to the other similes that constellate the episode.[79] In this episode, the Poet employs

---

[75] See Gaskin 2001, 151: "Lesky has shown that Dodds is wrong to describe Patroclos' death as overdetermined. The point is that the contributions of Apollo and Hector to Patroclos' death are not thought as independent inputs, each of which would have been sufficient on its own to kill Patroclos. The gods work with (sometimes through) men: the term 'overdetermination' misses the essential unity of such action." Yet it is an asymmetric, non-comparable unity, as I show in the following arguments.
[76] Janko 1992, 416: "The lion has no epithet, but the beaten boar is 'tireless,' an epithet reserved for the sun and the Sperkheios; this evokes the hitherto unbeaten Patroclos."
[77] The detail of the spear is incongruous with respect to the battle in the simile.
[78] In the "double motivation" formulation, everybody from Achilles to Patroclos to Apollo and Hector would be responsible for Patroclos' demise (see Janko 1992, 4), but the simile qualifies that formulation.
[79] This principle is described and is perfectly illustrated by Tsagalis in his work.

three analogous similes to comment on Patroclos' fight: a first simile at 487 ff. stages Patroclos as a lion that kills Sarpedon,[80] a bull. The lion is the symbol of royal *aristeia* in battle; the bull (the defeated Sarpedon) gets the epithet, "blazing and great-hearted."

A second simile follows (752 ff.) in which both Patroclos and Hector are compared to lions, and the last simile (823–28) reverses the conditions of the first: Patroclos is now the boar killed by Hector, the lion.[81]

In the second simile at 752 ff., Patroclos is twice compared to a lion. In the first part of the simile (752–754), Patroclos jumps toward Kebriones

> and the two fight in their pride like a lion, one who has taken a chest wound
> while ravaging a cattle pen – his valor
> is his undoing. So you sprang at Kebriones, full of fury, Patroclos.

The pathos of the wounded lion parallels the pathos of the new apostrophe: it is as if the Poet himself were seeing Patroclos' leap toward Kebriones,[82] whom he has just slain and who lies on the ground.

In the second part of the simile (756–61), Patroclos and Hector are compared to two lions that are fighting over the corpse of a deer: Patroclos is no longer a wounded lion, but is exactly like Hector: both fight on the summit of a mountain, both with huge pride,[83] and both are hungry. The fight between the

---

**80** On the connection of the "lion similes" to *aristeia*, see Schnapp-Gourbeillon 1981, 40. Probably this connection helps to explain the privilege and frequency of these similes —37 examples— in the *Iliad*. The semantic structure of the simile is complex. On the one hand, it assimilates the heroes to creatures other than themselves: they lose their individual traits and become undifferentiated symbols of violence. Through the assimilation of the champions to wild animals, the text not only eliminates the divine presence from the fighting event, but also suppresses most of the heroic motivations that stimulate the human fight. Even heroic values like *kleos* and *kudos* tend to disappear and cede place to a mere animal conflict in view of survival. On the other hand, the mirror image of the simile may reflect on the *comparandum*: the lion tends sometimes to appear as heroic as a hero: see for instance XX. 164–75, where the lion is modeled after Achilles rather than the inverse, creating a sort of floating 'signified.'

**81** The reversed figures are perfectly combined, and in the light of this chiastic reference, the realistic terms of the combat are insignificant: what is relevant is the image that terminates and closes Patroclos' *aristeia* with his death as a boar killed by Hector, a lion, the symbol of royal *aristeia* in battle.

**82** The "*tertium comparationis*" is the lion's and Patroclos' furious leap.

**83** μέγα φρονέοντε. This phrase grants the lions a slight human touch. Indeed, in many of this type of simile, the animals appear humanized, since the similarity works also in a reverse way. The beings of the whole world touch each other in an extraordinary transparency.

two champions is real: Patroclos and the Achaeans finally are successful and gain the corpse of Kebriones.

If we now return to the last simile (823–28), the one in which Patroclos is assimilated to a boar and killed by Hector, a lion, we meet some of the same descriptive details as in the previous simile:

> ...as when they both fight in their pride on the summit of a mountain
> over a little spring of water; they both want to drink,
> and the lion overcomes by force the all-panting boar...

The analogous and chiastic description of the animals' fight is meant to suggest that a real fight between Patroclos and Hector took place: this suggestion – strengthened by the parallelism with the simile at 756–61– goes against reality as it is represented by the Musean narrative.

There is indeed no account of a confrontation between the two heroes: a throw of the spears, a crossing of swords, etc. In the absence of this confrontation, we have the struggle between the lion and the boar, and Hector, since he is compared to the winning lion, gets the symbolic honor as the winner in a trial of *aristeia*.

The account of Patroclos' death is therefore split: on the one hand the Narrator, as if he himself were present, narrates the divine destruction of Patroclos; on the other, the same Narrator, through the simile, offers an image that claims a battle was truly fought between the two heroes in the total absence of divine intervention.

The divine intervention directs the action and obtains the results it intended to achieve; yet, in accordance with epic convention, the divine intervention was visible and operative only for its individual receiver, Patroclos.

## 3.4 Double Voices

> E come in fiamma favilla si vede,
> E come in voce voce si discerne,
> Quand'una è ferma e l'altra va e riede,
> Vid'io in essa luce altre lucerne
> Muoversi...
>     Dante, *Paradiso* VII. 16–20

Patroclos, the individual receiver of the divine interventions, was unaware – until the moment of his death – of being possessed by Zeus, who had inspired in him an uncontrollable fury. It is because of this fury that he exceeded the bounds of his allotted task and that he met the anger of Apollo.

He was also not fully aware of Apollo's attack against him. When he withdrew, he did not realize that he was deprived of his armor: the *diêgêsis* states, "*Atê* deprived him of his mind... and he stood astounded" (τὸν δ' ἄτη φρένας εἷλε, ... στῆ δὲ ταφών) (XVI. 804–5).[84] Though he reacted to the god's injunctions, he failed to notice that he was possessed by Zeus, and only the narrative account ensures us that he was not, in fact, in control of himself.

Only when he is dying and receives the prophetic gift does Patroclos recognize that he was subdued by the gods and thus asserts that Zeus and Apollo "stripped the arms from my shoulders" (845). As Hector fails to raise any objection, the narrative gives the Narratees confidence that the miraculous action was real.

Here are Patroclos' dying words (XVI. 844–50):

"Yes, Hector, now boast with big words: for the gods gave you
victory (*nikên*), Zeus Cronides and Apollo, who have subdued me
easily, since they themselves stripped the arms from my shoulders.[85]
If even twenty warriors such as you had come in against me,
all of them would have died here, subdued by my spear.
But my deadly destiny (μοῖρ' ὀλοὴ),[86] and the son of Leto killed me;[87]
and, among men, it was Euphorbus: you are my third slayer."[88]

The gods confirm Patroclos' version of events. They have a constant knowledge of their own interventions and are forever conscious of what really happened. Thus, when Thetis at XVIII. 450 ff. summarizes for Hephaistos the battle between Patroclos and Hector, she says that the Achaeans, under the command of Patroclos, "in that day would have stormed the city, if Apollo had not killed, in the first ranks, the strong son of Menoitios [i.e. Patroclos], who had accomplished such great damages, and then given shining triumph [*kudos*] to Hector" (XVIII. 454–56: Μενοιτίου ἄλκιμον υἱὸν / ἔκταν' ἐνὶ προμάχοισι καὶ Ἕκτορι

---

84 *Atê* is a different name and figure for the "destructive blindness" that invades Patroclos (see Ch. 4.3: The ruinous madness of *Atê*). Ultimately it is a cooperative figure and a manifestation of Zeus' *boulê*.
85 "Many analysts reject 846, because it refers to the removal of Patroclos' armor, but it is needed to contrast the gods' easy action with Hector's paltry deed (Reinhardt 1961, 323–5)." Janko 1992, 419.
86 "The ring formed by 845 and 849 confirms that Zeus and Fate are equated: these are two ways to explain the same event —it can occur because Zeus or the gods decide it or because it is simply one's portion in life." Janko 1992, 420. The "deadly destiny" (μοῖρ' ὀλοὴ) confirms the will of the gods (see 693), i.e. the will (*boulê*) of Zeus, the order of things, as it is recorded in the *diêgêsis* (I. 5) and in Zeus' words (XV. 64–66). For μοῖρ' ὀλοή, see also Ch. 2.2.
87 This is the unique example in Homer in which Apollo is defined only through his mother Leto. Perhaps it is a way for Patroclos to separate Apollo from his father Zeus, the ultimate ruler of events.
88 "Patroclos' speech is remarkable for its defiant tone. He denigrates Hector's achievement, and correctly prophesies his doom at Achilles' hands." West 2011, 328, n. 844–54. For the addresses by Hector, Achilles, and Briseis to Patroclos, see Kahane 1994, 139 ff.

κῦδος ἔδωκε).[89] Thetis, in stating that Apollo "gave *kudos* to Hector," means that Apollo gave Hector, who had merely been the god's final instrument in the destruction of Patroclos, the shining sign of victory.[90]

The inescapable conclusion is that what happens by miraculous intervention of the god is, for the Iliadic Muses' narrative, what truly happens, while the event as it unfolds through the Poet's simile and therefore before mortal eyes (XXII. 822) is essentially an obfuscated version of the real occurrence. It is presented devoid of the underlying miraculous realities: the human witnesses do not see the god stripping the armor piece by piece from Patroclos' body, but the stripping did occur, since Patroclos asserts it at his death and Hector does not deny it.

The position of Hector in this sequence is difficult to define, if not downright enigmatic. We quickly realize his contradictory stance: on the one hand, Hector attributes exclusively to himself victory over Patroclos (XVI. 833–6). Since Hector is not the recipient of divine intervention, it is correct that, in accordance with epic convention, he did not witness the progressive dismantling of Patroclos by Apollo. Hector's silence about Apollo's intervention is therefore expected: he did not see Apollo and did not need to see him. On the other hand, when he meets Patroclos —notwithstanding the simile— there is no real battle: Patroclos is naked. Furthermore, when at his death Patroclos tells Hector that Zeus and Apollo "stripped the arms from my shoulders" (845), Hector does not deny his enemy's assertion. At that moment, he silently agrees that Apollo demolished Patroclos.

The text tries to control all these ambiguous representations with the enigmatic expression that Apollo killed Patroclos and gave the *kudos* to Hector, through which some hybridism between the god's and the mortal's actions is achieved. The enigmatic semantics of the phrase is made evident by Achilles' use of an analogous phrase when he chases Hector (XXII. 205–7): by a sign of the head he prevents his soldiers from hurling their spears at Hector "for fear

---

[89] Achilles' immortal horses also attribute Hector's victory to Apollo (XIX. 414) with the same line as Thetis does at XVIII. 456. It is not clear what Apollo did in order to hide his responsibility and grant to Hector the splendid victory. It is probably impossible to be sure about the enigma of this hybridism.

[90] The verb Patroclos uses (850: ἐξεναρίζεις) literally means "you strip me of my arms." Literally, therefore, Patroclos sees Hector doing what Apollo began, and we need to take the verb metaphorically ("you kill me") in order for Patroclos' statement to correspond to what actually happened. Quite firmly, then, Patroclos denies Hector's independent action and sees him as simply a *longa manus* of Apollo. Patroclos would agree with Thetis' formulation of what happened. The game of ambiguities the text plays is endless.

the thrower might win the *kudos* (victory, triumph) and himself [Achilles] come second." It is obvious that for Achilles the slayer, the first thrower, wins the *kudos*, and the one who comes second wins nothing.[91] In accordance with this principle, Apollo wins the *kudos* for killing Patroclos and then transfers his *kudos* to Hector. As Patroclos perversely emphasizes, Hector is not the second but his third slayer, making Hector even more distant from the killer's *kudos* than the second assailant (XVI. 849–50):

> But my deadly destiny (μοῖρ' ὀλοὴ), and the son of Leto killed me (*ektanen*);
> and, among men, it was Euphorbus: you are the third.

Patroclos respects the principle which attributes *kudos* to the killer: Hector may boast about the triumph that was given to him by the god who actually killed Patroclos. Perhaps Apollo's transfer of his kudos to Hector means just this: he allowed Hector to put Hector's signature —so to speak— on his killing of Patroclos, though the slaying was already accomplished. Apollo allowed Hector to inflict a final blow to the dead body of Patroclos. But if it is so, then the 'killing' (849 *ektanen*) wobbles with an open, undecided, metaphorical meaning and *kudos* appears as a displaced attribute, a sort of empty image devoid of its supporting action. Through such semantic incoherence the text represents Apollo's and Hector's killing of Patroclos as a hybrid ambivalent action.

The points I am presenting lead also to the fundamental question about the relation that the *Iliad* institutes between the solid world of reality and the narrative that describes it. If we take seriously the essential notion implicit in the mythical premises, we should conclude that, for the archaic Narrators of the *Iliad*, the reality of the world was in some way communicated to men through the Muses, oracles, omens (II. 299–332), divine inspirations, old stories about the lives of the gods, and the divine aspects of nature (Zeus' storm, Poseidon's gales, etc.), and the world itself. The world of being therefore became known from the information that the divine and the world itself delivered to human beings. The world itself —being divinely permeated— manifested to men the image of itself, and men had only to receive and appreciate that image.

This apprehension is the opposite of the Cartesian principle —*Cogito ergo sum*— according to which it is human intelligence that opens the comprehension of the being of the world. It is by searching and meditating that humanity builds an image of the world. Through scientific and philosophical research

---

[91] The connection between the act of killing and the winning of *kudos* is made also by Athena a few lines later as she joins Achilles (XXII. 217–18).

men constantly modify and complicate the designs of that image. By itself, the world of being emits too many meaningful messages that are also too questionable. The scientific interpretation construes ever-changing images of the world from those messages that are often difficult to find and to understand.

I am purposely simplifying the immense complexity of the "cogito ergo sum" formula in order to draw a neater contrast with the Iliadic view. For, of course, the Cartesian formula implies something that is undeniable, i.e. the existence of consciousness as the source of knowledge about the being of humanity and of the world.

The Iliadic Narrators found themselves confronted with a tremendous amount of information from which they had to select, interpret, and elaborate. One of the first difficulties they met was certainly the lack of coherence and uniformity in the hypertext's mass of facts and ideas. The Narrators of the *Odyssey* had a different message than the Iliadic Narrators about the world and the role of Zeus. But the principle remained firm: information came from the world and not from humans' groundless elaboration and research. The divine emitted different messages, but that is of course the privilege of the divine. The multifarious, constantly moving, and diversified images always implied the permeability of human, divine, and natural voices, of earthly images and their divine counterparts. Narrrators interpreted and fashioned the description of events by hearing divine and human voices and by seeing earthly phenomena and their implicit divine nature.

In our episode, it is the divine voice that recognizes a sort of double version of the event: Apollo himself killed Patroclos, yet he exceptionally ceded to Hector the splendid reward of having been the killer. It is a lie of sorts, expressed by a semantic incoherence, but a lie that Apollo authorizes —the Muses do not explain how— and which therefore acquires divine truth. We have two truths, and the human characters, deprived of the Muses' narrative, perceived only that Hector was fighting like a lion against a boar, and inflicted the finishing stroke; they missed that Patroclos was already as good as killed by Apollo. This illustrates for the Narratees how the appearance of objective things can be duplicitous or defective and incomplete, since the appearance of events may efface divine action and causality.

The white lie, i.e. the hybridism, that Apollo authorizes justifies a belief in free will in the narrative's characters and hides from them the violence with which Zeus and Apollo have persecuted Patroclos, Achilles' companion, for no declared reason. That violence manifests to the Narratees the *mysterium tremendum et fascinans* of the world.

My final point develops an analysis of the peculiar ways in which Patroclos' behavior is represented by the narrative and the poetic voice.

There is an excess in Achilles' *therapôn*, an excess that parallels his lack of awareness. As he boasts to Hector about his tremendous force (XVI. 847–8), he is no longer inspired by Zeus and forgets or misses that the supernatural power he exhibited during the battle and on which he now grounds his boasting was dispensed to him by Zeus, and Zeus gave it to him only with the purpose of killing him.

Notice the difference between Patroclos here and Hector in his last monologue (XXII. 300–3), where Hector is aware that he has been the victim of continual, contradictory action on the part of Zeus.

Excess and lack, as we have seen, are the measures by which the supplement, the surrogate, the *therapôn* exceeds, replaces, and defers the original term. Patroclos deployed an excessive measure of power and lacked sense about what he did, being unaware of the paradoxical help he received from the god. Now, as he speaks, he continues to behave with excessive confidence in his power, and lacks any awareness of what it means to have that power.

The text seems tempted to describe his character and behavior with a dose of bitter irony. For instance, the narrative mentions twice Patroclos' being "equal to the gods," and it does so in contexts in which this role is emphatically false and ironic. Because Patroclos imagines that he is able to conquer Troy, not only does the text dress him with hyperbolic rhetoric, but it induces the Narratees to recall Achilles and his hallucinatory desire to conquer Troy together with Patroclos: a sort of not-fully-repressed parody emerges. Patroclos begins as a savior of the Achaeans and by his death he will also cause the death of his master.

With these remarks, I suggest that there is a minimizing intent that tinges the picture of Patroclos. He is described by Apollo as inferior to the tasks he takes (conquering Troy), to his master Achilles; he receives a lesson from Nestor, who reminds him also of the lesson that he received from his father Menoitios; he speaks through the language of others, through the consciousness he borrows from others; he is interpreted, and directed by the narrative, which never enters or focalizes his mind and feelings but wonders with pity and reproach about what he is doing. For the narrative his mind has a surrogate and dependent disposition, a sort of void to be filled by a responsible master, by the narrative itself. Even his human and existential consistency depends upon his pairing with his royal companion and on the companion's presence.

# Chapter 4

## 4.1 Achilles' Destiny and Zeus

> "The savage and inflexible temperament of Achilles is a constant extending all the way to *Iliad* XXIV, which marks the point where pity begins to set in and the ultimate heroic refinement of the Iliadic hero is about to be achieved."
>
> Nagy 1979, 110

The *Iliad* does not narrate Achilles' death, yet it foreshadows it in many passages. As he decides to avenge Patroclos and kill Hector, Achilles' death warrant is signed. The *diêgêsis* shows that Achilles freely accepts his immediate death and dismisses the long life that he could have had as an alternative (IX. 410–16).[1]

As concerns the double motivation for this development, Achilles' choice creates a convergence with the divine will, so that he is fully conscious and nobly prepared for his approaching death. Despairing and enraged at the death of his companion, Achilles prepares his return to battle and his revenge on Hector. He announces this decision to his mother, Thetis, and she warns him (XVIII. 95–100):

> "Then, my son, you will run to a short life,[2] by what you are saying,
> since, immediately [αὐτίκα] after Hector, your death is ready."
> Deeply troubled, swift-footed Achilles [πόδας ὠκὺς Ἀχιλλεύς] answered her:
> "Immediately [αὐτίκα][3] may I die, since I was not to protect my friend

---

**1** I translate the passage (IX. 410–16):
  "My mother Thetis, the goddess of the silver feet, tells me
  that two sorts of destiny carry me toward the day of my death.
  If I stay here and fight beside the city of the Trojans,
  my return home is gone, but my glory shall be everlasting;
  but if I return home to the beloved land of my fathers,
  my shining glory is gone, but I will have a long life,
  nor will death take my life quickly."
Achilles' life is inscribed in a divine, preordained plan, with two different outcomes that depend on his free choice. The dramatic narrative shows us that in a few occasions he could have opted out of his destined, premature death. Enraged against the Achaean elite, Achilles twice threatens to abandon the Trojan expedition (I. 169 ff., IX. 427–9); had he accomplished this project, he would have escaped his early, impending death.
**2** ὠκύμορος δή μοι τέκος ἔσσεαι: the compound ὠκύμορος —which is used again by Thetis at I. 417— by being placed at the verse's beginning, increases its pathetic force: it prepares the repetition of another temporal sign, αὐτίκα "immediately," and brings to vivid light the shortness, the quick rushing of Achilles' life. The compound adjective, moreover, makes a bitter and painful allusion to the most frequent epithetic phrase for Achilles, which the Narrator picks up at line 97: πόδας ὠκὺς Ἀχιλλεύς (hence my perhaps too literal translation of "run").

when he was killed. He died far away from his fatherland and lacked me to defend him from ruin."⁴

With his assertion, "immediately may I die," Achilles rashly rejects the chance of returning home and determines his destiny.⁵ His feeling of guilt for having caused the death of his friend is so deep that he refuses to continue living after having killed Hector: he wants to join his own friend in death.⁶ Before our own eyes, he accepts his own fate as a fate that he grants to himself; he is master, in some way, of his own destiny.⁷ He impersonates the theme of heroic death, as he runs to an early death in order to carry out his noble commitment. He is going, therefore, to live with the vision of his own death before his eyes.⁸ This

---

3 "The repetition of αὐτίκα 'immediately' from 96 is striking. While Thetis meant: 'straight away after Hector's death,' Achilles means: 'Now, now at once.'" Edwards 1991, 159. With this word, as Lohmann suggests (1970, 145), Achilles probably interrupts his mother's speech.
4 ἐμεῖο δὲ δῆσεν ἀρῆς ἀλκτῆρα γενέσθαι. The verb δέω —"to lack," "to miss," "to be in need of"— expresses literally the relationship between master and *therapôn*, the supplemental position of Patroclos.
5 "In contrast to the *Iliad*, which emphasizes Achilles' mortality and the tragic dilemma it entails, Cyclic epic highlighted his semi-divine origin and his special status as Thetis' son, painting a very different kind of hero." Tsagalis 2016, 115.
6 Zanker 1996, 97–98 writes with full understanding of Achilles' emotions: "Patroclos' death has made Achilles alive to the power of affective appeals... This sharpened awareness drives him to rejoin the battle in the full knowledge that reentering it will mean his death... so in a very real sense he is mourning his own death as much as his friend's. In book 9 death had cast doubt on the value of action and inhibited it, but we find Achilles now pushed beyond any such consideration, to the point where, paradoxically, death has totally lost relevance to his decision-making processes."
7 By inscribing certain epic motifs into the sphere of divine will, the text grants new force and a different color to traditional themes. For instance, Taplin 1992, 122 calls "the epic paradox" —in a different sense than the one I use— the mechanical sequence of the Narrative, according to which the victor Patroclos is killed by Hector, who is then killed by Achilles, who will be killed immediately after. Through Achilles' recognition of his destiny, the text provides the emotional scenario in which this sequence turns into a theological design bringing together the destinies of three different persons. I have already stressed that Zeus, through the paradoxical notion of "compensation", inscribes the mechanical sequence into a theological design (see Ch. 2.3).
8 Seaford 1994, 166–72 correctly finds that "Achilles' liminal participation in the state of death seems excessive in duration as well in degree." Usually the death-like state of mourners comes to an end, but for Achilles a complete return to normality seems excluded by a combination of abnormal ritual expressions of death-in-life with the knowledge that his own death has been made inevitable by the death of Patroclos. Seaford realizes that the constant and prolonged state of death for Achilles responds to the fact that the tradition places Achilles' death after that of Memnon: the *Iliad* accordingly has to combine the announcement that he will die "immediately" after Hector and his survival in order to agree with the already-established tradition.

vibration of anxiety and serenity that accompanies this attitude produces such an intense emotion as to grant the poem its immortal appeal.

Achilles becomes painfully conscious of collaborating with Zeus' dispensing of sorrowful destinies to Peleus (XXIV. 538–40) and to Priam (XXIV. 547–9). He shows this awareness when, in his theological speech in the last book of the *Iliad*, Achilles describes Zeus' exclusive control over human destinies and meditates on his own role within the various destinies Zeus has assigned to Achilles, to Achilles' father, and to Priam.

Achilles develops his illustration during a long speech with which he intends to console Priam, who in book XXIV miraculously reaches Achilles' dwelling and falls at Achilles' knees, begging him to accept a ransom for Hector's body.[9]

The image of the old and noble man at his feet, the memory of his old father, and the anguish for his dead friend Patroclos bring about Achilles' tears. After crying, Achilles produces the consolation speech which is grounded on the theme that human sorrows are unavoidable, since they are dispensed by Zeus: the only remedy against them is to accept and endure them. The gods are forever blessed,[10] but they "spun out"[11] an unhappy life for miserable mortals[12] (527–33):

---

This survival, however, prints in Achilles its peculiar pathos. Thetis did not need to declare the immediacy of Achilles' death: if the Poem has her declare so, it is because the Poem wants him in this permanent state of living-in-death.

9 Hermes suggests to Priam (XXIV. 465–67) that he embrace Achilles' knees and supplicate him in the name of his father, mother, and son. Priam brings this gesture of supplication to its greatest emotional force by adding a tremendously pathetic phrase (XXIV. 503–6):
"Revere the gods, Achilles, and pity me,
thinking of your father; I am still more pitiable:
I endured what no other mortal in the world ever endured,
to put my lips to the hand of the man who killed my son."
The *diêgêsis* had already used the phrase when describing Priam's gesture of supplication (478–9):
"[Priam] embraced the knees of Achilles and kissed the hands,
tremendous, murderous, that had killed many of his sons."
This text is stylistically more elaborate than the one used by Priam as he refers to his own lips —which by itself provides remarkable pathos. The Narrator's description creates a cruder effect through the enjambment, the double epithets, and especially the synecdoche that make Achilles' hands (that Priam kisses) the direct murderers of Priam's many sons.
10 Their blessedness is obviously without history and meaning for men: that is why, as the critics often repeat, the gods in the *Iliad* draw life only from their relationship with mortals.
11 The verb for spinning (ἐπεκλώσαντο) is used here without any literal connotation (Clarke 1999, 252): it is found only here in the *Iliad*, where it conceptually contradicts Zeus' act of dispensing gifts that Achilles here describes. The notion that "powerful Moira" spins a man's life at his birth appears at XXIV. 209–10 in Hecuba's words. The spinning of destiny is not an ex-

There are two jars that stand on the threshold of Zeus' halls full of gifts (*dôrôn*)[13] that he gives, the one full of evils, the other of blessings.

> If Zeus who delights in lightning[14] mingles them and bestows them
> on a man, this man sometimes meets with evils and sometimes with blessings.
> But when Zeus gives only sorrows, he makes a man an outcast:
> an evil starvation drives him over the shining earth,
> and he wanders honored neither by gods nor by mortals.

Zeus' dispensing of human destinies is here represented by a concrete image and by a universal operation. This image brings to completion that of the Goldens Scale that also represents Zeus as the master of destinies. Once more, Zeus provides no reasons and no motivations for his choices and follows no certifiable moral code.[15] Nor can men reject his gifts. This sort of sporadic and unmoti-

---

pression used by the gods in the *Iliad*. The *Iliad* does not know the *Klôthes*, the "spinning Fates," that the *Odyssey* mentions at vii. 197. The spinning metaphor is frequent in the *Odyssey*: see i. 17; iii. 208, where Telemachos says that the gods have not spun for him the happiness (*olbon*) of getting rid of the suitors; iv. 208, where Menelaus says: "Easily recognizable is that man for whom the son of Cronos spins happiness (*olbon*) in his marriage and in begetting children" – which seems to echo our passage at XXIV. 534–38, where, however, the notion of "spinning is missing,"; viii. 579; xi. 319; xvi. 64; xx. 196. The belief that Zeus dispenses (with a variety of verbs – *didômi, nemô* etc.) gifts (*dôra*), i.e. blessings and evils, to each man as he wants is a most common idea and feeling in Greek culture from Homer on.

12 ὡς γὰρ ἐπεκλώσαντο θεοὶ δειλοῖσι βροτοῖσι: Achilles has begun to speak to Priam (518) with the sympathetic and pathethic ἆ δείλ', "Ah, unhappy man!" Priam is the quintessential model of an unhappy, miserable mortal: he calls himself *panapotmos* (493) "totally helpless."

13 Evils and misfortunes are termed "gifts" (*dôra*) of the gods: Hesiod (*Erga* 718) calls "cursed poverty" a "gift of the gods," and so he also calls Pandora (*Theog.* 103). In Greek, the *dôron* ("gift," "present") can have a neutral connotation.

14 The noun-epithet "Zeus who delights in lightning" may appear here justified simply by the formulaic system, but the system seems to be purposeful: the god who delights in lightning is not a benevolent one.

15 The only Iliadic passage in which Zeus is openly qualified by a moral purpose is at XVI. 384–88: "As underneath a hurricane all the black earth is burdened on an autumn day when Zeus pours violent rain / in deep rage and wrath against men / who in assembly arrogantly pass crooked judgments / and drive out justice (*dikên*), caring nothing for the visit of the gods..." The passage is considered late, for the language is derived from Hesiod (See West 2011, 320, and below Ch. 6.1). Yet the features that most crucially prove that the passage is not representative of the metaphysics of the Poem are its isolation and its being uttered by the Poet in a simile. In the similes the Poet gives examples that speak to the experience of his present audience in the eighth and seventh centuries: this audience – or even himself –may believe that Zeus, god of the sky, punishes men for their injustice with a violent hurricane; but it is not a character of the poem, i.e. a character of the time of the Trojan War, who speaks in that way.

vated distribution of lots to men makes him a divine source that is inscrutable to mortals, unanswerable, in some sense, like blind destiny. It prevents Zeus from producing with the *Iliad* his own sacred book, a book that would found the supreme principles of his authority, mission, and governance of the world. His invincible hands make him a victor in brawls but provide no arguments for the supremacy of his spiritual principle – whatever that may be – concerning the being of the world. It is important to realize that every image that represents or symbolizes Zeus as master of human destinies displays a mute and speechless entity. The Golden Scales, the deadly *moîra* (XXII. 5), thunder and lightning, and now the two jars accomplish or provide or announce definite lots to men, but cannot emit any word that would explain, comment upon, or justify their choices. Nothing explains for what purpose and according to what principle Sarpedon, Hector, Patroclos, and Troy itself should now perish. Zeus dispenses the lots of miserable lives and the *diêgêsis* never reveals the monstrous urging that induces him to do so.

It is not clear how Achilles knows about these urns or jars: he might have heard of them from his mother, or he could simply have picked up a traditional mythical motif: the theme is popular in myth/poetry, as we find it again in the story of Pandora (Hesiod, *Erga*, 90–104). However, the jars, the box, and the whole operation could be read, though less felicitously, as a metaphorical scene. As such, the concrete image of the jars and Zeus' dispensing operation loses its dramatic intensity, hides the mortals' suffered effects, mitigates their terrific agent's role, and conceptualizes the blind and uncheckable events as merely universal rule.

It is remarkable that the *diêgêsis* presents the only image of Zeus devising and dispensing the lots of mortals within the narrative of a mortal, that of Achilles. Even if Achilles heard this account from his mother, he certainly did not know the god's strategies of distributing fates. No gods and no other character confirms Achilles' account. The text heaps up new evidence of Zeus' mysteriousness and solitary behavior. In the act of choosing and distributing the lots of mortals, Zeus is all alone. Some particular dispensations are attributed to the "gods" (534), probably as elsewhere, only to indicate the "divine agent" anonymously. Even the space in which this operation is produced is vaguely identified as Zeus' threshold. This description severs Zeus from the other Olympian gods, just as many other acts and much other behavior of his that we have seen. His pathetic appeal to the gods, asking for Hector's life, followed by their lack of

---

Nor is the simile dictated by the Muses. Lloyd Jones 1971, 6 misses this detail. See also Pelloso 2012, 94 n. 223 and 132 with n. 71 on the specific connotation of *dike* in this passage.

response, is a dramatic example of his exteriority and almost foreignness in the Olympian community. Again, a psychological portrait of Zeus does not support or literarily endorse this unique position: he is not shown as being aware of his isolation, as he is not made conscious of his tragic inner contradictions, or now of his tremendous responsibility in dispensing the lots of miserable human lives. His foreignness is inscribed in the structure of his role as master of destiny: his foreignness is analogous to the exteriority that marks the merely mechanic operation of the Golden Scales, an operation that Zeus himself provokes (XXII. 209: "and then the Father balanced his Golden Scales"). This is the response that Zeus receives, not from the Olympian gods, but from the order of things that he himself controls.

The evils and the blessings gathered in two different jars are already separated as bad and good, as if a neat contrast were always possible: in human life, often good things have some nasty angles and, vice versa, bad things may carry positive implications.

Zeus "who delights in lightning" recalls the non-anthropomorphic and celestial image of Zeus, and in this context it is proper to think that, in the vision of the narrative, the bolts of lightning are his celestial "gifts" to all men: they are always threatening and often announce his destructive will.[16]

Achilles offers to Priam an example of Zeus' distribution of blessings and sorrows with the life of his father Peleus (XXIV. 534–42):

> So too did the gods give splendid gifts (ἀγλαὰ δῶρα)[17] to Peleus
> from his birth: for he excelled all men[18] in happiness
> and wealth and was king over the Myrmidons,
> and to him who was a mortal they gave a goddess as wife.
> But even on him the god brought evil (κακόν). There was not
> any generation of strong sons born to him in his house,
> but he begot a single all-untimely child (ἕνα παῖδα τέκεν παναώριον)[19]

---

**16** It is Zeus' dispensation of evils that Plato (*Rep.* II, 579d1 ff.) attacks as Homer's "foolish mistake about the gods" and quotes some lines from this Iliadic scene (XXIV. 527–32. Of course, for Plato, god cannot be said to be "the cause of anyone's evils" (380b6–7).
**17** With some exceptions, the eight Iliadic examples of "giving ἀγλαὰ δῶρα" refer to divine gifts. These gifts are the immortal horses for Peleus (XVI. 381 and 867), the gods' armor for Peleus (XVIII. 94), Hephaistos' armor for Achilles (XIX. 18) and here (XXIV. 534) the advantages of the status as king of the Myrmidons for Peleus. As a whole these gifts increase the status of the fighter to whom they are bestowed: Zeus in our passage does not increase the status of a fighter but of the king.
**18** Notice the pleonastic figure: "all men."
**19** Παναώριον is a hapax in Homer: literally it means "[dying] completely out of season." It is a remarkable and impressive word, typical of Achilles' particular language: it comes in as a

and I give him no care as he grows old, since far from the land of my fathers
I sit here in Troy[20] and bring sorrow to you and your sons.[21]

Achilles dies young —totally out of season— because Zeus determined this condition as Peleus' disaster (κακόν).[22] Yet Achilles collaborates with Zeus in dispensing a negative destiny to Peleus, since Achilles —Peleus' only child, as Zeus has preordained— "gives him no care as he grows old." God and man autonomously cooperate to make the destiny of Peleus miserable, and together —each by his own will and purpose— create a negative destiny for the old man.

This consonance seems to increase the epic and religious stature of Achilles in the eyes of the Narratees, but in truth this consonance is only partial, for Achilles does not and will not know why he should die immediately after Hector's death.

Furthermore, Achilles cannot feel that he is willingly hurting his father without some sense of guilt. He could have chosen his alternative destiny (IX. 410-16) and lived a long life, taking care of his father, though without the

---

hyperbaton —i.e. separated from its substantive— at the end of the sentence, in *hephtemimeres caesura*, acquiring great emphasis. It has been chosen to parallel Priam's definition of himself as πανάποτμος (493: "totally helpless"), an expression that Priam also uses at 255-56 and that appears only in these two passages. Here, at XXIV. 493, Priam sees himself as a father deprived of all his children. It is in this context that Achilles raises deep pathos by showing that, by being Peleus' only child and "[dying] completely out of season," he places his father in a similar situation as Priam. See Renehan 1987, 114 who underlines the pathos of the expression.

20 The expression "I sit in Troy" would imply "I am idle." Macleod 1982, *ad loc.* comments: "There is a hint of colloquial speech in this use of the word [...] It is used of Achilles' *absence* from the battle in 1. 329, 416, 421 and above all in his own mouth in 18. 104. It is a bitter paradox that Achilles is now far from idle at Troy, when he is killing Priam's sons, doing to him the opposite of being idle. He now becomes aware of the disgrace of abandoning his father and causing grief to the Trojans. Achilles gazes at his ambition of heroic life from the point of view of its victims." Griffin 1980, 100: "Sitting with Priam in the last book, Achilles still sees the war in an unheroic light."

21 Macleod 1982, ad XXIV. 542: "It is [...] a fine touch that Achilles sees both Priam's and Peleus' suffering as embodied in one and the same person: himself. This reinforces the argument that the two old men's misfortunes are equal and it brings out how detached Achilles is from his role as a warrior and the best of the Achaeans."

22 Griffin 1980, 191 emphasizes the tragic aspect of Achilles' acceptance of his death. Indeed, Achilles becomes a source of pain for his father not only because he is far away, but also because, as he says, he dies prematurely (*panaôrion* 540). Zanker 1996, 121: "Achilles' concern with his death is no longer directed toward himself. It is directed toward Peleus and the suffering it will cause him."

shine of glory. He didn't: he wanted glory and, after the Achaean outrage, he wanted his honor to be restored at any price.[23]

As Achilles sees himself autonomously playing the role that destiny assigned to him and to Peleus, he feels guilty, and the consonance between Zeus' dispensation to Peleus and Achilles' subjective will qualifies Achilles' "heroic" status as a damaging and painful asset.

At this point, a modern reader —I mean an anachronistic reader— may feel a dramatic absence. During the whole poem, we Narratees have never witnessed Peleus' pain for his unique and short-lived son, but we have been exposed to the sorrows and regrets of Achilles' mother, Thetis, when she laments her son's short life.[24] This happens in a pathetic tone in the first and eighteenth books; in the twenty-fourth book we see her mourning with her divine peers for the approaching death of her son. Through Thetis' dramatic expressions, therefore, we feel that Achilles' destiny has caused his mother tremendous pain, but she is not mentioned. The reason is contextual: Achilles is describing Zeus' dispensation of destinies to mortal beings, and Thetis is a goddess, a class of beings not submitted to this action of Zeus.

The epic's ambiguous representation of the divine nature displays here its paradoxical aspects: though Thetis is a goddess, she suffers like a mortal, as the text has shown in dramatic scenes; but, since as a goddess she should not suffer like a mortal, she cannot be included among mortals who suffer mortal destinies. Yet the blessed immortals can paradoxically suffer anthropomorphic pains.

A specific consonance between his destiny and his willing actions occurs, then, in Achilles' life. In the quoted passage (XXIV. 541–2), Achilles sees himself as idle —"I sit here in Troy and I bring sorrow to you and your sons"— meaning to Priam, his people, and his sons: Achilles kindly avoids mentioning Hector. But as he closes his speech, he sees himself as the objective evil that the gods have dispensed to Priam (547–51):

---

[23] It is impossible to advance speculations on the psychological reasons behind Achilles' refusal to relent in book IX. Homer does not usually deliver psychological analyses (see Codino 1965, 137–39; Redfield 1975, 20; Griffin 1980, 70 ff. and many others). As we have seen, Achilles' "wrath" is his own and yet also has a long divine pedigree: it is advised by Hera and Thetis, and it becomes the immediate offspring of Zeus' *boulê*. For other examples and passages about the text's resistance to psychological inquiry, see Ch. 1.1; 3.1 n. 7; 3.2.

[24] As the mother of Achilles, Thetis has a fundamental role in the poem, as Nannini 2003, 72 reminds us.

> But now the Uranian gods have brought this agony [πῆμα] upon you,
> there is forever fighting about your city[25] and men killed.
> Bear up, do not mourn incessantly in your heart:
> you will get no advantage from grieving for your son,
> you will not bring him back, but suffer more pain.[26]

Since the gods, i.e Zeus, brought Achilles to Troy to be an agony (πῆμα) for Priam and his people, Achilles is correct to console Priam:[27] it is as if he were saying, "This slaying was preordained by the gods and I became the affliction that Zeus chose from his jar as an 'evil gift' for you, Priam."[28]

Clearly Achilles sees himself in two contexts and on two levels: as a regretful divine agent, accomplishing events imposed by fate, he, objectively speaking, has no responsibility for the agony he causes to his father and to Priam; but, at the subjective level, he feels guilty and disheartened because of the predicaments he encountered in the course of the heroic life he chose to follow. The unresolvable epic paradox is somehow resolved by Achilles' awareness of his double stance. For he recognizes the fatal preordained agony (πῆμα) he causes by destroying Priam's life and by betraying his father's expectations, and simultaneously he is aware of his willful wasting of time ("I am sitting... killing Priam's sons"), by which he fails to take care of his father. Here he reaches the view that his heroic life is simultaneously preordained by his destiny and willfully and absurdly chosen by him —when he had indeed a different option. He

---

**25** Notice the generalizing force of the nominal phrase.
**26** In the last three lines Achilles develops the theme of "endurance" for men, which was introduced by Apollo at XXIV. 49: "for Fate has given mortals an enduring heart." (See also Ch. 1.2).
**27** In book III. 164–5, Priam tries to console Helen using the same motif: she is not to be blamed, but the gods are responsible, "who drove upon me this sorrowful war of the Achaeans." Helen is anguished and feels regret for her elopement. Aphrodite did inspire Helen's erotic passion, in the third book, or Zeus did, according to Helen when she speaks of the evil destiny that Zeus assigned to Paris and herself (VI. 357–8):
> οἷσιν ἐπὶ Ζεὺς θῆκε κακὸν μόρον, ὡς καὶ ὀπίσσω
> ἀνθρώποισι πελώμεθ' ἀοίδιμοι ἐσσομένοισι.
> "to whom [Helen and Paris] Zeus assigned an evil destiny so that hereafter
> we would be matter of song for the men of the future."

Zeus is made ready to contribute to the Iliadic representation of Helen's destiny.
**28** πῆμα ("agony," "affliction") plays in another thematic opposition concerning Achilles, as Nagy 1979, 76–77 richly documents: Achilles is a *pêma* for the Trojans when he fights, but a *pêma* for the Achaeans when he refuses to fight.

does not eliminate the objectivity of his destiny: this would be an elimination that a modern, not an ancient, man might make.[29]

The opportunity that Achilles had to choose a variant destiny strengthens the sense the Narratees have that Achilles is in some way, and in some measure, master of his fate. This sense is definitively increased by the fact that Achilles does not care for his own determined death, but for the fate of those to whom he is inflicting sorrows. He becomes master of his own destiny to the extent that he has no fear of it, and becomes master of others' fate, since he is preordained by Zeus to give them sorrows which he accomplishes willingly but at the end, regretfully.[30] He becomes complicit in Zeus' bitter game and in agreement with Zeus' discrediting of heroic life. In this complicity, however, he deeply differs from Zeus, who sees heroism as nonsense because he has no experience and knowledge of death. This is why Zeus is not heroic, but a blessed immortal, while Achilles is lucidly and tragically heroic and suffers the objectively troubled nature of heroic life.

It remains true that the destiny according to which Achilles has to die young, and, specifically, immediately after Hector's death, is a divine imposition, a terrible gift Zeus dispenses to him, to his mother, and to his father, Peleus. He does not discuss or question Zeus' dispensation, probably because, as he hints to Priam, it does not make any sense to question necessity.

When Achilles tells Priam, "now the Uranian gods have brought this agony [πῆμα] [i.e. "me"] upon you" (547), or "I sit here in Troy and bring sorrow to you [Priam] and your sons," he refers to a metaphysical intervention and then uses colloquial and offhand expressions to describe what truly has been his terrible hatred for Hector and his violent rush to kill him. Zeus' plan surely preordained Hector's death at the hands of Achilles and dispensed this agony to Priam, but Achilles acted autonomously: he acted under the violence of a terrible grief caused by Patroclos' death and under an urgent need to punish Hector and himself.

All this seems now superfluous: now, speaking to Priam, a melancholic regret vibrates in Achilles' words: "I sit here in Troy [i.e. useless for my father, and for myself] and bring sorrow to you and your sons." These words are addressed to the enemy, with a deep sense of pain, and acquire a tremendous emotional force. This confession of having somehow committed a misdeed in the "heroic"

---

**29** Heidegger 1950, 83 ff. has elaborated a long analysis of the differences between the posture the Ancient Greek adopted in relation to the human's place within the existential sphere and the modern posture.
**30** See Ch. 4.1, n. 22.

accomplishment of defeating Hector turns the savage Achilles into a sensitive, humane, and disheartened man. He gestures toward the senseless nature of heroic life and, therefore, of his life. He interiorizes Zeus' dispensations and, by making them parallel to his own choices, bestows a vibrant immediacy to the objective impact of Zeus' dispensations on his life. He thus proffers a hybrid solution to the opposition between human and divine terms, without theorizing on its principle.

Within this context, the "heroic death" turns out to be only the noble disposition of confronting the unavoidable death as a glorious choice. The Poem displays, with Achilles, a different version of the wisdom that was left to Hector when he turned his fate decreed by Zeus into a noble and brave choice (XXII. 297–305). No sort of glorious life and death can compensate for or erase the amount of misery Achilles's destiny and his chosen heroic life have created, both for himself and for those around him whom he loves and respects. Achilles' analysis does not force him to refuse the heroic life, but only to show its painful and disastrous aspects. Achilles will die and die as the *aristos* that he is, and here he intimates that the moments of enduring harsh divine dispensations will necessarily arrive, during and before the consummation of a heroic life. It is necessary to accept those disastrous moments, those terrible dispensations of Zeus with noble resistance: this disposition of the mind is not less heroic than the glorious death. With these words of Achilles, the *Iliad* delivers its religious and moral message to its universal audience.

## 4.2 Zeus and Achilles' immortal horses

> "Kein Wunder ist, dass erst dort wo die Welt zu Bild wird, der Humanismus heraufkommt. Aber so wenig in der grossen Zeit des Griechentums dergleichen wie ein Weltbild möglich war, so wenig konnte sich damals ein Humanismus zur Geltung bringen."
>
> "No wonder, then, if humanism emerges only in the place where the world has become image. But just as a world image was hardly possible in the great time of Greece, so it was hardly possible at that time the appearance of a humanism."[31]
>
> Heidegger 1950, 86

Among the immortals, only the horses of Achilles truly weep and mourn for the death of their charioteer, Patroclos (XVII. 426–454): they are represented like a

---

31  My translation.

living gravestone set over the tomb of a dead hero.³² Or like mourning friends, who pour warm tears and soil their hairs with dust, so the horses roll in the dust and dung. In this way, they are shown to have a tight emotional relation with Patroclos' death and "long for their own charioteer" (XVII. 439: ἡνιόχοιο πόθῳ).³³ We can imagine that the immortal horses have been fascinated by the man who drove them: his personal grace and extraordinary kindness are traits that give him a unique identity in Iliadic poetry.³⁴

Pitying them, Zeus confesses to his heart the mistake he made when he gave the immortal horses as a gift to Peleus, a mortal man (XVII. 443-7):

Oh unhappy you! Why did we give you to lord Peleus,
a mortal man,³⁵ while you are ageless and immortal?
Was it in order for you to suffer pains among miserable men?³⁶
For there is truly nothing more wretched than man
among all the beings that breathe and walk on earth.

ἆ δειλώ, τί σφῶϊ δόμεν Πηλῆϊ ἄνακτι
θνητῷ, ὑμεῖς δ' ἐστὸν ἀγήρω τ' ἀθανάτω τε;³⁷
ἦ ἵνα δυστήνοισι μετ' ἀνδράσιν ἄλγε' ἔχητον;
οὐ μὲν γάρ τί πού ἐστιν ὀϊζυρώτερον ἀνδρὸς
πάντων, ὅσσά τε γαῖαν ἔπι πνείει τε καὶ ἕρπει.

With the immortal horses, Zeus dispensed a special gift —among the splendid ones he bestowed to Peleus (see XXIV. 534 ff.). The immortal horses do not know what death is, but they learn it at their own bitter expense when their

---

**32** Richardson 1993 quotes Fränkel 1921, 56 who speaks of the solemn immobility of death. Thetis is another exception: she ritually mourns for the death of Achilles while he is lamenting the death of Patroclos (XXIV. 83-86).
**33** "The *pothos* of the dead, the painful ecstasy of sobbing (XVII. 439, XXIII. 14, 97-98) [...] the all-powerful presence of the absent man, the unfulfilled desire must be replaced by the ever-renewed memory of the valor of those who have fallen." Loraux 1986, 47. This is the only example of *pothos* in the *Iliad* where we find in its place *pothê* —an older form of the same word— with the same meanings of "fond desire" for living people or "deep regret" for dead ones.
**34** See XVII. 669 ff. (*enêeiê* and *meilikhios*), 204; XXIII. 272, 281; XIX. 282 ff.; and cf. Codino 1965, 153–54. At XXIII. 279 ff. Achilles praises the kindness and grace of Patroclos and his care for the immortal horses. They still grieve for him and "their manes are swept along the ground as they stand with hearts full of sorrow" (XXIII. 283–84).
**35** The enjambment emphasizes the painful contrast between the solemn "lord Peleus" and "a mortal (man)."
**36** The rhetorical question contains a bitterly ironic assumption.
**37** This slow, mostly spondaic line has three omegas that give solemnity to the sound of the verse, a solemnity also sustained by the beginning and ending, which both reference death.

brave driver Patroclos dies. It is impossible for us to understand and express what a divine being who loves —anthropomorphic feeling— a human being, must experience when the mortal suddenly dies and disappears forever. Divine sentiments and dispositions are more mysterious and ineffable for mortals when they are ritualized and described as anthropomorphic attitudes. The paradox is then absolutely explosive. Let us feel the ontic weight of ὑμεῖς δ' ἐστὸν ἀγήρω τ' ἀθανάτω τε ["you are ageless and immortal"]), when Zeus asks himself with bitter irony why he ever gave these immortal beings as gift to a mortal man.

I will first analyze Zeus' radical expression used to define human destiny and misery: *oizuros* (literally "lamentable": "*somebody* or *something* deserving to be lamented with the cry 'ahi!'"). This word defines war, for instance (III. 112), and it is selected as the totalizing epithet to embrace the entire wretched story of Achilles (I. 417: "lamentable beyond all men") as well as that of Odysseus (*Od.* v. 105: "the most lamentable of all"). Here too the epithet resonates as an all-embracing epic description of the human condition.³⁸ Apollo makes this point explicit when he refuses to fight against Poseidon: it would be foolish for me, he says, to battle against you —another god— "in favor of the miserable mortals" (XXI. 461 ff.: εἰ δὴ σοί γε βροτῶν ἕνεκα πτολεμίξω / δειλῶν), "who like leaves now flourish full of fire (ζαφλεγέες)³⁹ and feed on the fruits of the land, but then again perish lifelessly."⁴⁰ This simile transports the human race into the seasonal domain of nature: they even eat the seasonal fruits of the fields: a future, after their short summer, is denied to them. Therefore, Apollo argues, immortal gods should not make efforts and risk pains by fighting in favor of mortal beings, dispensable and ephemeral as they are.

---

**38** In the *Iliad* there is another occurrence of *oizuros*, used to define the misery of mortals: the adjective is employed by the Narrator at XIII. 569. In our passage, however, we have a most expressive comparative form. Of the six Homeric examples in which the adjective characterizes a person, one is used for Achilles and five qualify Odysseus. The adjective describes and qualifies the protagonist of the epic poem. The adjective derives from *oizus* "lamentation," "suffering," from the verb *oizuô*, "I lament," "I suffer," and ultimately from *oizô* "I cry oi!" "I cry ahi!" The sound of the lament becomes the lament itself.
**39** The adjective ζαφλεγέες refers metaphorically to "men at their prime," but it is an odd figure in the context of men as leaves.
**40** The passage reworks the language and some of the metaphors of the exchange between Diomedes and Glaukos at VI. 142–9. Mortals eat the fruits of the earth, the natural produce which itself is perishable and therefore analogous to, if not the perpetrator of, their perishable life. Apollo is a loyal helper of Hector, and he will take care of his corpse, but when the Golden Scales determine his death, Apollo abandons him without a word of regret or pain (XXII. 213: "and Phoebus Apollo forsook him, λίπεν δέ ἑ Φοῖβος Ἀπόλλων). That is all.

The gods will always have cities sacrificing to them, building temples, and praying for help. Gods immersed in the unfolding of temporality appear paradoxical.

Since Zeus' utterance has no narrative necessity, its purpose seems schetliastic:[41] the scene begins with Automedon trying to lead the horses out of the battle and failing, despite threats and sweet words, to move them: they stand as still as a grave monument (XVII. 434). From here, Automedon momentarily disappears from the scene: he does not perceive that the horses are accomplishing a ritual mourning, and it is Zeus who enters the picture as he watches the horses' pain and feels pity for them: "But, now, seeing them weeping, the son of Cronos felt pity for them and, shaking his head, spoke to his heart: 'O unhappy you!...'" (XVII. 441–43).[42]

As Burkert 1955, 85 writes, Zeus realizes that human wretchedness obscures the life itself of the immortal horses. Zeus regrets what he did.[43] Rarely do the gods regret their mistakes. Understandably, the mistakes that both Zeus and Thetis lament consist in being emotionally involved with mortals. Though the *diêgêsis* makes no explicit inference, the endless pain of Thetis is an example of this painful incompatibility that is analogous to the pain that Zeus suffers.

Zeus must now help the horses and, if possible, relieve the sadness that holds them motionless as a gravestone. He cannot stop their ritual of grieving and mourning – they will still perform it during the games in honor of Patroclos – except by pushing them to fight. First Zeus forbids their meeting with other mortals and particularly with Hector, who has already taken possession of Patroclos' armor (XVII. 448 ff.). Then, instead of leaving them blocked by their mournful sadness, he instills in them a warlike fury so that they carry Autome-

---

[41] West 2011, 337 quotes the following two passages: "In an earlier version something like 426–55 might have been the immediate sequel to Patroclos' death, leading to Automedon's escape (Erhardt 331 ff.)." "A similar episode might have been related following the death of Achilles (Kullmann 133, n. 3, 134, 329)." In this passage there are some recent linguistic forms that could signal the popularity of the scene constantly recited and adapted until its fixation in writing.

[42] Pelliccia 1995, 165 emphasizes the double lack of contact – Zeus is physically remote from the horses, and it is impossible for the horses to answer – that characterizes this deeply moving sketliastic utterance.

[43] Thetis (I. 414) laments the disgrace of bringing Achilles to life, and at XVIII. 54–64 she cries for the disgrace of giving birth to the best hero and her inability to help him as he lives in pain. Thetis cannot save her own son and must suffer for the disgrace of being his mother, immortal but impotent as she is. She experiences with the most radical intensity the trauma of the immortal horses.

don safely to the ships (451–52). Treating them like immortal heroes, Zeus throws them again into the battle to divert their pain.

This healing treatment is typical of Zeus: he enhances the fighting fury of a hero as a "compensation" for the hero's subsequent death; and here he heals the horses' paralyzing sorrow of mourning by instilling more fury in their hearts. Of course, this cure will create more deaths and more mournings. Yet Zeus knows the senseless economy of the heroic life and he discredits it when he can or takes advantage of it when he must.[44]

Meanwhile he will give the Trojans "the splendid might (*kudos*) of killing[45] until they reach the strong-benched ships" (454–5: ἔτι γάρ σφισι κῦδος ὀρέξω κτείνειν, / εἰς ὅ κε νῆας ἐϋσσέλμους ἀφίκωνται) and as long as the day lasts.

I call attention here to Zeus' granting of *kudos*: he helps the Trojans with the momentary splendor of victory. The epic poem, by recording Zeus' attribution of *kudos*, celebrates his help to the Trojans: unfortunately, however, Zeus' intentions are again double. After bestowing *kudos* on the Trojans (XVII. 454–55), he changes his mind (546: "Zeus' mind [or purpose] had shifted") and sends Athena to help the Achaeans.

Zeus grants the Trojans the victorious shine of *kudos* often and frequently takes it away. In this way *kudos* shares the aberrant and paradoxical nature of Zeus' treatment of what he seems to understand as the senselessness of human heroic life.

The scene ends with the return of Automedon to the action. The text shows him standing upon the chariot (459 ff.): he has heard nothing of Zeus' utterance and decision, but he does not need to know that Zeus has given warlike fury to the immortal horses and that this is the reason why they brought him into the middle of the melee. The immortal horses do not fear death and bring their charioteer to the front line of the battle. Only men continue to die.

## 4.3 The Ruinous Madness of *Atê*

Ruinous madness or blindness (*atê*) is one of the many evils that Zeus dispenses to mortals, even if he does not hold it in his jar. A long time ago this awful *daimôn*, the oldest daughter of Zeus, was rampant even on Olympus, but one

---

[44] Zeus, for example, needs murderous battles to respect his commitment to Thetis; on specific occasions, he creates a bloodbath, such as when he needs to honor the death of his son Sarpedon at XVI. 563–8, 644–55, 686–91. He had an alternative but chose a bloody solution that, for the purpose of honoring, is also the regular epic practice.
[45] On *kudos* see Pucci 2010, 201–25.

day she blinded Zeus and he, enraged, threw her to the earth. Now Zeus can use her to inspire ruinous madness or blindness (*atê*) in the mind of a human character.

This sort of intervention unfolds through the process described by Agamemnon. Speaking with Achilles, he declares that he is not responsible for the outrage he brought about by stealing Achilles' girl. Agamemnon recognizes that often the Achaeans did reproach him for his misdeed, and kept finding fault with me:

> yet I am not responsible (*aitios*)
> but Zeus is and destiny (*Moira*) and Erinys who walks in the mist,[46]
> who during the assembly drove savage madness (*atê*) into my mind[47]
> on the day in which I stripped from Achilles his prize.
> Yet, what could I have done? God accomplishes all things to their very end."[48] (XIX. 86–90)

Against his "will," Agamemnon joins together the indisputable power of three divine beings: in the unfolding of the argument, Agamemnon combines the three authorities into that of Zeus (137–8):

> but since I was blinded [ἀασάμην] and Zeus stole my wits[49]
> I am willing to please and give back endless gifts.

---

[46] The triad is a traditional composition with the third term accompanied by an epithet: ἠεροφοῖτις Ἐρινύς. In this way, the triad occupies an entire line and acquires a sort of unity. In order to increase the power of the divine intervention, Agamemnon mentions three deities, among whom also Erinys, who has little authority in this context; yet this has referential importance, because she is mentioned with this epithet in Phoenix's story about Meleager (IX. 571), and this story might be the model of Achilles' refusal to fight. The emphatic position of Erinys and its epithet therefore may be intended to recall that episode.

[47] On the problematic etymology, religious significance, and disputed connotations of *atê*, the literature is large: concerning the latter issue, some scholars consider "damage, ruin, harm" to be its primary meaning (see for instance Dawe 1967, 96–97); others take that connotation to be secondary and consider "mental blindness" and synonyms to be its primary connotation (see, for instance Dodds 1951, 2 ff.). Thornton 1984, 118: "In seizing a man, *atê* imparts to him her own nature so that he is filled with blind madness and is harmed by what he does in that state." Here *atê* has to be understood as "ruinous folly" as the following words, μευ φρένας ἐξέλετο Ζεύς, indicate; and, on line 88, it is intended in the non-personified form as the verb ἀασάμην in line 137 also indicates.

[48] We are reminded of how Zeus inspires fighting fury in Patroclos' mind and erases, in this way, Achilles' warnings, for "the mind of Zeus is stronger than that of man" (XVI. 688).

[49] At IX. 119 Agamemnon, with the words, "I was blinded and listened to my heart's wretched persuasion," added his heart's "wretched persuasion" to his being blinded by *atê* and therefore pointed to a collaborative responsibility: see Clarke 1999, 207–9.

Zeus subsumes into himself the powers of Moira and Erinys, and therefore he is the one who stole Agamemnon's wits by driving *atê* (ruinous madness) into his mind. Though Zeus is the responsible agent, Zeus cannot, or shall not, compensate Achilles for the consequences of the Zeus-sent madness: Agamemnon must take care of the compensation by himself.[50]

With his last line (XIX. 90), Agamemnon declares his powerlessness to resist the divine impulse: as Pasquali (1968, 293) suggests, Agamemnon's assertion denies what we call "free will." However, the effect and the textual deployment of *atê* can qualify Pasquali's statment. *Atê* is recognized by its victims only *post eventum*: men and gods felt that they were acting freely at the moment of deciding and accomplishing the event.[51] It is therefore only after having seen and suffered the consequences of the action that Agamemnon discovers the influence of *atê* (he does not tell how)[52] and therefore claims that his decision was imposed by a divine power and was part of a larger divine plan. Achilles, in his immediate response to Agamemnon, states just this principle (XIX. 270–4):

> Father Zeus, great are the ruinous frenzies [*atai*] you dispense to men,
> otherwise the son of Atreus could never have stirred the passion in my breast
> so long, nor would he have taken the girl away from me,
> against my will, in his stubbornness; but Zeus
> wished death to come to many of the Achaeans.[53]

Achilles mentally addresses this reproach to Zeus himself, as if Zeus should confirm its truth, since Zeus also was cheated by *atê*. It is because Zeus desired to kill a great number of the Achaeans that he blinded the mind of Agamemnon and maintained Achilles' wrath for such a long time.[54] Achilles and Agamemnon

---

**50** Dodds 1951, 137–8 shows that Agamemnon does not evade his responsibility in the juridical sense. In the *Iliad*, mortals often indict the gods as responsible (*aitioi*) for human errors and foolishness (e.g. III. 164–65). This view is also shared by Achilles' immortal horse Xanthos (XIX. 409–10). He should know.
**51** See Naas 1995, 157 ff., Gaskin 2001, 155–56. This is clearly also the case for Zeus, who was himself blinded by *atê* and discovered it only later after foolishly falling for Hera's trick (XIX. 95–133).
**52** He, however, blames *atê* on previous occasions, II. 111, IX. 18, lamenting what he takes to be Zeus' false promise, and IX. 115–19.
**53** We recognize here the same language and motif as at XVI. 685 ff. when the Narrator (!) – not a character – comments on Patroclos' fighting fury: "Fool! He was really blinded! [ἀάσθη]" and connects Zeus' spurring Patroclos on with Zeus' desire to increase the massacre (See Ch. 3.4).
**54** It is improbable that, as Clarke 1999, 209 assumes, Achilles' words are "diplomatic." Achilles is dramatically serious, since he conceives Agamemnon's ruinous madness to be part of the plan that Zeus realized to give victory to the Trojans and to Hector against Patroclos.

agree. Zeus killed many heroes, among whom also Patroclos,[55] and Achilles should know why, since it was at his suggestion that Thetis asked Zeus to do exactly that, to kill many Achaeans. Through his own wit, and in some way illogically, Achilles combines the *atai* with Zeus' plan, which we Narratees know very well was a difficult undertaking for the god. No *atai* appear in Zeus' pursuit of his plan. All this sounds like an assumption that Achilles makes in order to explain or justify his obstinacy. Both heroes acted through violent, autonomous passion, and only later, when they uncover the disproportionate negative consequences of their initial decisions, do they retroactively define these decisions as being divinely planned. We could say then, taking seriously the heroes' frank confessions, that the god took possession of their minds, and that, as sometimes we have seen happen, the heroes did not realize their having been coopted. Patroclos, for instance, becomes aware of the intervention of Zeus and Apollo only as he is about to die.

Yet if Patroclos misses the impact of the divine intervention, the Narratees do not: in this case – and generally in cases of divine psychic intervention – the narrative reports the divine presence in detail: from the very inception of the intervention, the narrative mentions the name of the god, how he or she appears, and the message that the god delivers. No narrative accounts for *atê*'s intervention in Agamemnon's and Achilles' minds. Zeus incites fury in Patroclos (XVI. 688); the "deadly moira" binds Hector (XXII. 5), and Apollo essentially kills Patroclos with Hector's spear. We have a divine witness and objective account showing as a fact that the characters have been permeated by the gods' power or inspiration. Hector fails to realize the presence of Athena in the disguise of Deiphobus, but the *diêgêsis* informs us of Athena's trick.

On the contrary, the experience that Agamemnon and Achilles describe remains exclusively subjective, unsupported by any objective account; the divine intervention is grounded only on their later acknowledgment of the effects that their earlier action produced. This belated realization could even be subliminally self-serving.[56] Agamemnon's companions indeed kept finding fault with him

---

[55] As Corey 2009, 50 remarks: "Agamemnon does not mention any motivation of the gods' action."

[56] Naas 1995, 157 describes the process of *Atê*: "Guilt is thus assigned and denied, responsibility given and then taken away," and quotes Bespaloff 1947, 49: "Outside all sanctions of the moral order, outside all imperatives of divine origin, the vengeance of the Nemesis of Antiquity makes an act appear guilty in retrospect that at the time of its commission was not considered a sin." Janko 1992, 4: "By leaving an undefined area between free will and supernatural forces, Homer achieves two goals: his characters are seen to suffer for their own choices, which is clearly

and considered him responsible. The soldiers of Achilles were also muttering against his refusal to fight.

The *diêgêsis* offers other important evidence to suggest the subjective character of the two heroes' assumptions. At IX. 501 ff., *Atê* does not appear as a belated, recognizable agent but as a *daimôn* that strikes men who reject the Prayers, daughters of Zeus. *Atê* functions as the punishing agent against those who refuse and reject the Prayers. Phoenix explains this process to Achilles, and Achilles' refusal to accept the Prayers of his friends could cause him great damage: the Prayers would petition Zeus that *Atê* hurt Achilles. There would be here a remote anticipatory suggestion that *Atê* intervenes to punish Achilles for his obstinate rejection of his friends' Prayers: *Atê*, however, would not be the cause of Achilles' anger and obstinate rejection, as Achilles states at XIX. 270–4, but would be the *daimôn* who might punish him for his obstinate anger. She would, for instance, blind Achilles when he sends Patroclos to fight alone.

Achilles, just like Agamemnon, justifies his own predicament by inserting it into the large panorama, the *boulê* of Zeus, of which he feels himself to be a victim. He says it clearly: "otherwise [without *Atê*'s intervention] the son of Atreus could never have stirred the passion in my breast so long..."[57] Oddly enough, he does not mention Patroclos, though he must have been on his lips and heart.

It is perplexing that when Athena appeared to Achilles in the first book to stop his murderous fury, she took Achilles' violent reaction to be his own and calmed him with persuasive arguments that impressed themselves upon his mind and heart. Now it appears to Achilles that, actually, he was at that time not himself: had this been the case, Athena would have spoken to a mind co-opted by *Atê*, but neither Hera nor Athena had any such suspicion. Certainly they would have known if *Atê* had taken possession of Achilles' mind. Thetis too has no suspicion that Achilles' wrath is implanted in his heart by *Atê*. She even advises him to keep on being angry and refusing to fight. (I. 421–2): she, not *Atê*, encourages his obstinacy.

The conclusion to which I am driving is that the interpretation of *Atê* as the belatedly identified agent of calamitous passions is not given by the *diêgêsis*, i.e. by the Muses of the *Iliad*. It is only hypostatized by the two protagonists of

---

tragic, and yet the whole outcome seems beyond their individual control or even preordained, which is tragic in another way."

57 The subject who reinterprets his calamitous decision as a hidden and secret invasion of his mind by *Atê* implicitly assumes that a man cannot consciously act against his own interest and in view of his own misery. He saves his mental sanity.

the tale of wrath. The mythical source and foundation of their interpretations are not the voice of the Iliadic *diêgêsis*, but that of a poem on Heracles. Agamemnon recalls the trick that *Atê* played against Zeus at the time of Heracles' birth (XIX. 91–133). The story was certainly narrated in an earlier poem of which Agamemnon relates the plot: *Atê*, the oldest daughter of Zeus, blinded Zeus so that Hera could play an awful trick on him. According to Agamemnon's recitation or close quotation of the text, Zeus proffered a most boastful announcement before the assembly of the gods. Zeus' bragging words sound odd when compared with Zeus' behavior in the *Iliad* (XIX. 100–105):

> He, boastful, said to all the gods:[58]
> "Listen to me, all you gods and all you goddesses,[59]
> as I tell you the words that my heart orders in my breast:
> this day, Eileithyia, the goddess of birth pangs, will bring
> to light a man of the race of the people sprung from my blood.
> who shall be lord over all those who dwell around him."[60]

Zeus is referring to the fact that, at that very time, Alcmena is about to give birth to Heracles. Hera exploits the terms of Zeus' triumphant declaration and induces Zeus to swear that the first child born, on that day, among the people of his blood, shall rule over the people dwelling around him. Zeus has no reason not to swear what he proclaimed, but he has also no reason to swear, especially with that totally enigmatic formulation. Yet he swears. As he understands later, he was blinded by *Atê* and failed to see the opportunity that, through his oath, he gave Hera to cheat him. Hera immediately, on that same day, manages to delay Alcmena's delivery and to have the wife of Sthenelos give birth to her

---

**58** ἤτοι ὅ γ' εὐχόμενος μετέφη πάντεσσι θεοῖσι. On this "secular" εὐχόμενος implying boasting and pride, see Muellner 1976, 93 ff. Zeus' boasting about his new child, compared with the whole context of Zeus' Iliadic behavior, is close in style and theme only to the passage at XIV. 314–28 (see Ch. 5.3) in which he is seduced by Hera and by Aphrodite's girdle and recites the catalogue both of the great lovers he has had and of the famous children he has fathered. As we will see, that passage is amusingly ironic and belongs to an episode that is fully allusive, as this one, to the Heracles saga. Agamemnon emphasizes Zeus' innocent openness and frank behavior and his corresponding innocent and unsuspicious attitude in order to stigmatize *Atê*'s and Hera's deception. Notice the mention of "all the gods" three times in the two lines 100–101.
**59** These lines 101–02 return at VIII. 5–6, where Zeus forbids the gods from intervening in the battle scene and threatens violent punishment for any breakers of his order.
**60** The child whom Zeus intends to describe is, of course, Heracles.

seven-month-old child, Eurystheus.⁶¹ According to Zeus' oath, Euristheus will be the lord of the people of the region.

The text has perplexing details. First, it is obviously a quotation from a poem: Agamemnon cannot know the words of Zeus and Hera on Olympus. Moreover, while introducing Hera, the text makes a derogatory remark when it describes her (XIX. 96–97):

> yet Hera deceived him blind, female as she is, by her guile.
>
> ἀλλ' ἄρα καὶ τὸν Ἥρη θῆλυς ἐοῦσα⁶² δολοφροσύνης ἀπάτησε.

This type of generalizing derogatory remark, "female as she is," is unique in the *Iliad*, even if Hera's cunning is mentioned elsewhere.⁶³ It is unlikely a creation of Agamemnon's machismo, since Agamemnon recites or adapts an epic passage and therefore might have found the derogatory remark in the text to which he refers.

Finally, Zeus in this short drama appears incredibly gullible: he makes an unnecessary oath only to fall into the trap of *Atê* and Hera. Even if Agamemnon emphasizes the innocent attitude of Zeus, made blind and unsuspicious by the nasty game of *Atê*, so as to intimate also his own innocence, the essential plot displays Zeus' unbelievably naïve behavior.

According to Agamemnon, when Zeus recognizes the shameless trick of *Atê*, he throws her from Olympus to Earth, where she can now cheat and blind poor mortals such as Agamemnon.

Zeus too discovers the nasty intervention of *Atê* only later and only from the effects that she accomplishes by blinding him to Hera's deceptive intentions. Agamemnon finds this story seducing and instructive, for it provides a model for his own behavior as the defenseless victim of *Atê*.⁶⁴

---

**61** Leaf 1902 (ad XIX. 111): "It is simpler and sufficient to suppose that *ate* lies in Zeus' rashness in swearing an unconditional oath, limited to a single day, forgetting that Hera's function gave her some control in these matters." The name of the wife of Sthenelos is not offered by the text and the Greek mythographers offer several names.
**62** From Coray 2009, we learn that θῆλυς is used mostly to designate the sex of domestic animals; of a goddess only here besides the form of θήλεια θεός at VIII. 7.
**63** See δολοφρονέουσα "guileful" at XIX. 106, XIV. 197, 300, 329. Hera is "guileful" because she is made that way or because she needs to be so in that context, not because she is a "feminine being."
**64** Edwards 1991 *ad loc.* finely indicates the parallels that Agamemnon draws between himself and Zeus. See also Coray 2009, ad 95–133, with the bibliography for this point.

For these three characters coopted by *Atê*, the later discovery of *Atê's* maddening inspiration involves self-serving advantages and attenuates, to some extent, their sense of guilt and gullibility. Since Zeus, according to the poem quoted or referenced by Agamemnon, did behave in this same way, and for the same purposes, he appears as a comic victim of *Atê*, a funny and silly character, quite dissimilar from the Iliadic Zeus. My suspicion is that the Poet of the *Iliad* means to mock that representation of Zeus and to present a perverse picture of the god in view of two advantages. First, by making the gullible Zeus of the Heracles Poem the Zeus of the 'Bible' of Agamemnon, the Poet of the *Iliad* belittles the evidences Agamemnon can produce for his interpretation. Unfortunately, we cannot compare the text of the Heracles Poem and see whether the comic and silly atmosphere into which the Iliadic poet has plunged Zeus is a perverse reading and malevolent re-composition of the original scene.[65] It is possible that our Poet is making a polemical and amusing parody of the original text, creating pleasure for his audience: the pleasure, however, would not be exclusively textual, but substantial: making fun of the Bible of Agamemnon would entail making fun of Agamemnon's reading and belief.

I have assumed an analogous poetic strategy in other passages and scenes in which Zeus appears as a "former" Zeus and not the one that vibrates and acts in the *Iliad* (see, for instance Ch. 5.1; 6.2).

Agamemnon is perhaps "quoting" the very words of Zeus and Hera,[66] though this notion of "quoting" must be understood in accordance with the

---

[65] The exact nature and the tone of the adopted text remain impossible to determine: critics note the limited action of Atê in comparison to Hera (Edwards 1991, 249); and West 2011, 355 even assumes that "Ate's role in the birth story is an embellishment added for the present context." I have noticed, with Muellner 1976, the peculiarity of Zeus' boastfulness (XIX. 100) and the unusual anti-woman bias of the text. I would add to this the exceptionally strong wording describing Hera (XIX. 105–7): "her malicious delight in personally making Zeus aware of how she tricked him" (XIX. 120: Edwards 1991, 251), which again emphasizes Hera's, rather than *Atê's*, role. Two hapax uses (φρένα τύψε βαθεῖαν, 125; κεφαλῆς λιπαροπλοκάμοιο, 126) have some contextual peculiarity. The first could be ironic: the "depth of Zeus' mind" can only be praised mockingly after Zeus' display of such superficial thinking. The second phrase evokes the "glossy locks" of *Atê's* head that Zeus grasps to throw her off of Olympus: a gesture recalling Zeus grabbing Hephaistos by the foot, being itself probably a quotation from a "former portrait" of Zeus.

[66] Scholars of course recognize the peculiarity of a human character reporting deeds and even words of the gods. As Leaf (ad IX. 95–96) comments: these deeds and words "elsewhere are told only by the poet himself who knows them by direct inspiration. This was no doubt the case in the original *Herakleia*."

conditions of the epic composition: its orality, its ephemeral or relative stability, repetition as a means of composition, and of adaptation of an episode to a different context, etc.⁶⁷

The poetic voice uncovers the two characters' awareness of having gone too far in their actions and simultaneously presents their assumptions of having been dominated by *Atê*: if this assumption is interpreted as a psychological gesture in order to control their sense of guilt, the Poet would have accomplished an extraordinary creative act. The Muses' narrative had made Agamemnon fully responsible for his exaggerated reaction and had distributed Achilles' responsibility for his wrath —as a replacement for his murder— to various divin-

---

In our story, Zeus' love affairs are twice indirectly mentioned: his paternity of Heracles with Alcmena (mentioned on line 99) and his paternity of Perseus (116, 123, with no mention of the mother). The mentions of Zeus' love affairs in the *Iliad* seem always to echo a traditional story of the hypertext.

67 Nagy 2003 kindly criticizes my use of the words "text" and "writing" for what he calls and interprets as the traditional and evolutionary performative composition of the epic poems. This interpretation responds to his interest in the diachronic process of epic composition and its progressive performance and fixation. For him, therefore, the Homeric "cross-referencing must be appreciated within the larger context of a long history of repeated performances" (p. 16). I use "writing" in the structural sense of a practice that records meaning and signification through a system of signs. By using this word, I imply that the oral system of signs is open to most of the deconstructive features that the "sign," both written and oral, generates. I do not assume, by using the word "writing," that Homer —i.e. the traditional Poet(s)— knew how to write and composed though writing, though I imagine that when, at some point, someone — alone or in a community— fixed the monumental poem— might have. With this definition I mean to erase the metaphysical idea of an oral performance divinely blessed by a sort of immediacy between the sign and its reference, and I mean to introduce that distance and that perplexing problematic that criticism habitually attributes to the written sign, the ostension that the sign makes of itself through rhetoric, specific conventions etc. A sign is a "supplement" that generates a semantic process through which, simultaneously, reference to and difference from something is taking place. I am analyzing the epic "composition" as a "text" that marks its creative form and literary conventions with constant repetitions that may be semantically always different; a construction grounded on the utopian conciliation of paradoxical forces, mortal/immortal and their consequential terms; a creation that appears to hybridize its paradoxical composing forces and makes them, even through linguistic tricks, more or less compatible and complicit. Yet, the text through tricks and deployment of opposite forces cannot hide their irremediable conflict and paradoxical contrasts, so that "the text", in a very deconstructive way, seems to leave undecided for the readers whether the real final purpose of the whole creation is to impose the mythical compatibility of the asymmetrical terms, or to reveal the revolutionary exposure of their irreconcilable nature. I read it as the Monumental Poem that arrived to us through a long, perilous, and complex history; and it is to its monumental form that I address my literary analysis. Nagy did this in a masterful way, for instance with his *The Best of the Achaeans*.

ities: Athena, Thetis, and finally Zeus. For the Muses, therefore, no loss of free will in these characters is implied. Since the Muses, however, record that Agamemnon and Achilles identified Atê's effects in their behavior, we must recognize that for the Muses the two heroes indeed used this subjective belief as a self-serving means to attenuate their sense of guilt and excess during their disastrous reciprocal hostility. The Muses bring to light the humorous divine support that Agamemnon and Achilles could appeal to in order to explain —now that they realize the nonsense of their violent hostility— how they were abused. All the people around them, soldiers and friends knew correctly that they were fully responsible: to manifest to themselves, and to their companions the real cause of their foolishness, Agamemnon and Achilles borrow the comfortable teaching of Zeus' experience. If it really happened to him, couldn't it have happened to them as well?

## 4.4 The *Odyssey*'s Reaction to the Iliadic Zeus

Let us open a short parenthesis. The Greek philosophers, beginning with Xenophanes, raised the question of whether gods need to be honored by cults. In the Platonic dialogue *Euthyphron*, Socrates elaborates a negative answer to this question. Gods, insofar as they are gods, do not gain any advantage from what men offer them, and it is questionable whether human holiness (*to osion*) consists solely in cult offerings (*Euthyph.* 14 d–15 a).

In the *Iliad*, Homer certainly does not assent to the Socratic position, since he has Zeus praise Hector's frequent sacrificial practices elaborately. But the other mind of Zeus, the one that directs human destinies, points to a role that empties prayers and cult practices of any real purpose.

Only through a disingenuous, tricky textual strategy (double truth, smart silences, characters' forgetting, etc.) is Homer able to preserve a surface unity and coherence within the divine character of Zeus: during each manifestation or illustration of Zeus' contact with, and control of human destinies, the Poet, according to his dramatic need, hides or adapts one of the conflicting images of Zeus.

The image of Zeus with his two immense jars, impassive dispenser of blessings and miseries, deaf to any ethical exigency and unable or unwilling to change any destiny that he allotted —for he is accountable to no one— is the figure of Zeus that was upsetting to the poets and the myth-makers around the time in which the *Iliad* was composed and began to be performed. The Poems of the Epic Cycle, the *Odyssey*, and Hesiod's works in particular, elaborate images of Zeus that contrast deeply with that of the Iliadic Zeus. A neat, almost explicit reaction against the upsetting figure of Zeus of the *Iliad* explodes forth in the

*Odyssey* —a text, for external and internal reasons, very close to the *Iliad*. Odysseus, the Poet says,

> desired to save his companions but could not,
> for they perished through their own recklessness,[68]
> fools! Who devoured the cattle of Helios Hyperion,
> and he took from them the day of their return.

The divine power punished a reckless, inappropriate human action: the god determines what is correct behavior, and chastises whoever breaks his orders. This is a different god than the Zeus of the *Iliad*, who does not punish, since heroes always do what is implicit in his will.[69] The Iliadic Poet may raise his voice to reproach Patroclos for forgetting Achilles' orders and thus running to his death (XVI. 686); but this reproach comes neither from a companion nor from Zeus. Zeus is precisely the one who induces Patroclos to forget Achilles' orders.

The poetic voice of the *Odyssey*, with an apostrophe, calls the reckless men of the *Odyssey* "fools" and justifies this insult by stating that they devoured the cattle of Helios Hyperion (i. 8, νήπιοι, οἳ κατὰ βοῦς Ὑπερίονος Ἠελίοιο ἤσθιον). If we compare the analogous apostrophe of the poetic voice of the *Iliad* when it reproaches Patroclos for neglecting Achilles' warning, the text immediately adds that the mind of Zeus is stronger than any human mind. The Poet combines the two motivations and produces a hybrid parallelism whereby Patroclos is simultaneously a foolish man and a victim blinded by Zeus (See Ch. 3.3). In the opening lines of the *Odyssey*, the men of Odysseus are treated as fools because of their own foolishness: the god does not contribute to their madness and correctly punishes the men for their recklessness. They deserve the insult, and no pity.

As I have argued in my essay "The Proem of the *Odyssey*" (1998, 19), not only does the Poet exculpate Odysseus for the loss of his companions, but also asserts that his companions offended the god, knowing very well that they were doing so, and thus paid for the offense with their death.

---

**68** The line is found at *Il.* IV. 409, where Sthenelos says, "our fathers died for their recklessness," implying their military arrogance; the line is echoed also at XXII. 104, where Hector says that he ruined the army through his recklessness, meaning his excessive confidence in his military power and in Zeus' help. These are the only two examples of the word *atasthaliai* in the *Iliad*.

**69** Human characters sometimes imply that Zeus, through *atê*, may punish people who deny prayers (see for instance IX. 511–12); but this is the characters' opinion and we do not hear or see Zeus in the *Iliad* punishing any hero.

That the *boulê* of Zeus in *Il.* I. 5 is treated as a foil by *Od.* i. 7, and therefore gives value to the Odyssean point of view, is recognized by Maehler 1963, 23.

The Poet editorializes the story in favor of Odysseus, and provides an intimation of Zeus' ethical figure. Indeed, a few lines later, during the first divine assembly (i. 26 ff.), the Poet stages Zeus to recall the recent revenge that Orestes took upon Aegisthus, and declares (i. 28, 32–40):

And among them the father of men and gods began to speak[70]
...
"Alas! It is astonishing how mortals blame the gods![71]
They say that their evils come from us, but they even by themselves,
through their own recklessness, have sorrows beyond [what is ordained in their] destiny (ὑπὲρ μόρον).
Just as now Aegisthus beyond [what was ordained in] his destiny
took the legitimate wife of the Atrides and killed him on his return
though he knew of sheer destruction since we had told him
through the message of Hermes...
that he should neither kill the man nor woo his wife,
for vengeance would come from Orestes..."

It is tempting to assume that, in the first lines (i. 32–34), Zeus responds exactly to Achilles' theological principle at *Il.* XXIV. 527–33 or, at any rate, to the *Iliad*'s representation of Zeus as master of human destinies, a role that makes him the

---

[70] τοῖσι δὲ μύθων ἦρχε πατὴρ ἀνδρῶν τε θεῶν τε. The staging line repeats the line at *Iliad* XXIV. 103 which the Narrator uses to introduce Zeus' order to Thetis to have Achilles put an end to the outrage of Hector's corpse. What is remarkable is that this line is repeated only once again in the *Iliad* (XXII. 167 – the line introduces Zeus' lament for Hector), and never again in the *Odyssey*. This unique presence of the line in the *Odyssey*, at the moment when the Narrator introduces Zeus' polemic words in argument against the Iliadic view of Zeus as master of human destinies, may be, besides a convenient staging line, sign of the intended reference.

[71] θεοὺς βροτοὶ αἰτιόωνται recalls Priam's line (*Il.* III. 164): θεοί νύ μοι αἴτιοί εἰσιν; Xanthos' line (XIX. 410): οὐδέ τοι ἡμεῖς αἴτιοι, ἀλλὰ θεός τε μέγας καὶ Μοῖρα κραταιή; and of course, Agamemnon's at XIX. 85–89. In the *Odyssey*, Telemachus considers Zeus responsible for the ruinous home return of the Achaeans (i. 347–49); Odysseus attributes Ajax's and Achilles' deaths to Zeus (xi. 558–60); and Nausicaa makes Zeus the dispenser of those human lots that he wishes, referring to Odysseus' unhappy condition (vi. 188–90). An Iliadic theology emerges in these passages: it is perhaps not meaningless that they refer to events or characters of the *Iliad*. A line repeated four times expresses with a different metaphor —"these events lie upon the knees of the gods"— a vague theological principle, a generic trust or hope in the gods' help or assistance in the upcoming events: *Iliad* XVII. 514 and XX. 435; *Odyssey* i. 267 and xvi. 129. In all four passages it is a character who speaks —at i. 267 it is a goddess, Athena, and of course she gives divine authority to the principle.

impassive organizer of the order of things.⁷² The Odyssean Zeus protests precisely against that human view of the gods; not we gods, but men themselves, Zeus says, by their own faults, add evils to their initial portion of destiny. In their wantonness men even dismiss the useful advice that the gods dispense to them —as he exemplifies with the case of Aegisthus. Men still have a prescribed destiny— a sort of portion attached to each individual person —and Zeus knows it, but men by their free will can change that destiny, even against a god's advice. For Zeus in the *Odyssey* is a master and guardian of the ethical values that human society treasures.

Critics and scholars all agree that the theological principle in the *Odyssey* is different than that in the *Iliad*: it depicts Odysseus as an ethical character;⁷³ a divinity is ready to help moral men, is fair and merciful, does not hide his/her purposes, and sustains ethical values.⁷⁴ Aegisthus' ruin in the opening lines of the poem announces in advance the destruction of the suitors, at the end of the poem, a destruction that, because of their crimes, is equally deserved.⁷⁵ The contrast with the *Iliad* is eloquent: in the opening of the poem, the *Iliad* stages its own Zeus, monotheistic, master of destinies, and closes with the theocratic image of the two jars, dispensing blessings and terrible evils to mortals.

---

**72** Rutherford 2001, 132: "It is not clear to me ... that this [Zeus' complaint about the mortals' belief] is a specific allusion to the *Iliad*. The allusion, if there is one, is insufficiently signaled, the polemic too generalized... Zeus' speech sets the *Odyssey* in contrast with more negative presentations of the gods (and more tragic presentations of mankind) in general, rather than in opposition to the *Iliad* in particular." The author remains consistent in his skepticism about "allusion" and prefers to refer to countless contemporary representations of the gods that are more tragic than those of the *Iliad*. Whatever Homer's authorial intentions may have been, a contrast exists, and though to install a dialogue between the two contrasting texts might be too postmodern for austere philologists, this dialogue nevertheless exists and offers rich critical insights: see Mondolfo 1958, 81 ff.; Pasquali 1968.

**73** See for instance Griffin 1980, 164–5: in the *Odyssey*, "The hero is helped through his tribulations by a goddess and the justice of his actions goes with divine favour and with eventual success." Notice the presence of the word "justice." See de Jong 2001, 217 and my review in *Classical Philology* 2003, 86. Rutherford 2001, p. 132: "What the passage [*Od.* i. 32–40] clearly does is to establish the ethical tone of the *Odyssey*, with its emphasis on righteous dealing rewarded and rash or wicked behavior as self-destructive."

**74** When Zeus agrees to help Odysseus' return, he does not simply praise Odysseus' piety, but also his intelligence (*noon*) greater than all mortals' (i. 66). He also justifies his and the gods' lack of intervention by recalling Poseidon's hostility to Odysseus. Zeus explains the ethical and practical reasons for his decisions.

**75** As Stephanie West remarks, the suitors too, like Aegisthus, dismiss divine warnings (ii. 146 ff.) and, as Aegisthus is killed by Orestes, they will be killed by Odysseus.

This scholarly agreement on Odyssean theology is on the whole correct, but often it does not give sufficient consideration to the fact that ethical principles sometimes work inconsistently and contradictorily across the rugged surface of the Odyssean text. It is enough to mention the affair between Ares and Aphrodite, the cheating of Athena, the monsters in Odysseus' narrative, and the not-completely-unified body of the Olympian gods. The first assembly of the gods can decide in favor of Odysseus' return home because it takes advantage of Poseidon's absence, as he is among the Aethiopians: had he been present, he would not have agreed.

The text makes clear that the *Odyssey*'s Zeus accepts what Zeus in the *Iliad* would not, for in the *Iliad* Zeus would not allow this distortion of human destiny because of a man's will. The expression ὑπὲρ μόρον or ὑπὲρ μοῖραν[76] is found in a context in which Aegisthus threatens to act "against the ordinance of his/her destiny." In the *Iliad*, whenever this threat appears, Zeus or one of his peers prevents the menace from succeeding. In the Odyssean text (i. 34), this expression ὑπὲρ μόρον shows that Aegisthus acts against his destiny, kills Agamemnon and possesses his wife. The gods warn him against overstepping his own destiny, but do not take any action when he does so. This linguistic exception, at the very opening of the poem, is significant.

Furthermore, Zeus' entire speech, though obviously intended for the Narratees, is addressed to the divine assembly: Zeus' first declaration in the *Odyssey* appears polemical and didactic. The Poet uses the voice and the authority of Zeus to communicate to the Narratees the Odyssean theological principle. Zeus displays a sort of pedagogic and paternal attitude, in a fully anthropomorphic dimension: "Ah me (*Ô popoi*)! Look at these mortals, how they blame us."

Compare him to Zeus in the first book of the *Iliad*, when he says to Thetis (I. 526–27):

> what I bent my head in assent to shall not be revocable,
> nor vain, nor unfulfilled.

---

[76] The Greek expression ὑπὲρ μόρον designates a violence waged against a mortal's destiny. In the *Iliad*, this expression and ὑπὲρ μοῖραν indicate an action that threatens to violate the order of human destiny but that does not succeed thanks to a divine intervention: XX. 30 and 336, XXI. 517, and exceptionally v. 436. I have translated the expression as Murray/Dimock do, since I use so often similar metaphors to describe the content of destiny —its "ordering," "its inscription" etc.

He has given his assent to the provisional victory of the Trojans, with all its wretched and heroic consequences which he will supervise through and through.

Evidence that the Odyssean Zeus is concerned with justice and that he aids just causes is offered immediately, during the assembly, when he agrees with Athena that Odysseus should be allowed to abandon Calypso if he wants to. The decision is made to send Hermes to the nymph with the order to let Odysseus to leave the island.

There is in this image of Zeus no hint of a negative theology. (See other arguments on the Odyssean Zeus in Ch. 6.5)

# Chapter 5

## 5.1 Zeus challenges the Divine Assembly

I will now examine Zeus and his *boulê* in relation to the other gods' wills and reactions. I divide this theme, for mere convenience of exposition, into various sections: in the first, I gather the episodes of Hera's, Athena's, and Poseidon's rebellion against Zeus' order; in the second, the collaboration between Zeus and other gods to achieve a specific end; and in the third, Zeus' taking into his hands what could be called an Olympian project, in book XXIV.

In book VIII, following the assembly in the first book (see Ch. 1.2), Zeus gathers the gods for an important decision. Zeus firmly bans the gods from helping or assisting either side in the war (VIII. 11: ἢ Τρώεσσιν ἀρηγέμεν ἢ Δαναοῖσι). This order implements —after the pause created by books III–VII— the action that Zeus promised to Thetis: the granting of a provisional victory to the Trojans. Scholars often consider that, in the original *Mênis of Achilles*, this divine council (VIII. 1–52) would have followed after the second book and would have led directly into the battle of the eleventh book. The scholarly discussion on these issues and on the relative newness of the book and of its parts leaves many crucial questions open.[1]

Some of the religious details in this council of the gods are, as Chantraine argues, very archaic. This does not ensure the archaism of the whole passage, but rather entails that the composer of the passage, at whatever moment of the tradition he composed it, was quite familiar with the entire range of epic diction and thought it coherent to use traditional, archaic components, finding them appropriate to his epic episode.

The council begins in the following way (VIII. 2–4):

> Zeus made the assembly of the gods, Zeus who delights in thunder,[2]
> upon the highest peak of rugged Olympus.
> As he spoke, all the gods were listening to him.[3]

---

[1] See Chantraine 1934, 281–296; Shipp 1972, 262, n. 1; West 2011, 199–200.
[2] I leave the original word order, Ζεὺς δὲ θεῶν ἀγορὴν ποιήσατο τερπικέραυνος, and I increase the emphasis by repeating the name Zeus. The reasons for this are that this is the only example in Homer in which this epithet is in its nominative form —which appears otherwise three times in the *Iliad*, two times in the *Odyssey*— and is separated from its name; furthermore, the text auspiciously employs the "thunder" epithet as to announce the three other times in the same book in which Zeus' thunder will be mentioned (75–6, 133–35, 170–71), while he thundered at the end of the preceding book to terrorize both Achaeans and Trojans (VII. 478–79).

Zeus is presented in full epic panoply: his epithet and the mention of the highest peak, as at I. 499 and V. 754. In those books, Zeus' position on the topmost peak is distinct from his palace, where the gods otherwise assemble (XX. 4–12). In the first book, as we have seen, his isolated highest seat is symbolic of his theocratic power to impose on his peers changes in the order of things: the text had accordingly given a terrific image of his control over the assembly and over the world's events. That the second line, which stages the scene, ends with the epithet, "who delights in thunder," is contextually quite appropriate, since Zeus will soon adopt a menacing posture concerning the use of his lightning bolts or concerning himself in the form of lightning.

Now, in book VIII, Zeus intends to give victory to the Trojans and accordingly bans the gods from helping or assisting the fighters in the war. He does not give any explanation for the reason of his ban, however: he simply threatens awful punishments to any god who dares disregard his order.[4] Either the hypothetical rebel would return to Olympus in bad shape, having been struck by lightning, or would not return at all: Zeus will dash him or her to dark Tartarus where the abyss under the earth is deepest. By threatening to treat them as he treated the Titans, he opens up the memory of a full-out fight among the gods, with all the danger that entails, as in the myth of his succession. He ends his threat by adding (VIII. 17): "Then you shall know[5] by how far I am the strongest of all the gods."

These threats sound arbitrary because no explanation for the ban is given: yet explanations would open a discussion and weaken the force of the command. Explanations would also reveal his position as god of Fate, master of events, and, as he states at I. 449–50, he desires secrecy to keep his promise to Thetis. He acts now, therefore, as the dictatorial ruler of the Olympian gods, whom he masters through the deterrence provided by the threat of his physical force. This is the position that Derrida, 2003, 38, analyzing the "difference de force" calls 'ipsocratic'.

Zeus' last boast, "Then you shall know by how far I am the strongest of all the gods" (VIII. 17) could possibly ring empty: a strong god, as he is, should not need to assert that he is strong. Zeus, however, needs to utter a violent threat:

---

3 The line is a hapax.
4 He demands that his peers accept, or approve (αἰνεῖτ', l. 9), his ban. Elmer 2013, 267 n. 27 writes that the verb "suggests the temporary coordination of divergent interests rather than a proper consensus." Of course, Zeus means '"accept" my order or it will be very painful for you.' There is no deliberation and no negotiation.
5 Or, reading γνώσετ'[αι], "he [i.e. the one who dares to transgress my ban] shall know." The plural "you" sounds stronger.

he has no legitimate, ethical, or contractual grounds for justifying his ban and for sustaining his position as ruler of the gods. He is not like Yahweh, who in Psalm 82 —as West recalls (1997, 370–71)— issues a similar threat to the gods, but can substantiate the ethical reasons for his displeasure:

> How long will you give unjust judgments
> and show favor to the wicked?

Yahweh is a god of justice; see also *Amos* 3–7 where, in some passages, the prophet asserts that the Lord is ready to uphold justice, to punish the sinners and "to tell his secret to his servants the prophets" (see for this last point 3,7). Zeus, on the contrary, keeps secret the motivations and the extensions of his decisions.

Zeus proves his superior physical force by a curious claim: he challenges the gods to play tug-of-war with him (19–27): all of them – even the gods who are on his side – competing against him alone, would not be able to pull the rope to bring him down, while, as he boasts, he would draw the rope and win the game. By this assurance, he intends to give factual evidence for his superior force (19–27):

> Hang a golden rope from the sky,
> and lay hold of it all you gods and goddesses,
> yet you would not drag down, from sky to ground,
> Zeus the highest counselor,[6] not even with your great effort;
> while whenever I too earnestly wished,
> I would drag you up with the whole earth and the whole sea.[7]
> And then I would tie the golden chain around a horn
> of Olympus and in that case everything would dangle in midair:
> to such an extent am I stronger than the gods, and stronger than men.
> [τόσσον ἐγὼ περί τ' εἰμὶ θεῶν περί τ' εἴμ' ἀνθρώπων.]

---

**6** Notice the use of the self-referential third person. Muellner 1997, 152 writes: "here the personage is at the center of the social hierarchy and applies to himself honorific epithets. Because the third person is neither an I nor a You, speakers who refer to themselves as third persons are placing themselves on another level of being apart from their interlocutors." For the self-referential use of the proper name see also van Hille 1938, 253 ff. and Kelly 2007, 84–85. Though Zeus boasts about being a strapping champion, he still wants to be what he is, especially now that he gives an order: "the uppermost adviser" (22: Ζῆν' ὕπατον μήστωρ').

**7** Zeus imagines himself as being high up on Heaven-Olympus, dragging up the gods who are thought to be on earth and attached to the golden rope; he would drag up the earth and sea with them. Leaving the gods suspended in midair means removing the gods from heaven — earth and sea are dangled in midair with the gods— and therefore it means placing them in a non-place.

Critics emphasize the comic and bizarre idea of this sportsman competition and of its purpose.[8] They are right, but we should keep in mind the different nature of the audience to whom the challenge is addressed and distinguish the effects that the text of the challenge produces. For the divine characters, as we will see, it constitutes a serious menace involving the whole Olympus; but for the audience of the Poem, Zeus' challenge appears as a humorous defying gesture that inscribes his figure into a superior and hilarious context.[9]

After the *personal* threats (VIII. 10 ff: "Any god I perceive... he shall go whipped by lightning..."), Zeus needs a strong deterrent for the *whole Olympian community*, one that demonstrates that he alone is stronger than all of them together, and moreover a deterrent that carries strong symbolic references. The match of tug-of-war is such a deterrent: it constitutes an aggressive challenge, a purposeful mockery of the Olympians, while symbolically it evokes Zeus' mastery of the skies and of the world. It is a clever diplomatic solution, since Zeus cannot declare a war such as he waged against the Titans: Zeus' peers, as a group, are not his rivals, and what he asks of them is only a temporary obedience. The game of tug-of-war is a perversely ironic and diplomatic choice.[10]

Zeus stresses the opposition between the totality of the gods and himself (see lines 5, 9, 17, 18, 20, 22, 27). He isolates himself from the group and projects himself into the third person, defining himself as "Zeus, the highest counselor" (22), the chief and wisest god.

---

[8] Burkert 1985, 126–27: "The sportsman's brag is marvelously fused with cosmic fantasy and the divine glimmer of gold: the golden chain became the subject for manifold interpretations by the ancient exegetes. The other gods may protest against Zeus, they may attempt to disobey him or even plot against him, but nothing can seriously threaten him —he remains far superior." Willcock 1978, 260 also considers the passage ironic or amusing ("It is not to be taken seriously"). West 1997, 371 singles out "this extraordinary vision" as being quite unique in early Greek literature and quotes some of the Babylonian texts that could be the sources of inspiration for this vision. West (2011, p. 200) refers to his previous work and defines our passage (VIII. 18–27): "A phantasy of Babylonian inspiration."

[9] Aristarchus (Arn/A) and modern critics suggest that this image could come from traditional sources that were already difficult for the ancients to identify. Possibly this representation of Zeus echoes some analogous picture that appeared in the Heracles saga. For the hypothetical hypertext concerning the story of Heracles, see Kirk 1990, ad V. 396–97 and, for Babylonian sources, see West 1997, 371.

[10] Zeus' ironic distance from his peers comes to the fore in other circumstances, for instance at XXI. 388–90, when he takes pleasure and laughs at seeing his peers come together in strife.

Without frustrating the Narratees' expectation of a potential dramatic rebellion,[11] the poetic voice offers a Zeus who mocks the gods' impotence and inability to contest him. On lines 21–24, Zeus, speaking directly to the gods, tells them sarcastically that they are a bunch of powerless individuals: they, all together, would not move Zeus from his place by a step. Here, as often, the poetic voice manages that Zeus' violent menace to his peers be felt by the audience of the Poem as a threatening speech with a simply deterring intention. In addition, Zeus' surrealistic defiance carries a tone that produces comic effects that palliate and, in some way, transform the sheer physicality and brutality of a menacing use of force.

Zeus' power to challenge the whole assembly in this sarcastic way shows that the Iliadic Zeus has no serious competitors and that the assembly of the Olympian gods offers simply a resonating wall for his public display. Nothing could more crucially showcase the will of the Narrator to stage a completely new Zeus than this scene.

In the eyes of both the gods and the audience of the Poem, the serious aspect is the symbolic meaning of the tug-to-war challenge. Zeus, the supreme ruler of the skies, clouds, lightning, and thunder, would remove all the gods from Olympus, "where the seat of the immortals is" (VIII. 456), and suspend them in midair.[12]

Zeus begins the picture he paints in these lines (23–26) with a temporal adverb: "but whenever I too earnestly wished to drag you up," meaning from the earth —he mockingly places them on the earth, already far from Olympus—, and declares that his desire to have them move up would be contingent on his mood and mind-set.

In the eyes of the Narratees, Zeus' choice of the game to demonstrate his absolute power may sound humorous, especially because the game, played on the cosmic dimension, acquires a funny and surrealistic grandeur and it is in this hilariously distorting mirror that the text exhibits to its audience Zeus' physical and spiritual hyperbolic ego.

---

**11** There is no suspicion of plots or sedition when at I. 518 ff. Zeus tells Thetis that assenting to her request will be a "disastrous affair," for he tells her that the disaster will consist in his entering into conflict with Hera. He does not mention any hostility, discontent, or unease among the gods. And indeed, it is only Hera that immediately (I. 540 ff.) assails Zeus.

**12** The symbolic force of the game has been well caught by Bonnet 2016, 123: "Zeus places before us an assembly in a vertical line, hanging on a thread: Zeus on the top, alone, and all the other gods below. Even worse: all this creation dangles in the void, under the eyes of the master." Bonnet then refers to the great success that this image has in the following literature and philosophy.

Zeus' tactics grant him complete success: the gods, struck silent in surprise, listen to Zeus' order (28–29):

> So he spoke and all of them remained in deep silence,
> stunned (ἀγασσάμενοι) at his words: for he had spoken very boldly.

Zeus' physical force is the necessary basis of his authority over the Olympian gods; he nonetheless never needs to employ it and only mentions it as a deterrent, either as a possible threat in the future or as a deed of the past.

The text invites the Narratees to stand on the side of Zeus against the gods, and therefore to enjoy his mockery of the gods and appreciate his unique authority. The trembling silence of all the gods, scared by the tug-of-war challenge, displays the Narrator's spiritual freedom and creativity in fashioning such a god as Zeus. We are reminded of certain scenes in Aristophanes' *Birds*.

The text's irony spreads out on the whole picture of the divine community gathered in the assembly. Its consistency is virtual and lasts until the needed effect is achieved. Indeed, a little after Zeus' words and the assembly's frightened silence, when everything seems settled in accordance with Zeus' will, Athena intervenes with a surprising request and obtains an even more surprising response (30–34):

But now, after a while, the goddess grey-eyed Athena spoke to him:

> "Son of Kronos, our father, preeminent among the mighty,
> [ὦ πάτερ ἡμέτερε Κρονίδη ὕπατε κρειόντων][13]
> we too know well [εὖ νυ καὶ ἡμεῖς ἴδμεν][14] that your strength is dauntless.

---

**13** The line addresses Zeus with his full epic panoply: "son of Kronos, father of the gods, and preeminent among the mighty," has notable features: the reference to Kronos entails a specific allusion to the same hierarchical role of the father and to the superior force of Zeus who defeated Kronos. The expression Κρονίδη ὕπατε κρειόντων in the vocative is unique in the *Iliad*, and occurs three times in the *Odyssey*. Only Athena uses this staging line in the four Homeric passages (i. 45, 81, xxiv. 473, and VIII. 31), an odd specificity that is difficult to explain. It could sustain the assumption that the passage VIII. 31 ff. comes from a non-Iliadic tradition where the affectionate relationship between Zeus and Athena would be more constant than in the *Iliad*.

**14** Of course, "you do not need to make such a display of your strength: we too know it." It is not clear in the whole passage 31–37 to whom Athena's "we" refers: to all the gods, to some of the gods, or simply to Athena herself and Hera. It is evident that not all the gods are evoked: when Athena says, "But even so we are sorrowful for the Danaan warriors / who must complete an unhappy destiny and perish," she should speak only for a portion of the gods. When she promises to keep clear of the war she can only promise for herself...; with "we" she does not speak as a representative of the gods, but of only herself.

But even so we are sorrowful for the Danaan warriors
who must complete an unhappy destiny and perish."

Then Athena promises obedience and asks for an exception, whether the gods can give good counsel to the Achaeans (35–37):

Yes, we will keep clear of the war, as you command,
but we will offer the Argives advice that may help them[15]
so that not all of them will die because of your wrath.

Athena recognizes without hesitation Zeus' undefeatable force, but this is just what troubles her (see line 37: "...to the Achaeans so that —and here Zeus might be smiling at her repetition of his own phrase —not all of them will die).[16] She knows that Zeus agreed to honor Achilles,[17] but she does not know the specific nature of the plan and the depth of Zeus' anger.[18]

To Athena's request to be allowed to advise the Achaeans, Zeus unexpectedly answers smilingly and states that his speech was not spoken with serious intent (or "heart") and consents to her demand (VIII. 38–40):

Then, with a smile, cloud-gatherer Zeus answered her:
"Take heart, Tritogeneia, dear child! I am not saying this
with zealous heart, and with you I want to be kind."

These lines trigger critical embarrassment from antiquity to our days. By Athena's request and by Zeus' unlikely concession —the critics argue— the text enfeebles the strong image it depicted of Zeus' hegemony and absolute power.[19]

---

**15** Private advice from the gods does occur: Zeus himself sometimes enacts this practice: for instance, he advises Hector to avoid fighting until Agamemnon is wounded (XI. 182–209). Hera herself inspires Agamemnon at VIII. 218–19 and by this inspiration she saves the ships of the Achaeans (215–17).
**16** The expression "all of them will die" is a rhetorical exaggeration: she cannot believe that the death of all the Achaeans is Zeus' goal.
**17** See VIII. 370–72 where even Athena knows of Zeus' promise to Thetis to honor Achilles. Hera must have informed her.
**18** Only in book XV, after Hera's erotic deception, will Zeus present the large outlines of his plan, but even then he will present his plan not for consultation or discussion but as a *fait accompli*, an undisputable decision. A most partial hint at his plan occurs at the end of the eighth book in the new divine council, after Hera and Athena's aborted attempt to help the Achaeans (VIII. 471–77).
**19** The lines "are open to the strongest suspicion. That is because his [Zeus'] relenting undermines his whole position, making his spectacular threats pointless, even absurd and being

Since, however, the face-saving explanations for this embarrassing passage seem unrealistic,[20] the alternative solution is to accept it and try to make sense of it.

It is impossible to state with certainty whether or not Athena's request and Zeus' answer are borrowed and attached here from other scenes depicting Zeus' and Athena's relationship.[21] This borrowing is possible (see for instance XXII. 183 ff.),[22] but it cannot be substantiated, since its internal inconsistency is only relative. The conjectured interpolator would have had a reason, a purpose for this addition and we have to search for it and find it. If we find it we no longer need to excuse the text by means of an interpolator.

First, Athena's request and Zeus' consent legitimize Hera's intervention and her saving advice to Agamemnon at VIII. 218–19. Yet what really justifies both request and tone in the exchange between Zeus and Athena is the sudden, though unannounced, change of scene and context. This short dialogue must occur in the context of the family relationship, even if it follows immediately after the assembly.

The tonal and stylistic jump from one setting to another is certainly deep and unexpected: Athena's and Zeus' sudden switch into a private dialogue marginalizes or even effaces the presence of the assembly, its divine atmosphere and its dramatic purposes. Athena's "we" does not include the assembly of the gods, but is a "we" that bestows to her private views a general and collective reference: sure enough, not all the gods are sorry for the death of the Achaeans; only she —and nobody else— can promise to behave as Zeus commands. She clearly speaks for herself: the text is tricky because with her "we" (and with her

---

contradicted by his undiminished hostility to the two goddesses later in the book (e.g. 447–456)." Kirk 1990, 299–300.
20 See Kirk 1990, 300. The attempts to adapt the text with some coherence to what precedes begins with the different ways of retouching of the translations. In Zeus' statement, "I do not speak with zealous [or serious] heart" (οὔ νύ τι θυμῷ πρόφρονι μυθέομαι), θυμῷ πρόφρονι has received various translations: "In no way I speak with full purpose of heart" (Murray); "for I say this not in outright anger" (Lattimore); "I do not speak my full intent" (Fitzgerald); "Nothing I said was meant in earnest" (Fagles); "non parlo così per mio gusto" (Cerri); etc.
21 Athena demands permission to advise the Achaeans and obtains it from Zeus, yet she will never be shown to accomplish this task. Hera, however, will intervene with an appropriate piece of advice for Agamemnon at VIII. 218–19, and will be allowed to fulfill what Athena demanded. Hera requires the same permission at VIII. 462–68, but Zeus, as we will see, denies it.
22 Lines XXII. 183 ff. repeat lines VIII. 39–40: they are part of a long scene in which Zeus first wishes to save Hector, then he accepts Athena's rejection of his desire (see Ch. 2). When the Golden Scales confirm the necessity of Hector's death, Zeus sends his "dear child" to proceed with her plan of supporting Achilles.

epic address on line 31) she speaks as being still part of the assembly. With this trick, the text grants a fake plurality to her single voice.

The text, in this way, introduces the conflicting relationship between daughter and father that, as we will see, unfolds toward the end of the book and displays Athena's resentment against Zeus.

Zeus is made to interpret and confirm the change of setting, atmosphere, and context when he addresses her as "dear child": the assembly is no longer there, he is smiling and he can say that he did not speak seriously: he spoke seriously to the gods and to her; yet in a direct conversation with his dear daughter, he would give the order in another fashion, of course, because he is kind to her. He would no longer need to impress her with the tug-of-war challenge. And to begin with, he allows her to advise the Achaeans so that not all of them will die.

The Narrator felt that Zeus' display of violent threats as a deterrent had to be followed by some drama: the drama could develop only if certain gods challenged his arrogant tone; yet this challenge could not destabilize Zeus' ban. Accordingly, he placed Athena on the stage, the character who, with Hera, will attempt to break the ban, without, however, endangering Zeus' authority.

The Narratees, of course, do not yet know all of this. For them, the sudden switch from the assembly to a domestic scene is a surprise. This Iliadic Zeus, master of the world, ruler of destinies, now appears like a familiar and affectionate father, in a sort of fourth role for Zeus, who is already accustomed to an exchange of favors and kindnesses with his daughter.

## 5.2 The Breaking of Zeus' Ban

Toward the end of book VIII, Hera feels pity for the Achaeans and enlists Athena for an armed intervention. Athena, unexpectedly for the poem's audience, agrees and justifies her attitude by expressing deep hostility toward her father as she recalls recent events (VIII. 360–73):

> But it is my father who furiously rages in his rotten mind,
> hard, always wicked, thwarter of my plans.[23]
> He has no remembrance of all the times I rescued his own son

---

[23] This strongly abusive line, for whose clumsiness see Kirk 1990, at VIII. 361, suggests obstacles that Zeus created for Athena's plans. Yet it is impossible for us to identify them. A probable assumption is that she refers to her commitment to the destruction of Troy, of which she is the designated planner (XV. 71).

> as he was distressed by the labors Eurystheus imposed on him
> and time and again Heracles would cry out loud to the heavens
> and Zeus would send me down from the heavens to help him.[24]

[366–369: Athena recalls her rescue of Heracles from his adventure in Hades.]
370–74:

> And now he [Zeus] hates me and accomplishes the wishes of Thetis
> who kissed his knees[25] and grasped his chin with her hand,
> begging him to honor cities-sacker Achilles.[26] Yet[27] the time
> shall come when he calls me again his dear "grey-eyed" [daughter] [φίλην γλαυκῶπιδα εἴπῃ]

From whatever niche of the Heracles saga these themes depicting Athena's help to Heracles derive, they help to construe the Iliadic context. First, they justify, though from external circumstances, Athena's radical change of mood. For, after the kindness Zeus showed to Athena in lines 39–40 ("dear daughter ... with you I want to be kind"), the text needs to introduce a new context in order to justify Athena's alliance with Hera in transgressing Zeus' will. The new context is Athena's disappointment that while Zeus induces her to help him in all his plans, even the questionable ones, he is constantly thwarting her own plans, and in particular he is now frustrating her wish that the Achaeans win and destroy Troy (see XV. 70–71). She realizes with horror (see lines VIII. 358–361) that Zeus' new policy favors Thetis' plan.

The text connects Athena's disappointment to the Heracles saga, which is also one source of Hera's traditional hostility toward Zeus and his son (XIV. 250–5, XV. 15–30, XVIII. 117–19). Athena's new emotional attitude does not ensue from a coherent psychological development, but is imposed on her from an external event, belonging even to another saga. Here, as often in the *Iliad*, the event leads to a psychological explanation, while the psychological

---

**24** These reminiscences correspond metapoetically to borrowings from or allusions to the hypertext's Heracles saga: Athena reminisces about the recent past and the Poet reminisces about the hypertext. Athena's assistance to Heracles is attested for us at *Od.* xi. 626, Hes. *Theog.* 318, *Scut.* 1225–27. In Pisander's *Heracles and Theseus*, fr. 7, Athena helps Heracles at Thermopylae by sending forth hot springs for him.
**25** "Athena's remark that Thetis kissed Zeus' knees is just her malicious exaggeration." Edwards 1987, 184. Against Aristarchus' athetesis of 371–72s, West 2001, 202–203 defends the lines, adding that "371 in Athena's mouth has a fine touch of sarcasm."
**26** Harmonizing with the exaggeration of the tone, Athena calls Achilles "cities-sacker." In the *Iliad* he is not programmed to sack Troy.
**27** Strong asyndeton contrasting "He now hates me" (370).

development does not lead to the emergence of an event. After the analysis of the "quotation" technique in book XIX, through which Agamemnon is made to recite a piece of a Heracles saga (see Ch. 4.3), we can see that Athena is obviously made to quote from the same or another saga of Heracles. Through this borrowing strategy, the text attributes the non-Iliadic aspects of Athena (or of Zeus) to their hypertextual mythical image. With this I do not mean that Athena in the role of furious dissenter and hater of Zeus cannot be an Iliadic Athena, but that, for the Poet, this contrast with the role that in the *Iliad* is most consistently hers, as Zeus' collaborator,[28] is useful in making his Narratees feel some strangeness, some alien aura around her. The text identifies for its Narratees the external source when, for instance, it recalls Heracles' descent to Hades in order to steal the dog (VIII. 367–69). The entrance of this resentful Athena dramatizes the contrast between a text, the *Iliad*, and another text concerning the Heracles saga, and employs this contrast to its full force: such an Athena, borrowed from another text, will stand no great chance and have no real authority in her venture.[29] The assuredness that she habitually exhibits in the *Iliad* turns void, her penetrating mind —which she extols here at 366— fails to warn her of the vanity of her gesture, her collaboration with Zeus becomes her resentful obedience, and her enthusiastic and joyous mockery turns into a bitter smile. This attitude and role end when Zeus reprimands her and Iris insults her in the most brutal terms. Simultaneously, such an Athena, borrowed from another poetic horizon, provides the most dramatic action that the daughter of Zeus could ever accomplish in the poem. If some god had to depart from the rest of the gods' passive obedience to Zeus' order and create waves, Athena's doing this would be the most surprising and, on a personal level, the most offensive. Her rebellion against Zeus' ban provokes a crisis in the expected order of loyalties, strengthens and exacerbates the impact of Hera's and Poseidon's revolt, yet never constitutes a genuine threat to Zeus' power. The Narrator has followed a mythical model that he had already employed at I. 396–406, where Achilles mentions the story according to which this same rebellious triangle, Hera, Poseidon, and Athena, are at the head of the Olympian gods' rebellion against Zeus.[30] That

---

**28** For Athena as an embodiment of Zeus' success and power, see Kelly 2007, 423.
**29** Kelly 2007, 423 quotes Hirvonen 1968, 63: "The poorly planned expedition (sc. in VIII), so untypical of Athena, is obviously based on an older tradition in which Athena may have been more powerful than Hera and may have challenged even Zeus for power."
**30** For Kirk 1985, 93, the digression is probably Homeric. The perpetrated assault on Zeus' rule belongs to the succession myth which is prevalent in Hesiod. In the *Iliad* it appears only as an event of the past and possibly is itself an allusion to another saga. See Ch. 1.1, n. 24.

conspiracy, however, appears to have been more dangerous, and partially more successful, than the new one that Hera and Athena here organize.

When Athena says, "<u>now</u> he [Zeus] hates me," the narrative has given no indication to its Narratees that this is actually the case: on the contrary, a few moments before, Zeus had smiled on her and granted her the concession she wanted. Athena may have reasons to resent Zeus' concession to Thetis, but these reasons become clear only now, from line 361. She feels that his excess is unbearable. As Athena bitterly smiles at Zeus' affectionate words (373: "he will call me again 'my dear grey-eyed daughter'"), she implies that he tends to take advantage of her love for him. This has been true both now and in the past, in this text and in the others where the same epithet is used: her loyal alliance to Zeus functions only in his favor, never in hers (see line 361). Accordingly, his affectionate words are only a flattering rhetoric used to obtain from her what he wants.

As she says, "he will call me again 'my dear grey-eyed daughter,'" the text signals that this epithetic form for Athena is the conventional way the epic tradition refers to her and characterizes her relationship with Zeus. The *Iliad* uses the epithet (θεά) γλαυκῶπις Ἀθήνη dozens of times —once it even stands for her name (VIII. 406)— but the affectionate φίλην ("dear") is found only in this verse (VIII. 373); otherwise Zeus addresses Athena with φίλον τέκος "dear child" (VIII. 39 and XX. 183). The latter, however, is a generic form of affectionate address used also by older persons without any paternal identity when speaking to younger people. The whole affectionate expression, φίλην γλαυκώπιδα, is unique in the Poem; in his addresses to Athena, Zeus is thrifty in using the adjective φίλη. By sarcastically flaunting it as Zeus' usual form of affectionate address for her, Athena refers to a universal use, even if in the *Iliad* it is documented only three times.

The motivations and earnestness in Athena's and Hera's hostility to Zeus' plan become immediately evident as the text depicts Athena's arming scene (VIII. 384–91). She goes, as is her custom when she arms herself (see V. 734–47), to her father's palace and there she slips off her elaborate dress and dons her father's military equipment (VIII. 387–91).[31] She becomes like him. This is a curious, paradoxical detail: even in the act of betraying Zeus, her father, she still derives her military power from him and identifies herself with him. This paradox is not surprising: the arming scene in Zeus' palace with Zeus' weapons repeats the scene in book V. 733–37, 745–47 (= VIII. 384–88, 389–91), in which

---

[31] Scholars tend to consider the arming scene at VIII. 384–91 as the model of the analogous scene at V. 736–47: see West 2011, 167.

Hera and Athena intervene, with the full blessing of Zeus, against Ares, who is mangling the Achaean army. Athena arms herself in Zeus' house, donning the same description of her military implements, though here the process lasts longer, after which she and Diomedes wound Ares. This is the Athena who operates in the *Iliad* with Zeus' blessing: the repetition of the arming scene in book VIII has a specific textual purpose. The text wants to invest her with the familiar poetics of the *Iliad* and has her act as she does in the *Iliad* when she acts in agreement with Zeus and in accordance with her usual Iliadic role. Now she arms herself against him in his own house: the paradox makes sense. It is as an insider that she arms herself to act as an outsider; it is in accordance with her Iliadic persona that she plays a non-Iliadic character.

The paradoxical touch that I am illustrating becomes ostentatious in the last line of the arming scene when, at VIII. 391 (= V. 747), Athena is evoked as "the daughter of a mighty father" (ὀβριμοπάτρη): this word, in the *Iliad*, is found only in these two passages —three times in the *Odyssey*— and it sounds therefore strongly allusive. While in the first passage the evocation adheres harmoniously to the blessing of Zeus' agreement, at VIII. 391 it sounds doubly humorous: since Zeus is mighty, Athena has no chance, and since he is her father, her transgression is somehow perverse and unnatural.

Zeus becomes aware of Athena's and Hera's transgression and becomes intransigent. He sends Iris to stop them and warns them with the harshest punishments. Through Iris' message, he threatens them with lightning

> so that my grey-eyed [daughter] may learn what it means to fight against her father.
> But with Hera I am not so outraged and irate –
> it is always her way to thwart my will, whatever I command. (406–08)[32]

Zeus is deeply upset by Athena's behavior and threatens only her. The text displays the exceptionality of his indignation by this unique distinction, never made again, between Hera's dissenting role as banal and insignificant and Athena's as grievous. But Athena's behavior is crucial for the Iliadic Zeus.

---

[32] Some scholars have found suspect these two lines and the passage 420–25 that contains them, as Iris' message to Athena and Hera. See West 2001, 203 who brackets 421–4: among his arguments, he asserts that Iris should not repeat lines 407–8 as Zeus' message, since, as West fathoms, these two lines 407–8 in Zeus' speech "could be taken as a comment for Iris' benefit rather than an integral part of the message she is to deliver." If I understand well, this is a weak point: even in the interpolator's mind did Zeus change his tone of voice to indicate to Iris that these two lines were a private, confidential comment, a complicit nastiness? Whoever composed these lines, they had to be repeated by Iris to Athena. On line 420, Iris, repeating Zeus' words, uses γλαυκῶπι, the unique vocative example of the adjective (Taplin 1992, 142).

Zeus' serious reproving of Athena may even suggest a metapoetic purpose on the part of the Poet, that of announcing that his borrowing of such an image of Athena from another text is over, that this figure of the goddess is terrific, but finally employable only in her alliance with Hera. In this context, despite her force and intelligence, Athena assumes Hera's weaknesses and Hera's usually humiliating failure of her projects.

An allusive concern also emerges in Zeus' emphatic use of Athena's epithet "grey-eyed." This specific epithet connects Zeus' passage with Athena's own use of the epithet "grey-eyed" to evoke Zeus' affectionate relationship with her at VIII. 373: "there will be a day in which he will again call me 'my dear grey-eyed [child],'" implying of course that Zeus will again flatter her to obtain a new favor. Zeus sarcastically employs this endearing epithet that same day to indicate that his love for her will not prevent him from harshly punishing her if she betrays him.[33] Both complain about the abuse that the other makes of his/her affection: it is a bitter reciprocal relationship built around an endearing, but ironic, epithet. It is a reciprocal accussation of abuse, built around and endearing but ironically used epithet.

Iris, instead of ending the message with Zeus' last two lines (VIII. 407–8), adds something of her own mind, and she screams at Athena (VIII. 423–24):

> But you are an insolent, brazen bitch, if you really
> dare to raise the huge spear against Zeus.

This violent curse against Athena's unimaginable treason declares again the exceptionality of Athena's behavior in this episode.

Iris stigmatizes Athena's rebellious behavior with an authority that certainly does not come from her being a messenger, but from the Poet, who implies that indeed the behavior of Athena in this scene threatens to stand absolutely contrary to her Iliadic role.[34]

Athena's disgraceful end emphasizes Zeus' victory over his rebellious daughter: the drama is high, but the real danger for Zeus has never been too serious.

---

**33** The epithet "grey-eyed" connects a third passage to the two we are analyzing here: at VIII. 30, when Athena intervenes after Zeus' menacing speech to the gods, the poet in a formulaic verse defines Athena as "grey-eyed." A red thread runs through the three passages and creates mirroring textual effects. The Narrator knew and employed the "quotational" or "allusive" function of the epithets, even of those most commonly used.

**34** When the Narrator adds to Iris' message some point or action that her sender had not made, it is the poetic voice that sends the message to the Narratees: see, for instance, III. 139–40 and Pucci 2003.

Zeus, the father and the husband, exits smiling and triumphant. Zeus takes his place on the golden throne, and under his feet vast Olympus is shaken (VIII. 442–43):

> Meanwhile, Zeus himself, the god of the deep-thundering voice, was sitting
> on the golden throne and vast Olympus under his feet was shaken.[35]

While Zeus is presented to the audience as the lord of Olympus, Athena and Hera are staged as sitting apart, where they "did not speak nor raise questions" (οὐδέ τί μιν προσεφώνεον οὐδ' ἐρέοντο) (445). This line and the following one are used also at I. 332–33 to indicate the hesitation and worry of the embassy approaching Achilles to carry away Briseis: in our analogous scenario, Hera and Athena reveal their worry before the powerful master whose order they had planned to break.

In his mind Zeus knows their worry (VIII. 446) and addresses them by name, mockingly (VIII. 447–56):

> Why so crushed, Athena and Hera?
> Surely you did not tire yourselves in the glorious battle
> by slaughtering Trojans for whom you have horrible hatred (κότον αἰνόν);[36]
> At any rate, such is my force and so invincible are my hands (καὶ χεῖρες ἄαπτοι),
> that all the gods in Olympus would not turn me backward,
> while you! trembling, took hold of your shining limbs[37]
> before you could glimpse war and the horrid deeds of war.[38]
> For so I will speak and it would now have been accomplished:

---

35 The shaking of vast/great Olympus underlines Zeus's preeminence (see I. 530): the epithet εὐρύοπα Ζεύς often emphasizes Zeus as an inspirer of strong feelings, the giver of *kudos* and other special gifts, chief in the assembly, and master of his plan. The epithet can be translated with a reference to Zeus as master of thunder. On the other hand, literally it could also mean "of the wide glance." Line 443 is the same as Hes. *Theog.* 842, ποσσὶ δ' ὑπ' ἀθανάτοισι μέγας πελεμίζετ' Ὄλυμπος, where Zeus, in full epic glory, comes after Typhoeus with strong thunderclaps while earth, sky, Ocean, rivers, and Tartaros resound terribly. It is impossible to know who repeats whom; what is clear, however, is the portentous figure of the master. At VIII. 199, as Hera stirs in the throne, endeavoring vainly to persuade Poseidon to sedition, Olympus is shaken: an ironic sign of her delusive royalty?
36 By singling them out by name from the whole assembly, ridiculing their vain plan, and mentioning the punishments they risked receiving, Zeus produces a humiliating attack about which Athena feels savage anger (460), but wisely remains silent.
37 In this almost formulaic line, "trembling" (*tromos*) takes the mortal warriors as they face a terrible menace in a heroic danger or in some other analogous danger: such trembling never grasps a god, and a divine message causes a mortal to tremble once, when Priam encounters Iris.
38 πρὶν πόλεμόν τε ἰδεῖν πολέμοιό τε μέρμερα ἔργα. "The repetition of πόλεμόν and πολέμοιό emphasizes their avoidance of it." Kirk 1990, 333.

Once hit by the lightning bolt, you could not come back
on your car to Olympus,³⁹ to the place of the immortals.

His violence and sarcasm are easily won, just as his victory has been. Here he repeats the boast of his physical force when there is no real necessity to do so. He threatens them with the same violent punishment as earlier (VIII. 401–05), now that it is no longer necessary to accomplish it. It is a sort of reverse deterrent.

His whole assault, however, is merely verbal, mocking, and self-comforting: he speaks to his wife and daughter with a tone that carries at once the violence of political aggression —he speaks before the assembly— and the intimacy of a family quarrel. This ambiguous tone of address marks the disparate roles of the addresser and the addressees, and the passage is not one of the most felicitous poetic performances of the Iliadic dramatization of Zeus. The mocking insolence is too facile and the assertion of the escaped punishment unduly vengeful and violent.

By emphasizing Zeus' divergent evaluation of Hera's and Athena's insubordinations, the external textual source of Athena's role, and Zeus' easy victory, my interpretation contests the reading that attributes to Hera and Athena the greatest threat to *dios boule* as Kelly 2007, 337 and 422–24,⁴⁰ for instance, assumes.

Hera cannot contain her rage and asks Zeus whether she and Athena can help the Achaeans by offering useful advice (VIII. 462–67).⁴¹ She demands the same favor that Athena obtained from Zeus at VIII. 31–37: she uses almost the same words, but with some modifications: she refuses to address Zeus with full epic panoply, as Athena had done at VIII. 31. She instead uses the standard line that she repeats whenever she disagrees with Zeus: "Most terrible son of Kronos, what sort of words have you spoken?" The contrast between the two addresses is intentional and qualifies Hera's address as disrespectful of the divine ruler.⁴²

---

39 Zeus means that their car would have been utterly destroyed by lightning.
40 "Athene's action in book eight comprises a serious challenge to Zeus' hegemony, for it is the rebellion of a figure who represents the very things guaranteeing his power." Kelly 2007, 423.
41 The text intends Hera still to be provoking Zeus and, full of rage (461), attempting to match his power. Notice on line 466: "if you order so," instead of what Athena had said (35): "as you order," by which Hera would still question the reality, legitimacy, etc. of Zeus' ban. See Kirk 1990, ad 463–8 who finds the passage unobjectionable: "its tone of modified defiance providing a motive for Zeus' further threat at 470 ff. on what he will do on the morrow."
42 αἰνότατε Κρονίδη ποῖον τὸν μῦθον ἔειπες. This line is used six times by Hera (I. 552, IV. 25, VIII. 462, XIV. 330, XVI. 440, XVIII. 361) as Hera contests points presented by Zeus. In the *Iliad*, it is in these six lines that the epithet Κρονίδης is used in the vocative. The name "Zeus" is not

This different form of address reveals immediately the difference in tone and context between the two repeated passages (463–8 = 32–37). This repetition, with its insistent use of quotation as merely formal and passive, emphasizes the text's disregard for the different occasions, contexts, and psychological identities in the passages. It produces in the audience, therefore, the effect of strong narrative surprise: Hera's request is unexpected and sounds like a jarring impropriety. Hera does not give up, and wants at least to be able to continue to do what she did with success when she advised Agamemnon, after Zeus consented to Athena that she could engage in this practice. Yet the context here is completely unfavorable to Hera's request and the narrative traps Hera by producing a result that does not repeat the success of the earlier passage.

We realize the textual irony of leaving us uncertain about the result of this repeated request, until the text traps Hera (and us) by the surprise of her abject failure and humiliation.

For, instead of receiving Zeus' consent, as Athena did, Hera receives a violent rebuke with the promise of a massacre of the Achaeans by the Trojans (VIII. 470–82):

> At dawn, my ox-eyed queen Hera, you will see,
> if you want,[43] an even more omnipotent son of Kronos
> vastly destroying the army of the Achaean warriors:
> strong Hector will not refrain from fighting
> until the quick-footed son of Peleus has been stirred to action
> beside his ship, on the day when at the sterns of the ships[44]
> they will be fighting in most dreadful distress over dead Patroclos.
> For so it is divinely ordained (ὣς γὰρ θέσφατόν ἐστι),[45] and for you and your anger I care not.

---

mentioned and only this patronymic appears with the qualification "most awful." It is difficult here for the Narratees to fathom the specific connotation of her reference to Kronos: is Zeus as violent as Kronos was? And even more violent, since he crushed his father? Athena uses once the vocative *Kronidê* at VIII. 31, as we have seen, with full epic panoply.

**43** An analogous way to introduce a prophetic event is used by Achilles at IX. 358–61: but Achilles does not use the third person to speak about himself and, contrary to Zeus' prophecy, he will not act in the way he promises. Zeus indeed accomplishes what he announces.

**44** Zeus uses overstatement to cow Hera: at XVIII. 172 the fighting goes on "in front of the ships." Macleod 1982, 96. However, Nannini 1995, 76 presumes that in a primitive version the duel between Hector and Achilles took place around the body of Patroclos and close to the ships.

**45** Zeus identifies his own decision with a divine decree, i.e. with himself, since, of course, he is the initiator and guarantor of that fate. On the meaning and significance of this word see

This is the first time in the poem where Zeus declares his decision (*boulê*) to the gods and offers scanty details of some events in his plan. And he does so by speaking of himself in the third person, the non-person: "you will see...an even more omnipotent son of Kronos" (καὶ μᾶλλον ὑπερμενέα Κρονίωνα): the force of this syntax excludes the subject from the interaction between the "I" and the "You." Zeus is now inaccessible to dialogue and persuasion. Of course, he was already so before, but now his open sarcasm tinges his autocratic position with an explicitly self-conscious tone. He is the one placed outside and above the interaction of his family circle.[46]

He defines himself as "the son of Kronos" (καὶ μᾶλλον ὑπερμενέα Κρονίωνα) which now is not an epithet, but his specific definition of himself from an objective point of view: of course, he wants to emphasize both his royal role as Kronos' son and his own greater force.

Then Zeus turns to Hera and blasts her with a brutal dismissal (VIII. 477b–83):

> not even if you should reach[47] the lowest regions
> of earth and sea, where Kronos and Japetus sit
> enjoying not a ray of Hyperion Sun, not a breeze,
> and the depth of Tartarus surrounds them:
> not even if you should go and wander there, I care nothing for you
> and your anger: none is a meaner bitch than you.[48]

Here Zeus' marital and political tones are identified and form a straightforward, insolent attack. Zeus means that he does not care if Hera, by behaving as she does, should be sent to Tartarus. He threatens to end their marriage. The mention of Tartarus is rare in the *Iliad* and its theme appears to be an archaic one (Chantraine 1934, 288): it alludes to the punishment of the Titans and we may assume here —as at VIII. 12–17— that Zeus considers the god who would potentially dare to break his order as a challenger to his power and thus as one who deserves the same lot as the Titans.

---

Ford 1992, 182: "Zeus in particular is the god who can pronounce or know what is *thesphatos* (e.g. *Il.* 8, 477, Hesiod fr. 193. 8 M-W)."
**46** He had already used the third person to speak of himself in line 22: see Muellner 1997, 152.
**47** On the conditional sentence with the subjunctive often accompanied by *ke*, see Chantraine *GH* II, pp. 279–80.
**48** Kirk 1990, *ad loc*. notices the ring-composition of the passage. Indeed, it ends with a much stronger statement than at its beginning. The "bitch" is an image that insults a traitor: Helen uses the same image against herself, the betrayer of Menelaus and Sparta.

## 5.3 Sex without Love

It is difficult to fathom Zeus' attitude toward Hera: he at once threatens her with the strongest punishments and dismisses her as a sort of obsessive, but insignificant, antagonist, as he compares her to Athena (VIII. 407–8):

> Yet with Hera I am not so angry, neither indignant,
> since it is ever her way to thwart whatever I order.

It is only after her useless sexual aggression that Hera becomes helpful and protects Zeus' role as dispenser of destinies, as we have seen in Sarpedon's episode. Yet, before that attack, Hera is the one who tries to organize a subversive alliance against Zeus' ban, not only with Athena, but also with Poseidon. She tries to enlist an important god, a good fighter. As she hears Hector's triumphing words (VIII. 185–97), she feels anger and

> she stirred in her throne and caused large Olympus to shake (ἐλέλιξε δὲ μακρὸν Ὄλυμπον)[49]
> and she spoke to the great god Poseidon:

She is represented in the act of manifesting her royal power and ambition, but her ambition sounds much stronger than her power.

Turning to Poseidon, she reminds him of the Danaans' cult for him, of his "desire for their victory" (σὺ δέ σφισι βούλεο νίκην)[50] and proposes to him a subversive alliance against Zeus' ban (205–207):

> If all of us who are helping the Danaans were ready and willing
> to push back the Trojans and restrain deep-thundering Zeus,
> he would sit there all grieving, alone, on Ida.

This is a gesture of open challenge to Zeus, a gesture grounded on the only authority Hera possesses, that of being Zeus' wife. The tremendous force of that adjective "alone," in "grieving alone on Ida," suggests her ambition of reversing the privilege of power: Zeus would be abandoned by the gods and she could

---

**49** Kelly 2007, 425: "Like Zeus… she shakes Olympos *tamquam vir* before attempting unsuccessfully to persuade Poseidon to join her." All Hera's attempts to play a monarchic role, fail.
**50** Kelly 2007, 124: This expression, σὺ δέ σφισι βούλεο νίκην, is generally used by the narrative in the third person. This (VIII. 204) "is the only occasion where a god mentions to another a determination in this regard. Hera's appropriation and manipulation of this figure as a persuasive device is a poor choice [in light of the frequent lack of success of this device] and so doomed to fail" (p. 425). She tries but fails to use traditional syntax *quasi in loco poetae*.

then gain his hierarchical role. The text introduces this plan by having her cause the shaking of Olympus on 199: ἐλέλιξε δὲ μακρὸν Ὄλυμπον, and by using the same words at the end of the line as at I. 530, where Zeus causes the shaking of Olympus when he manifests to Thetis his resolution to honor Achilles.[51] By repeating that manifestation of power, the text shows Hera as a pathetic copy of Zeus and grants her a "delusive royalty," as Piettre correctly says.

Poseidon immediately rebukes Hera (VIII. 209–11):

> Hera, of the reckless word, what sort of word have you spoken!
> I am not willing to fight against Zeus, son of Kronos,
> I and the others, since he is by far much stronger.

Part of line 209 recalls the line that Hera throws against Zeus six times, when she rebukes him for one of his proposals: the text wants us to see how Hera can easily be parodied in her postures and pretensions.

The fact that Poseidon, in this specific context, calls Zeus "son of Kronos," may help us understand the connotative substance of this epithet. For Poseidon is himself a son of Kronos, and if he calls Zeus "son of Kronos," it is evidently not to remind Hera that he himself is the brother of Zeus, but to attribute to Zeus the political and hierarchical role that Kronos had among the gods.[52] Yet, more importantly, Poseidon evokes Kronos here to remind Hera and the gods that Zeus crushed him and keeps him captive under Hades.[53]

The *Iliad* must silently imply that there is a consensus among the gods in Olympus to hold the Titans in captivity in Tartaros where Zeus has placed them after having defeated them —according to the Hesiodean version— in personal combat. The memory of the Titans surfaces occasionally in the poem: a specific and significant allusion surfaces in the episode of Hera's seduction of Zeus. The Titans represent, of course, the divine hierarchy governing the world before Zeus and the Olympians; they evoke the shadow of an order that Zeus has replaced and which can never return. Their imprisonment causes no regret and no sense of guilt in any of the Olympian gods.

It is perhaps significant that the memory of the Titans in their captivity surfaces at least twice in relation to Hera's rebellious aims and activity, as we will see in the next chapter.

---

[51] Piettre 1996, 72–73 takes this example as another instance of Hera's "royauté décevante."
[52] As I have already remarked, the text never attributes to Poseidon the patronymic epithet recalling his descendance from Kronos, save once in a dual form, together with Zeus (XIII. 345).
[53] The bibliography on aspects of Hera as character is immense and is listed by Kelly 2007, 424, n. 18. Add Pirenne-Delforge/Pironti 2016 and Pironti/Bonnet 2016.

The long scene during which Hera induces Zeus to make love with her, so that he falls asleep (XIV. 153–XV. 77), is today interpreted as a moment of pleasing intermezzo between the war scenes. It evokes that side of the divine world that, in balanced contrast to its sublime tension, is defined, since Reinhardt, as its "frivolity."

The lightly comic element, the humor, the sensuousness of the episode are praised by Leaf (1902, 2. 62); Janko is no less eloquent when he writes: "The deception of Zeus is a bold, brilliant, graceful, sensuous and above all amusing virtuoso performance, wherein Homer parades his mastery of the other types of epic composition in his repertoire.[54] [...] Hera's intervention...entirely fulfills its aim – to retard further Zeus' plan, while the ships' fate hangs in the balance." This interpretation of the episode as an amusing intermezzo has sometimes contributed to the critical view that the gods in the *Iliad* are a poetic source of comedy.[55]

The episode is more festive than frivolous, surreally ironic rather than amusing, with very serious implications as the subtext of the fantastic story: it elaborates old mythical themes which, if they were not treated by the *Iliad* with an ironic tinge, would undercut the Iliadic Olympian structure.

The episode belongs to the general theme of the tense relationship between Zeus and Hera. This theme, as we have seen, is anchored in the hypertext from which our text derives and re-elaborates, with specific intents, the tone and certain motifs of its source. I underscore here the point that Hera in the *Iliad* does not undermine Zeus because of her jealousy and resentment for his rich progeny of great characters, but exclusively because she dissents from Zeus' management of the war. Hera's jealousy is recalled in past episodes, but never as a present inducement to act.

This is the last episode in the poem about the tense relationship between Zeus and Hera. At the end of the episode Hera is frightened and humiliated (see

---

54 Ancient and modern interpreters have tried to explain the divine erotic farce as an allegory or otherwise, see Lamberton 1986. Pironti 2016, 85–110 refuses the literary definitions and the anthropomorphic moral judgments as the interpretative frames of the story, and points to the polytheistic effects of the interrelation of the divine figures and to the echoes to and from other mythical stories that the episode emanates.

55 See for instance Redfield 1975, 76: "The gods in the *Iliad* are lacking in numen: they are in fact the chief source of comedy in the poem. We can, I think, explain this difference most easily by assuming that the gods in the *Iliad* belong to the conventional world of epic and were understood as such by the audience. Just as the epic tells, not of men, but of heroes, so also it tells stories, not of gods conceived as actual, but of literary gods." Herodotus would not agree with Redfield.

XV. 90) and agrees to collaborate fully with Zeus. She begins, indeed, to follow his instructions and, starting with her suggestions in Sarpedon's episodes, she substantially collaborates with Zeus' governing role until the last book.

The scene begins with a double and contrary glance by Hera "of the golden throne"[56] (XIV. 153 ff.): a look full of sympathy for Poseidon, who is helping the Achaeans ("she rejoiced in her heart"), and a bitter glance at Zeus, sitting on mount Ida ("in her heart he was hateful").

The Narrator uses Hera as the focalizer (*eiseide* 153 and 158, *egnô* 154 etc.) in the description of the situation. Poseidon receives an almost full line of epithets (154): αὐτοκασίγνητον καὶ δαέρα ("her very brother and her husband's brother"), an expression that is unique in the *Iliad*, while in the next line Zeus' name is mentioned without any epithet.[57] The emphatic family relationship that through the paternity of Kronos comes to light recalls Zeus' brotherly and equal status with Hera and Poseidon. Hera's clever choice of the epithets inserts Zeus into a network of family relations and eliminates his roles as a monotheistic ruler and master of destinies that are his distinction in the *Iliad*. Through her focalization, the text shows us that Hera embraces an earlier mythical reference, when the roles of the gods on Olympus were still undecided.

This treatment anticipates the coming into the foreground of Poseidon and the removal of Zeus and of his sovereign power from the center of action. We recall that, at VIII. 197 ff., Hera had attempted to enlist Poseidon in a rebellion against Zeus' orders, but he had refused, because, as he said, Zeus is more powerful than all the gods. Now, on the contrary, taking advantage of Zeus' distraction due to his cosmic duties (XIII. 1–10), Poseidon in secret (XIII. 352 and 357) helps the Achaeans. A double conspiracy emerges when Hera decides to beguile Zeus' mind and make him fall asleep. Both conspirators fear Zeus' force and act against him while taking care not to be perceived in their fraud. The text, therefore, intimates Zeus' omnipotence by displaying his antagonists' humiliating fear as they attempt to avoid having to confront him.

By showing Hera's and Poseidon's weakness and fear of confronting Zeus, the *diêgêsis* may allude to the traditional myth of succession, in which Zeus'

---

[56] In the archaic period, this epithet χρυσόθρονος, besides having the meaning "of the golden throne" (from θρόνος), may have meant "draped in gold," with a possible reference to the nuptial coat, from θρόνα "ornaments woven on a clothing, flower": see Chantraine, *DELG* on θρόνα and Pirenne-Delforge/Pironti 2016, 26–27 who assume the possibility of a polysemy for the ancient audience. The epithet qualifies Hera when she is in close proximity of Zeus (I. 611, XV. 5 or making eye contact with him XIV. 153): this epithet defines her at the beginning and the end of our episode. Otherwise, in the *Iliad*, only Artemis has this epithet (IX. 534).

[57] The accusative form *Zêna* is unique in the entire *Iliad*.

monarchic role is threatened by competitors such as Poseidon or others.[58] Even after Zeus' victory, rivalries unfold: Earth produces the last dangerous enemy, Typhoeus, and Prometheus' provocation contests Zeus' supreme power. The *Theogony* and part of the *Works and Days* unravel as an important theme the consolidation of Zeus' authority against Prometheus' provocations.

In the *Iliad* there are no real threats from divine successors (see Collobert 2011, 38–39). Even during the episode of Thetis' supplication in the first book of the *Iliad*, there is no explicit allusion to the danger —which the audience may have recognized— that Zeus' having a child with her would pose to him. There is, however, the recollection, by Achilles, of an old story that belongs to the traditional succession myth. According to Achilles' account, it was a familiar topic in Peleus' house —a story ensconced in the hypertext?— that Thetis had saved Zeus from the subversive plot of Hera, Poseidon, and Athena (I. 396–406). If they should conspire anew against Zeus' *boulê*, Zeus will now need no help to defeat their plot. He will succeed all alone, which is what will happen and what audience and readers expect him to do. They know from the first assembly that Zeus' monarchic command over the Olympian gods is stable and sure.

Homer invites his readers to realize that Hera's, Poseidon's, and Athena's plot is a past event that has become a family legend and that commands no authority in the days of the action narrated in the *Iliad*.[59] My suggestion that Poseidon's fear of being discovered by Zeus is an ironic allusion to past myths of succession is sustained at the end of the episode when Poseidon is shown to be immensely relieved that he can avoid fighting against Zeus without losing face. The *Iliad* proves here again its newness and its pleasure in destabilizing and smiling ironically at other versions of the hypertext.

The *diêgêsis* steeps Hera's decision —to seduce Zeus sexually— in a "typical" *mermerizein* scene (scene of introspection and decision) (XIV. 159–62):

And then she pondered, ox-eyed lady Hera (βοῶπις πότνια Ἥρη),
how she could deceive the mind of aegis-bearing Zeus;[60]
and in her heart this came to light as the best plan,
to go to Ida, to adorn herself beautifully...

---

**58** See Louden 2005, 97 ff.
**59** Thetis' supplication to Zeus makes a covert allusion to the help she gave to Zeus on that occasion, but the reference does not move Zeus and when she reiterates the supplication she avoids alluding to it again.
**60** As Bakker shows (1997, 198), the two lines 159–60 are so built as to contrast the two epithets at the end of each line.

With the epithets of 159–60, the text now displays the Narrator as a focalizer who is favorable toward Zeus. Through the metrical parallelism of the two epithetic phrases, the text brings into relief differing images of the two figures: an archaic and theriomorphic image depicts Hera (βοῶπις πότνια Ἥρη), while Zeus appears with the mind/intelligence of an unconquerable fighter (Διὸς νόον αἰγιόχοιο):[61] of course, the owner of the aegis, the god with invincible hands.

The Narrator could have used a metrically parallel epithetic phrase to describe Hera's white splendor and beauty and fill line 159: θεὰ λευκώλενος Ἥρη ("the goddess Hera of the white arms"). This epithetic phrase would have depicted her more appropriately for her seductive task than the theriomorphic image of "ox-eyed lady Hera." Pirenne-Delforge/Pironti 2016, 25 assume, without any evidence (see p. 47, n. 90), that the theriomorphic epithet celebrates Hera's large and beautiful eyes. But the prevalence of the theriomorphic epithet in contexts where Hera stands in an antagonistic relationship with Zeus invites one to think that the Poet saw in the theriomorphic epithet a connotation not improper in these contexts.[62] In the whole episode (XIV. 153–353), the text uses the theriomorphic image three times (159, 222, 263): in two of them θεὰ λευκώλενος Ἥρη would have been possible, but it occurs only once, on 277, in a conventional introductory line repeated four times in the poem.

---

**61** The expression "blends the formulae Διὸς νόος and Δ. αἰγιόχοιο" (Janko 1992, 173). See *Hymn to Aphrodite* 36, where Aphrodite καί τε παρὲκ Ζηνὸς νόον ἤγαγε τερπικεραύνου, "led astray the mind of Zeus that delights in the thunderbolt." And compare with XIV. 217, where "persuasion" lies in Aphrodite's magic strap: ἥ τ' ἔκλεψε νόον πύκα περ φρονεόντων, "steals the mind away even of thoughtful men."

**62** Hera's purpose here of seducing Zeus would suggest that the Poet should choose the epithet that directly enhances Hera's beautiful splendor: θεὰ λευκώλενος Ἥρη; but he does not, as Hera is concocting a plan against Zeus. Where Hera acts without contesting or even in accordance with Zeus' plan, the Poet selects the "white arms" epithet to celebrate openly and explicitly her beauty. This is evident at I. 55, 195, 208 where the epithet θεὰ λευκώλενος Ἥρη celebrates Hera's beauty. Even more evident is the whole scene in which Hera, with the consent of Zeus, brings help to the Achaeans together with Athena: this epithet is used five times in the fifth book (V. 711, 755, 767, 775, 784), a repetition that is sometimes taken as an example of oral composition (see Rossi 1994, 41), while the other epithet, βοῶπις πότνια Ἥρη, never occurs. The Poet made a choice and in depicting Hera's cooperation with Zeus chose θεὰ λευκώλενος Ἥρη and rejected the other. He must have felt stylistic and connotative reasons for this selection, attributive features that escape us. Perhaps the Poet understood a specific value in the theriomorphic epithet; maybe he valued its archaic, evocative force, placing her in a, for us, unknown mythical time and configuration; or he preferred the generalizing epithet πότνια —which is also used as "mistress of the house" for highly esteemed mortal ladies (VI. 413, etc.)— instead of θεά; or for other reasons that are unavailable to us. See also Ch. 1.2 n. 59.

Hera's "best decision"[63] is to adorn herself, go to Ida, and induce Zeus to lie in love with her, so that he then falls asleep (163–65). It is an odd and unexpected decision: we would imagine that she might join Poseidon, already busy on the battlefield, since a little while earlier (VIII. 199–207) she had asked him to join her to fight in favor of the Achaeans.

Hera moves to her chamber and begins her toilette and wardrobe: the description of her toilette comes close to the toilette of Aphrodite in *Hy. Aphr.* 58–65, as Janko (1992, 171) shows, singling out the same lines: *Hy. Aphr.* 60–63 = XIV. 169–72.

Since Hera's toilette presents its charms in the narrative of the *Iliad*, it becomes structurally analogous to the arming scenes of the champions as they prepare themselves for battle (*e.g.* XI. 16–48, XIX. 369–91).[64] Janko touches on certain comparable echoes: for instance, Hera's final headdress recalls the helmets in the military dressing scenes, and by itself suggests the different contexts of the *Iliad*'s and the *Hymn*'s narratives. I note that also the political effects are deeply different.

First, Aphrodite does not seek out any secrecy when composing her toilette (the Charites wash her and anoint her, 61), while Hera's secrecy is strongly emphasized (167–69): it recalls the same prudent behavior of Poseidon and creates an atmosphere of deception around her initial gesture.[65] Of course, this is her goal, and we should not view her purpose with moralizing eyes: Zeus, Athena, Aphrodite, and other gods deceive in order to achieve their goals.

Aphrodite dresses in a very simple robe and carries a limited number of ornaments in her toilette: there is no "girdle with one hundred tassels," as there is in Hera's toilette (XIV. 181: ζώνῃ ἑκατὸν θυσάνοις ἀραρυίῃ): this girdle is a mismatch with the peplos (Janko), but reminds us of the tasseled aegis of Zeus – the god is mentioned as "carrier of the aegis" on line 160.

Aphrodite's toilette that aims to seduce Anchises has no military allusions: she wants to seduce him because she is in love with him; on the contrary, Hera's toilette functions as her weapon to seduce Zeus so as to conspire against his policy. The two toilettes stem from, and nurse, opposite feelings and have opposite purposes, peace and war respectively.

---

[63] "Surprisingly, the first part of 159 (5x Hom.) precedes 161 nowhere else; *Il.* 3–5 is the closest parallel." Janko 1992, 173. Pironti 2016, 89, n. 5: "among the gods, the line [161] is exclusive for Zeus (*Il.* II. 5) and Hera; and in both contexts their *boulê* turns out to be a deception."

[64] Taplin 1992, 171: "Hera girds herself for 'battle' with items of toilet that play on an arming scene (14. 175–86)." See also Reinhardt 1961, 291; Edwards 1987, 247ff.

[65] At line 189, Hera correctly wants to speak secretly with the goddess of love because Hera is inventing a false purpose for obtaining the miraculous strap.

Hera's fragrance spreads from Zeus' house and fills "earth and sky alike" (XIV. 173–74: Διὸς κατὰ χαλκοβατὲς δῶ / ἔμπης ἐς γαῖάν τε καὶ οὐρανὸν ἵκετ' ἀϋτμή), an effect that is hyperbolic and, therefore, a source of epic grandeur. What sort of grandeur in this case? May it subtly suggest and at once undermine Hera's universal ambitions? She can only fill the world with her fragrance, not with her voice, lightning bolts, will, and plans, as Zeus does. Another undercurrent is possible: by what Milman Parry called a calembour, *autmê* "perfume" could echo *autê* "cry of war," which often is described as "reaching heaven" (e.g. XIV. 60: ἀϋτὴ δ' οὐρανὸν ἵκει). This echo would invite the Narratees to connect the spreading of the perfume with the military correspondent of spreading the war cry.

The hyperbole continues to aggrandize the magnificent quality of her toilette: the adjective *ambrosios*, with its vast epic meaning ("divine," "immortal," "excellent") occurs four times in ten lines (170, 172, 177, 178).

Athena —the sometime colleague of Hera's conspiracies— is mentioned (178), but only as a weaver who created the robe for Hera:

> she dressed in an ambrosian robe that Athena
> had made her, with art and with many figures on it.

It is difficult to tell how the audience interpreted this allusion to Athena. It reminds us of Athena's role in the creation of Pandora (Hesiod, *Works and Days* 63–64), rather than of the Athena of the *Iliad*. Just as the initial mention of Hephaistos —"her son"— who built the *thalamos* for her (166–67) —evokes the domestic, familiar, and peaceful Olympian life, so also Athena as weaver emphasizes this precise connection. These surprising and jarring narrative touches may be intended to bring out more forcefully a contrast with the goddess' subversive motivation for her action.

The headdress —which generally functions as a symbol of chastity— here emphasizes the splendor of Hera's whole etiquette (XIV. 184–85):

> and the lady goddess covered her head with a headdress,
> beautiful, new, shining like the sun.

> κρηδέμνῳ δ' ἐφύπερθε καλύψατο δῖα θεάων
> καλῷ νηγατέῳ· λευκὸν δ' ἦν ἠέλιος ὥς·

The last clause is a simile posited by the Poet and is "typical" of the toilette scene (Janko). This is a flattering compliment by the Poet, who adapts with some perversity that "typical" theme. Often, in the description of armor, the Poet singles out, through a starry simile, a piece of the armor, the shield or the helmet or the spear (see for instance XI. 44–45, XXII. 317–19). Here the headdress would be the equivalent of the helmet. Its shining like the sun is a new hyperbole that crowns the description of her toilette with flattering tones. If I am correct, the perversity of the whole description lies precisely in the false innocence and questionable purpose that constantly underlies Hera's toilette. The poetic voice purposely stages the traditional theme of a woman beautifying herself for marriage and stages it in a context in which the beautifying theme is employed to betray the spouse and damage domestic tranquility. The scene unfolds little by little as the repetition of Hera's and Zeus' marriage, but even in this exciting descriptive repetition, Hera's hostile purpose is never completely absent. If I have emphasized certain notes that seem to echo Zeus' characteristics, it has been in order to underline Hera's ambivalence: I am far from intimating that she takes possession of his figure, but rather simply imply that her performance obliquely suggests something of her husband's grandeur.

After arming, champions go forth to meet the enemy, and here Hera goes to meet Aphrodite, who, in the general context of the *Iliad*, is an enemy of Hera in the war and her rival in beauty; but now she acts as a helper and gives Hera the magic erotic charm.[66] Some Narratees may find it odd that the extraordinary display of Hera's rich and seductive toilette is not sufficient to achieve her purpose and that Hera needs additional help, professional help, as it seems, from the goddess of love. But this double type of help occurs elsewhere: Achilles, for instance, succeeds through his spear and Zeus' initial help in adapting Hector's armor. Analogously, Hera succeeds through her beauty and through the magic of Aphrodite's charm.

Hera's visit to Aphrodite opens up a scenario in which her deceit becomes explicit and her role of supplementing Zeus acquires new allusive connotations. The process begins with Aphrodite's staging address to Hera (194): Ἥρη πρέσβα θεὰ θύγατερ μεγάλοιο Κρόνοιο ("Hera, ancient goddess, daughter of great Kro-

---

**66** Again, some modern critics take the scene of the visit as a product of the epic machinery. Janko 1992, 178: "With a minimal preamble, we find ourselves in the first of two unheralded developments, all the funnier for their unexpectedness —Hera's request for Aphrodite's magic love-charm. Metaphorically, she needs Aphrodites' aid, if Zeus is to desire her, just as she needs Sleep if he is to slumber, but this is imagined as usual in anthropomorphic terms." Hera needs Aphrodite's real aid and the real magic strap. It is this magic band that seduces Zeus and that affects his wise mind. In Janko's interpretation, the imagined scene is the anthropomorphic dramatization of a metaphor —what is also called epic machinery, or beautification— and gives fictional, dramatic life to a metaphor. In my reading, the scene is real: Hera actually visits Aphrodite. "Hera's invented purpose of the strap is also a real event: it evokes the divine world before Kronos and Zeus and shows the direction of Hera's imagination."

nos"), which answers Hera's maternal "dear child" (190). Aphrodite's epithetic line identifies Hera as a goddess of the old generation, like Zeus and Poseidon, and as the daughter of "great Kronos," the earlier king of the gods.[67] Zeus, as Hera's husband, will be mentioned later. The same line in the same vocative form is used later by Sleep on XIV. 243 and in the nominative form by the *diêgêsis* on V. 721 and VIII. 383. Pirenne-Delforge/Pironti 2016, 30 underscore the importance that this description attributes to Hera, since it seems to grant her – as she certainly believes – a share in Zeus' authority: "Sa position généalogique en tant que fille de Kronos est un élément crucial pour comprendre la nature et le fonctionnement du couple qu'elle forme avec Zeus, dont elle partage les mêmes parents. [...] Elle est même plus proche de lui que ne le sont ses frères, Poséidon et Hadès, dans la mesure où elle semble participer de l'autorité souveraine de Zeus." It is just this participation that Zeus denies her (see I. 549–50, 561–67) and that she will never obtain. In the tradition, Zeus gained his exclusive position through his victorious fights against the Titans and against successive pretenders, and he preserves it through his greater force.[68]

Hera turns to Aphrodite (197–99):

> Then, with deceiving purpose, mistress Hera replied her:
> "Give me love and desire with which you subdue all
> immortal gods and mortal men."

The Narrator – in accordance with the Muses – is the focalizer who, knowing well Hera's intended trickery, grants her a sort of hymnic tone. We are again reminded of the *Hymn to Aphrodite* (see 2–3, 33–35 and in relation to our episode 33–44) and of the segment of absolute power that each god holds in his/her own domain. Soon Hera will praise Hypnos as "lord of all gods and all men" (233), and we think of Zeus as "father [i.e. "ruler"] of gods and men." The multivalent mights of the respective gods could not be better represented and aggrandized. It may happen that one god's power overwhelms the absolute power of another, as occurs in the *Hymn to Aphrodite*, where Zeus induces Aphrodite to fall in love with a mortal, against her will (45–55). Zeus is, then, stronger than Aphrodite even in her domain of love.

The gods' absolute control in their respective domains is not a stable and objective theological status, since the different poetic genres and different poems within each genre confer specific powers to their gods. The singular might

---

[67] Of course, Hera's relation to Zeus her brother is asserted with pride by Hera on several occasions (see IV. 58–9) or mentioned by the *diêgêsis* (XVI. 432 etc.).
[68] See Hera's assertion about her equality of genealogy and rank with Zeus at IV. 57–61.

of each god is therefore a poetic attribution, such that different genres and different poems may well disagree on the specific and exclusive power of the gods whom the poetic creation is about to celebrate.

Propounding her lie to Aphrodite, Hera says that she intends to stop the hostility between Okeanos and Têthus and to reestablish love and sexual relations between them. In Hesiodean terms, this would mean rekindling Ouranos' sexual visits to Gaia and renewing their symbolic meaning —the conjunction of earth and sky. In diverging myths, the first separation, anthropomorphized as a quarrel, was between either Sky and Earth or, as here, between Sky —Tethys is the daughter of Ouranos— and Ocean, a liquid version of earth. In our passage, "Homer extracts humor from the idea that if their quarrel ends, the world will revert to the primitive chaos" (Janko 1992, 181). Hera's project is a lie and the Narratees know that she has no intention of reinitiating the intolerable pressure of Sky upon Earth, but Aphrodite believes her, approves the idea, and gives her the magic love-charm. Aphrodite, as the goddess of love, is not an adversary to that sexual relationship. Furthermore, Aphrodite may think that if Hera, who "sleeps in the arms of Zeus who is the best" (213),[69] has so decided, there must be a valid reason.

Accordingly, even if audiences and readers recognize the lie and the great menace inherent in Hera's project, they understand from Aphrodite's reaction the consistency of that insane project. Her purported project evokes the return of the original chaos —the destabilization of the whole universe, a new division of spatial powers, and the establishment of a new royal dynasty. It is a false scheme, of course, but the text allows us to see through what sorts of paths Hera's imagination moves. Accordingly, it is hard to fathom whether "the ancient narratees found Hera's project humorously or bitterly ironic."[70]

Trusting in Hera's purpose, Aphrodite gives her the magic "broidered strap" (κεστὸν ἱμάντα, 214), a charm carried hidden around her breast. In this magic object "all the enchantments reside" (XIV. 215–17):

> in it there is love, in it there is desire; in it love-whispers
> and dear persuasion that steals the mind away even of thoughtful beings.[71]

---

**69** Griffin 1980, 66: "Aphrodite lends the charm with the unconsciously ironical remark that 'It would not be right to deny your request, for you sleep in the arms of mighty Zeus.'"
**70** I agree with Kelly's interpretation (2007, 424) of Hera's invented project: "...the whole scene abounds with undercurrents of *stasis*, not the least of which is Here's mention of the marital difficulties between Okeanos and Thetys...".
**71** ἔνθα δέ οἱ θελκτήρια πάντα τέτυκτο.

A quick comparison of this description with the description of Zeus' "aegis" at V. 738 ff. shows that the magical content of the "aegis" is itemized analogously to the magical list of powers in the embroidered strap:

> the betasselled aegis,
> terrible, that Terror crowns all around,
> and in it there is Fight, there is Force, there is heart-freezing Rout,
> and there is Gorgon's head, the horrible monster,
> terrible and awful, portent of Zeus who carries the aegis.[72]

Aphrodite's "embroidered strap" is a "unicum," just as the "aegis" is: both are the property and portents of a specific god; both consist in an assemblage of all the forces that universally relate to their specific action. The one makes people unable to fight and paralyzes their courage, the other makes men and gods unable to resist sex and paralyzes their sound mind. These two objects materialize the specific might of their respective gods, just as the Golden Scales materialize the course of destiny that Zeus controls.

We understand why Zeus falls immediately under the power of Hera's seduction (294: "As he saw her, Eros encompassed his wise mind" (ὡς δ' ἴδεν, ὥς μιν ἔρως πυκινὰς φρένας ἀμφεκάλυψεν).[73] Through the magic of the strap, the specific power of Aphrodite is transferred to Hera, so that she —as the wife of Zeus— her body, and her toilette acquire Aphrodisian seductive powers. We will analyze the whole scene later.

Having obtained the formidable erotic charm, Hera needs the help of Hypnos (Sleep), "brother of Death" (XIV. 231): as she meets him, she presents her request[74] (XIV. 233–37):

---

ἔνθ' ἔνι μὲν φιλότης, ἐν δ' ἵμερος, ἐν δ' ὀαριστὺς
πάρφασις, ἥ τ' ἔκλεψε νόον πύκα περ φρονεόντων.
Taplin 1992, 171 compares the strap to "a shield or baldric which with its terrifying motifs is ornamented appropriately for its function."
72 αἰγίδα θυσσανόεσσαν
δεινήν, ἣν περὶ μὲν πάντῃ Φόβος ἐστεφάνωται,
ἐν δ' Ἔρις, ἐν δ' Ἀλκή, ἐν δὲ κρυόεσσα Ἰωκή,
ἐν δέ τε Γοργείη κεφαλὴ δεινοῖο πελώρου
δεινή τε σμερδνή τε, Διὸς τέρας αἰγιόχοιο. (V. 738–42)
73 Janko (1992, 179) makes the same remark, and adds: "bT thinks the charm also arouses Sleep's desire for Pasithea."
74 See Janko 1992, *ad loc.* for the hymnic resonance in Hera's request that sounds like a "prayer." I turn my attention to the perverse and dissonant words and intimations that suspend or infringe upon, during Hera's conniving, the real status quo presently existing on Olympus.

Hypnos, lord over all gods and all men,
as before you listened to my word, so now also
do as I ask. I shall be forever grateful to you.
Put to sleep the shining eyes of Zeus under his brows
as soon as I have lain beside him in love.

Here Zeus, "the ruler of men and gods," is about to become the victim of Aphrodite's power and her magic strap, and of Sleep, "lord over all gods and all men." But with the entrance of Hypnos we abandon the hymnic genre and return to the epic, dramatic genre, within which Hypnos relates a personal episode. He begins his answer with the same staging line used already by Aphrodite: "Hera, noble goddess, daughter of great Kronos..." (243). As we learn, Hypnos accomplished the same favor that Hera now requests when she was persecuting Heracles. On that occasion he caused Zeus to fall asleep so that Hera could accomplish her evil designs: filling the sea with blasts of wracking winds, she dragged Heracles to Kos, far away from his friends (XIV. 249–56). Once woken, Zeus furiously tried to find and punish Hypnos, but could not, because Hypnos was saved by his mother, Night.[75] Because of that earlier event, Hypnos refuses now to make Zeus fall asleep, so that Hera's new trick is nearly foiled.

The Iliadic text recalls for its contemporary audience a traditional episode from the Heracles saga: they may know and recall it, or find it new, in the wake of analogous stories in the large mythical-epic panorama which they control. The text gave the Narratees the privilege of measuring the differences in narrative details and tone between the passage and the Iliadic exploitation of it. For instance, in Hypnos' version of Hera's first request, it is not indicated whether she made love with Zeus before Hypnos' intervention. A textual game was proposed to the Narratees, in which they enjoyed the emotional repetition of the scenes and savored the critical use that the *Iliad* made of its borrowings. If they found the episode new, they enjoyed the invention of the story that enriched their mythical-epic panorama. We have lost the ability to confirm this possibility and cannot be sure whether our perception that the text re-channels a story

---

**75** The story could be invented by Homer, but the exact terms of the events seem to refer to and summarize a longer narrative which could derive from an earlier *Gigantomachy* or *Herakleia*. In either case, the narrated event emerges from a rich mythical soil in which many versions of Hera's tricks aiming to stymie Heracles were narrated. Zeus' threat could be taken from Hephaistos' experience. See Janko 1992, 192. Night in line 259 is *dmêteir(a)* "with power over gods and salvation for men," a unique epithet in all of Homer. She is, of course, the exact opposite of Zeus, who is light.

from another epic poem is certain, and, if it is true, how that story is re-elaborated by our text.

It remains appealing to question what the critical purpose or effect is that the text aims at by re-channelling certain old stories about Zeus, some of them being unedifying, even if entertaining.

The best option seems to me that the narrative quotes, integrates, or simply echoes traditional stories with the intent of granting them new edifying perspectives or of making fun of the traditional versions. From a comparison between Hera's two recourses to Hypnos' help, it becomes evident that in both cases she achieves what she wanted, i.e. to have Zeus fall asleep so that she can challenge Zeus. It is not, however, certain whether Hera made love to Zeus before he fell asleep or rather trusted the intervention of Hypnos pre-sex and rushed to raise the gusts of winds that drove Heracles to Kos (XIV. 254–55). It is probable that she slept with Zeus, just as in our present episode. There are some distinct differences, however: in the earlier story she, in her jealous fury, is persecuting Heracles, while in the present one she wants to save the Achaeans from the murderous attack of the Trojans. The political rivalry contained in her present purpose is of a less private and emotional sort than her earlier jealousy. Assuming, then, that Hera slept with Zeus to make him fall asleep, we may better imagine the difference: in the earlier story Hera perhaps aims to rekindle Zeus' love for herself in a conflictual situation in which Hera's jealousy is the determining stimulus of her hatred for the bastard Heracles; Zeus is proud of his son born from his adultery with Alcmena; Hera's bitterness is justified and her weapons —making love with him and causing him to sleep in order to distress his son— are coherent. On the contrary, to reignite Zeus' amorous desire in order to allow Poseidon's help to the Achaeans to last longer seems more artificial and incongruous.

We do not know whether the erotic scene occurred in the earlier episode nor, if it occurred, how extensive it was, but probably in the 'new' version it has been heightened through collaboration with Aphrodite; moreover, Zeus' recitation of the catalogue of his lovers is wholly Iliadic and suggests a certain provocative grandeur.[76]

---

[76] Concerning the anthropological epoch and ethos of Zeus' catalogue of lovers, see Lucci 2011, 36, for whom this catalogue would be a good example of "...quello che si può definire un passaggio da un sistema endogamico e matrilineare a un sistema esogamico e patrilineare come criterio della strutturazione dei rapport fra divinità. Un buon esempio è fornito dal Catalogo delle amanti di Zeus (XIV. 315–28): la relazione fra Zeus e Era, così come quella con le altre figure femminili, si conforma poco a poco a un modello patrilineare,

Back to the narrative, Hypnos needs to be sure he will receive what he wants and asks Hera to make an oath that is far from jocular (270–79):

"Come on, now," Hypnos urges her, "swear to me on Styx's inviolable water.
With one hand take hold of the richly nourishing earth,
with the other of the shining sea, so that all the gods beneath
who are around Kronos may be witnesses to us.
Swear that you will give me one of the young Graces,
Pasithea, the one I have always desired."[77]
So he spoke, and white-armed Hera did not refuse
but swore as he ordered, and called by their names
all the gods down in Tartaros who are called the Titans.

Referring to Hesiod, *Theog.*, 383 ff., Janko (1992, 194) explains that if Hera "neglects her promise, the entire divine order is to be overturned; her plot imperils Zeus' rule." Rousseau (1995, Ch. V. 13) writes: "Sommeil interprète correctement la contradiction dans laquelle Hera est prise ...: en se revoltant contre Zeus, Hera restaure symboliquement la souveraineté cosmique des Titans."

The readers of the Poem remember that in book VIII. 13–14, Zeus threatens to send the god who might potentially disobey his order down to Tartaros, where the Titans are imprisoned. Hera does not merely symbolically restore the order of the Titans; she also displaces the *Iliad*'s narrative and replaces it with other mythical stories. It is not that these stories are not true, but they have been buried by the *Iliad* under Tartaros with their characters and do not have any relevance for the Zeus of the *Iliad*.

All these disquieting vibrations in the scene of the oath, while coloring Hera's subversive attitude, display simultaneously the out-of-place nature of her strategy and paint her doomed ambitions.

The reason why Hypnos requires Hera to call the Titans as witnesses of her oath could be that Hypnos belongs to the beginning of life in earth and heaven, and for him Zeus is only a recent god who simply replaced the ones with whom Hypnos and Night were familiar.[78] Hypnos has no respect for Zeus, as he is

---

caratterizzato dal dominio del dio." For the gods' anthropomorphism in the *Iliad* see I.1 n. 13, and Appendix 2.

77 Commentators notice the cute transformation of *kharis*, the "thankfulness" Hera promises to Hypnos (235), into *Kharis*, the "Grace" Pasithea that Hera promises him (Χαρίτων μίαν 267) after his refusal and explication.

78 See Hesiod, *Theog.* 211–12. Hypnos is identified on *Iliad* XIV. 231 as "brother of Death" and also in this relationship he must have appeared at the moment life occurred on earth. He is stronger than his brother, since his brother cannot affect the gods.

ready to work against him for the second time. His figure and role evoke a remote order to which Zeus is really a late comer, but over which he has taken control.

As Hera reaches Zeus on the peak of Gargaros, the text emphasizes the immediate effect that Aphrodite's erotic charm produces on him (XIV. 293-96):

> ... And Zeus who gathers the clouds saw her,
> and as soon as he saw her, love encompassed his wise mind[79]
> as much as on that time when they first went to bed together,
> and lay in love – all unknown to their parents.

Suddenly Zeus is no longer the monarch of the gods and the lord of fate, no longer the immortal being untouched by the phases of age: he appears as the lucky youth accomplishing what his parents ought not to know, his first intercourse with Hera. In the textual elaboration, the intercourse that is about to occur repeats that first encounter of the young lovers and gains from this repetition a greater strength, and more joyous excitement.[80] Hera reenacts this renewal of her first intercourse with him in a context that she did not expect: she is drowned beneath the tremendous mass of erotic encounters he celebrates while paying her the greatest compliment, namely that she is the most pleasing and seductive among all his lovers. This makes her the only goddess worthy of being selected as his wife. He produces a magic garden of love that is unique, therefore, a place reminding them of the first and unsurpassable experience (*locus amoenus*). From that specific frame, the scene derives also the freshness and joy that their first amorous encounter inspires: their hiding from their parents is a marvelous touch that evokes their youthfulness, innocence, and pleasure.

Zeus does not even listen to her motivation (301-311), and breaks out (313-16):

> Hera, you may go there later:
> but now let us go to bed and make love,
> for never has love for a goddess or a mortal woman
> overcome me in such a way, spreading in my heart…

---

[79] The line echoes that of Paris at III. 442: "for never desire encompassed so powerfully my mind," beginning an allusion to the passage in which Paris declares his desire for Helen: of course, Zeus largely outdoes in sexual energy and creativity the human lover. In this line, Zeus' heart/mind is called "wise," an epithet missing in Paris' line. A peculiar feature of the magic amulet is that it acts, so it seems, only on males. Hera wears it, but she is not affected by its seductive power.

[80] "Greater and more joyous" because the memory of the first occasion increases the analogous pleasure of its repetition. Zeus will indeed say that his desire for Hera was never so strong as it is now.

The Narrator has Zeus assert a greater intensity of desire than the same Narrator had attributed to him at 294–96: now Zeus recites the catalogue of the women he loved (317–328) and declares, following the rhetorical scheme of a priamel, that not even at that time of his first love with Hera was his desire so strong as it is now. The Muses and the Poet have not sufficiently taken into account the effect produced by the Aphrodisian seduction. Zeus' eyes are full of Hera (293–94): "Zeus saw her / and as soon as he saw her, love encompassed his wise mind..." The repetition of the verb "to see" accurately describes the conventional idea that love passes through the eyes and suggests the total loss of Zeus' wisdom at that moment.

The effect of the Aphrodisian presence stimulates the grand catalogue that Zeus delivers about his erotic performances[81] and his fatherly productivity (XIV. 314–23, 327–8):

> Now, let's go to bed, let us turn to love!
> Never has such a love for goddess or mortal woman
> flooded my heart and overwhelmed me so.[82]
> Not even then, when I made love with Ixion's wife
> who bore me Pirithous, rival to all the gods in wisdom.
> Not even when I loved Acrisius' daughter, Danae, with marvelous ankles,
> and she bore me Perseus, the most glorious of all heroes;
> not even when I loved the daughter of far-renowned Phoenix
> who bore me Minos and Radamanthus, like a god; [...]
> not even [I loved] you, so much
> as now I love you and sweet desire[83] has taken hold of me.

The features that punctuate the portrait of Zeus as he displays the effusive catalogue of his lovers are various: the formal priamel of his list of lovers, the questionable form of love declaration, and the fact that some of his lines echo those that Paris utters at III. 441–42 (see XIV. 314–15) when a burgeoning desire for Helen takes hold of him. I begin from this last point. Paris too states that he never felt so much love for her as he now feels (III. 446 and XIV. 328 mirror each other). But the recalling of that passage might emphasize the immense difference between the immediate desire of a mortal lover and the god's eruption of

---

[81] The poetic form of the catalogue was a virtuoso performance for the epic poet and pleased to the audiences as Plato's Ion states. See Doherty 1995, Steinrück 2016, 12.
[82] The *diêgêsis* describes the effect of the erotic charm as that of stealing away mind/ heart even of the thoughtful persons (XIV. 217).
[83] The word *"himeros,"* indicating a desire that requires immediate satisfaction, appears here after *philotês, eros* and the verbs derived from *eros* denoting love and passion of love without the pressure of *himeros*. See Weiss 1998, 50.

volcanic erotic experience and endless creativity. Nothing in Paris' comparison between his earlier and present lust comes close to Zeus' dashing bluntness with which the father of men and gods flaunts to his wife the passion he felt for his many lovers. The intensity of the catalogue, the flow of the intercourses, the magnitude of the heroic names and epithets, all this textual erotic fullness translates into Zeus' erotic *aristeia*, celebrating his tremendous sexual energy and immense productivity.

The catalogue can also be viewed as the Poet's humorous response to Hera's traditional obsessive jealousy: her jealousy of Alcmena and hostility to Heracles become ridiculous themes as the Iliadic text heaps up the names of dozens of Zeus' lovers and of his magnificent children.

The style creates an epic grandeur: the catalogue proceeds, line by line, evoking legendary names of famous and beautiful ladies and singing their children's noble and sublime epithets: almost each line rings out as a three-part ascending line that gives great emphasis to the last epithetic part; each incident is marked by a heroic birth, so that, already in its partiality, the catalogue gives birth to half a world of Greek mythological lore. Quantity becomes quality and acquires an epic, monumental sublimity. The catalogue produces a sort of sexual apocalypse.

The festive aspect of the almost endless catalogue lies in its unexpected candor,[84] surreal length, and in its possible echoing of heroic practices. Just as during their *aristeia* heroes sometimes mention their previous deeds, so here Zeus, before moving to the great sexual act, festively proclaims the catalogue of the lovers he has enjoyed.

The catalogue functions also as a sort of theatrical or lyrical performance. For Zeus recites the catalogue of his conquests through the hyperbolic priamel (315–28), it is an often-formalized lyric structure, a recognizable rhetorical piece. This priamel could continue forever and this possible openness is certainly a source of some comedy: let us see when he can stop...

Some of these stylistic features are not appropriate to epic, but the grandeur of the whole performance, the apocalypse of his mythical productivity, are consonant with the Iliadic Zeus.

---

[84] If I am correct, the Poem mentions an erotic deed of Zeus at VI. 198–99, where —though without any explicit erotic allusion— Sarpedon's birth is announced, and at XIX. 101–105, where Zeus announces the birth of his son Heracles; his son Perseus is mentioned at XIX. 116. Otherwise, the text tends to be silent about his affairs, even when they might be expected and perhaps appropriate.

Hera is silent, either overcome and surprised, or embarrassed by the list: to be the best and most seductive partner among the endless list of great and seductive lovers distinguishes her only within an unavoidable crowd of rivals: she is at the summit of a hierarchical series, just as Achilles is better than Ajax, Diomedes, and all the others; and yet they all possess the same specific virtues and qualities.

Hera's jealousy was implicit in the Hypnos episode from a Heracles' saga (250-51), but the Iliadic text[85] produces great parodic pleasure by burying the traditional jealousy of Hera under the avalanche of Zeus' lovers. Hera's persecution of Heracles becomes a senseless action caused by a senseless feeling, as she hears Zeus recite in glorious paternal tone the names of Peirithoos, Perseus, Minos, Radamanthys, Heracles, Dionysos, and others, all Zeus' bastards. She knows all of them. The Iliadic text keeps her tranquil and silent under this flood of adulteries, allowing the Narratees to enjoy the erotic *aristeia* of the god.

Zeus' productivity is again exalted, though in a different register, when Zeus creates a *locus amoenus* on which he and Hera may lie in love, a flowery spot, covered by a golden cloud, and deprived of all suggestions of evil or loss, just as the *locus amoenus* in its rhetorical and symbolic frame most often intimates.[86] Unless, of course, Hera's tricky purpose lies under the beautiful and flowery bed as a reminder that even this most miraculous *locus amoenus* is ensnared by some nastiness.

Yet this perverse streak of the *locus amoenus*' rhetoric may be silenced here by another more present and innocent connotation: as Griffin 1995, 12 writes, "Beneath them the holy earth sets up fresh growing grass and dewy lotus and saffron and hyacinth thick and soft.... The union of these two is still the cosmic marriage of heaven and earth which makes the whole world fruitful." If this evocation of Zeus and Hera —as Heaven making the Earth fruitful— is legitimate, it contrasts most eloquently with the threatening image that Hera evoked when she stated that she was going to stop the hostility between Okeanos and Tethys and to reestablish love and sexual relations between them. The fruitful earth magically flowering under the bodies of Zeus and Hera dispels all imagined menaces, while a beautiful golden cloud covers them and glimmering dew

---

[85] The allusions to Heracles are frequent in the *Iliad*: besides XIV. 250-51 and 323-34, see XIX. 96-133: Hera's deception of Zeus, on the day Semele was to beget Heracles; XV. 25-26: once more, Hera's persecutions of Heracles; VIII. 362-69: Athena's saving of Heracles from Hades; XV. 639-40: Heracles' service under Eurystheus; XX. 145-49: Heracles and Troy; V. 392-94: Heracles wounds Hera; XI. 690: Heracles attacks Pilos.

[86] In *Od.* v. 63-75, the *locus amoenus* on Calypso's island is described with its admirable beauty, but in this same paradisiacal spot, Odysseus sits weeping and groaning (v. 82-84).

descends. It is in this space that separates them from the world of which they are the source and the masters that "the son of Kronos caught his wife in his arms" (XIV. 346). The *diêgêsis* reestablishes the conventional epithets and roles.

In the last two lines of the episode, we see Zeus sleeping serenely in the arms of his wife (XIV. 352–53). We have to wait for the beginning of book XV to see him awakening, granting victory to the Trojans, and persuading Hera to collaborate with him.

## 5.4 Zeus Restores the Order of Things: The Credentials of Monarchic Power

When Zeus wakes up, he first restores his authority over Hera and retains her cooperation. Then, through Iris, he induces Poseidon to leave the battlefield. Finally, with the help of Apollo, he brings Hector back to the fight (XV. 4–270).

His first move is to threaten "uncontrollable Hera" harshly, reproaching her for the "nastily designed trick" (14). He describes the terrible and humiliating punishment that he inflicted on her when, a long time ago, she, through a similar trick, was able to mistreat Heracles (XV. 18–33). The text, again, displays the violence that Zeus committed in the past (I. 590–94, XIV. 256 ff.), following the narration of this violence in another text. Zeus now narrates that former punishment as a deterrence for the future. For the present, however, Zeus does not touch Hera and enacts no punishment. It is certainly the Poet's good taste, as West, for instance, opines (2011, 300), that prevents him from enacting such violence. Yet there exists a supplementary textual purpose concerning Zeus: the text borrows heavily from the Heracles saga,[87] not only because this story describes Hera's hostility toward Zeus, but especially in order to show how different the Iliadic Zeus is. The narrative does not aim to show Zeus' adoption of a milder and more diplomatic mood over the course of time; but it does — shockingly— contrast its Zeus with the same character agent of the Heracles saga. In that saga, Zeus was represented as violent and physically brutal: through Zeus' narrative, the Poet recalls the cruel details of Zeus' punishment of Hera —the anvils attached to her feet, the chain around her hands, etc.— though Zeus is almost oblivious of having himself been the one who accomplished such tortures. He was still himself, of course, but in another adventure, with other purposes, told in another narrative. The contemporary Narratees remember well

---

[87] This borrowing is not technically a borrowing, since the total permeability of the hypertext suggests a rather process of free re-performance.

those passages and see their abject semantics. The Iliadic poet imputes relevance to this other narrative by quoting it and its storyline (XV. 24–300), and by emphasizing the sadistic details attributed to the other Zeus. Simultaneously, however, the same poet enhances the purpose of this recollection —it is merely a deterrent— and the hope it brings of a reconciliation with Hera.

The Narratees, however, cannot deny that Zeus' recollection of the brutal punishment that he, in the other narratives, inflicted on Hera also exhibits Zeus' pleasure with the terror that his menacing produces in Hera. Let us examine some passages.

Zeus, "looking terribly and scowling at her,"[88] begins with a sinister false question to himself (16–17):

> I do not really know if you are the first to profit
> from this evil plot and if I should whip you with strokes.

Zeus is obviously sarcastic... Hera may be scared, but the Narratees know both that Zeus will not touch her and that Hera's "profit from this evil plot" is aggressive, abject rhetoric.[89]

Zeus goes on (18–20):

> Don't you recall the time when you hung in midair and on your feet
> I slung two anvils and around your hand I drove a golden chain,
> unbreakable...

As Janko writes (1992, 229): "Zeus underlines the reality of this threat by citing a precedent. Yet, precisely, by giving the full story, he undercuts its force." I would add that this precedent is buried in a saga that the Iliadic poet has already evoked in the context of Hera's jealousy: through the catalogue of Zeus' lovers, the Poet invited the Narratees to smile at Hera's ferocious hatred for Zeus' infidelity with Alcmena (see Ch. V.3).

Zeus certainly finds some nasty pleasure in the game of frightening Hera and tastes the sweetness of his victory after suffering the bitterness of Hera's victory. The gesture of suspending Hera in midair is brutal, and the Narratees recall that Zeus employed the same threat when he threatened the Olympian

---

**88** On the scowl, see Holoka 1983, 1–16. It is a male feature and Zeus is the only god in the *Iliad* and the *Odyssey* who looks with a scowl.
**89** At I. 410 and VI. 353, the same sarcastic expression is followed by negative consequences, but the warnings implied by the sarcasm are generic and exist in an undetermined future.

gods through the game of tug-of-war: he would draw the gods from the earth and suspend them in mid-air (VIII. 24–26):

> while whenever I too earnestly wished,
> I would drag you up with the whole earth and the whole sea.
> And then I would tie the golden chain around a horn
> of Olympus and in that case everything would dangle in midair.

Zeus' surreal autocratic imagination loves to see his potentially rebellious peers hanging somewhere, far from Olympus, the seat of the immortals (VIII. 456), lacking place and roles. I say surreal, because the Iliadic Zeus stands supremely above the reality of the other gods: he takes pleasure in imagining a displacement of the standard and familiar spots as a revolution of the hierarchical order.

Back to the narrative, Zeus contextualizes and justifies his recollection of violent punishment (XV. 31–33):

> I remind you of all this so that you stop your deceits
> and may see if you got any profit from love and sex
> as you laid with me, when you came from the gods, and it was a deception!

Zeus explains the hopefully educative purpose of his recalling past punishment and repeats the sarcastic expression: "if you got any profit from your deception." There is an accent of reproach and disappointment in Zeus' recognition that Hera's making love with him was done with the intent of deceiving him. Even the master of the order of things is sensitive to feelings of betrayal and disingenuity.

Both the characters and the Narratees of the poem might perceive certain ironic conciliatory touches in Hera's response to Zeus' utterance (XV. 36–46). She appeals to him as κελαινεφές ("dark-clouded," 46), an epithet often used in prayer and therefore considered by its users to be flattering. Shuddering, she pronounces a solemn oath, swearing that she did not incite Poseidon to intervene in favor of the Achaeans. She adds that she is ready to advise Poseidon to leave the battlefield. She is right in proclaiming her innocence, but she fails to recognize that by causing Zeus to sleep she allowed Poseidon to prolong the duration of his help to the Achaeans. Zeus, "the father of men and gods," certainly understands this, and smiles (47).

As Janko writes (1992, 233): "we are left to wonder whether Zeus smiles because Hera agrees, or because he sees through her wiles, or for both reasons."

In the *Iliad*, Zeus sometimes has a tolerant opinion of Hera's opposition: it is political and not erotic resentment and her resentment has a habitual ring when he says to Iris at VIII. 407–08:

> But with Hera I am not so outraged and irate –
> it is always her way to thwart my will, whatever I command.

In light of this, Zeus' smile, after Hera's oath and promise to collaborate, indicates his recognition of her habitual tendencies: but now, as we are going to see, she makes a promise to collaborate that is new. New also is Zeus' explicit prophecy about the following events that culminates in the destruction of Troy. This commitment must satisfy Hera.

Hera's oath here neatly contrasts with the oath she gave to Hypnos at XIV. 271–79, when she swore on the Titans, the adversaries of Zeus, as witnesses: now, pronouncing the oath before Zeus, she adopts the correct, standard divine formula and adds to it as witnesses, "your sacred head and our legitimate bed" (XV. 39).

It is difficult to imagine a stronger reversal of authoritative witnesses and a more direct example of *captatio benevolentiae*.

Zeus accepts, with only a shadow of suspicion, Hera's collaboration and asks her to go to Olympus and tell Iris and Apollo to come to see him on Mount Ida. Zeus begins by saying (49–55):

> True, if you, lady Hera of the ox eyes,[90] hereafter
> were to take your place among the immortals[91] thinking in accord with me
> then yes, Poseidon —even if he has other plans—
> would soon turn his mind to follow your and my heart.[92]
> If now you really speak truthfully and frankly,[93]
> go among the ranks of the gods and summon
> Iris and Apollo, the famous archer, to come here to me...

---

**90** Zeus uses the same epithet —βοῶπις πότνια Ἥρη— that the *diêgêsis* uses on the previous epiphanic introductory line (34). As we have seen in Ch. V.3 and n. 62, the text seems to give some functional significance to the choice of this epithet. In this new episode, the metrically equivalent epithetic phrase for Hera, θεὰ λευκώλενος Ἥρη, appears as soon as Hera reaches Olympus (78), after having come to an agreement with Zeus, and remains the same for the unfurling of the scene on line 92. It is a hypothetical assumption that the Poet intended an ethical, functional difference between the two epithets of so distant literal significance. See also Janko 1992, 238.
**91** Zeus means: sitting in the assembly or on other occasions when decisions are made.
**92** As West 2011, 300 notices, "For the motif that if Zeus and Hera agree, others will fall into line, cf. IV. 62, i. 76–9."
**93** ἀλλ' εἰ δή ῥ' ἐτεόν γε καὶ ἀτρεκέως ἀγορεύεις. Zeus adds ἐτεόν to the formulaic phrase that follows. He intensifies the connotations of truthfulness in his request for truth.

Zeus takes the opportunity to invite Hera to become his collaborator rather than his political opponent: he implies that her constant resistance facilitates the other gods' plots against his plans. Through serious decisions and scenes of extravagant omnipotence, he has shown that he can secretly decide what he wants. He needs neither her nor the other gods, but he may still use diplomacy with a hint of prudent skepticism to obtain her agreement.[94]

He prolongs his diplomatic gesture by confiding to Hera the next development of the war (64–77): Achilles will rouse up Patroclos, who will kill many young men —and among them even Zeus' own son, divine Sarpedon. Hector will cut down Patroclos; as revenge, Achilles will kill Hector. From that moment on, the Achaean counterattack will dominate the field until Troy is captured "through the plans of Athena" (XV. 71: see Ch. 2.1 and 3.2). After this announcement, Zeus warns Hera that he will help the Trojans and prevent the gods from helping the Achaeans until he has accomplished the promise he made to Thetis —the promise that on XV. 598 the *diêgêsis* defines as "Thetis' disastrous prayer."

Hera does not answer what should be for her most welcome news, and instead leaves in order to execute Zeus' request.

Zeus remains on Ida to direct Iris and Apollo.

It is a prudent and diplomatic decision for Zeus to send Iris to Poseidon with the order to leave the battle: in this way, Zeus avoids a direct clash with his brother over the question of the basis of Zeus' authority over his brother. The encounter between Iris and Poseidon does indeed achieve a dramatic suspense as the god denies the legitimacy of Zeus' authority. We follow the entire dialogue.

Iris reports "aegis-bearing"[95] Zeus' message, which, with few alterations, is the one she received from him (XV. 176–83):

---

[94] How correct his skepticism is depends on how we read Hera's performance at the assembly (XV. 87–112) where she announces Zeus' "evil decisions," possibly referring to Zeus' continuous support of the Trojans, then she blames her own and the other gods' foolishness to resist or contravene Zeus' will: in the serene awareness of his greatness, she says, he cares nothing; Hera thus provides a beautiful image of Zeus' fatal power and superiority. Finally, she announces the death of Ares' son: since he has been killed by Deiphobos (XIII. 516–20), Hera cites this death possibly to prove the evils of Zeus' continuous support of the Trojans. Hera's performance does not sound like a full agreement with Zeus' plans, yet she recognizes the vanity and the foolishness of opposing Zeus and sends Iris and Apollo to see him.

[95] Iris presents the message of *aigiokhos Zeus* (175), employing an epithet that instantly makes Zeus stronger than Poseidon.

he commands you to quit the war and the battle
and to go back to the ranks of the gods or to the divine sea:
if you do not obey his orders but despise them
he threatens to come in person here to fight against you,
strength against strength, and warns you to avoid
his hands,[96] since he says that he is far greater in fight than you are
and he is firstborn too. Yet your heart does not hesitate
to call yourself his equal,[97] of whom the others are afraid.

Zeus is ready to exercise violence in order to be obeyed. We might think of the Hesiodean Zeus fighting with lightning against the Titans, his adversaries, in order to take the place of Kronos.[98]

We have heard Zeus show full control over the assembly (see for instance VIII. 28–29) and we have heard Poseidon himself recognize Zeus' superior power at VIII. 209–11. As if this recognition were not sufficient, the Narrator both informs us that Poseidon takes advantage of Zeus' distraction to help the Achaeans in secret (XIII. 352), and then explains (XIII. 353–7):

---

**96** Here Iris changes the wording given to her by Zeus (163–65):
 "if he does not obey my orders but despises them
 then let him consider in his mind and heart
 that he might not, strong though he is, be able to stand up
 to my attack, since I say that I am far greater in fight than he is
 and that I am firstborn..."
With her text, Iris makes the potential conflict more physical and shocking: the expression ὑπεξαλέασθαι χεῖρας is unique in Homer. Iris directly mentions an open threat instead of inviting Poseidon to think about this warning. She gives Poseidon a sense of greater and more immediate physical battle and announces more clearly the argument through which she will finally persuade Poseidon to leave.

**97** The text repeats, in part verbatim, the accusation that Agamemnon makes to Achilles at I. 186 ff.: "so that you may learn / how greater I am than you and another man may shrink back / from calling himself my equal..." The verbal parallels may be intentional, and in this case it is difficult to imagine their intended purpose(s). Perhaps the repetition suggests the immense distance between Agamemnon's insulting boast and Zeus' justified assertion of his real force. See Janko 1992, 245.

**98** Indeed, a few lines later, Zeus narrates to Apollo that Poseidon has given in and therefore has escaped Zeus' terrible wrath —otherwise those "other gods who gather around Kronos beneath us" would have known the battle (XV. 224–25). Yet from the same description (XV. 226–8) it seems improbable that Zeus would have used the lightning against his brother Poseidon. He says to Apollo: "This business would have not finished without sweat", an expression that might imply that Zeus and Poseidon would have used similar means of force.

> he [Poseidon] was terribly angry at Zeus:
> indeed they were of the same generation and of a single father,
> but Zeus was the firstborn and knew more.[99]
> Therefore Poseidon shrank from defending them out in the open
> but, in secret, in a man's likeness, kept stirring them up throughout the army.

The narrative grants Poseidon the legitimacy of being angry at Zeus' supremacy and simultaneously mentions the grounds —Zeus' superior knowledge, his being the firstborn, and his force— on which Zeus justifies his order to Poseidon to leave the battle. For the Narratees, therefore, the nature and force of Zeus' position are well known and seem compelling: the Narratees expect that there will be no clash. Yet they cannot evaluate Poseidon's proud reaction against Zeus' monarchic violence. The drama explodes when Poseidon rejects Zeus' order: he begins his protest by expressing strong indignation (XV. 184–6):

> But the famous Earthquaker in anger answered her:
> "What outrage! Noble as he is, what an insolent word,
> if, against my will, he wants to control me by force, me, equal to him in honor."[100]

Poseidon follows his spectacular expression of indignation by demonstrating that he and Zeus enjoy the same honor (187–93): the monarchic control of the universe was split, through a casting of lots, between the three brothers, Poseidon, Zeus, and Hades:[101] this account proves that the three gods have equal honor or station and that Zeus has no authority to impose his will on Poseidon.

After asserting their equal honor and recalling the division of the world among the three brothers, Poseidon goes on (XV. 194–9):

> Therefore I shall not live by Zeus' wits, but let him, tranquil and strong
> as he is, remain in his third part of the world:
> and let him not try to scare me with his hands

---

**99** In the four cases in the *Iliad* of πλείονα ἤδη – with other persons and times of the same verb– (XIII. 355, XIX. 219, XXI. 440, XXIII. 312), greater knowledge is connected with being born earlier and therefore with being older.
**100** ὦ πόποι ἦ ῥ' ἀγαθός περ ἐὼν ὑπέροπλον ἔειπεν
εἴ μ' ὁμότιμον ἐόντα βίῃ ἀέκοντα καθέξει. (XV. 185–86)
The equality of honor and right between the brothers could be the theme preluding a fight between them in view of gaining supreme power. This anthropological and narrative motif is so well-known by the audience (for instance in the case of Atreus and Thyestes) that they may expect this hostility to explode. Yet, Poseidon's restrained and secret form of disobedience intimates his fear of Zeus' force and suggests that the *Iliad* does not assume that the fight between brothers against the *Kronides*, *Kroniôn* Zeus, father of men and gods is a serious menace.
**101** For the oriental parallels of this division of the worlds among gods, see West 1997, 109 ff.

as if I were a coward. It would be better for him to blame
with arrogant words the daughters and the sons he begot:
they shall obey his orders, by necessity.

With this statement, the *Iliad* has Poseidon give a neat formulation of the motif that Zeus has no more legitimate, superior power over the world and human destinies than do his brothers and sisters. He denies him his supremacy on Olympus and his role as god of fate. This motif surfaces in Hera's oath and in the feeling of hostility against Zeus during the episode of sexual aggression.

Poseidon rejects the two arguments on whose grounds Zeus claims to give orders to Poseidon: Zeus' stronger force does not frighten Poseidon —it is humiliating to be treated as a coward— and Zeus' position as firstborn does not give him any real authority. Zeus is not Poseidon's father; Zeus can give orders to those over whom he has legitimate power, his daughters and sons.

A consequence of the brothers' equal honor and station is that each of the brothers is master only in the region that the lots attributed to him. Let then Zeus swagger in his own domain, not on the earth where, as Poseidon asserts (193), each of the three gods has the same rights.

Iris astutely understands that, though Poseidon may be scared by Zeus' superior force, he will not yield on that ground: it would be too dishonorable for him to give in to fear. Accordingly, she argues (201–204):

So then, oh Dark-haired and Earth-holder, am I really to carry
such a harsh and strong word to Zeus, or will you change a little?
The minds of the great can be bent:
you know that the Erinyes always stand by older brothers.

By hinting that, in a potential fight, the Erinyes —who protect family relations[102]— would favor the firstborn, she gives Poseidon an honorable reason for giving in.

Poseidon is immediately relieved and praises Iris (206-7):

Now, divine Iris, you said the quite proper word:
it is a fine thing when a messenger knows what is fitting.[103]

---

[102] The Erinyes are *daimones* who punish and therefore are divinities who use violence (XIX. 259–60).

[103] Ἴρι θεὰ μάλα τοῦτο ἔπος κατὰ μοῖραν ἔειπες·
ἐσθλὸν καὶ τὸ τέτυκται ὅτ' ἄγγελος αἴσιμα εἰδῇ.

Αἴσιμα properly means "appointed by the will of the gods," such as, for instance, the "fatal" day, the day of death (VIII. 72), and "agreeable to the decree of fate," therefore "fitting to the specific occasion" and "contextually correct, appropriate."

The praise so explicitly betrays Poseidon's pleasure at the honorable rescue Iris offers him that it appears humorous to the readers and suggests the text's mocking intent.[104]

Poseidon then explains his change of mind (XV. 208–17): he says that he feels a terrible pain from the fact that Zeus tries to reprimand with irate words someone who is equal to him in rank and is endowed with equal station; yet this time Poseidon will give in, with a threat, however, that if Zeus, against Poseidon's desire and that of Athena, Hera, Hermes, and Hephaistos, spares Troy and does not bestow great victory on the Argives, he should know that he must face Poseidon's and the other gods' implacable anger.

After these words, Poseidon leaves the Achaean army and merges into the sea (228–29).

Poseidon is a powerful god, earth-holder and earth-shaker, and, as Zeus confesses to Apollo, a fight with him would have been hard and strenuous (XV. 226–28):

> it has been much better for me and also for him
> that, for all his earlier indignation, he has yielded
> to my force, since all would have finished not without sweat.

This litotes allows us to imagine the great efforts that such physical wrestling would entail: luckily Poseidon has yielded. And even after Zeus' eventual victory, it is not clear that he would have been able to send Poseidon to Tartaros.

Zeus ends the episode by speaking as Fate and announcing future events (XV. 62–77): he envisions the series of dead heroes with superb objectivity, and he recalls the bending of his head in assent to Thetis' request: a simple gesture that shapes the whole story of the *Iliad*. When later he tells Apollo (XV. 221–35) how he will organize the events after the provisional defeat of the Achaeans, he says (XV. 234–35):

> from that moment, I myself shall think of the action and the word
> so that again the Achaeans take breath from the defeat.

---

**104** Once more, the Poetic voice endorses Zeus' provisional support of the Trojans and meta-poetically smiles at Poseidon's fear and weakness as he faces the power of Zeus. The Iliadic Poet has made clear from the beginning of the Poem that his Zeus approves the destruction of Troy (see Ch. 6.1) and no philo-Achaean audience will resent this representation of Poseidon. Scodel 2017, 89–90, misses how, in the previous lines, the narrative emphasizes the humiliation of Hera and, in our passage, derides Poseidon's fear. The narrative has emphasized that both Hera and Poseidon conspire secretly —because of their fear of Zeus.

We recognize the same absolute control of the events ("action and word"!), his total autonomy ("I myself shall think of"), and the secrecy of what "the action and the word" will be.

Through the contrast with Poseidon, the figure of Zeus acquires fresh traits that confirm and emphasize his greater force, his invincible hands, his superiority in the game of tug-of-war. Yet it may appear odd or inexplicable that these are also the only grounds that allow him to decide, without serious contestation, debate, or agreement, the Trojans' temporary victory and the final defeat of Troy through Athena's will. Poseidon's desire to save the Achaeans is simply denied, negated, made impossible. Zeus' superior *kratos* guarantees the success of his dictatorial role as monarch of the gods and lord of human destinies, whereby he is the impersonation of the Golden Scales and the dispenser of human blessings and evils from his jars. We imagine that, through the measuring, weighing, and combining of destinies that these images and symbols evoke, a subjective choice is necessarily involved. And we know that this is so, since we have seen Zeus decide with heavy hesitation in favor of Thetis. Zeus finally mentions that occasion and tells Hera that his granting victory to the Trojans is done with the intent of honoring Achilles (XV. 72–77); yet the reasons for honoring Achilles in that way, with its harsh and contradictory consequences, remains unexplained. Furthermore, his larger plan, the capture and destruction of Troy, is left to the planning of Athena, again with no declared motivation. No shown act of measuring, no deliberation or choosing, no justified combining ever take place.

On this account, it is to be expected that even Poseidon, who desires the Achaean's victory and the capture of Troy, does not justify Zeus' solution on any grounds: he might mention an objective ground (the superior force of the Achaeans, for instance), or subjective beliefs (the need to punish Paris' rape of Helen, for instance). Not at all: Poseidon imposes his solution by menacing that, if his plan be not agreed upon by Zeus, he and his allies will engage a violent conflict against Zeus (XV. 211–17). The paradox is that both Poseidon and Zeus desire the capture and destruction of Troy, but the Narratees will never know whether the brothers have the same or different motivations for this goal. Had a minimal political interchange between Zeus and Poseidon taken place, we would know.

Political games do not exist for the Iliadic Zeus: his personal solutions are never contemplated and discussed, but directly taken and imposed through the deterrent threat of boxing matches. Only concerning Hector's funeral does a sort of debate arise among the gods, and Zeus imposes his view through persuasive arguments. The gods' way of imposing their will on Zeus is softer: they warn of the withdrawal of the other gods' consensus (*epainos*).

Politics thrives among the mortal characters: for them, politics means deliberation, as, for instance, when in the second book the elders discuss and accept Agamemnon's proposal. Politics means that some truth may be seen in the position of both opposing parties, as Nestor is able to see when he intervenes between Achilles and Agamemnon at I. 247 ff. Politics requires the acceptance of suggestions from higher powers, if the suggestions protect the interests of the persuaded subject. Achilles in book I, under Athena's suggestion, rejects the idea of murdering Agamemnon and, by retiring from the war, will force Agamemnon to negotiate with him. For more on the theme of politics and consensus among the mortal characters of the Poem, see Elmer 2013. I am less convinced by his evaluation of politics among the gods, and especially concerning the monarchic role of Zeus.

# Chapter 6

## A New Story of the Trojan War

> "The characters in Homeric epic are all striving for attention: their ultimate goal is immortal fame, *kleos*. But this is achieved not by them, but by the future generations who sing and hear about them."
>
> Taplin 1992, 5

## 6.1 A Perverse Comedy

The truce between the Achaeans and the Trojans is an episode (books III and IV) that would occur, presumably, in the first part of a war, and accordingly belongs most likely to the events of the early years of the war (Coray 2009, 38–39). And, in fact, it is placed in a section of the poem that is not marked by the story of Achilles' anger. As West (2011, 53) writes, "Where Zeus appears (in IV. 1–72), he shows no consciousness of the plan he is supposed to be implementing." Achilles, however, is not present on the battlefield: accordingly, the Composer(s) have adapted these episodes to the larger plot of the wrath of Achilles.

The episode of the gods' breaking of the truce therefore belongs to the so-called "expanded" part of the *Iliad;* it was re-elaborated at the time of the monumental composition of the poem. The Composer(s) realized that the passage — which they probably found among, or elaborated from, the hypertext's stories on the Trojan War— offered a powerful enticement due to its dramatic aspects.[1] For me, Zeus' identity remains the important question: how do his role and nature in this episode compare with those in the story of Achilles' wrath?

I begin with a few remarks on the duel between the two champions, Menelaos and Paris, who fight, in accord with the terms of the truce, for the possession of Helen and the end of the war. The gods, sitting around Zeus, have watched the battle from Olympus while feasting and drinking (IV. 1–4). They were enjoying "nectar," a non-natural drink,[2] in golden cups, and venerable Hebe was serving them. She is the goddess of youth and her explicit presence as the dispenser of nectar marks the gods' immortal youth. Their description as they pleasantly watch a fight between humans would characterize the gods and

---

[1] On this issue, see Bakker 2017. He proposes that narratives preceding the *Iliad* and used by the *Iliad* are recomposed by the Poet.

[2] *Nectar* is the counterpart of *ambrosia*, the food of immortality: the reference is clear, although the etymology is contested and not established. One interpretation reads it as "triumphing over death" (see Chantraine, *DELG*).

their performance as frivolous according to Reinhardt and others. Calasso, in the same vein, writes that "war for the gods is nothing but a spectacle."³

As we know, the gods cannot understand the heroic nature of the human battle, since they do not experience or know death; moreover, they are hardly interested in the outcome before the battle started, since they know that they could always change its results. This is the vision of the gods' attendance presented by the Muses.

The duel will also be a spectacle for the Narratees. They experience the fight on two different registers: according to the human characters' experience, and simultaneously according to the Muses' voice, which deforms the battle into a comic event, over and above the knowledge of the characters. Menelaos is the fighter through whose hope and feelings we will follow the duel: the duel constitutes for him the most serious and sacred occasion to take revenge on Paris who wronged him. He means to kill the despicable man.

Through an almost parodic deformation, the text mocks the dramatic gravity of Menelaos and the other soldiers, and attempts to show the vanity of an action —the truce— of which the gods do not approve. This fight is, for the Narratees too, a sort of spectacle, for they do not experience the battle from the point of view of Menelaos' anger, but through the epic deformations and parodic variations that the text brings to light. We are induced to imagine that the duel will have no serious outcome. We reach this conclusion because we also know that both Menelaos and Paris will remain alive for the rest of the poem.⁴

The text begins the comic manipulation of the fight by displacing a major epic device: it attributes the arming scene to Paris (III. 330–38), the weaker warrior who is destined to be defeated,⁵ while, according to epic convention, the major arming scenes always introduce the hero's *aristeia*.⁶ No audience of the Poem can expect Paris to be the winner or the better of the two warriors; yet, since Paris' arming scene closely resembles that of Patroclos, the text seems to

---

3 On the scandal about the fact that the gods enjoy watching the events of the war, a scandal that the scholiasts already denounced, see Griffin 1976, 5 ff. The Narratees of the Poem enjoy the narrative just as the gods do: the gods' presence and enjoyment of the events both grant truth to the events and function as a mediation of the audience's pleasure.
4 Paris will kill Achilles; Menelaos shall return home victorious after the war.
5 Carey 2009, 119 realizes that the arming scene, by being short and by contrasting Paris' lamentable failure and Menelaos' superiority, does not enhance the figure of Paris.
6 The major arming scenes in the Poem, as Kirk (1985, III. 380–88) describes them, are attributed to Paris, Agamemnon, Patroclos, and Achilles. The extraordinary discrepancy between Paris and the other names does not need to be stressed. These arming scenes resemble each other in composition and in the use of many formulaic lines.

want to confer to Paris an analogous heroic expectation. But this is only a perverse irony of the narrative, which intends to misplace Paris and to make him occupy a role that he cannot sustain. The text mocks Paris' bravery, as it will do again in the course of the gods' violation of the truce. The text exhibits two contradictory versions of the event on the same page and in the same lines: in one version, we read of Menelaos' heroic actions and expectations; in the other, we read the parodic deformation —of which Menelaos cannot be aware— of the epic narrative rules and realize that these rules do not take seriously Menelaos' heroic commitment.

Through this devious strategy, the narrative displays its collusion with the gods' violation of the truce.

Menelaos' invocation to Zeus is uttered with full and justified passion (III. 351–54):

> Lord Zeus, grant that I punish the man who first wronged me,
> divine Alexander,[7] and kill him through my hand;
> so that anyone, even of the men to come, may shudder
> at doing ill to a host who has given him friendship.

> Ζεῦ ἄνα δὸς τίσασθαι ὅ[8] με πρότερος κάκ' ἔοργε,
> δῖον Ἀλέξανδρον, καὶ ἐμῆς ὑπὸ χερσὶ δάμασσον,
> ὄφρα τις ἐρρίγῃσι καὶ ὀψιγόνων ἀνθρώπων
> ξεινοδόκον[9] κακὰ ῥέξαι, ὅ κεν φιλότητα παράσχῃ.

The solemn invocation to "Lord Zeus" and the epithet itself, *anax*, are rare (eight times in the *Iliad*, once in the *Odyssey*). Characters address an invocation to Zeus in decisive moments: Achilles, for instance, invokes Zeus when he sends Patroclos to fight (XVI. 233), with a most elaborate and enigmatic series of epi-

---

**7** δῖον Ἀλέξανδρον: the epithet picks up the nominative form δῖος Ἀλέξανδρος of III. 329, the whole line of which returns at VII. 355 and VIII. 82. At III. 329, the whole line reads δῖος Ἀλέξανδρος Ἑλένης πόσις ἠϋκόμοιο ("divine Alexander, husband of lovely-haired Helen"). This line introduces his arming scene and links him with Helen, daughter of Zeus, as he prepares to fight against her previous husband. These connections with a heroic context and indirectly with Zeus may perhaps suffice to justify the epithet. At III. 352, Menelaos is made to employ the epithet as he prays to Zeus: if the audience feels that the epithet is contextually inappropriate, it may understand its sarcastic denotation: "your divine Alexander" (See the Appendix).
**8** In principle, this ὅ of the autonomous relative clause could be understood as a conjunction: "since…" Ruijgh 1971, 273, 322.
**9** ξεινοδόκον "who receives a guest" is hapax in the *Iliad*. Without mentioning the function of Zeus Xenios, this word of course suggests it.

thets. In this case, as in that of Menelaos, Zeus does not satisfy the prayers, because both heroes are asking for something that contradicts his will and his determined order of things.[10] After Achilles' prayer, the text (XVI. 249–50) informs the Narratees that Zeus did not consent to the return of Patroclos to Achilles. Here, after Menelaos' prayer, the text does not need to report Zeus' negative response, since the Narratees know from III. 302 that the prayer will not be fulfilled: Menelaos' throw fails to wound Paris. There is no need to make explicit what the action makes evident: Menelaos attacks with his sword, but his sword breaks in his hands in three or four pieces. Obviously, Zeus rejected Menelaos' request and his claim at a sort of moral and anthropological right to kill Paris.[11]

Menelaos' indictment of Zeus' intervention, as his sword breaks in his hands (III. 365: "Father Zeus, no god is more baleful than you!"), implies a miraculous event whose author the text does not need to name: the Narratees know that the sword does not break by mere chance when Menelaos hits Paris' helmet. It is a sudden flash without any duration and leaves no witness unless it be the unique one for whose fate the miracle has been accomplished. It is at this point that Menelaos "raises his glance to wide heaven," a rare gesture found exclusively in the *Iliad*,[12] and, understandably, launches an invective against the god (III. 365–67):

> Father Zeus, no god is more baleful than you!
> (Ζεῦ πάτερ οὔ τις σεῖο θεῶν ὀλοώτερος ἄλλος)[13]
> Here I thought I was punishing Paris for his wickedness
> and now my sword is broken in my hands.

Suddenly the text stages heaven as dishearteningly empty, in Menelaos' eyes. The Narratees are not surprised: even his gesture of raising his eyes to heaven

---

10 Paris will kill Achilles (XXII. 358–60), and Patroclos will not return to Achilles because Zeus has determined his death (XV. 64–65).
11 The traditional causes of the Trojan War are supported in the *Iliad* by Menelaus, Agamemnon, the old men of Troy (III. 156–60), and even Hector (XXII. 116). See also IV. 163–68, and my Ch. 6.1 and n. 25.
12 I have analyzed this iterative syntactical unity ("raising the eyes toward the wide heaven" ἰδὼν εἰς οὐρανὸν εὐρύν) in Pucci 2011: it is found only five times and only in the *Iliad* and it carries a singular religious intensity. It "means explicitly both to seek a mental contact with Zeus, as the next invocation confirms, and figuratively to scan heaven imagining Zeus' unfathomable figure. The parallel ritual gesture of 'raising the arms in prayer' (χεῖρας ἀνασχών, see, for instance, III. 275) represents the same attempt at a symbolic contact, but it misses the graphic and emotional power that the scanning of the wide heaven with the eyes felicitously carries" (p. 429).
13 With the same insult Achilles reproaches Apollo who has tricked him (XXII. 15: ἔβλαψάς μ' ἑκάεργε θεῶν ὀλοώτατε πάντων).

appears to them superfluous, since they know that Zeus is gazing at the battle and, as Menelaos suspects (III. 366–67), causes Menelaos' sword to break into pieces. The miracle has no visible agent but, as for analogous interventions by a visible god —for instance Apollo against Patroclos—, constitutes a violation of the human action, introduces an asymmetry in the relation between mortals and immortals, and leaves unexplained what human characters, beside Menelaos, saw and felt. This divine intervention jusitifies Menelaos' anger and displays his vain bravery, but it is also a very good trick for achieving a bitter and perverse parody of the heroic fight, whose superfluity is necessary for the continuation of the war and of its poetic narrative.[14]

The scene ends with farcical humor, as Menelaos grabs hold of Paris' helmet and drags him toward the Achaeans, while the strap under Paris' throat strangles him (III. 373–82):

> he would have dragged him away and won an unspeakable triumph,
> had not Aphrodite, daughter of Zeus,[15] been watching sharply.
> She broke the chinstrap [...]
> and the helmet came away empty in the heavy hands of the Atrides [...]
> He turned against his man, determined to kill him
> with the bronze spear. But Aphrodite snatched Paris away,
> easily, since she is a goddess, and hid him in a thick mist
> and set him down again in his own perfumed bedchamber.

The text plunges us into a farce. The passage begins with the usual contrary-to-fact conditional sentence that is used to annul a heroic and sublime deed, and it ends in a way in which no heroic battle would ever end (see Corey 2009, 131). Aphrodite, "Zeus' daughter" (373), breaks the chin strap that was suffocating Paris, snatches him away and sets him down in his perfumed bedroom. Given that the gods are watching and Zeus does not intervene, it may be reasonable to argue that Zeus is in agreement with Aphrodite that the battle should end without Paris' death.

Aphrodite brings Paris to his own perfumed bedchamber not to give him rest or comfort, but in order to organize his amorous encounter with Helen, an intercourse somehow symbolic of the first one that the goddess originally prom-

---

**14** See Zeus' first rejection of the truce at III. 302: the *diêgêsis* asserts that Zeus vouched no fulfillment to the prayers of the Achaean and Trojan soldiers. The *Iliad* will not show Paris killing Achilles nor the death of Paris: according to the *Little Iliad*, he will be killed by Philoctetes.
**15** The epithet, notwithstanding its frequency (seven times in the *Iliad*) becomes here contextually significant: Zeus does not stop Aphrodite, since she accomplishes that which conforms to his will.

ised to Paris and brought about by persuading Helen. Aphrodite repeats the scandalous gesture that is at the origin of the Trojan War. Rescuing Paris means not only saving his life, but also ensuring that Troy continues to protect Helen and refuses to give her back. Aphrodite's gesture intimates that Paris did not rape Helen, but that she came to him under the goddess' pressure.[16] This is the reason why the text ends the duel by crowning it with a scene of seduction and love between the two fatal lovers.

It is after Paris and Helen make love that in book IV the gods face the question raised by Menelaos' victory. According to the terms of the truce, the Trojans should now give Helen back to Menelaos with a rich recompense and the war should end.

However, neither Zeus nor Hera or Athena want the war to stop. The stage becomes exclusively divine and a dialogue develops between Zeus and his wife in the presence of his daughter. Given the agreement on the destruction of Troy (XV. 70–1) between the three divine powers, the Narratees might expect an easy and unanimous decision. Yet this is not what happens: the Poet takes the occasion of their agreement to show the basic differences in their views of Troy and their inability to negotiate directly a resolution. A resolution will finally be reached, but only after constant attacks and provocations, by which each god will assail or ridicule the unalterable position of the other. The gods are individual Powers ("Puissances," as Vernant used to call them), not political, negotiating Beings.

Zeus launches a provocation at Hera (IV. 5–19 and 31–34): the provocation will rouse her anger; Zeus knows that she will succumb to her anger and will request that the war be unconditionally continued until the final destruction of Troy. The *diêgêsis* defines Zeus' ironic provocation (IV. 5–6):

> immediately the son of Kronos tried to provoke [to rise the anger of] Hera, speaking deviously with sneering words.
>
> αὐτίκ' ἐπειρᾶτο Κρονίδης ἐρεθιζέμεν Ἥρην
> κερτομίοις ἐπέεσσι παραβλήδην ἀγορεύων.

---

[16] On the ambiguous role of Aphrodite, goddess of love but also lover of Ares, see Pironti 2007, and on the goddess' particular ambiguity in this scene, see Bouvier 2016, 255–56. Bouvier also suggests that Aphrodite, by pushing a resistant Helen to make love with Paris, repeats and renews her first intervention, when she gave Helen to Paris. The suggestion is very attractive, for it is supported by the preceding dialogue between Helen and Aphrodite and by Aphrodite's zeal to provoke the erotic encounter. In the *Iliad*, however, Helen does not feel she was Paris' victim when she departed with him, despite his word "ἁρπάξας" "I carried you off" (III. 448). In this renewed scene, she ends by participating in the pleasure of love.

Zeus speaks deviously "because he really needs to get the fighting restarted to fulfill his promise to Thetis" (Kirk 1985, 332),[17] and to ensure his larger plan, the defeat of Troy. We will see later why the text makes Zeus play this pantomime. Zeus begins by touching the sensitive chords of Hera's and Athena's tempers (IV. 7–14):[18]

> Two among the goddesses are supporters of Menelaos,
> Hera of Argos and Alalcomeneis Athena:[19]
> And, of course, sitting from afar they enjoy [Menelaos' success],
> watching him, while smile-loving Aphrodite forever
> stands by the other man and defends him from death:[20]
> and even now she rescued him when he thought that he would die.
> Yet, truly, the victory goes to Menelaos dear to Ares:
> let us then think how things will be accomplished.

Zeus begins by naming the three goddesses: they cannot be mentioned together and their actions cannot be compared without some implicit reasons. He evokes the names of the three goddesses involved in Paris' judgement and implies that Aphrodite won again – by saving Paris, she prevented Menelaos from killing him and insured the happy continuation of the affair that she had concocted. With this simple evocation, Zeus provokes the bitter reaction of Hera; when he argues that Menelaos is the victor (14–15), and that the goddesses and Zeus must consider what to do, he, with a mocking emphasis, appears to opt for peace (IV. 17–19):[21]

> If then this [i.e. peace] were somehow sweet and pleasing to all of us,
> the city of lord Priam may still be lived in,
> and Menelaos may lead away Argive Helen.

---

**17** On the evocation of Zeus as "son of Kronos" and its possible allusion to the theomachia, see Louden 2005, 17. In the *Iliad*, gods provoke, irritate, and cause anger through the verb *erethizô* more often than do human beings.
**18** Though Zeus speaks to Hera and Athena, he mentions them in the third person, as an objective observer or as the Poet would, with their epithets in a chiastic sequence (line 8).
**19** Hera and Athena are the goddesses who have a special concern for Paris and Menelaos, the two contenders, and the two men who, because of Paris' rape, are, in some versions, the cause of the war. The emphatic beginning, "Two among the goddesses," is uttered in contrast to the one, i.e. Aphrodite: the contrast is reminiscent of the dramatic, older one.
**20** Zeus is made to avoid the name "Paris" as the name corresponding to "Menelaos" and indicates him only with "the other." The name "Paris" would have made the allusion to the judgment too obvious; the mention of the two goddesses seen in opposition to Aphrodite was sufficient to recall it.
**21** Ameis-Hentze 1913, *ad loc.*: "in spottischem Tone"; Kirk 1990, *ad loc.*: "The sarcastic tone comes out in the stress on 'all' and 'sweet and pleasant...'"

Peace pleases neither goddess (and, of course, not even Zeus). The optative mood in lines 18–19 is potential and delivers almost a "wish," which allows Hera to suspect that Zeus is on the side of peace. Her suspicion shows how duplicitous Zeus is and what an untalented a reader of others' minds Hera is. She fails to see that Zeus is disguising his real view on the question. The suspicion triggers her outrage (24: "she could not contain her rage"[22]), which explodes with a scandalized question (IV. 24–29):

> Awful son of Kronos, what sort of speech is this one?
> How can you wish [ἐθέλεις] to make wasted and fruitless the fatigue,
> the sweat that I have sweated in toil, my horses worn out,
> gathering my people[23] and bringing evil to Priam and his children?
> Do it, then, but not all the rest of us gods approve you.[24]

She gives no reason for her destructive commitment, no grounds for her relentless hatred that induced her to harm the Trojans with tremendous physical efforts. At line 27, "the sweat that I have sweated in toil" (ἱδρῶ θ' ὃν ἵδρωσα μόγῳ), her language contains an excessive emotional charge: this etymological figure with "sweat" occurs only here in Homer, and the mention of "sweat" appears only in regards to Hephaistos as he works (XVIII. 372); otherwise it refers to horses, and once to a deer. The tone sounds menial, undignified for the sister and wife of Zeus, whose high status she celebrates (IV. 58–61).

The text contrasts her explicit motivation to act with Zeus' reticence. Although Zeus knows the source of her hatred against Troy, mockingly, he asks her the source of such rage (IV. 31–33):

---

[22] She is often represented in this way, unable to contain her rage: VIII. 461. Elmer 2013, 147 writes: Zeus' speech "according to the Narrator is intended to 'provoke' Hera." It does indeed provoke Hera and is the cause of her violent accusation.

[23] According to Wilamowitz 1916, 30, here the text has Hera refer to a poem about the beginning of the war. This assumption seems to me most probable: in the *Iliad* we do not see her fighting and recruiting soldiers.

[24] Hera's utterance includes the formulaic first (24) and conclusive (29) lines that she uses at XVI. 440 and 443: this pattern seems to indicate to the audience that Zeus will acquiesce to the goddess, Hera, who uses it. We know that Zeus will certainly acquiesce to Hera in our passage, since he manipulates Hera so that she requests to restart the fighting. On the line, "Do it, then, but not all of us other gods approve you," Elmer 2013, 149 has a subtle comment, in harmony with the thesis of his book: "the rhetoric deployed on both sides clearly articulates the decisive function assigned to *epainos*" (consensus, collective approval). It seems to me that this rhetoric is vividly present in Hera's blind view of what Zeus is aiming at, but it is not seriously intended in Zeus' game, since his dissent is a fiction and a provocation (IV. 5–6). He is not opening a political debate, but using a tricky disguise to take her where he wants.

> My dear, what could be all the great evils done to you
> by Priam and the sons of Priam, such that you are so obstinately
> furious to destroy the strong-founded city of Ilion?

As expected, Hera does not answer this question, but everybody in the audience knew the response. For what harms, evils, and disrespect did the Trojans commit against Hera to deserve her obsessive hatred, unless it be the infamy of her defeat in Paris' judgment? Unless it be the protection that the Trojans still grant to Paris, as Aphrodite's last involvement again ensures? The whole mythical story of Paris' judgment and its function in promoting the Trojan War emerges in Zeus' mocking tone.[25]

Zeus insists and transforms Hera's obsession into a mental disease through an image that, for its brutality —"the savagery of Zeus' sarcasm" (Kirk 1990, 334)— is shocking (IV. 34–36):

> if you, after crossing the gates and the large walls [of Troy],
> would devour Priam raw,[26] and the children of Priam,
> and the other Trojans, only then would you cure your rage.
>
> εἰ δὲ σύ γ' εἰσελθοῦσα πύλας καὶ τείχεα μακρὰ
> ὠμὸν βεβρώθοις Πρίαμον Πριάμοιό τε παῖδας
> ἄλλους τε Τρῶας, τότε κεν χόλον ἐξακέσαιο.

Zeus diagnoses that the only medicine for Hera to recover from her hatred would be a beastly raw devouring of the entire population of Troy.

---

**25** Nothing of Zeus' dismissing or even mocking the mythical ground of the fall of Troy is to be found in Allan (2006). Zeus' praise of Troy contradicts the accusations that Menelaos and others launch against the Trojan violation of the norms of hospitality, connecting this with the cause of the war: see for instance I. 152–62; III. 154–60, 171–180, 354–60; IX. 337–40, etc. Lloyd Jones 1971, 5 quotes a passage with Menelaos in support of the idea that Zeus is the god of justice in the *Iliad*, but Menelaos knows nothing about Zeus unless it be the traditional myth of Zeus Xenios, whose function and whose sense of justice are here fully neglected. See De Cristofaro 2014, 39. The hypertext produces at least three motivations for the war: either Zeus' desire to punish Troy for Paris' abduction of Helen and the violation of the law of hospitality; or his will to destroy the heroic race (see Hesiod, *Cat. of Women* fr. 155). Rousseau 1995 accepts this premise as Zeus' final purpose. Or perhaps Zeus desires to lighten the burden of humanity's weighing on mother Earth (*Cypria* fr. 1: see Tsagalis 2016, 104). Kullmann 2012, 15 returns to his earlier view that the phrase Διὸς δ' ἐτελείετο βουλή (I. 5) is an allusion to the legend that Zeus had caused the Trojan War in order to relieve the earth from the burden of mankind.

**26** The verb *bibrôskô* "I devour" occurs only one other time in the *Iliad* (XXII. 94) and denotes a snake's act of devouring; in the *Odyssey* too, out of two examples of the verb, one (xxii. 403) implies a lion's act of devouring.

This anthropophagous motif is employed in the *Iliad* by human characters: both Achilles and Hecuba express the desire to devour their respective enemies who have brought upon them the most devastating sorrow. Their brutal desire hyperbolically represents the intensity of the pain they suffered from their enemies.²⁷

This epic theme is deployed to shock the audience, but it is understood that it will never be implemented.²⁸ Likewise, Zeus assumes here that Hera's desire to eat the Trojans raw will not be fulfilled: once again, it is only a very brutal and expressive epic *façon de parler*.

The expression that Zeus is made to employ, κεν χόλον ἐξακέσαιο (36), metaphorically means "you would appease your rage," but literally means "you would heal your rage," almost as if her rage were a pathological disease.²⁹ There is no comparable example in the *Iliad* of Hera's beastly hatred for mortals: for a god, such a feeling is odd, inexplicable, and only by a polemical or mocking husband is it described as a disease and a folly.

The Narrator continues to develop the comparison between Zeus' silent motivations for the destruction of Troy and the violent urgings of Hera. Two different natures or casts of mind are compared. Both depict a negative theology, but with diverse features, one more anthropomorphic than the other, though they both have the same finality. It becomes clear why the Narrator decides to have Zeus disguise his agreement with Hera: this disguise and aggressive pantomime allows Zeus to attack Hera's inappropriate motivations for the destruction of Troy, which are also the traditional ones. The Narrator uses Zeus' mockery of Hera in order to support his polemic against the tradition, while having Zeus stay silent about his own motivations. It is as if the text refused to imagine any anthropomorphic reasons or any other reason for Zeus' decision to destroy Troy.

---

27 Achilles (XXII. 347 ff.) tells dying Hector that he wishes his fury would drive him to cut Hector into pieces and eat him raw, then he tells him that he will give Hector's body to bitches and birds; Hecuba in XXIV. 212 ff. tells Hector that she wishes she could set her teeth in the middle of Achilles' liver and eat it.

28 Analogously, the motif, "to give the corpses of the enemies for the delicate feasting of dogs and birds," which occurs in the proem of the poem (I. 4–5) and elsewhere, is never accomplished.

29 Kirk 1985, *ad loc.* stresses this point: "Only through having devoured them [the Trojans] she would cure her rage —which is thus implied to be a kind of disease." Among the translators, Fagel prefers the literal connotation, "you just might cure your rage," as does Lasserre: "guérirais-tu ta bile."

Hera will not answer Zeus' sarcastic question and condemning remarks, and for good reason: both her hatred and its nature are, in her eyes, proper and in need of no apology.

Continuing his speech, Zeus, with a gesture of false magnanimous comprehension, yields to Hera's will of destroying Troy ("do as you want, so that this decision may not become a source of quarrel between us," 37–38). He places his concession to Hera within a confession that he loves Troy: he is therefore allowing her to destroy a city dear to his heart. He means to underscore the generosity of his concession by emphasizing the pain of seeing Troy destroyed. He then tries to explain why, though he feels such sympathy for Troy, he still allows her to destroy the city. Zeus introduces an odd argument: he requires that Hera make no opposition whenever he wishes to destroy a city dear to her heart, since he has now granted her the destruction of Troy, which is a city dear to him (40–49):

> Whenever I too might wish to destroy that city,
> as I please, the one in which men born there are dear to you,
> do not detain my anger, but let me do it [μή τι διατρίβειν τὸν ἐμὸν χόλον, ἀλλά μ' ἐᾶσαι]:
> since willingly I granted you (ἐγὼ σοὶ δῶκα) this with my unwilling heart.[30]
> For as many cities where earthly men live
> under the sun and the starry sky,
> of these, none has ever been honored nearer in my heart than sacred Ilion
> and Priam and the people of Priam of the good spear,
> since my altar never missed fair feast,
> the libation and the fat: for this is the honor we get."[31]

---

**30** This oxymoron shows the troubled position of Zeus. Marks 2001, 53–56 sees Zeus' claim as part of his deceptive game. Elmer 2013, 153 cherishes the reading option that "Zeus is not merely at odds with Hera and the other pro-Achaean gods, but at odds as well with himself; he both understands the necessity of Troy's destruction and regrets its demise."

**31**  αἴ γὰρ ὑπ' ἠελίῳ τε καὶ οὐρανῷ ἀστερόεντι
ναιετάουσι πόληες ἐπιχθονίων ἀνθρώπων,
τάων μοι περὶ κῆρι τιέσκετο Ἴλιος ἱρὴ
καὶ Πρίαμος καὶ λαὸς ἐϋμμελίω Πριάμοιο.
οὐ γάρ μοί ποτε βωμὸς ἐδεύετο δαιτὸς ἐΐσης
λοιβῆς τε κνίσης τε· τὸ γὰρ λάχομεν γέρας ἡμεῖς. (IV. 44–49)

Line 44 does not recur again in the poem in this exact formulation and creates, also through its novelty, a striking emphasis; the locution ἐπιχθονίων ἀνθρώπων is found only here in the *Iliad*; lines 48–49 are repeated by Zeus at XXIV. 69–70: the word λοιβῆς appears twice in these two passages out of its four occurrences in the *Iliad*. The attribution of δαιτὸς ἐΐσης to gods would be improper if the *geras* did not emphasize the symbolic nature of the offering. Usually, the phrase is used for men's "equally divided feasting." But the offerings on Zeus' altar are neither

This passage introduces complex points and requires a detailed analysis.

1. Zeus assumes as a mere hypothetical eventuality that someday he too would feel a passionate wish to destroy a city dear to her (ὁππότε κεν καὶ ἐγὼ μεμαὼς πόλιν ἐξαλαπάξαι τὴν ἐθέλω... 40–1): Hera would then feel pain because of Zeus' urge to destroy such city, and yet she should not prevent him from destroying it, just as he now does not prevent her from destroying Troy, a city dear to him. This hypothetical example has the immediate purpose of lending perspective to Hera about how Zeus now feels as he consents to the destruction of Troy. But, in fact, this convoluted passage tells Hera that she has the right (ἐγὼ σοὶ δῶκα) to destroy Troy even if Zeus is pained by it. As Zeus grants her this right (ἐγὼ σοὶ δῶκα) of destroying Troy, he implicitly confirms a sort of principle: gods have the right to follow their anthropomorphic feelings in rescuing or destroying cities. Yet he is silent about the condition that controls this legitimacy: if the gods' feelings do not correspond to the destiny of the city, their feelings will be vain. Zeus is the evidence of this: the destiny of Troy is to be captured and destroyed —of course Zeus knows this (XV. 70–1)— thus Zeus' feeling of sympathy for the city must be vain. For the audience of the Poem, Zeus' concession explains why cities, even when they are pious and devoted to the gods, may end in ruin and destruction. Both the hatred felt by a particular god — whatever its motivation may be—and destiny explain and determine the destruction of great cities; to mortal eyes, of course, this condition appears unjustified and unfair, as indeed it has no other source than the explication given by Zeus.

2. Hera has the right to destroy Troy if she wants, but she needs Zeus' consent. When Zeus consents to the destruction of Troy, he acts as the lord of human destinies.

The oxymoron (IV. 43: "I willingly granted you this with my unwilling heart") accounts for two equally powerful but contradictory urges. Zeus avows that the urge of his desire to agree with Hera is just as powerful as his desire to avoid the destruction of Troy: yet he agrees with her. He does so because as lord of destiny he has preordained the destiny of Troy and knows that no feeling of sympathy can save the city (XV. 70–1). He can therefore make the generous —

---

divided nor feasted upon, as men do with their own food: they have a devotional and symbolic intent. The passage gives the impression of having been composed for this exceptional and unique context. Kirk 1985, 333 notes that the audience may wonder why, given this affection, Zeus allows the city to fall, and he answers that the city is punished because of Paris' offense against hospitality —which is protected by Zeus as Xenios. But, as I am showing, the text stages a Zeus who pays no attention to his specific role as Xenios.

and purely rhetorical— gesture of consenting "willingly" to Hera's urge. In fact, the contradiction lies in himself: if he had not determined the destruction of Troy, he could save the city and deny his consent to Hera.[32] His concession is pure posturing.

When Zeus faces Sarpedon's and Hector's deaths, the *diêgêsis* makes him oblivious of his responsibility for their death, and makes him aware only of his fatherhood of Sarpedon and of Hector's piety. No inner conflict emerges and only the gods prevent Zeus from saving Sarpedon and Hector. On another occasion, as Zeus gazes at the Immortal Horses as they mourn for Patroclos' death (XIX. 443–7), he strongly expresses the conflicted condition of an immortal being who loves a mortal being (see above Ch. 4.2). Zeus perceives and describes that conflict as an objective phenomenon, but not as his own experience.

On the present occasion, we have a new version of that conflict. Zeus feels and formulates in a specific rhetorical figure the conflict between the two commitments; his deep appreciation for Troy's piety and the unavoidable destruction of the city. As he says "I willingly granted you this," implicitly he must think something like "I cannot do otherwise, since I preordained that destiny for Troy." Then he adds: "Yet I do so unwillingly." He should have felt this pain when he decides, for now it is too late. As god of destiny, however, his decision could not be motivated by his emotions. Accordingly, Zeus recites before Hera the scene of a difficult, even costly, decision, when in fact he has now nothing to decide and, if he suffered a dramatic internal conflict, it only occurred when he preordained the defeat of Troy previously. We Narratees do not know how "willingly or unwillingly he took that original decision, yet we know that finally, even if regretfully he made it; we, however, seeing how unproblematic it is for Zeus to kill the pious Hector, the exclusive defender of the most pious city, doubt that he had any moral, psychological, or sentimental troubles when he condemned the city. The lord of destiny acting with the impassive disposition of the Golden Scales cannot entertain that sort of feeling.[33]

---

**32** I do not need to clarify that, in the prospective of the composition of the Poem, Zeus' determination to destroy the city corresponds to the hypertext' representation. The Iliadic Zeus does not suspend, but rather leaves some fluidity in this representation by giving partial and provisional victory to the Trojans. Even if the Narrative is aware of this pre-Iliadic situation, it immerses Zeus and his peers into a full experience of the conditions they have authentically chosen in this Poem.

**33** In XV. 65–67 Zeus announces the death of Sarpedon with the recognition —perhaps with a touch of pathos— that he is his son, and he announces the death of Hector and the defeat of Troy (XV. 71) with the most impassive tone: see Ch. 2.1 and n. 6, 7.

The conclusion to which I am driving is that the pathos of Zeus' oxymoron is an impressive rhetorical device by which Zeus is made to appear as feeling the pain for a decision that has already been made, and as suffering the pain of a conflict that he cannot really suffer at present: the rhetorical force of this representation consists in detaching him from the choice that he made at the time in which he preordained the capture of Troy, and yet to represent him with the pathos that is imaginable if he were now deciding and choosing the destiny of Troy, before Hera. The splitting of Zeus' personality allows the Poet and the Muses to showcase for the audience the destruction of a great and pious city from two points of view. This event can be viewed in the context of negative theology and of historical necessity: in such context, it creates no other human reaction than the recognition of the nonsense of the event, the *mysterium* under which mortals live; but within a second context, that of the recognized and appreciated force, value, and greatness of the destroyed city, human consciousness cannot avoid to cry for the scandal of the event and for the misery of such a precious loss. Zeus' split personality symbolizes both contexts and their incommunicability. Steeping the pathetic moment into a context in which no real choice is possible, increases the poetic force of regret, and despair: it also brings to light that one of the alternatives —saving the city for its piety— may never have existed.

At the level of Zeus' personality the conflict remains inoperative and cannot unfold as a psychological crisis, as the inability to decide and act, and therefore as a tragic impasse. It can only resolve itself in the form of a regret: Zeus authorizes Hera to destroy the city though he regrets this destiny. There never was, *at that moment,* any other solution.

The praise Zeus offers in honor of Troy is very high: in the whole world, Troy is the city he honors most, because of her ritual devotion to him. As, however, Zeus' care and honor for Troy are ineffective in the face of destiny ("I willingly grant you..."), these feelings take the shape of an abstract stance and sound like the expression of a powerfully rhetorical regret. Hera will interpret his emotional and ethical stance as a false posture intended to bother her (see points 3 and 4). Simultaneously, Zeus' effective avow: "I willingly grant you..." opens the manifestation of his real power in the following phases of the debate.

3. Hera realizes that Zeus is consenting to her urge to capture Troy and that, concerning the gods' relationship with mortals, he shares her opinion. She enthusiastically accepts the barter (IV. 51–56):

> Very well: I have three dearest cities,
> Argos, Sparta, and Mycenae of the wide ways.[34]
> Destroy them utterly whenever they become hateful to your heart:
> I will not stand up for these against you, nor begrudge you.
> For even if I prevented you and did not allow you to destroy them,
> I would not succeed in preventing you, since you are far stronger.

> ἤτοι ἐμοὶ τρεῖς μὲν πολὺ φίλταταί εἰσι πόληες
> Ἄργός τε Σπάρτη τε καὶ εὐρυάγυια Μυκήνη·
> τὰς διαπέρσαι ὅτ' ἄν τοι ἀπέχθωνται περὶ κῆρι·
> τάων οὔ τοι ἐγὼ πρόσθ' ἵσταμαι οὐδὲ μεγαίρω...
> εἴ περ γὰρ φθονέω τε καὶ οὐκ εἰῶ διαπέρσαι
> οὐκ ἀνύω φθονέουσ' ἐπεὶ ἦ πολὺ φέρτερός ἐσσι.

Though Zeus has demanded Hera not to oppose the destruction of one of the cities dear to her, she offers him three cities. At the psychological level, this block of cities would seem to emphasize the essentially limitless extent of Hera's ferocious hatred, as she is ready to trade three for one. These three cities are Hera's dearest, and they are the cities respectively of Agamemnon, Menelaos, and Diomedes.

She seems to increase purposely the horror of her concession in order to display Zeus' awfully rapacious appetite. For Hera deals with Zeus' proposal in an ironic and amused tone: she clearly intimates that Zeus' barter is meaningless, since she would not be able to prevent him from destroying whatever city of hers he would wish to: you ask me, she tells him, to abandon to your wrath, without protesting, one city I love: excellent! I give you three of them, since you could destroy them if you wanted, even if I were "standing up for these against you, or begrudging you." She mocks the force of the care Zeus displayed for Troy, while he consented to her destruction of Troy: "why bother me with your 'unwilling heart'?" she tells him, increasing the number of the doomed cities: "I could be in deep despair, yet you would not care for it and would destroy the cities I love." She says with a mocking imperative: "Destroy them utterly!" She smartly realizes that Zeus' injunction, "whenever I too might wish to destroy a city dear to you, you should not detain my anger," proves that the really monstrous god is not her, but him.

---

**34** The text uses what is called an "augmented triad that has a fixed way of selecting three names, and composing them in a sort of unity, both metrical and conceptual." See West 2011, p. 140 with reference to p. 87 n. 145: "The line made up of three names, the third of which carries an epithet, corresponds to a common IE pattern: *IEPM* 117–19 ('augmented triad')." This effect is the reason why these three cities have been mentioned together in the classical tradition as Hera's cities.

Zeus has no response.

Hera takes Zeus' hypothetical hatred for a city loved by her as an actual fact and derives from it her mocking of all his pious and self-righteous postures. She implicitly teases Zeus' faked longing for the establishment of peace through Menelaos' victory; she teases Zeus' hesitation about destroying a dear city – dear because pious —and exposes his habitual dictatorial behavior. While he does not reveal why an unavoidable destiny —of which he is the ruler— may lead to the destruction of a city dear to her, he declares that his reason for destroying it would be hatred and anger, exactly what Hera feels for Troy. She realizes that his whole pantomime was only a game intended to irritate her; while the Narratees realize that the pantomime allows the Poet to exhibit Hera's and Zeus' different disposition of mind toward divine responsibility for the destiny of the cities.

There is no longer any need to bicker or dissent. Since Zeus is the most powerful god among all the gods, he could, —in a hypothesized contingency— without any hesitation or concern, destroy any city dear to whichever god. Again, no politicking is involved: power speaks, decides, and acts.

4. Since the power to destroy a city and the legitimacy of doing so are the privileges of each god, Hera now supports her own perfect privilege. She extols the power due to which she can carry out her plans even without his consent: I am a goddess as you are a god; I have the same legitimacy as you (57–67):

> Yet you must make my labor not unaccomplished,
> for I am a god too and both I and you are of the same race,
> for crooked-devising Kronos generated me as most honored
> in both ways, because of my birth and since I am called your consort
> and you are the lord of all the immortal gods.
> Fine! May we yield on this matter to each other,
> I to you and you to me: the other immortal gods
> will follow us. And you immediately command Athena
> to go to the cruel battleground of the Trojans and Achaeans
> and seek that the Trojans be the first to offend
> the exulting Achaeans by breaking the sworn truce.

Hera asserts the same prerogatives of power that Zeus has and ends as a winner in the dialogue: "Fine!" she says, "you know my right, and you have already given me your consent: then send Athena to violate the truce."

Zeus acquiesces and, turning to Athena, orders her to accomplish that task, using Hera's exact words (IV. 71–2).

Hera's irrepressible hatred of the Trojans emerges again when she plots that the Trojans be made responsible for the violation of the truce (66).

Given her personal and narcissistic motivation, Hera's violent hatred could be judged, by human minds, as being disproportionate to the offense.[35] Yet the Iliadic narrative leaves some fluid examples: Achilles asks whether Apollo shoots at the Achaeans for nine days straight because he blames them "for the sake of some vow, some hecatomb" (I. 65). Since the Narrator in all these cases never notices any scandalized reaction on the part of his characters, we may assume that what might appear to human eyes to be excessive, is for the characters only the effect of shortsighted and distorted visions: men cannot imagine what it means to be an immortal, polyvalent Force. Yet in the case of Hera's monstrous hatred for Troy, we have Zeus' assessment that her behavior is excessive. Zeus mocks and satirizes Hera's sick and obsessive hatred for Troy and, with an ironic question, alludes to Paris' judgment and her offended vanity. Nothing can explain the bestial desires of Hera's hatred unless the resentment caused by her defeat has become a monstrous disease (IV. 30–35). In this way, through the authority of Zeus, the *diêgêsis* supports the Narrator and the Narratees' feeling that, if the Trojan War and the destruction of the city were justified by the goddesses' vanity, the war and the sack of the city were badly and wrongly motivated. Of course, we do not know whether Zeus' motivations are decent and right. In his hypothesized future scenario, they certainly are not. We only realize that Zeus' reticence manifests his role as master of destinies; his total indifference toward those who, like Hector, are trying to save Troy give some sense and direction to the secrecy and mysteriousness of his reasons for destroying this most pious city.[36]

After such a long analysis of the effects and tensions the dialogue produces between the two characters, it may be convenient to look at the compositional and theological advantages the *diêgêsis* derives from such a complex and problematic debate. The subtle strategic move of the text consists in the hypothetic concession Zeus gives when he assumes that "I too, some day, might wish to destroy that city, as I please." This concession places him on the same level of personal motivations as Hera. Because this concession is given as a mere hypothesis, the text leaves open to the Narratees the idea that this event may never occur. The irresolvable contrast between Zeus' two sorts of motivations —his

---

**35** While on the mythological register Paris' judgment silently justifies Hera's readiness to sacrifice her three favorite cities in return for the destruction of Troy, "in human terms, in terms that might satisfy Homer's audience, there is no sufficient reason." O. Taplin, 1992, p. 132.

**36** In the theological terms of Bouvier 2016, pp. 259–61, the inevitability of the war can be read in the fact that, though Zeus hates Ares, finally they are shown to sit together, for no apparent reason, surrounded by a common blessedness (V. 906). It is a perfect image that gives the appropriate linguistic form to the inextricability of Zeus' double posture.

humanlike ones (= these of Hera) and the mysterious ones of the master of destinies— is inscribed in that syntactical movement of the hypothesis. It is this open and unrestrainable movement that controls the opposition between the higher order of things, of which Zeus is master, and the personal interest of a god: the irresolvable contrast fails to explode and remains in the realm of the conjectural. Therefore, the hypothesis functions here as a textual trick that eludes the certainty of Zeus behaving like Hera. It parallels the other analogous textual tricks by which the text places mortal and immortal natures in direct contrast but succeeds in suggesting or simply saving their permeability. The most explicit case we have commented upon is the double identity that mortals and immortals attribute to the slayer of Patroclos. The gods assert that Apollo killed Patroclos and gave the *kudos* to Hector (XIII. 454–56): it is through this enigmatic formulation that Patroclos' killer remains perfectly ambiguous. (See Ch. III. 3-4).

The conspicuous textual exhibition of Zeus' two contrasting roles occurs in the oxymoron, through which Zeus appears to be conscious of the inextricable roles of his divine activity. Yet, human feelings are changeable and ineffective. Not only, in a future hypothesis could they become negative and change love into hatred, but even in their positive disposition they may be powerless. We have seen that one of two commitments —Zeus' love for Troy' ritual devotion to himself— creates a high emotional effect without real corresponding psychological, theological and conflictual consequences.

The assumption implied in Zeus' pantomime is an example that Zeus offers to Hera to make her conscious of what a god may feel when his dear city is destroyed by another god's will. Of course, Zeus knows that his example dismisses or simply obliterates the control that destiny has over all the cities.

This dismissal leaves the Narratees surprised: the day in which Zeus would act as Hera might never arrive, but how to be sure? Hera takes him seriously and asserts with a polemical irony that neither she —nor any other god— would be able to stop Zeus if he were to decide to destroy a city.

The tricks and devices of the text designate the conscious textual fashions of representing and giving a form to the imponderable secrecy of the divine. Here the oxymoron and the syntactical hypothesis function as the appropriate forms chosen by the text of the Muses to intimate some aspects of the inextricable and secret nature of Zeus. The oxymoron turns out be the expression of a painful "regret" and the hypothetical syntax leaves open the potentiality of both roles. By giving an appropriate linguistic form to the imponderable and the unknowable, the text endorses the mythical collaboration of men and gods, assumes the contradictory presence in Zeus of anthropomorphic and supernatural aspects, and recognizes its unresolvable nature. Since the language of the Muses can afford to give an appropriate form to Zeus' oxymoronic mind set, and suspend his two different roles, it depicts a truth that vibrates deeper —perhaps uncomfortably— than any straightforward assertion or denial.

Zeus' pantomime also justifies his consent to Hera's desire, with precise theological terms. According to these terms, every god has the right that Hera exercises; namely, to destroy any city that the god hates, on the condition, however, —never announced as such, but constantly implicit— that the order of things allows it. Zeus attenuated the open assertion of his will because he was about to agree with Hera in deciding to break the truce, and to ensure the continuation of the war until the capture of Troy. He first used some teasing about Hera's hatred of Troy: with Zeus' support, the *Iliad* openly smiles at the mythical motivations —as Paris' abduction of Helen, for the capture and destruction of Troy. After the teasing, Zeus preferred to show that his motivation for the destruction of a city could conjecturally be taken as being just as anthropomorphic as that of Hera. Yet he did not specify the reason of his eventual hatred for a city: his motivation remained secret and it is imaginable that, unlike Hera's, it was not the fruit of a simple wounded pride.

Another effect the text derives from the elaborate dialogue is to attribute to Hera the decision to make the Trojans responsible for the breaking of the truce (IV. 66–67 and 71–2). With Athena's intervention, the Trojans need no longer respect the obligations that the truce demanded of them as the defeated party — the restitution of Helen, and an appropriate compensation. Objectively, however, they would be the party to gain the greatest advantage from the truce, even as losers. It would have been more convenient and logical for the Trojans to respect the truce and for the Achaeans to break it, since the Achaeans' desire to pillage the wealthy city, and to see the simple return of Helen, even with some additional compensation for nine years of war, would not have satisfied them. Agamemnon has no difficulty in asserting this point. To attribute to the Trojans the scandalous breaking of the truce is therefore a partisan decision that is caused by Hera's hatred for the Trojans and is supported by Zeus. Hera's hatred and its effects also justify the Trojans' senseless refusal to give back Helen and end stop the war.

1. Troy had already disappeared by the time the *Iliad*'s compositional poem was created and, from what the Poem tells us, the city had been destroyed as Zeus preordained (XV. 70–1). The Narratees may thus feel shocked by the fact that Hera and Zeus —in his hypothetical conjecture— have such an urge to destroy human cities due to personal motivations or without any motivation at all; but they should not be shocked by the fact that cities are destroyed in spite of

their temples, their sacrifices, and their cults for the gods, since the course of history does not obey ethical or religious principles. In the Narrator's eyes, the world does not exist as human beings would like it to be. It is the world itself, with its gods, that the Narrator manifests to men —even through silence.

2. The violation of the truce by the gods seems like an irreverent and nasty gesture. The three gods are irreverent regarding their own function and status, as if mortals' devoted ritual practices had no weight on the gods' will and actions. Achaeans and Trojans had established the truce with stern commitment: they had accomplished the ritual in the name of the gods, through a sacrifice supplemented by a provision of divine punishment for the potential violator (III. 276–80); Zeus himself had been invoked by the anonymous crowd who begged him that the violator's brains and the violator's sons' brains be spilled on the ground and his wife be taken by others (III. 300–01).[37] The text comments on this prayer (302): "So they spoke, but the son of Kronos did in no way fulfill their prayer" ("Ὣς ἔφαν, οὐδ' ἄρα πώ σφιν ἐπεκραίαινε Κρονίων).[38] Now, Zeus himself orders Athena to violate the truce (IV. 70–72) and he certainly does not grant their wish that the violator's and the violator's sons' brains be spilled on the ground, nor that his wife Hera be subjected to others.

It is improbable that the poetic voice aims at such a derisive implication: it raises not even the shadow of a reproach against the gods' dismissal of human hopes, rituals, and curses. Rather, it identifies with the Muses' narrative to show how remote human hopes and expectations are from divine decisions and to hint that Zeus, from the very start, is opposed to the truce. Accordingly, all that has been done to make the truce sacred, the promises, the ritual, etc., was not and will not be considered by Zeus to be compelling. A ritual is rightly compelling if the god agrees with its purpose.

After Zeus' disregard not for a ritual but for the entire pious culture of Priam and his sons, Zeus' dismissing the oath during the celebration of the truce seems a trifle.

To transpose human feelings into anthropomorphic divine characters means to qualify these feelings as absolute and inevitable. The text, through its representation of Hera, shows the human reasons for the war, the feelings that frequently nourish the war, i.e. hatred and resentment. Hera, then, is manipu-

---

**37** This curse "has a parallel in the Vassal Treaties of Esarhaddon and another in Jeremiah 8.10, where Yahweh says of those who have rejected his word, 'Therefore I will give their wives to others, (and) their fields to new owners.'" West 1997, p. 358.
**38** The same line is used for an analogous context of cheating at II. 419, where the *diêgêsis* announces Zeus' rejection of Agamemnon's prayer.

lated by Zeus to display in a grotesque and monstrous form precisely these motivations for the war, her unstoppable resentment for the offense she has received.[39] If the gods have these feelings and if even Zeus can imagine identifying with them, these feelings must truly be ingrained in the world.

3. Concerning the differential features that characterize this Zeus in relation to the Zeus of the "Wrath" part of the Poem, my analysis shows that the character is marked by some differences. The first novelty consists in Zeus' virtuosic game of disguising his intentions and leading the argument where he wants. The Narrator takes the risk of immersing Zeus in an odd and ambiguous role, that of the impassive lord of destiny and of the sensitive god who appreciates men's devotion to him.

In Zeus' ambiguous role, we recognize the god who in books XVI and XXII feels pity and love for Sarpedon and Hector. The strategy of the text consists in making Zeus oblivious of his role as master of destiny to avoid him having a conflict of interest. The gods prevent him from saving the heroes without causing in him of a conflict. In our episode, on the contrary, a conflict is recognized and formulated by Zeus through an oxymoron. We have seen how this rhetorical figure functions and how it points both to an unresolvable conflict and to its resolution under the form of a "regret." A psychological, tragic conflict is avoided, but the tension between the two terms continues to vibrate. He seems to be searching within himself his own motivations for the unpleasant destruction of Troy, and lacks the dictatorial posture with which the Zeus of the *menis* carries out his *boulê*.

Two other features separate this Zeus from the Zeus of the *menis:* he raises the conjecture that someday he could hate a city and, under the compulsion of this feeling, could destroy it. First, by assuming the chance of behaving some day just like Hera, he minimizes his role as god of human destiny. After the powerfully poetic oxymoron in which he sees himself split between his agreement to the final day of Troy and regretting it, he confesses an anthropomorphic motivation —his eventual hatred— that annuls the conflict and makes him resemble any common god rather than the god of the first book of the Poem. Indeed, his role as master of human destiny in the whole dialogue is more presumed than openly declared. This weakening and marginalization of Zeus' dictatorial power as god of destiny makes him slightly different from the Zeus of the *menis*. Though, not declaring the reason of his hatred, he accepts that an

---

**39** See Bassett 2003 (1938, 1966), pp. 223–24: "With a single exception, her [Hera's] actions and words spring from a single passion, hatred. This hatred is directed not against Paris, but against the Trojans..."

anthropomorphic feeling similar to that of Hera *could* determine his decision. This confession is delivered in a hypothetical syntax and, accordingly, it sounds as Zeus' strategic move to reach his goal with Hera. To this extent, here Zeus does not violate the serious reticence that he has about his motivations in the rest of the Poem when he speaks as god, master of destiny; yet the assumption is made that hatred could determine his decision. The hypothetical syntax and the limited description of the motivation convince me that the text does not violate the normal reticence of Zeus, but comes close to doing so.

I would say that these differences stage a god who is not yet determined to grant victory to the Trojans, and who does not need to impose his will onto Hera. It is fine for him to deride Hera's hatred and her desire to punish the city of Paris, but when he declares that some day he might behave just like Hera, he loses most of the power of his amusing or derisive image of her.

## 6.2 The Breaking of the Truce

As Athena comes down to earth to violate the truce, the human stage is marked by the divine presence: during the duel between Menelaos and Paris, the scene was seen through Menelaos' despear, and the gods' amused and jovial spectatorship; but now the action fully unfolds through the goddess' interventions. The humorous and, in a way, perverse parody of the epic deeds that the gods' spectatorship encouraged the *diegesis* to offer, returns, but now under the direction of the goddess.

Athena descends from Olympus to earth with a miraculous leap (IV. 74–80):

> And she went, darting down from the peaks of Olympus.
> As a star that the son of crooked-thinking Kronos sends,[40]
> a portent to sailors or to a vast host of warriors,
> a shining star: many sparks burst from it;[41]
> similar to this, Pallas Athena jumped onto the ground
> and leaped in the middle. Amazement took hold of all those who saw it,
> the horse-taming Trojans and the well-greaved Achaeans.

---

[40] After Zeus' ambivalent behavior in the previous scene, the text could not choose a more appropriate epithet for him. The epithet, as often, has here too an almost synechdotal function, it describes the part for the whole in a specific context.

[41] The simile does not announce either favorable or unfavorable function of the meteor for sailors or soldiers, but Athena's purpose is certainly not good for the Trojans.

βῆ δὲ κατ' Οὐλύμποιο καρήνων ἀΐξασα.
οἷον δ' ἀστέρα ἧκε Κρόνου πάϊς ἀγκυλομήτεω
ἢ ναύτῃσι τέρας ἠὲ στρατῷ εὐρέϊ λαῶν
λαμπρόν· τοῦ δέ τε πολλοὶ ἀπὸ σπινθῆρες ἵενται·
τῷ ἐϊκυῖ' ἤϊξεν ἐπὶ χθόνα Παλλὰς Ἀθήνη,
κὰδ δ' ἔθορ' ἐς μέσον· θάμβος δ' ἔχεν εἰσορόωντας
Τρῶάς θ' ἱπποδάμους καὶ ἐϋκνήμιδας Ἀχαιούς.

Athena has been sent by Zeus into the midst of the battlefield (IV. 68–72), and she becomes similar to a star, a meteor, which is a luminous body of Zeus' domain. This is the basic connection of Athena to Zeus in the upcoming episode with Athena, Pandaros, and Menelaos. Athena plays here an analogous role to that which she plays when she deceives Hector in book XXII,[42] but in the present episode the tone is light and comic. Zeus is less directly responsible than in the episode of the death of Hector.

This is to be expected in this part of the poem, before the eighth book. Zeus, however, is the one who sends Athena, just as he sends meteors; and though Athena does not need encouragement, lines 74–78, through the ring repetition on the verb *aissô* ("jump," "dart") and the star simile bring to light the swiftness and enthusiasm of Athena's leap and Zeus' blessing of her flight. The lines display also the divine nature and the epic mission of the goddess: the text often attributes the splendor of light to heroes, especially to the heroic Achilles. If this epic function is perceivable in Athena's fire, the simile would aggrandize Athena's action and lead to the expectation of a great deed —which, in fact, however, will have no real epic grandeur. The text seems to continue to misuse ironically its epic artifices and devices.

It is no wonder that Athena, who reaches the ground in the form of a meteor, provokes the army's amazement (θάμβος) and is considered a portent (*teras*).[43] The earthly stage is anxious: because stars may be harmful signs (XXII. 25–31, XI. 62), this meteor too may be baleful. At the view of the portent, the soldiers on both sides realize that they may soon face sweat and death again (IV. 81-4):

Amazement took hold of all those who saw it,
the horse-taming Trojans and the well-greaved Achaeans,
and someone, at this sight, would say to his neighbor:

---

[42] Bakker 2017 analyzes the relationship between the two episodes and derives important conclusions for the compositional technique of the *Iliad*.
[43] Carastro 2006, 84–5 shows that this amazement (θάμβος) in the epic poems is almost always caused by a divine sight.

> "either the bad war and the awful fight
> will come back, or Zeus who controls the human war
> bestows friendship between the two peoples."

At the sight of the meteor's fire, the anonymous crowd utters, with the same words, the alternatives that Zeus presented to the goddesses (IV. 15 ff.): with this textual device —even if encouraged by the formulaic composition— the Narrator wants the anonymous choral voice to repeat Zeus' alternatives and even his own words. The purpose, or, better, the effect of this repetition is debatable. Since in the context of IV. 15 ff. the text asserts that Zeus is speaking in a provocative and disingenuous way, as in fact he seems to desire peace and not war, the repetition of Zeus' words by the anonymous crowd would, on the contrary, take seriously Zeus' absolute mastery over the alternative between war and peace. He is rightly the master of human destinies. This interpretation would intimate the candor of the anonymous soldiers.

The same crowd will not see how this divine light transforms itself into the Trojan hero Laodokos, who will be the character that Athena embodies. The question that can be asked is whether the dialogue between Athena as Laodokos and Pandaros develops as a simple human scene or is in some way marked by the divine power of the goddess. It recalls the scene in which Athena, disguised as Deiphobos, cheats Hector and persuades him to face Achilles.

Athena, disguised as the Trojan hero Laodokos, comes close to the great archer Pandaros and speaks to him "with winged words" (93–103):

> Would you be persuaded by me, brave[44] son of Lycaon?
> Would you dare to shoot a quick arrow against Menelaos,
> and you would receive gratitude and triumph[45] from all the Trojans
> and among all of them especially from prince Alexander?
> First, you would gain a splendid gift from him,
> when he should see Menelaos, the warlike son of Atreus,
> struck down by your shaft and hoisted onto his pyre.

---

[44] It is difficult to decide which meaning Athena gives to the epithet δαΐφρον "wise" or "brave" (93): the first would be ironically bitter, since Pandaros' decision is foolish, as the Narrator declares at line 104: τῷ δὲ φρένας ἄφρονι πεῖθεν ("Athena persuaded the mind of the fool"). The translation "brave" would be in line with Pandaros' courage and fighting ability, but tremendously ironic because of his final failure that Athena, as she knows while speaking, will ensure.

[45] The combination of χάριν καὶ κῦδος ("gratitude and triumph") is unique in the *Iliad:* what greater sign of gratitude can he receive from his people than their gift of κῦδος? Κῦδος is most often granted by the gods. Here Athena seems to speak like a goddess rather than like Laodokos.

> Come on, shoot at Menelaos full of glory
> and pray to Lycian Apollo, famous for the bow,
> that you will sacrifice a magnificent hecatomb of firstling lambs
> when you return home to the city of holy Zeleia.

The untold logic of Athena's argument still depends on the premise that the Achaeans fight in order to gain Helen back. Alexander would be ecstatic to see Menelaus dead since otherwise, having lost the fight with him, he would be forced, in accordance with the truce, to return Helen to him.

Athena's advice to pray to Apollo is both deceptive, for she will ensure that Pandaros will not return home, and perverse, since he would ask Apollo to succeed in what Athena plans to frustrate. Athena takes control of the action and Pandaros obeys: without a word, he begins to prepare the assault against Menelaus.[46]

Laodokos ought to have authority over Pandaros, and his argument is persuasive. Of course, the ambition of the archer and the promise of favors and gifts coax him, but the argument also provides the strong incentive of finishing the war. Menelaos' death could induce the Achaeans to abandon the war (IV. 169–175), so that peace could return to Troy. This point is not made by Athena, but it is implicit in Athena's/Laodokos' words; it is recognized immediately after by Agamemnon (IV. 169–75) and sounds sufficiently reasonable. It is only because Athena brushes aside Pandaros' arrow that the implied result is not attained. And this is the true deceit of Athena, not that of having persuaded the fool Pandaros, but that of preventing his arrow from achieving what she advised him to try to do. In the episode with Hector, the text makes Hector fully innocent and unaware of Athena's deceit: the text even underscores Athena's

---

[46] In the context of "persuasion" (*peithein*) the text in all cases shows that the persuaded character immediately accomplishes what he has been persuaded to do (e.g. IV. 68 and more than other twenty other examples). In the present passage, Athena/Laodokos begins to speak to Pandaros with a formulaic invitation (IV. 93: "would you be persuaded by [or obey] me?') that, in principle, would open the possibility for Pandaros to express his agreement or disagreement: but, in fact, Pandaros does not, for, in accordance with formulaic examples, this possibility does not occur. The Poet, becoming the commentator of Pandaros' silence, in a line that is unique (IV. 104), says: "So Athena spoke and persuaded the mind of the fool." For the poetic voice, it is not Zeus and Athena but a fool who breaks the truce and condemns Troy to war. The poetic voice considers that Pandaros could have been clever enough to say no to the goddess, which is, however, impossible, as the convention connected to the formulaic invitation (IV. 93) also confirms. The narrative therefore aims at minimizing the indecency of Athena's deceit and collaborates with Zeus' and Hera's decision to have the Trojans appear as the breakers of the truce.

deception on line XXII. 247. In Pandaros' episode, on the other hand, the text emphasizes Pandaros' foolishness as if he were an idiot who followed a proposal worthy of reproach in the pursuit of immediate benefits. He did follow the proposal for his own immediate interests, yet, had Pandaros been the wisest and most unselfish man in the world, Athena would still have found the appropriate argument to persuade him. It is impossible that she would have failed to persuade a mortal. The narrative not only cooperates explicitly with the gods' violation, but also with their decision that the responsibility for the breaking of the truce must be the Trojans'. To this effect, the text not only makes and depicts Pandaros as the foolish breaker of the truce, but, when Athena deflects the course of Pandaros' arrows, does not stress Athena's trickery and deception. Instead, the text breaks the continuity of the action with a most perverse apostrophe and ironic simile (IV. 127–31), as we will see.

The text aims at teasing the Narratees' expectation that Pandaros will not seriously hit Menelaos with an impressive epic description of Pandaros' preparation for the surprise attack: it attributes twenty-one lines (105–26) to it. Pandaros is a warrior "blameless and strong," close to "his strong ranks of shield-armored men" (IV. 89–91: ἀμύμονά τε κρατερόν τε· [...] ἀμφὶ δέ μιν κρατεραὶ στίχες ἀσπιστάων / λαῶν).[47] The description of the preparation of his bow takes seven lines (105–111): it does not simply fill the *horror vacui* of the epic diction, but also displays the large and perfect weapon destined to kill Menelaos and then carefully positioned in order to achieve that goal (111–26). The description of the murderous arrow deserves commentary (117): "never shot before, winged, transmitter of dark pains" (ἀβλῆτα πτερόεντα μελαινέων ἕρμ' ὀδυνάων): the first epithet is hapax, the second rare, and the whole line unique in all of Homer.[48]

This whole warlike seriousness about the attack is rhetorical filling. The Narratees may admire the newness of describing in detail such an unreal situation, or enjoy the almost parodic use of epic descriptions and appreciate a rhetoric that delays the arrival of the important moment, Pandaros' shot. Therefore, this rhetoric perversely and amusingly fills the expectation of an event that is

---

[47] The line is repeated on IV. 201, but without the repetition of the adjective "strong" as in the previous line. Here, on lines 89–91, strength is emphasized. And with reason.
[48] For Pandaros' Lycian connection as a great archer and his bow as a gift of Apollo, see Tsagalis 2012, 239 ff.

destined to end in a void: the void of a false attack, the void of the truce, destined to be broken, so that the war may continue and Troy may be destroyed.[49]

As the bow groans, and the string sings high, Athena brushes the arrow away (IV. 127–31):

> Nor did the blessed gods forget you, Menelaos,
> the immortal gods, and first among them Zeus' daughter, the spoiler
> who standing in front of you fended aside the sharp arrow
> and brushed it away from your skin, as when a mother
> brushes a fly away from her child who is lying in sweet sleep...

> Οὐδὲ σέθεν Μενέλαε θεοὶ μάκαρες λελάθοντο
> ἀθάνατοι, πρώτη δὲ Διὸς θυγάτηρ ἀγελείη,
> ἥ τοι πρόσθε στᾶσα βέλος ἐχεπευκὲς ἄμυνεν.
> ἣ δὲ τόσον μὲν ἔεργεν ἀπὸ χροὸς ὡς ὅτε μήτηρ
> παιδὸς ἐέργῃ μυῖαν ὅθ' ἡδέϊ λέξαται ὕπνῳ...

The text forcefully interrupts the narrative of the surprise attack with the unannounced[50] apostrophe that the poet addresses to Menelaos: it is as if the poet, viewing Menelaos now threatened with death, could not restrain himself from telling him his sympathy for his situation.[51] Of course, it is a void sympathy, since the Poet knows —and knows that his audience knows— that there was never any real danger.

The Poet congratulates Menelaos that the blessed, and moreover, immortal gods of Olympus, and first among them Athena, did not forget to save him. The perverse irony explodes. The poetic voice focalizes the pleasurable tone of the rescuer who is simultaneously the persecutor: the voice stages the paradoxical game and enjoys the poetic relish of voicing its victorious end.

---

49 Often the epic narrative, as Auerbach showed, breaks the audience's expectation of a forthcoming event with a description of something that could appear to be unimportant, but, of course, the tension increases from the main event being delayed. "Here the extended account of the bow (and the process of shooting from it, 116–126) underlines the significance of the moment. In II. 827 Pandaros was said to have been given his bow by Apollo." West 2011, 141. See also Austin 1966.
50 The Scholiasts comment on what they consider to be an abrupt transition from narrative text to speech, see de Jong 1987, 11.
51 "In making a more personal apostrophic address, the narrator has chosen to speak to characters who significantly relate to his protagonist, but are closer —because of their slightly vulnerable states— to real life human beings..." Kahane 1997, 260.

The victim of this amusing trick is the great archer, Pandaros, the fool who obeyed a lord of his army, being unaware that this lord was not Leodokos but the goddess Athena, sent by Zeus to break the truce.

The second victim of this amusing divine and poetic ambush against the Trojans and the Achaeans is Menelaos, who is wounded and whose blood suddenly flows from his thigh. In the Poet's simile that follows, the great hero, unexpectedly wounded, looks like a child whose mother fends a nasty fly away. The poetic voice smiles at its pleasant game, played via the epic diction and style: the voice has described a heroic action only to dismantle its heroism from the inside: the Narrator turns epic style into humorous self-parody. The full epic panoply of gods who did not forget Menelaos but rescued him produces an action no different than that of a mother removing a fly from her sleeping child. The irony of these lines functions on two registers: Athena, "the spoiler," textually becomes a protective mother; yet, by breaking the truce, this tender mother allows the war to continue until Troy is taken. As Zeus has decided, the destruction of Troy will happen "through the design of Athena" (XV. 71).[52]

The fascinating story produces serious effects, but its ironic tone allays and attenuates their gravity: the continuation of the war is what the gods finally want, the Narrator wants, and the Narratees want. Since Pandaros wounds Menelaos, the truce is broken and the crime is attributed to the Trojans, as had been established in Hera's and Zeus' plan (IV. 66–67 = 71–72). The Achaeans will then accuse the Trojans of being the initiators of the violation,[53] and Agamemnon, at the sight of Menealos' wound, expands on this theme in a long lament (IV. 158–168): he asserts with full confidence that Zeus "will be angry at this deception" (τῆσδ' ἀπάτης κοτέων, 168) and will punish the Trojans:

> Zeus, son of Kronos, who sits on high, dwelling in heaven,[54]
> will shake with his own hand the black aegis over all of them,
> angry at this deception: all this will come to pass.

---

52 Brouillet 2016, 193 ff. interprets the simile in an analogous way.
53 See for instance Idomeneus on IV. 268–71: "…since the Trojans have broken / their oaths; thus death and sorrow will come to them / in the future, since they were the first to violate the oaths."
54 Ζεὺς δέ σφι Κρονίδης ὑψίζυγος αἰθέρι ναίων. The line is unique in the *Iliad* while part of the line: αἰθέρι ναίων is found only here and on II. 412, in a very solemn prayer offered by Agamemnon. What unites the two lines is that both characterize Zeus while what is attributed to him or requested from him will not occur. It is somehow odd to place Zeus' dwelling in the highest and purest part of heaven while asking him to intervene with his hand on earth.

Earlier the text had displayed Menelaos' naïve belief in Zeus' ethical and educational purposes (III. 351–54), only to show him bitterly contradicted by Zeus' denial; now the text exposes Agamemnon's similar attitude. Agamemnon's candid presumption that Zeus acts according to an ethical principle is savagely derided by the text's exhibition of Zeus' fraudulent behavior.[55] Rarely does a Greek text so cynically display evidence of foolish human beliefs about the gods' moral behavior.

At the same time, the text withholds from the Narratees the true motivation that leads Zeus to ensure the destruction of his beloved Troy and to play this mystifying game in front of the credulous eyes of mortals. Were Zeus' mind readable, we would have an image of the order of Being in the world. The world would be encased in an image and would be penetrable by human requests.

Returning to the text, one target of the narrative's irony is, among others, Agamemnon's and the other chiefs' candor. Agamemnon's ideological presumption is that he is the commander of an army pursuing moral ends, fighting for just and divinely supported goals.[56] The *Iliad* shows that the Trojans are no traitors, neither in the violation of the truce, nor in Paris' abduction of Helen. Had the Achaeans listened carefully to what Helen herself says about her elopement, they could have ceased to incriminate the Trojans.

In the most unexpected way, Agamemnon suddenly abandons his trust in Zeus' punishment of Troy and, as he sees the blood flow from Menelaos' thigh, shudders and, in panic, laments his brother's death: he imagines that the Trojan expedition is over and sees himself returning home without Helen (173–75):

> and we would leave to Priam and to the Trojans the Argive
> Helen to glory over; while your bones will rot under the ground
> as you lie dead in Troy, on a venture that went unaccomplished...

Agamemnon's imagination runs free and uncontrolled: he even invents the proud speech that a Trojan will make when he presses his foot on Menelaos' tomb (169–82). His imagination is richly nourished by his constant anxiety about the Trojan expedition. The Narrator shows Agamemnon's obsessive and embarrassing fear of failure: first in his assurance that Zeus, in anger, will pun-

---

[55] This is an inevitable consequence, since Pandaros cannot be considered autonomously responsible for the breaking of the truce.
[56] The Achaeans, and especially Menelaos and Agamemnon, reproach Paris and the Trojans for their betrayal of laws and norms (III. 100, 351–54; IV. 165; XIII. 620–25, where Menelaos mentions Zeus Xenios).

ish the Trojans and destroy them, and then in his seeing everything lost with his brother's death.⁵⁷

This portrait of Agamemnon is recognizable across the whole poem, but here, far from the tension and the disasters produced by Achilles' wrath, the Narrator enjoys underlining with irony the irresolution, anxiety, and mourning of the hero: his picture acquires deep relief and creates disturbing and comic effects.

The reader's embarrassment at the gods' behavior has induced some critics to seek out guilt in Pandaros, so as to find a sort of double and parallel responsibility between the goddess and the human being.⁵⁸ Zeus and Athena could even simply be figures of the epic machinery that creates divine support for fully human feelings and decisions.⁵⁹ As I have indicated, it is unthinkable that the goddess should fail to persuade Pandaros. This unavoidable condition makes the question of Pandaros' responsibility inappropriate. Athena's argument, finally, is not a foolish one. Pandaros is made to play the double of Alexander, as Tsagalis has shown (2012, 141): both are great archers and breakers of social or religious norms. Accordingly, had his arrow hit Menelaos as he intended it to do, he would have not only broken the truce, but changed all the terms of the conflict.

With the breaking of the truce, the three gods' long intervention to ensure the continuation of the war is over. Levity, parodic relish, and intellectual irreverence mark the interaction between the poet, the characters, and gods. The characters are involved in epic actions and turn out simultaneously to be the victims of divine deceptions and of the epic parodic virtuosity.

This collaboration does not surprise us, since both the gods and the Poem need the same result: the continuation of the war.

The relish with which the narrative teases its own expressive tools by perverting their meaning and revealing their arbitrariness shows the mastery the

---

57 Griffin 1980, 71–2 sheds light on this double mood.
58 The text seems to encourage critics to find fault in Pandaros by defining him as "fool" *aphroni* on line 104: Ὣς φάτ' Ἀθηναίη, τῷ δὲ φρένας ἄφρονι πεῖθεν. It seems that Athena could persuade him because he was unwise and foolish.
59 Yet the miraculous features of the episode are necessary for explaining the action and cannot be eliminated: Pandaros' failure to kill Menelaos after the praise of Pandaros' excellence and the careful preparation of the shot makes sense only through the intervention of Athena; the incredible exposure of Menelaos as a visible and immobile target serves the miraculous events; the undetermined position of the Achaeans and the Trojans, as they seem to be still gathered together (see 79–80), though Pandaros' attack implies that they must be separated, designs an unrealistic space, etc.

text feels it holds over its own means and its ability to color the events as it wants. It would be possible to assume that the Poet, in the act of recreating for his own *Iliad* a previous epic narrative on an analogous "breaking of the truce," takes pleasure in parodying that model —but obviously this can only be speculation. Yet the comedy and the parody are justified by the theme itself: the text's festive abuse of its own heroic style intends to discredit the epic seriousness of the truce. The argument that Hector and other Trojan princes advance — according to which Paris, by holding Helen in Troy, is the cause of the terrible war— is too obvious, too embarrassing, and needs to be dismissed once and for all. The *Iliad* produces a perverse version of this attempt to give back Helen to the Achaeans. Not only does the text display the hostility of the gods toward the truce that would necessarily have given victory and Helen to Menelaos, but at every moment it immerses the duel into a sort of farce, showing its improper and derisive epic style, and therefore its impropriety as a serious epic event. As Athena enters the human stage, the text celebrates her with a heroic simile; she enchants Pandaros and deviates Pandaros' arrows. The text comments on this gesture by honoring her with another heroic simile, yet one that is derisive, that evokes the domestic scene of protection, and that is violent due to its implicit consequences. The text makes the inoffensive wounds that Menelaos receives into the source of ridiculous, pathetic responses and into the cause of a false reading of Zeus' intentions. The Trojans are not the violators of the truce: the gods are; but the magnificent chiefs of the Achaeans miss what the text brings to light so clearly for the Narratees. The textual purpose of this comic mistreatment of the text's own epic devices is to reveal that the truce, the restitution of Helen, and the end of the war could not find correct epic place and form – therefore, that they could not have any chance of succeeding.

One god remains outside this paradoxical and parodic horizon: this god is Zeus. He ends his intervention once Athena enters onto the human stage.

## 6.3 Zeus Closes the Poem

Cities fall and their heroes must die: this is the law of heroic life that Zeus supervises. He assumes other names and images, the Golden Scales, Oloiê Moira, he appears to operate above and outside the rules of Olympus, and he is always Zeus, the master of human destinies. As the heroes lie dead, they enter into the sphere of the cult, and Zeus, as a god who receives a cult, loves the mortals who honor the gods with rituals on the appropriate occasions.

In the last book of the poem, Zeus organizes the conditions for Hector's funeral and fulfills them. He killed Hector, the defender of Troy, making possible therefore the capture of the city by the Achaeans in accordance with his and Athena's *boulai* (XV. 71); now, however, Zeus wants Hector to be honored in accordance with the appropriate sacred rituals.⁶⁰ The unbalanced relation of power between men and gods, between the anthropomorphic and the superhuman aspects of the gods, forms here another paradoxical pattern: Zeus is completely indifferent to the fact that he contributed to Hector's death, but now he wants Hector to be honored by men and by the rituals through which also the gods are honored.

To refuse these rituals would mean to act in a savage way, as Achilles does when he denies the restitution of Hector's body to his family and city. Apollo makes this precise indictment (XXIV. 39–41):

> This murderous Achilles who has no sane mind,⁶¹ whose will
> cannot be bent in his breast, whose thoughts are fierce like a lion's.

In organizing the means for Hector's funeral, Zeus acts in accordance with the monarchic position that he enjoys among the gods on Olympus: he no longer needs to exhibit his physical force to obtain the gods' obedience, but derives power from the persuasiveness of his plan and from the collaboration of his close associates. With this performance, Zeus leads the Poem to its conclusion.

The book begins with Achilles' desperate mourning for Patroclos (XXIV. 3 ff.): his lamentations will be echoed by those of his mother, who sits in a grotto at the bottom of the sea (XXIV. 83–86) and who offers to the Narratees a dramatic image of maternal sorrow for the close death of her son. The Poet cannot avoid anticipating the tremendous pathos of an event that he cannot present in his poem. Thetis' divine mourning at the bottom of the sea in the absence of the mourned corpse (XXIV. 83–86) appears as an unrealistic and sublime ritual of pain.

The solipsistic figure of Achilles emerges in the very first lines, still crying for his companion, still far away from the common life of all the others, close to

---

**60** Zeus never justifies his killing of Hector nor his plan of destroying Troy. Whether the text means to offer a theologically positive image of Zeus through his commitment to honor Hector is difficult to say, for the Narratees cannot forget that Zeus himself adapted Achilles' armor to Hector's body.

**61** The adjective in the Greek φρένες ... ἐναίσιμοι is connected with *aisa*, "destiny, sort" and may assume various connotations such as "ominous," "fateful"; when applied to omens, "favorable"; and to persons, something like "righteous."

death-like liminality,⁶² untouched by human physical needs, and still dragging Hector's corpse around the tomb of Patroclos with his chariot. He is troubled by the barbarous and obsessive intention of punishing the killer of his friend and taken by the hope of overcoming his own guilt⁶³ —and finally, succeeding in none of this. The mourning rituals of Thetis and Achilles are parallel, furthermore, to some of their abnormal aspects.

As Apollo, feeling pity,⁶⁴ continues to protect Hector's body from any disfiguration (XXIV. 18–22), Achilles must have realized the invulnerability of his enemy's corpse. Yet, as we know, the effects of divine contact with mortals remain always indescribable and ineffable. The dragging of Hector's corpse around the tomb of Patroclos was for Achilles, possibly, a sufficient shaming of his enemy, quite apart from the condition of the body. A worse treatment would have been that of cutting the body into pieces and giving these to the dogs, as Priam fears (XXIV. 408–09).

Even so, most of the gods are dismayed by Achilles' behavior, and would have asked Hermes to steal the corpse had not Hera, Athena, and Poseidon, the regular trio of opponents, rejected the idea.⁶⁵ Zeus (notwithstanding line 25) was

---

**62** See Seaford's (1994, 168 ff.) eloquent pages on "Achilles' excessive liminality," by which the author defines Achilles' proximity to death after Patroclos' death. Note in particular the following point: "... for Achilles a complete return to normality seems excluded by the combination of abnormal ritual expressions of death-in-life with the knowledge that his own death has been made inevitable by that of Patroclos. The death-like liminality of the mourner seems in this case to acquire the permanence of real death."
**63** XXIV. 2–18: "... the rest of them took thought of their dinner and sweet sleep and its enjoyment: but Achilles was weeping for his friend, remembering him... All-subduing sleep could not take him [the paradox underscores the exceptionality of Achilles' torment]... he turned and twisted, side to side [a very realistic and intimate detail, rare in the *Iliad*], he longed for Patroclos' manhood and his great strength and all the toils he had gone through with him... At dawn... after he would draw three times [Hector's corpse] around Patroclos' tomb, he would leave it to lie sprawled on its face in the dust... So Achilles in his madness outraged divine Hector."
**64** φῶτ' ἐλεαίρων – καὶ τεθνηότα περ (19–20): "Apollo pitied Hector – dead man though he was" (Fagles). We recall that Apollo, at Zeus' request, washed the corpse of Sarpedon and that he has been protecting the body of Hector (XXIV. 33 ff.). Here he seems to act autonomously: Apollo is a god who has a very large, polyvalent, and independent sphere of action. He has massacred many Achaeans, without any regard for the pro-Achaean gods, in order to honor his own priest Chryses.
**65** Elmer 2013, 173 underlines the verb *handanein* (25: ἔνθ' ἄλλοις μὲν πᾶσιν ἑήνδανεν, "the plan pleased all the others," but not Hera, nor Poseidon, nor Athena), which "carries distinctly counterconsensual overtones in so far as it signals individualized, as opposed to collective, volition."

probably opposed to the project (see 71–73), for, had he approved of the stealing, he would have imposed it, as later he will impose his own preferences. He remains silent and lets the proposal fall. The narrative does not remain reticent but qualifies Achilles as furious in his mistreatment of Hector's body (XXIV. 22).

It is in connection with Hera's and Athena's hatred for Troy that the text explicitly mentions – for the only time in the Poem – their personal motivation, their resentment toward Paris' judgment (XXIV. 27–30).[66]

Twelve days after, in a new divine assembly, Apollo accuses the gods of being pitiless and cruel in their indifference toward Achilles' inhuman behavior: it forbids Hector's family and city from performing funeral rituals. Infringing all civilized norms, Achilles behaves, Apollo says, like a fierce lion, acting pitilessly and shamelessly toward a pious man.

Apollo blames the intolerance and the excess of Achilles' mourning (44–54):

Achilles has lost all pity and shame,[67]
which does much harm to men or profits them also.
I suppose that it can happen to a man to suffer a dearer loss than his,
a brother from the same mother or a son,
but in the end he stops weeping and grieving,
for Fate has given mortals an enduring heart.[68]
But Achilles, after he has deprived divine Hector of life,
ties him to his horses and drags him around his beloved
companion's tomb: that is not honorable nor advantageous for him.

---

**66** The text attributes Athena's and Hera's hatred for Troy to Paris' judgment. This judgment is the hidden subtext of various scenes, for instance on the occasion of Aphrodite's and Helen's meeting (III. 383 ff.), and in the discussion between Zeus and Hera at the beginning of the fourth book. On the spirited defense of this passage's authenticity, see the dramatic phrase by Reinhardt (1938) 1960, 33: "Ohne Parisurteil, keine Ilias."
**67** ὡς Ἀχιλεὺς ἔλεον μὲν ἀπώλεσεν, οὐδέ οἱ αἰδώς. The two words "are linked again at 207–8; XXII. 123–24, referring to Achilles' implacability. When they recur finally in 503, Achilles responds to the appeal." Macleod 1982, p. 92. The verb ἀπώλεσεν can be translated, besides "he lost," also as "he killed": see Burkert 1955, 101; Nannini 1995, 97–99 for a discussion on the double meaning of the verbs in other Homeric passages. Brügger 2009, 36 underlines the emphatic expression of ἔλεον which is hapax in Homer.
**68** τλητὸν γὰρ Μοῖραι θυμὸν θέσαν ἀνθρώποισιν. For the principle of the *tlêmosynê* (endurance) dispensed to mortals by the gods, see Archil. fr. 13, 5–7. Achilles will accept the principle of endurance and teach it to Priam (XXIV. 449–51). It cannot escape the readers that the funeral rituals are a sort of sacralization of the principle of acceptance and endurance. In the quoted passage we find the unique case of the plural Μοῖραι in Homer: it must refer to the three Μοῖραι attested in Hesiod *Th.* 217–19, 904–06. In the singular, ὀλοιὴ μοῖρα (XXII. 5) refers to Zeus, but μοῖρα by itself is at XX. 127–28 the spinner of each mortal destiny from the day of the mortal's birth; it is connected with Zeus and Erinys on XIX. 87 (See Ch. I. 2; IV).

> Let him take care that, noble though he is, we do not get angry at him,
> for in his fury, he is offending the dumb earth."[69]

It is a unique case, if I am correct, of a god in the *Iliad* considering human toils and sorrow from the human perspective, as Apollo does by placing himself on the level of human experience and recognizing "endurance" as the remedy that men have against incurable evils. Apollo goes deeper than Zeus when Zeus sympathizes with the pain the immortal horses feel for the death of Patroclos and recognizes the greatest misery of the human condition.

Oddly enough, "endurance" or perhaps "tolerance" is also a mode of resistance that the gods know and practice. Dione tells her daughter Aphrodite of the hardships and pains that many gods had to "endure" from mortals and from other gods (V. 382–400). Events that demand divine endurance are rare and occasional, while humans have endurance as a permanent dispensation from the three Moirai.

The question can be raised whether a patient, enduring, and resigned attitude is heroic according to the Iliadic code: if it is not, Achilles has been constantly heroic, since he was never resigned but rather implacably refused Agamemnon's compensation (see IX. 631–38) and in his excessive, barbarous ways of mourning expresses no forbearing acceptance. His refusal to eat and sleep, i.e. his practicing what implies "proximity to death", are existential heroic modes of facing sorrow and distress. The difficulty in defining the correct measure of heroic behavior is due to the porous nature of the "heroic" that in the epic code borders on superhuman, almost divine behavior: this porousness between the heroic and divine blurs the limits of human heroic behavior. Achilles, in particular, as he takes revenge for the death of Patroclos, crosses these limits and alone defeats the whole Trojan army. Athena had to intervene to prevent him from killing Agamemnon.

There is an excess in human heroism: Hector, believing in Zeus' support, brings his own army to ruin, and himself recognizing Athena's deception, runs to meet his death while gazing at his future glory. Thetis invites Achilles to moderate his absolute denial of the vegetative aspects of life, which implies his spiritual communion with the death of his companion (XXIV. 128–32). Achilles' brutality toward Hector at the moment of Hector's death and in the treatment of his corpse exceed human measure. Even so, it is problematic for the epic code to

---

[69] "Dumb, inert earth, i.e. the corpse, since man is made of water and earth..." Macleod 1982, 94.

indicate at which point heroic behavior becomes excessive, pre-divine, or even bestial: it is clear from the similes that even beasts may acquire a heroic stature.[70]

Later, at XXIV. 503–6, Achilles responds positively to old Priam's appeal to be pitiful and respectful of the gods and, at XXIV. 549, Achilles invites Priam to "endure" his implacable destiny. This reversal does not imply that Achilles has become suddenly unheroic: yet he has become able to view the heroic life as a source of wretched destinies for all who embrace it.

Apollo ends his speech by hinting at a divine punishment, when he says that Achilles should fear the rage of the gods. The gods should put an end to Achilles' mad and furious actions.[71] Apollo does not suggest how the gods should effect this punishment.

This attack allows the narrative to construct a semblance of a quarrel between Apollo and Hera, a sort of repetition of the quarrel among the gods at the end of the first book.[72] But the protagonists are different: Hera and Apollo instead of Hera and Zeus; and the substance of Hera's objection fails to create a real dissension: she argues that Achilles, the son of a goddess, and the mortal Hector should not have equal honor, but she does not offer any clue on what to do with Achilles. It would be inappropriate to imply that she would approve of Achilles' continuing or worsening the outrage of Hector's body. She does not offer any solution. Essentially she is angry (χολωσαμένη, 55) with Apollo because of his negative portrait of Achilles.[73]

---

[70] The extension and meanings of *tlêmosynê* in the heroic mode are not easy to define. The heroic quality of *tlêmôn Odysseus*, a repeated noun epithet in the *Odyssey* and present also in the *Iliad* (e.g. X. 231, 498 and see V. 670), complicates the shades of its meaning. See for instance *Od.* v. 221–24 and Pucci 1987, p. 43: what the *Iliad* cannot accept "is a certain passivity in Odysseus' sense of heroism, a somewhat vulgar pride in, as it were, exhibiting the marks of his griefs, blows, humiliations, defeats, and survivals and so great tolerance for these injuries that his already long record could be indefinitely lengthened."

[71] There is here (perhaps) a veiled allusion to Apollo's future participation in the defeat and killing of Achilles.

[72] The last book extensively echoes themes and motifs from the first book, with the intent of showing their final deployment and resolution. It suffices to think of the replaying of the first episode that set the Poem in motion —a father coming to ransom his child— to realize the crucially mirror-like play of the narrative. Now the ransoming is successful (see Wilson 2002, 132; Elmer 2013, 178), since it is imposed by Zeus. See on these often-debated critical issues among recent works the superb commentary by Macleod 1982 and the all-embracing one Brügger 2009.

[73] Her main argument has no relevance to the situation: the fact that Achilles is the son of a goddess (see Pirenne-Delforge/Pironti 2016, 80, 270–74), and that the gods were present at Peleus' wedding rites, do not change the mortal nature of Achilles, perfectly equal in this to Hector. As Brügger 2009 ad 58 remarks, birth as a source of *timê* ("honor") seems to be found only here. It is not through the word *gonos* (59), which in the *Iliad* is employed only for the

Zeus, the cloud-gatherer (64), finds the solution. First he[74] upbraids Hera for her anger toward the gods (65): "Hera, be not utterly angry with the gods!" The verb ἀποσκύδμαινε ("be angry") recalls the scene at VIII. 484 where Zeus dismisses Hera with the strongest discharge: "I do not care about your anger, since no one is a meaner bitch than you."[75]

Zeus positions himself among the gods with whom she is angry, indicating through silence his opinion on the matter. And though he recognizes that Achilles and Hector do not deserve the same *timê* (honor, status, social privileges) —a feeble concession to Hera— he defines Hector as "most loved by the gods among all the men who live in Troy," because of his piety and devotion to Zeus himself. Birth and social privileges yield to personal values.

Without any other motivation, Zeus rejects the inefficient idea of stealing Hector's body and decides to summon Thetis and urge her to convince Achilles to release the corpse.

Some critics (see Corey 2009) argue that Zeus reconciles Apollo's and Hera's positions. This view appears to me to be unsupported by the text: Zeus upbraids Hera but not Apollo; he appreciates Hector's piety exactly as Apollo does (see 68–70 and 33–34); he approves the idea of stopping Achilles' behavior as Apollo demanded (see especially 53–54): both Apollo and Zeus are concerned with the humanly appropriate behavior of mortals. Finally, both Apollo and Zeus are ready to threaten Achilles with the gods' anger if he does not release the body (53–4 and 113–14).

Besides, Apollo has protected the body of Hector ever since Achilles began to brutalize it: Apollo is therefore justified in reacting with indignation against the gods' indifference. Furthermore, by preserving the freshness and beauty of Hector's body, Apollo facilitates Priam's and Achilles' reconciliation.

Apollo's protection of Hector's corpse from any disfiguration imbues the whole episode of Hector's release and funeral rites with an aura of magic and

---

"child" of gods, that Achilles becomes immortal. However, Achilles' divine connections that Hera mentions raise his portrait to an almost divine being. Hera ends her speech by insulting Apollo as "treacherous": see the superb commentary by Macleod 1982 and the all-embracing one by Brügger 2009.

74 On the syntactic unit Τὴν δ' ἀπαμειβόμενος προσέφη ('answering [to her ....] said'), see Kahane 2018, pp. 30–1, who emphasizes the functional force of this often repeated unit through its various specific aspects, and its being used by important gods and heroes.

75 οὔ σευ ἔγωγε
σκυζομένης ἀλέγω, ἐπεὶ οὐ σέο κύντερον ἄλλο.
The verb σκύζομαι is only a phonetic variant of (ἀπο)-σκυδμαίνω.

divine sympathy for Hector's merits and for his people's pain. The Poem ends by displaying the benevolence of the gods within an edifying horizon.[76]

The gods employ their care and magic in order to ensure the correct performance of funeral rites, and thus in order to safeguard the respect for "the mute, inert earth" with which the human body is composed. The gods can approach and sense human death through these rituals, in which the mute earth is burned and vanishes from the terrestrial surface. The ritual brings about a final and immutable change, closing forever a living process.

Zeus exaggerates Thetis' control over Hector's body ("she is always near him night and day," so that it is impossible to steal Hector's body secretly, 71–73). Zeus appeals to a "force majeure," which in fact does not exist since Iris finds Thetis "inside the hollow of her cave" (82–83). Zeus does not need to evoke a "force majeure" —he is more powerful than any "force majeure"— in order to sell his own plan, but he invents a fib probably so as to quickly dismiss any other solution that in any case would have been incorrect.[77] He presents his plan (74–76):

---

[76] Zanker 1996, 147, calibrating the magnanimity of the gods in the *Iliad*, singles out Zeus and Hermes in book XXIV. He assumes that the gods are induced by "moral constraints to insure the kindly treatment of Hector's body," and that these constraints "are presented more forcibly by Apollo." The notion of "moral constraints" seems to me to be too engaging: Zeus and Apollo respond benevolently to Hector's piousness and sacrificial practices; Hector respects, as Zeus says (70), the *geras* ("honor" that is proper to the gods); both Zeus and Apollo defend the rituals that would satisfy Hector's family and people and blame the inhumanity of Achilles, who has lost pity and shame (44). Zeus' and Apollo's motivations do not ensue from their duty to support specific values: both of them react on the grounds of their interests as receivers of the cults that man owes to the gods and in favor of norms that characterize men as being different from beasts (41). Again, these norms ensure the human resignation to evils —so often sent to them by the gods— and their respect for the divine world. Men too recognize their own piousness toward the gods not as a "moral duty" or constraint but as a possible advantage, as Priam in this same book tells to Hermes (425–28): "the gods have remembered him [Hector] even in his destiny of death." Achilles makes the same point at I. 218.

[77] Zeus' assertion that Thetis is always near to Achilles may simply be a metaphor: see for instance IV. 10–11 where Zeus says that Aphrodite is always near to Paris, using the same expression: τῷ δ' αὖτε φιλομειδὴς Ἀφροδίτη / αἰεὶ παρμέμβλωκε καὶ αὐτοῦ κῆρας ἀμύνει, as in our passage at XXIV. 72–73: ἦ γάρ οἱ αἰεὶ / μήτηρ παρμέμβλωκεν ὁμῶς νύκτάς τε καὶ ἦμαρ. Aphrodite is always near to Paris metaphorically, that is, when he needs her to be saved from the danger of being killed. Analogously, Thetis is always near to Achilles, even if she sits in her cave, for if ever somebody should try to steal his booty, Hector's body, she would intervene immediately. Furthermore, the text may evoke Zeus' assertion to indicate that Zeus —contrary to line 25, but more in agreement with lines 107–09— could not have been favorable to the stealing of Hector's body.

> Let some of the gods summon here Thetis
> in order that I tell her a strong word, that Achilles
> must receive the due gifts from Priam[78] and release Hector.

Zeus' synthetic prolepsis is emitted as an order: he editorializes and characterizes his own command as the "strong word" (πυκινὸν ἔπος)[79] that Thetis must convey to Achilles. Furthermore, the summoning and the collaboration of Thetis are elicited by a command and are irrefutably taken for granted.[80] No other god but Zeus —"that great god" as Thetis calls him (XXIV. 90)— could deal with Thetis with such cool directness.

Presented in this way, the solution to the difficult situation appears to be simple: the mere word of Zeus suffices to stop Achilles' mad behavior. The other gods do not feel like commenting: the following events occur through their silent collaboration.

Zeus has barely finished the last word and Iris is already traveling to bring his appeal to Thetis at the bottom of the sea (77–88):

> So he spoke, and quick as stormy wind Iris rose to bring
> the message, and between Samos and rocky Imbros
> she dove in the black sea:[81] the surface of the water groaned.
> And she plunged down to the bottom as a lead weight
> that, set over the horn of an ox grazing in the field,
> goes down bearing death to the raw-eating fish.
> She found Thetis inside the hollow of her cave and around her
> the other sea goddesses were sitting together; and she amidst them

---

**78** The expression δώρων ἐκ Πριάμοιο λάχῃ implies that the gifts are due to Achilles for the release of Hector's corpse: see Perpillou 1996, 168 who translates: "pour que lui dise le fin mot qui fera qu'Achille recevra son du de cadeaux de Priam et rendra le corps d'Hector." Notice also, in line 76, the hysteron-proteron order of words that gives prominence to the reception of the gifts. It seems at this point that Achilles will simply have to accept the conventional exchange of gifts for the restitution of the corpse. Zeus, however, will grant him a shining triumph (*kudos*) for the acceptance of this exchange (110).
**79** The adjective is itself enigmatic in this context: "a close word" (Lattimore); "solemn, sound decree" (Fagle); "saggio consiglio" (Cerri); "klug" or "massgeblich, or "(ge)wichtig" (Brügger 2009, stating that the nuance of the adjective is difficult to be determined). The figura etymologica increases the indetermination since it repeats the same connotation in the two words εἴπω πυκινὸν ἔπος.
**80** The syntax of line 74 presents a wish clause as a mild form of command, see Brügger 2009, 74. The appeal to Iris, in its anonymous and indirect expression, may be simply "diplomatic" (Macleod).
**81** The unit μείλανι πόντῳ is a hapax and sounds emphatic at the end of the phrase that is followed by a pause.

> mourned the fate of her blameless son who was destined
> to die soon in fertile Troy, far from his fatherland.
> Coming close to her, quick-footed Iris told her:
> "Rise, Thetis: Zeus who has immortal thoughts calls you. ..."

This is an extraordinary description: economic in relating the actions —as Homer's best and rightly celebrated style is— but relaxed, even sumptuous in focusing on the surrounding contextual details; musical in its lines and internal sounds; pathetic, after the muscular energy of Iris' descent into the sea, as it presents Thetis and the goddesses in the grotto, lamenting Achilles' oncoming death.[82]

This is the unique instance in *Iliad* in which Iris must dive into the sea in order to deliver a message. The description stresses a certain violence in her swiftness: her feet are fast like winds in a storm, and her diving breaks the surface of the sea and causes the water to groan (79: ἐπεστονάχησε δὲ λίμνη).[83] She inflicts pain on the sea as she breaks it.

There is something blunt and painful in this embassy, as the Narrator makes nearly explicit through his simile, according to which Iris descends from heaven into the dark sea water, similar to the lead bait that "bears death to the raw-eating fish" (80–82).

It is hard to see how the purpose of the fishhook may compare with the purpose of Iris' message.[84] Odd as it may seem, I think that the simile suggests some parallelism: Iris carries to Thetis a direct order (88) that forces Thetis to move out of the black sea (79 – for darkness, see 93–94) to heaven: "Rise, Thetis: Zeus

---

**82** XXIV. 77–86:
> Ὣς ἔφατ', ὦρτο δὲ Ἶρις ἀελλόπος ἀγγελέουσα,
> μεσσηγὺς δὲ Σάμου τε καὶ Ἴμβρου παιπαλοέσσης
> ἔνθορε μείλανι πόντῳ· ἐπεστονάχησε δὲ λίμνη.
> ἣ δὲ μολυβδαίνῃ ἰκέλη ἐς βυσσὸν ὄρουσεν,
> ἥ τε κατ' ἀγραύλοιο βοὸς κέρας ἐμβεβαυῖα
> ἔρχεται ὠμηστῇσιν ἐπ' ἰχθύσι κῆρα φέρουσα.
> εὗρε δ' ἐνὶ σπῆϊ γλαφυρῷ Θέτιν, ἀμφὶ δ' ἄρ' ἄλλαι
> εἵαθ' ὁμηγερέες ἅλιαι θεαί· ἣ δ' ἐνὶ μέσσης
> κλαῖε μόρον οὗ παιδὸς ἀμύμονος, ὅς οἱ ἔμελλε
> φθίσεσθ' ἐν Τροίῃ ἐριβώλακι τηλόθι πάτρης.

Notice the subtle sonic echoes on lines 77, 79, 81–82, 83–84.

**83** Piettre 1996, 66, describing the supernatural ways the gods move, writes: "et quand Iris saute dans la mer pour une ambassade à Thetis, la plaine liquide sous le choc gémit."

**84** Macleod (ad 78–82) sees a reverse simile. The notion of "reverse simile" comes from Foley 1978.

who has immortal thoughts calls you."⁸⁵ Iris, who, when the text needs it, can be very diplomatic, is blunt here, interrupting Thetis' mourning and leaving her no alternatives but to obey Zeus. Thetis approached Zeus in the first book and induced him to cause the disasters brought about by honoring Achilles: now she will go to Olympus and obey his immortal thoughts.⁸⁶

Thetis reacts immediately and resists the order to go to heaven (90–92):

> Why does that great god call me? I feel shame
> to mingle with the immortal gods [μίσγεσθ' ἀθανάτοισι] now that I have unending woes in my heart.
> I will nevertheless go. No word shall be in vain, whatever he says.⁸⁷

The blunt unsuitability of the Olympian intrusion is suggested by Thetis' definition of Zeus as "that great god," which may imply various connotations of distance between herself and him. It certainly implies her recognition of Zeus' greatness, but also the deep unrelatedness between their reciprocal positions. This bluntness hints at a mingling of opposite horizons, from the extreme sides of the kosmos (heaven, earth, and sea): the description of the "lead weight set over the horn of an ox grazing in the field" evokes another death, that of a bull; the quick descent of the lead attached to the bull's horn implies the expedient way to reach the "raw-eating" fish. It is a hunting instrument that captures prey, removes it from its habitual place, and facilitates, in this way, its death.

The simile does not parallel each feature of Iris' intrusion in the sea and of Thetis' world, but it essentially parallels Iris' violent descent into Thetis' hollow cave to "capture" her while she is mourning the death of her son. Iris pulls The-

---

**85** ὄρσο Θέτι· καλέει Ζεὺς ἄφθιτα μήδεα εἰδώς. The imperative form and the lack of any epithet for Thetis are harsh touches. Iris' indifference to Thetis' mourning is unkind and contrasts with Zeus' care (104–06). This noun-epithet, "who has immortal thoughts," is used only here in Homer. Macleod 1982, 98: "Hesiod uses it three times in twenty lines to stress Zeus's superiority over Prometheus, the would be deceiver of the god (*Theog.* 545, 550, 561)." The use of this attribute extends through epic poetry from Hesiod to the Hymns. Though the adjective means "immortal," translators try to use synonymic alternatives: "infinite" (Lattimore), "infallible" (Cerri), and see Brügger 2009. The "immortality" of Zeus' thoughts re-semanticizes on a different conceptual register Zeus' irrevocable and unfailing words, never uttered in vain, and anticipates Thetis' evocation of Zeus' definition of his own word (92).
**86** Letoublon (1987, 138 ff.) shows a chiastic relation between *Iliad* I: Achilles – Thetis – Zeus, and XXIV: Zeus —Thetis— Achilles.
**87** With these two lines 90–91, Thetis seems to refuse the order of Zeus, but with the next line (92), "I will nevertheless go..." she yields. Di Benedetto 1994, 137–38. Macleod 1982 comments on the μέν in 992: "μέν stresses the assertion, here with an adversative implication: I *will* go, despite my misgivings."

tis out of her ceremonial lament for the death of her son though Thetis is unwilling and guides her to Olympus where she will receive orders concerning Hector's corpse.

In spite of Thetis' misgivings and Iris' blunt intrusion, Thetis will go listen to Zeus (92): "I will nevertheless go. No word shall be in vain, whatever he says." She recognizes the voice of Zeus and with a subtle evocation she brings to light the fact that, when he promised her to honor Achilles, he defined his word as unfailing, irrevocable, and all-accomplishing.[88] From the first to the last book of the Poem, the fatal word of Zeus is recognized as something never uttered in vain.

Why Thetis laments Achilles' death at this very moment is not clear. Scholars remind us of previous examples of Thetis' laments for her son's death. At XVIII. 35 ff., Thetis hears Achilles' desperate cry as he learns of Patroclos' death, and she, at the bottom of the sea, begins a lamentation for Achilles' death that responds to that of Achilles for Patroclos' death. The marine goddesses join her, before she runs to meet her son. At XXIV. 83 ff., however, no explicit communication from Achilles provokes Thetis' mourning. The text is reticent, but I have assumed that a certain parallelism between the two mournings consists in their abnormality and excess. Achilles oversteps human measure in his proximity to death-like liminality and in making himself the punisher of the killer of his friend. In the dark marine grotto, Thetis, weeping for the still inexistent death of Achilles, cares nothing about what creates the anger and the scandal of the gods in heaven —Achilles' offending Hector's body as blunt, inert earth, and preventing the ritual mourning for the Trojan hero from being celebrated.

Going back to the narrative, when the two goddesses depart from Thetis' cave, they look like both anthropomorphic and divine beings belonging to the natural world (93–96):

> [...] the divine one among the goddesses [Thetis] seized a black veil
> – and there is no darker garment – and she went,
> and in front of her rapid wind-footed Iris
> guided her. And the wave of the sea yielded before them.

By covering herself with a black veil, Thetis makes public her feelings and her state of mind, and indeed the veil speaks to the gods.

---

**88** Richardson, *ad loc.* and Brügger 2009, 54 cleverly notice that Thetis, by saying, "No word shall be in vain, whatever he says," makes a subtle allusion to what Zeus tells her about his own words at I. 524–28: Zeus' word is always fulfilled.

With this last remark, I complete the emphasis that I have placed on the funeral rituals that Achilles on his side and Thetis on her own accomplish. By brutalizing Hector's corpse, and by mourning for the death of her still-living son, Achilles and Thetis practice rituals that are unconventional and conducive only to more anguish. This is why Thetis does not care about Achilles' torturing Hector's body. These rituals evoke a dark, gloomy atmosphere and a desperate tone and depict this climate with dark colors and violent intrusions. Thetis' gesture of covering herself with a dark veil as she goes toward Olympus and its blessed gods carries the color of death to heaven: "I feel shame," she says, "to mingle with the immortal gods [μίσγεσθ' ἀθανάτοισι] now that I have unending woes in my heart."

This gloomy attitude, with rituals that solicit unending sorrow, contrasts with the appropriate rituals in honor of Hector that the Olympian gods are making possible: the rituals will produce in the minds of the participants an acceptance of death and an internalization of sorrow. This process begins as soon as Achilles accepts the ransom for Hector from Priam.

The contrast I am drawing constitutes furthermore a gesture by the Poem in favor of the conventional, socially performed rituals and beliefs. The text seems to assign deeper and truer intensity to Achilles' and Thetis' despair than to the conventional rites, for indeed nothing can remedy the loss of a person one loves, nothing can reduce the shock that an exceptional being like Achilles should die so young. The text's representation of Achilles' and Thetis' desperate, irrational, and distorted reactions produces a stronger impression than the ceremonial deployment of conventional rituals. The Poem, however, knows that life needs to go on and that it is necessary to control and internalize those desperate feelings.

Professional poetry participates in the funeral rituals, and indeed the *aoidoi* sing a tune of lament at Hector's funerals (XXIV. 720–22). No wonder that the poetic voice upholds Zeus' decision and actions in favor of a proper funeral, during which poetic words will soothe the mind of the participants.

Iris and Thetis' exit from the sea is made easy by the waves that recede on either side (XXIV. 96) and contrasts with the intrusion that is described on line 79. It is probably the presence of Thetis that produces a calming effect and an easier path.[89]

---

[89] Indeed, the same effect is produced for Poseidon at XIII. 27–29: "the sea creatures sported in his path [...] and did not fail to recognize their master, and the sea stood apart before him, rejoicing."

As Thetis, covered by the black veil in sign of mourning, arrives in heaven, she finds Zeus, εὐρύοπα Κρονίδην, "the deep thunder-voicing son of Kronos."[90] Through the exact repetition of expressions, the text emphasizes the parallelism between the gathering of the sea goddesses around Thetis (XXIV. 83–84: "all the other sea goddesses were sitting together around her and she in the middle of them was crying...") and the physically analogous gathering of the gods around Zeus (XXIV. 98–100: "and around him, all the other gods were sitting together[91] in their immortal blessing. She then sat down beside father Zeus..."). The exact parallelism brings out the spiritual contrast. Zeus and the rest of the gods are banqueting:[92] Athena leaves her seat to allow Thetis to sit beside Zeus, while Hera offers Thetis a golden goblet and comforting words. The text stresses the superimposition of the two climates and worlds that Zeus invites to come together.

At the sight of Thetis' black veil, Zeus does not need his immortal comprehension of things to understand her embarrassment, hesitation, and misgivings (104–05):

You have come to Olympus, goddess Thetis, even if you are in pain,
since an unforgettable grief preys on your heart —I know it well myself.[93]

---

**90** The initial part of the line, εὗρον δ' εὐρύοπα Κρονίδην, is found only three times in the *Iliad*: I. 498, XV. 152, and here XXIV. 98. The combination of the two epithets must grant a particular power to the expression, since in all three passages Zeus is engaged in very important operations. Of course, it is also possible that the initial verb εὗρον has facilitated, even suggested, the continuation with the εὐρύοπα epithet. At any rate, the reuse of the phrase from the first book when Thetis finds Zeus and makes her request seems hardly a chance or a mechanic repetition. The same for XV. 152, where Iris and Apollo reach Zeus and reestablish the order of things after Hera's and Poseidon's violation of Zeus' plans.
**91** The text emphasizes the "togetherness" of the marine goddesses and of the Olympian gods (ὁμηγερέες, 89, 99) and the contrast between the marine goddesses' mourning and the Olympian gods' pleasant collaboration.
**92** Lines "98–99 are deliberately worded like 83–84 to contrast the happy gods and the mourning Thetis. The phrase μάκαρες θεοὶ αἰὲν ἐόντες, which occurs four times in *Od.* but only here in *Il.*, is chosen to stress the same contrast." Macleod, *ad loc*.
**93** οἶδα καὶ αὐτός. In the *Iliad* we have twice (XX. 201 and 432) the phrase, ἐπεὶ σάφα οἶδα καὶ αὐτός, when a speaker assures that he too knows well the taunts and the insults his adversary has thrown against him. In the *Odyssey*, the formula οἶδα καὶ αὐτός prepares for an objection (e.g. x. 457). In our passage, form and context are, for the *Iliad*, unique: Zeus wants to assure Thetis that he is fully aware of what she feels, yet he will tell her what he wants from her, implying, "though this might be unsuitable to your state of mind."

When Zeus says, "I know it well myself," he realizes something that we can only imagine; he knows that Thetis has no concern for Hector and his funeral rites and that she is mourning for her son who will die very soon. She already lives with a sorrow that effaces her sense of any other event.

Even so, Zeus delivers his order (106–119):

> but even so, I will tell you why I summoned you here.
> For nine days the immortal gods have quarreled
> over the body of Hector and over Achilles, destroyer of cities:
> they kept on urging clear-sighted Argeiphontes to steal the body.
> I, however, am granting Achilles this shining privilege (τόδε κῦδος),
> while safeguarding your respect and friendship for the future.
> Run immediately to the camp and instruct your son:
> tell him that the gods are angry, and I, more than all the other
> immortals, am wrathful because in his madness (φρεσὶ μαινομένῃσιν):
> he holds Hector by the ships and does not give him back:
> [tell him] if indeed he might fear me and might give back Hector.
> Meanwhile I will send Iris to great-hearted Priam,[94] [telling him]
> to ransom his dear son, to go to the ships of the Achaeans
> and bring gifts to Achilles, which may placate his anger.[95]

Zeus' message unfolds through three moments: the engaging prologue (104–05), the Olympian quarrel over Achilles' detention of Hector's body (106–09), and Zeus' own resolution of the problem (110–19).

1. (103–05): The epiphanic formula that introduces Zeus' words at line 103 reads:

> τοῖσι δὲ μύθων ἦρχε πατὴρ ἀνδρῶν τε θεῶν τε·

The formula, "the father of men and gods," emphasizes Zeus' wide-ranging authority (see Ch. I.1). Brügger 2009, 58 remarks: "Since here Thetis has the role of mediator between men and gods, the epithet is especially suitable."

---

[94] Zeus sends Iris to Priam immediately, implying or expecting that Achilles will obey the order. Zeus' anticipation allows the simultaneous deployment of the other actions. Through Iris' miraculous speed, Zeus obtains the same results that we enjoy today thanks to modern instruments —and can simultaneously be in touch with all the characters he needs. The fact that technology is able to perform what the ancients thought to be miraculous and divine invites us to consider another difficulty in the definition of what is "human." The different stages of human civilization provide different identifications of what is human and divine.

[95] This last phrase, τά κε θυμὸν ἰήνῃ, is understood by interpreters along two different connotational lines: either "which may gladden his heart" (Macleod *ad loc.* and Brügger 2009) or "which might soften his anger" (Lattimore, and analogously Fagles, Cerri).

Thetis does not answer with any word[96] and instead rushes to satisfy Zeus' request. The Narrator chose a rapid deployment of the scene to underscore the accomplishment of Zeus' whole program, proving his narrative virtuosity. He goes to the heart of the action with a great sense of economy for what is important, and dismisses all the inessential details as, for instance, Thetis' odd lack of reaction to Zeus' bitter reproaches against Achilles.

When Thetis speaks to Achilles, she tells him Zeus' order, word by word (XXIV. 133 ff.), just as Iris, Zeus' messenger, would do. It is through the order of the "great god" that the contact between the divine will and Achilles' mortal will and consciousness takes place. Thetis tells Achilles to return to a human form of life,

> since you will not be with me long, but already
> death and powerful destiny stand closely upon you.
> Come, listen closely to me, for I come from Zeus with a message. (XXIV. 131–33)

As Achilles listens to Zeus' order and rage he suddenly becomes disarmed. Achilles ceases to relive symbolically Patroclos' death, stops punishing the killer of his friend, and, by seeing his own death, understands the sense of Zeus' order: he should return to a human and mortal measure. He should —and indeed this is what will unfold in the following scenes— dismiss the violent behavior of the hero, the more-than-human attitudes, close to divinity and bestiality, and consider his own being, and indeed question the very nature of the heroic life.

This means returning to the rituals of human life, the sacralization of life's events, dialogue and exchange with friends and enemies. Through Achilles' conversion, the text resolves, without dramatic contradictions, the asymmetry and impermeability between the divine and the human wills. The text no longer needs to resort to rhetorical tricks in order to combine the two distant terms: it is sufficient that Achilles abandon the rigid ethics of heroic epic life, and that he accept the destiny Zeus sends to him. But something unexpected happens.

Zeus expects Priam to bring a large ransom to Achilles, and Priam will do it, but Zeus does not expect the friendly, comforting dialogue between the two men. As Macleod (ad 119, p. 100), with great acuity, writes: "what [Zeus] does not predict is the fellow-feeling which will join Achilles and Priam. This is true

---

96 Lines 520–21: "So he spoke and the goddess, silver-footed Thetis, did not disobey him, / but descended with a leap down from Olympus..." The text chooses the syntactical unit οὐδ' ἀπίθησε, after which the persuaded person always rushes, without a word, to accomplish the request he or she received.

to Homer's vision of the difference between gods and men..." Of course, a dialogue such as that between Achilles and Priam would be impossible between a god and a man. Death remains a total otherness, an empty phantom for the gods.

Through this dialogue even the heroic ethic will be examined and seen in its paradoxical nature.

2. (106–09): By mentioning the gods' proposal of stealing Hector's corpse with the help of Hermes, Zeus stresses his rejection of that plan and the novelty of his own solution: "I, however..." (110). Stealing the body of Hector both meant accomplishing an offensive act and presumed that the gods felt convincing Achilles to be impossible: the new step is to have Achilles' willing collaboration.

3. (110–19): After the kind words and before spelling out his command, Zeus assures Thetis of his respect and friendship.

> I, however, am granting Achilles this splendid favor (τόδε κῦδος),
> while safeguarding your respect and friendship for the future.

The assurance sounds like an allusion to the support that Zeus promised to give, and indeed gave, her and Achilles in order to restore the latter's honor (*timê*) (I. 505–10). Specifically, Zeus' phrase, promising respect and friendship to Thetis, seems to assure her that what she feared when she said (I. 515–16), "so that I may learn how much I am the most dishonored goddess among all of them," has never been and will not now be the case.

Zeus deems that he has to give Thetis the assurance of his respect and friendship, for he will be blunt in his argument. He declares his anger at Achilles' behavior, showing to the Narratees a stronger passion than he had displayed when talking to the gods.[97] He declares to Achilles' mother, without any hesitation, that the man has lost his mind (114), and he sounds courteous when he seems to ask if Achilles, after hearing Zeus' command, might fear Zeus and release Hector's body (116).[98]

---

[97] Letoublon 1987, 130 ff. The phrase ἐμὲ δ' ἔξοχα πάντων ("and I, more than all the others") returns three times in the *Iliad* (XIV. 257, XXIV. 113 and 134) and it is always employed by Zeus.
[98] See Adkins 1975, 239 ff. who finds the line "presumably ironical. There is no likelihood that any mortal, however great and powerful, would attempt to defy a direct command of Zeus in Homer and Achilles does not." Macleod, on the contrary, takes it as "an expression of studied courtesy in the mouth of Zeus... It is designed to soften the peremptory tone of 112–15." It is difficult to decide: Zeus' courtesy makes him into a more noble figure than would a use of irony, and his courtesy is coherent with his respect for Thetis.

It is Achilles who now has to do something for Zeus, and not the reverse as happened in the past.

Zeus assumes of course that Achilles will fear his authority and is ready to accomplish a magnanimous gesture by granting to Achilles *kudos* (110).

There is a displacement of connotations in this use of *kudos*: in its common connotation and context, *kudos* implies the favor of the gods, the shine of a light that surrounds a victorious hero on the battlefield, and implies a limited duration of presence. It seems to imply a touch of sacredness in the moment of an extraordinary military event.[99] Again, as in all the other contexts in which a human receives the blessing of a divine agent, the subjective effect this contact produces, how it marks the mind, and the emotion of the mortal who receives it, remain ineffable and unable to be reckoned.

Zeus is, as always, reticent and inscrutable about the reason and grounds for his decisions: does he mean that Achilles will receive this touch of holy favor because he fears Zeus and obeys Zeus' order, or does Zeus also intend to bless with his favor the understanding attitude that Achilles will display to Priam? We will never know if he acts for the one or the other or both reasons:[100] in the eyes of the Narratees, Achilles certainly deserves this favor for both reasons.

The textual strategy in this scene consists in placing Zeus at the center of the action and in making him the exclusive power capable of closing the plot in a harmoniously thematic sequence. The Narrator wishes to replay Thetis' and

---

[99] See Pucci 2010. Often scholars interpret *kudos* in this passage as a synonym of *timê* (see Macleod, 27 and ad XXIV. 110 and Brügger 2009, *ad loc.*); but the semantics of the two words are very different. *Timê*, in contrast with *kudos*, when concerning men, is granted mostly by humans to their chiefs, kings, or colleagues; it involves specific duties and compensations and it may be permanent. When *timê* is accorded to men by the gods, it often implies a recognition of their sacred position as king or leaders; when is coupled with *kudos*, the 'honor' increases the divine assistanceand displays the open words but only trace the most obvious differences. *Kudos*, on the other hand, connotes a favor, a mere sign of sacredness without any concrete advantage and compensation. It is not permanent and here illuminates the new personality of Achilles. I am offering here a more open interpretation of the passage than in my essay "Honor and Glory in the *Iliad*" (1998, 179–230, 208 ff.).

[100] See Macleod (ad 119): "Zeus expects that Achilles will be pleased with the gifts and will fear the divine command (116); what he does not predict is the fellow-feeling which will join Achilles and Priam." Perhaps in saying that Priam will bring gifts to Achilles "that may placate his passion" (119: δῶρα δ' Ἀχιλλῆϊ φερέμεν, τά κε θυμὸν ἰήνῃ), Zeus foresees not only Achilles' friendly and emotional reception of Priam, but also a relaxing effect produced by the gifts, a reconciliation with himself and a deep concern for the old king and for his father, Peleus. The verb *iainô* implies the "melting" of the passion, its total relaxation, but it could also mean "to cheer the heart" of Achilles, though I would not choose this translation.

Zeus' actions in the first book through a reverted process and through a sort of ring composition so as to put an end to the violence of the wrath.

The edifying and beneficial role of Zeus ensues easily and richly from his ritual and monarchic roles: Zeus, in this function, does not act alone but with the concerted help of his peers (Apollo, Iris, Hermes); this role silences his other role that brought him to decree the death of many heroes, among whom was even Hector, of whom Zeus now organizes, with grace, the funeral.

## 6.4 Closing Remarks

In the *Iliad*, the mythical collaboration of gods and men begins with the Muses' privileged association with the Poet. Through a jump of centuries, this association also pervades Olympus and heroic human society.[101] The Poem aims at combining divine might and mortal forces into a sort of hybrid collaboration. Men and gods indeed collaborate; their aims, however, are different, and the characters of the Poem fail to recognize where Zeus, the master of their heroic destinies, leads them. When they finally perceive it, it is too late, and destruction ensues.

Zeus' theological and historical role as master of destiny turns him into an extraordinary, formidable, odd, and strange divine figure that makes the *Iliad* the Poem it is. This role splits Zeus' personality, causing difficult connections among different psychological dispositions he feels and needs in order to exercise the other two roles: Zeus as Olympus monarch, and Zeus acting on the human stage. He finds himself contrasted by some of his peers, especially his brother Poseidon and his sister/wife Hera: they cannot compete seriously to conquer his power, but they violate some of his orders and try to oppose his actions. It is in this relation that he appears as a god of brutal physical force. Yet this force is never actually enacted, because an appropriate discourse manages to display the menace of the force as a deterrent, show its parodic allusions, or produce comic effects. In other words, Zeus' physical violence is always spoken of and brought to light through a speech or a discourse that governs and controls it. Finally, as god of cult, Zeus is psychologically responsive to human

---

**101** The traditional stories narrated in epic poems and hymns constitute the hypertext that is constantly enriched by, and constantly at the disposal of, the oral poets. This hypertext came into being essentially through poetry, as Calame 2015, 28–29 writes: in Greece, the narrative we moderns call mythical "est par essence poétique."

death, needs, and prayers. In this role, he often encounters poignant human situations for which he feels pain, and of which he has been the cause.

Exercising his first role, that of the Golden Scale, Zeus cannot even delay his own son's death which, as god of destiny, he has decreed. The text must trick its audience and make Zeus oblivious of his fatal responsibility, when, animated by love for his son, he sees Sarpedon running to his death. If at this point, when Zeus feels love for Sarpedon, the text had made him conscious that he had preordained his son's death, a tragic conflict would have emerged and would have destroyed any chance for a hybrid and harmonious relationship between the anthropomorphic and the superhuman perspective, even for Zeus himself. It is in order to safeguard this happy relationship that the text manipulates its character's consciousnes, by making him oblivious, and manages that the Narratees will be fully gained by Zeus' emotion and love for his son.

When and if the wishful purpose of this textual strategy becomes obvious, the Narratees realize the terrible frailty of the relationship of these two contrasting reactions in Zeus himself. In the Poem Zeus becomes the most authoritative model of the impossible cooperation of what is human, anthropomorphic, and mortal with what is superhuman, immortal, and cosmic. It is only by employing various tricks and strategies, that the Iliadic text safeguards the wishful hybridism of these contrasting spheres.

Had the text granted Zeus the tragic awareness of being the killer of his son, it would have created a new religious figure; but since it represents Zeus as being unable to act in accordance with his fatherly love and grief, the text depicts his negative theocratic power.

The *Iliad* shows Zeus inspiring warlike fury in the great heroes, elevating them to a pitch of heroic excess, and then, paradoxically, pushing them to their respective catastrophic falls. He even intervenes with his own hands to kill Hector while praising him as the most pious man. This represents total nonsense according to human logic. The victims of such conspiracies escape the humiliation of being defeated and they meet death while gazing at their glory, or through the supreme dignity of enduring the meaningless will that operates above them.

Even as master of human destinies, Zeus faces conflicting purposes, for he preordains and controls two contradictory plans: the first one, to grant partial and provisional victory to the Trojans, and the second, to insure the final collapse of Troy. While the first plan violates the representation the hypertext gives of Zeus' pro-Achaean stance, the second reassures the audience that the history and the tradition of the fall of Troy are not betrayed. The narrative manages to sustain Zeus' new commitment, and consequently it enlarges the vision Zeus has of the human world and depicts a non-providential image of the divine destiny. Zeus in the *Iliad* can appreciate the piety of Hector and the innocence of the city of Troy. The Poet makes his audience realize that in the logic of Zeus qua embodiment of destiny, defeat, destruction, and disasters strike people and communities even when they have not necessarily merited them. This is the terrifying role of destiny in human history and Zeus, by impersonating that destiny, acts accordingly, silent about the motivations behind the terrifying human condition, and morally indifferent to the scandal of this situation. It took great lucidity of mind and great courage for the Poet to invest the main god of Olympus with this terrible role.

For the human characters and for the audience of the Poem, Zeus incarnates the *mysterium tremendum et fascinans*. *Mysterium* is the correct word. Zeus never describes the structure, the meaning, the connotations of the order of things, the ground on which he elaborates and imposes his will, his *boulê*. His words to the gods are rare and reserved. He never speaks to the human characters; he communicates his orders to them through messengers or through the roaring of thunders and the frightening flash of lightning. Such cosmic interventions signal orders or approvals, but no explanation. Zeus' eagle too brings messages to men: its flights are meaningful, but often deliver ambiguous signs. There is a certain savagery in the nature of these messengers.

Zeus, as can be expected, has no humor, yet, when he speaks polemically to his peers, his tremendous energy translates into teasing and sarcasm. Compared to the hypertext's accounts of his traditional quarrels with Hera and other gods, the Iliadic Zeus clearly belongs to another world. The text gives to the Narratees the impression that it reworked, not without parody and irony, old images of Zeus and then changed them into the shocking new one I have depicted. An exotic stranger in his Olympian community.

This portrait of the Iliadic Zeus must be completed by revisiting the traits and earmarks that characterize what we generally call "divine."

Immortality makes Zeus and the gods unable to comprehend any human value and makes mortals unable to comprehend the nature of what is divine.

On the one hand, Zeus and the other gods fail to understand the values of life, survival, and in particular, heroism. They do not have a life, they simply "are," existing forever, as the text never tires of repeating. They cannot evaluate what it means nobly to face death, which is what we call heroism.

In the radical forms of this incomprehension, Zeus, Hera, and other gods are totally indifferent to human life and to the survival of cities: the greatest achievements of humankind mean nothing to them and even the temples built in honor of gods do not safeguard a city that the gods decide to destroy for personal reasons.

On the other hand, men fail to comprehend divine nature: this incomprehension is another general pattern that is formed by the impossible, and yet textually wishful, permeability between divine immortality and human mortality.[102] The Muses themselves cannot explain what "divine" (*theos*-like) really means. Gods appear to mortals in human form, voice and feelings and help them physically and mentally. Apollo rescues Hector, Aphrodite rescues Paris, etc., but no trace of the divine presence, of its superhuman essence remains in these mortals' awareness. The divine exists, is named with the names of gods and operates before the eyes of human beings, upon both men and natural phenomena,[103] but remains ineffable and inexplicable. It can only be narrated by immortal witnesses —by the Muses— and is soon forgotten, or barely and sporadically remembered, by those who encounter it. It remains without a human story.

Yes, Zeus is there, manages events, and decides the destiny of all men and cities: his total governance remains suspended to his paradoxical and contradictory will, sometimes sympathetic and occasionally even providential but finally destructive, giving hopes and betraying them, with no scruples at all. Human beings in their ignorance expect a better Zeus than the Poem shows him to be.

The *Iliad*, with its Zeus, does not fulfill in Greece the function of the Bible, the Gospel, the Koran. Zeus does not deliver a readable order, or a promise of salvation, but he impresses upon human life the terrifying feeling that something called god, supernatural and immortal, controls everything, and may grant, but more often denies, what men most want.

It would be an enriching reading if we could solve the question whether the text, by using the strategies that safeguard the potential collaboration of mortal

---

102 This incomprehension is unavoidable for many reasons, and among them the fact that the gods speak, feel, act, and socialize like humans, even if in these similarities they are completely different from them.

103 I have already remarked, following Parker 2011, 77, upon the difficulty of understanding the line between the god as the cause of a natural phenomenon and as the natural phenomenon itself.

The natural phenomenon supplements the human-like role of the god. On VIII. 130–36:
"there would have been havoc...
if the father of men and gods had not seen clearly:
he thundered terribly and sent a blinding lightning bolt
[βροντήσας δ' ἄρα δεινὸν ἀφῆκ' ἀργῆτα κεραυνόν]
and dashed it to the ground in front of Diomedes' horses
and a ghastly blaze of flaming sulphur shot up and the horses,
terrified, both cringed away against the chariot."

and immortal issues, means to attain this goal or, on the contrary, to expose the terrible frailty and asymmetry of this collaboration as the text finally reveals. The text can attain this mythical goal only by ruse and deception. But to solve this question would take us to more enigmatic questions: it is impossible to detect the true intentions of a text, especially when this detection means thwarting and deconstructing a myth while working with mythical elements.

When we realize the way in which the text is straightforward and direct in staging Zeus' negative theocracy —his readiness to condemn, unmotivated, Sarpedon, Hector, Patroclos, Troy etc.— we are tempted to favor a reading according to which the text's clever strategies ironically deflate its mythical assumptions. Yet this interpretation would defy and contest the edifying concern of the text as it stages Zeus' love and grief for his son. The text extols Zeus' anthropomorphic feelings, which the Narratees expect from him as divinity honored by a cult, and as traditional father of the young hero.

By soothing, hiding and even eliminating conflictual features between mortal and immortal issues, the text appears to pay respect to the myth of mortal and immortal hybridism and it is not certain that the text grants the readers a legitimate ironical and skeptical reading of the goal of the myth. It is not easy to determine where textual agreement with myth stops, especially if we are conditioned to argue against the myth with mythical premises and assumptions. Once again, the double reading is possibly truer than the one establishing an assertion or a denial.

The textual parody that smiles at the traditional figure of Zeus could be read as a revolutionary gesture that would aim at showing the instability of the divine figure, the ease and the pleasure of mocking some of its earlier aspects, the whole being immersed in a sort of divertissement. Yet again, to select and privilege the intellectual novelty means to grapple with the myth inventiveness and rich semantic nature.

While the Poem survived as a most fertile source of figures and images of the permeability between divine and human worlds, and of the greatness and misery of heroic life, the mysterious and terrifying figure of Zeus became a constant source of research, reworking, and meditation within archaic Greek culture, without fully imposing itself as an image of the providential architect of the order of things.

In the previous pages, I have briefly touched upon the mostly providential and comforting image of Zeus that one reads in the *Odyssey* and in the works of Hesiod, possibly as a reaction to the *Iliad*'s theological image of Zeus. It would take a special inquiry and a closer investigation to analyze whether a real polemical reaction takes place or whether there exists simply a different theology within the *Odyssey* and other parallel epic works. I cannot begin here such an investigation, and I would like only to offer new evidence for the extraordinary originality of the Iliadic figure of Zeus.

In the closing lines of the *Odyssey*, Zeus cares for "the reciprocal love" of the citizens, for the "peace and prosperity" of the city, as he tells Athena (xxiv. 482–86: τοὶ δ' ἀλλήλους φιλεόντων / ὡς τὸ πάρος, πλοῦτος δὲ καὶ εἰρήνη ἅλις ἔστω). In contrast, we can think of Hera and Zeus arguing about their divine desire to destroy one —or three— beloved cities. Odyssean Zeus' commitment to the city's survival is so serious that when Athena encourages Odysseus and his party to massacre the hostile citizens (xxiv. 516 ff.), he throws a lightning bolt in front of the goddess to stop her (xxiv. 539–40). This lightning bolt contextually recalls the one that Zeus throws to stop Diomedes and save the Trojans in *Iliad* VIII. 132 ff.[104] The close reference to the Iliadic passage betrays a similar context and emphasizes that Zeus' final aim in the *Odyssey* is different: the lightning in both texts is meant to stop an unwanted assault: Iliadic Zeus wants to save Hector, whom he protects to keep his promise to Thetis, but Odyssean Zeus wants to insure life for the whole city of Ithaca. In the *Odyssey*, Zeus does not prevent a mortal's action, but Athena's, the warring goddess, never tired of fighting, who is here quite ready to help Odysseus continue the killing. With this gesture —a very rare intervention on the part of Zeus against another god in the *Odyssey*— Zeus seeks to establish a long-lasting truce and love between Odysseus' party and all the other Ithacans. The *Odyssey* does not close with Zeus' organizing the funeral of the man he himself helped to kill, condemning Troy to destruction, but with the god's decisive action to make possible a truce and safeguard peace for all the city's citizens.

In Hesiod's *Works and Days*, Zeus is the father of Dike. In its concrete meaning, this word implies "the right, straight verdict or judgment," but as a name and as a personification it designates "justice." Zeus and his daughter Dike cooperate (256–62):

---

**104** if the father of men and gods had not seen clearly:
he thundered terribly and sent a blinding lightning bolt
[βροντήσας δ' ἄρα δεινὸν ἀφῆκ' ἀργῆτα κεραυνόν]
and dashed it to the ground in front of Diomedes' horses
and a ghastly blaze of flaming sulphur shot up and the horses,
terrified, both cringed away against the chariot."

> Present is virgin Dike [Justice], daughter of Zeus[105]
> who is honored and respected by the gods who dwell on Olympus.
> And whenever someone hurts her by crookedly scorning her,
> she sits down at once beside her father Zeus, son of Kronos
> and sings to him of the mind of unjust human beings, so that he will take
> revenge upon the people for the wickedness of their kings
> who, evil-minded, bend judgments (*dikas*) by speaking crookedly.[106]

This quotation is sufficient to measure the distance between the Hesiodean Zeus and the Iliadic one, although the question of Justice is extremely difficult and complex in the Hesiodean poem (see Pucci 1977, pp. 45–81).

Hesiod's and Homer's texts constituted for the ancient Greeks a series of "revelations" or "apocalypses" about the gods, as Rudhardt (1992, pp. 231–32, and 2008) strongly emphasizes when he goes so far as to assimilate the poets' authority to that of the oracles.

As these few remarks on Zeus in the *Odyssey* and in Hesiod's work intend to stress, it is a serious misunderstanding of some modern scholars and ancient Greek readers to fail to distinguish, in a neat and sharp way, Zeus' autocratic, indifferent, and mysterious behavior in the *Iliad* from the almost providential figure in Hesiod and in the *Odyssey*. The traditional attribution of the two poems to Homer should not induce us to minimize the essential differences between them.

The misunderstanding that I am mentioning is not recent, as it is found in most of the Presocratic philosophers and in the historians of the fifth century. It is sustained by the dramatic, anthropomorphic figure of the gods that archaic epic poetry proposes. Herodotus attests this when he writes (2.53):

"Not till the day before yesterday, so to speak, did the Greeks know the origin of each of the gods, or whether they had all always existed, and what they were like in appearance..." They [Homer and Hesiod] were the ones who created a theogony for the Greeks [οὗτοι δέ εἰσι οἱ ποιήσαντες θεογονίην Ἕλλησι], gave the gods their epithets [καὶ τοῖσι θεοῖσι τὰς ἐπωνυμίας δόντες], divided out honors and functions among them, and described their appearance.

Herodotus, therefore, identifies Homer and Hesiod as the creators of the Greek theogony, of the dramatic personal aspects of the gods, and of their "anthropomorphic way of life" —for instance their family and social relationships, names and epithets, etc. Herodotus does not relate the gods' fusions with or

---

[105] Δίκη, Διὸς ἐκγεγαυῖα. "There is no doubt in my mind that Hesiod wants to show how the name *Dike* is formed from *Dios*." Pucci 1977, 80, n. 25.
[106] Hesiod plays on the double meaning of *dike* "judgment" and *Dike* the goddess.

connections to natural phenomena, but he does not deny them either. To this extent Herodotus is correct, but the distinction between the *Iliad* and the other epic poems cannot acquire any visibility under the investigatory light of epic anthropomorphism in general. As we have seen, a more exacting light shows that Iliadic Zeus' anthropomorphism is different from that of Zeus in the other poems, at least to the extent that in the *Iliad* he is identified with the Golden Scales, the *oloiê moira*, and remains reticent and mysterious about the aims of his actions. His weaponry, the lightning bolts and thunder, dehumanize him since he can be thought to be either throwing them or embodying them.[107]

Xenophanes too unites Homer and Hesiod in his criticism of the anthropomorphism of the epic gods: this generic criticism fails to recognize the difference between the specific images of Zeus in the different poems.

Greek tragedy is entirely involved with the metaphysical questions raised by the immortal gods' interventions in mortal affairs. The immortal might manifests and imposes its will in the form of plans, judgments, praise, punishment, etc. Here too, the troubled, bewildering Iliadic permeability of the two worlds, with all its paradoxes and tensions, outshines tragic conflicts and human ignorance. The direct divine voice, however, sounds more rarely than in the *Iliad*, though through oracles and prophets it is equally determining and absolute. The direct voice of Zeus and his figure as a character are practically absent in tragedy. Yet as the other gods make irreversible decisions for the individual protagonists, community, city, etc., the presence of Zeus is never far away. When Athena, in the last drama of the *Oresteia*, fails to persuade the Erinyes, she resorts to a veiled menace and informs them that she alone among the gods has access to the spot where Zeus keeps the lightning: it is with this mention of Zeus and of his possible violence that the Erinyes become persuaded.

The issue of Zeus' relationship to destiny and necessity is complex, among other reasons because it is treated in different ways in different dramas sometimes he is conceived as a form of necessity in accordance with the *Iliad*, but sometimes he is himself subject to Necessity.

On the whole, the tragic Zeus is closer to the ethical Zeus of the *Odyssey* and Hesiod than to the Zeus of the *Iliad*. However, this is not the place to illustrate

---

**107** Montanari 1992, 82 comments: "In realtà l'opinione di Erodoto attribuisce ai due poeti un ruolo formatore dell'impianto mitico-religioso greco che pare eccessivo, ma non si può mettere in dubbio il valore paradigmatico assunto dalla codificazione epica, entro una cultura la cui religione non possiede testi sacri ispirati, né alcuna rivelazione, e che invece riconosce ai poeti il ruolo di teologi e sistematori dell'educazione e delle credenze religiose."
For other formal aspects of the influence of Homer on the historians, see Rengakos 2006, 183–214.

the function of the gods and of Zeus in tragedy, and therefore I end here my hasty notes on the traits of Zeus as they appeared in texts contemporary or immediately after the *Iliad*.

In contrast with many of those texts, the *Iliad* has the lucidity and the daring to refuse a comforting and providential image of Zeus, while yet simultaneously avoiding the suggestion of any other divine principle as a criterion of Zeus' choices and interventions. Wisely, the *Iliad* leaves Zeus silent, so as not to speak in his place —and this is the Poem's most eloquent silence.

# Appendix 1

## δῖος Ἀχιλλεύς. The Notion of Divine as Applied to the Heroes

The expanded, hybrid, and polyvalent notions that define the immortal Greek god (*theos* – "divinity," "god"), also qualify what Homeric language understands with the words that derive from *theos*, i.e. that express the idea of "divine." Thunder, rain, fountains, a wall (XXI. 526), trees, and most parts of the natural world are "divine," "sacred" for the Homeric characters and for the gods. The divine nature of the gods essentially lies in their immortality, eternal youth, and extraordinary might, while the definition of nature as divine depends on its possessing some of those divine prerogatives through identification with a god or through sharing some of them. Human beings —the women and the heroes— are themselves often called "divine," "godlike," "equal" or "similar to gods," "fostered by Zeus," and "descending from Zeus," etc.[1] They are viewed as such in the eyes of the Muses and of men, who define each other in this way. Of course, the divine nature of the gods —their immortality, eternal youth, and extraordinary powers— is not signified by these expressions: rather, these images suggest a certain resemblance with some aspects of the gods' divine nature —beauty or wisdom for instance— or even a real descendance from a god, as heroes often boast of a divine ancestor, whether close or extended. Achilles is the direct son of the goddess Thetis and is "divine" only in this connection, for, in all other aspects, he is mortal.

The adjective *dîos* is very often employed as an epithet of various heroes, women,[2] and natural phenomena ("Ether" XVI. 365; "Dawn" IX. 240; "Sea" I. 141; "Earth" XIV. 347, "where the epithet is justified and XXIV. 532 where it is only formulaic," Chantraine, *DELG*). It is difficult to fix its precise meaning not only because it is generic but also because its etymology can emphasize a

---

[1] I refer to the noun-epithet phrases in which a mortal man or woman is defined as *theios* (divine), *isotheos* (equal to a god), *theoeidês* (with a divine aspect), *theoeikelos* (similar to a god), *epieikelos athanatoisi* (similar to the immortals), *daimoni isos* (equal to a daimon), *dîos* (divine), *diogenês* (born from Zeus), *diotrephês* (fostered by Zeus), etc.

[2] The feminine form is substantivized and in the epithetic phrase δῖα γυναικῶν it is translated by "goddess," "queen," "la plus belle among women"; while in the epithetic phrase δῖα θεάων it is translated by "shining among goddesses," "glory of goddesses," "divine among the goddesses," with the same inconsistency. Helen is defined by this epithetic phrase three times out of the four occurrences of the phrase. She is the daughter of Zeus.

"shine" or a direct connection with Zeus (Chantraine, *DELG*³) and therefore can mean something like, "belonging to Zeus," "descendant from Zeus." This latter meaning is evident at IX. 538 and is very well attested in Greek tragedy. Yet as Latacz 2000, 23 comments: "In Homer, it drops to a pure stereotyped function (Formelhaftigkeit) ('bien né, noble'): it is an expression of the highest excellence to which no specific signification is associated. Whether the original force of the expression could have been revitalized by the audience [...] remains without answer. On the possibilities of diagnosing its rivitalization (with probability) see De Jong 1998. Homeric Epithet and Narrative Situation. In *Homerica. Proceedings of the 8th International Symposion on the Odyssey* (1–5 Sept. 1996, ed. Païsi-Apostolopoulou, Ithaca 1998, 121–135.)" What may revitalize this epithet's near etymological connotation is the context.

I begin with the example on which Latacz 2000, 23 writes the quoted commentary. In the first lines of the poem, the text invites the Muses to sing the wrath of Achilles and Zeus' accomplishment of his plan (I. 5–7):

> [...] And the will of Zeus was accomplished
> since the time first when there stood in division of conflict
> Atreus' son, lord of men, and *dîos* Achilles.

> [...] Διὸς δ' ἐτελείετο βουλή,
> ἐξ οὗ δὴ τὰ πρῶτα διαστήτην ἐρίσαντε
> Ἀτρεΐδης τε ἄναξ ἀνδρῶν καὶ δῖος Ἀχιλλεύς.

The three central characters of the poem enter onto the stage: while Zeus has no epithet, Agamemnon and Achilles each have the epithet that specifically characterizes them in their conflicting roles and essences. As Pagliaro 1956, 37–38 argues, Agamemnon's epithet has here a unique and exceptional position; it otherwise appears thirty-seven times between the trochaic caesura and the end of the verse: ἄναξ ἀνδρῶν Ἀγαμέμνων. With this displacement, the Poet intended to grant the epithet a qualifying —and not merely ornamental— function, characterizing Agamemnon as a man of power, as opposed to Achilles, qualified as *dîos*. How to understand this last word and how to translate it? The following translations have been offered by various translators in various languages: "brilliant," "noble," "divine," "godlike," "glorious." The translation "divine"

---

**3** "'La forme grecque' peut dériver de *di-e-w-o* 'celeste', mais il est aussi naturel d'évoquer Skr. *div(i)ya-*. Dans ce cas δῖος reposerait sur *dî-F-ios* qui s'appuit sur mycénien *diujo*, *diwija*, etc." Latacz 2000, 23: "Im Myk ist δῖος in den Formen *di-u-jo*, bezw. *di-wi-jo* belegt und bedeutet dort noch "appartenant à Zeus" bei Heroennamen wohl "descendant de Zeus."

that I have chosen, although the epithet's meaning of "son/daughter of, belonging to, loved by Zeus etc." is not supported by his birth, refers nevertheless to a supernatural aura and even to the connection with his mother.

The noun-epithet δῖος Ἀχιλλεύς on *Il.* I. 7 is placed in a chiasmus and therefore with contrasting force in graphical opposition to Agamemnon as a man of power. In the previous line 5, the genitive of the name Zeus, Διὸς, notwithstanding its different syllabic quantity, provides a very strong assonance and may evoke or provoke the revitalization of the etymological Mycenian connection of the adjective with Zeus.

Assuming now that all this really brings back to the ears and mind of the audience Zeus' evocation, the question arises how we, the Narratees, should translate the adjective when it refers to people.

As is clear from what precedes, the expression δῖος Ἀχιλλεύς can be read according to three different premises: as a mere metrical aid, as ornamental diction (merely "noble," "brilliant"), and finally, as adding some functional significance ("divine"), or a full significance (son/daughter of Zeus, etc). All three premises may be present at once in each occurrence of the expression, if the context intimates or helps to revitalize its semantic function. If the context intimates its semantic function, the expression constitutes a supplement that covers over the mere human nature of the hero and grants him/her a divine pedigree. Of course, this supplemental force would render opaque the other two ways of reading without fully effacing them.

When in translation we use the word "divine" and revitalize its semantic function, we recover the resonances of the Homeric divine and its multiple associations with immortality, agelessness, superior physical force, miraculous efficiency, violence, natural phenomena, the mastery of human destinies, its presence among men, its beauty and shine. However, because the divine is, for humans, limited, provisional, and permeable, the divine quality that this epithet attaches to Achilles —as to other heroes— both enhances the hero's stature and simultaneously evokes a sort of lack, void, and incompleteness. This lack figures in two accounts: as a frequently repeated and generic epithet, *dîos* often connotes only a vague title of honor; when it evokes a connection with the divine, it may mock or even increase the hero's pains or the menace of death impending upon him.

Perhaps we should also look at the frequency of these divinizing epithetic phrases in a specific context. In book XXII during the first 405 lines, which describe the combat between Hector and Achilles, Achilles is described by impressive similes that compare him to a star, and specifically to the star Sirius, the brightest star in the sky (25–32), or that compare his spear to Hesperos, the most beautiful star in the sky (317–20). In the same passage, Achilles is evoked eight times by the epithetic phrase δῖος Ἀχιλλεύς and once by θεοῖς ἐπιείκελ' Ἀχιλλεῦ (279: "god-like Achilles"):[4] in all eight passages the epithetic phrase is effective and has a semantic function.

In the same book, Hector receives the epithet δῖος only four times and in contexts that revitalize the qualifying function of the epithet. I present an example. After killing Hector, Achilles turns to the Achaeans and cries out to them (393–95):

> "We have gained a great triumph: we have killed divine Hector [Ἕκτορα δῖον],
> to whom the Trojans in the city prayed to as to a god [θεῷ ὣς εὐχετόωντο]."
> So he spoke, and now he thought of a shameful treatment for divine Hector [Ἕκτορα δῖον].

It is impossible to miss the qualifying function of the epithetic phrases: on 393, Achilles aggrandizes Hector, making him godlike in order to magnify the importance of his victory over a mighty enemy who is dear to Zeus: he stresses this point by adding, as if as evidence, that the Trojans treated him like a god. Then the poetic voice takes over and focalizes the passage with bitter sarcasm —or compassion[5]— showing how violent and unbearable the treatment is to which that "divine" man is submitted. The poetic voice shakes and deconstructs the wishful and edifying assumption that the permeation between the human and the divine may be easily achieved, and constructive.

Renée Piettre 1996, p. 116 invites us to listen to something "unbearable" in the divinizing noun-epithet phrases: these expressions show "the shine often unbearable of the human body in the fullness of its beauty. The gods are the measure and the limit of the human grandeur. [...] What should be done in order to describe the divine grandeur itself? On this matter there should be no other limit than language's artifices and the conceptualization."

All this does not prevent the gods from manifesting themselves in human bodies and does not prevent men from presenting themselves with a divine shine.

---

[4] As De Jong 2012, 129 explains, this is "a regular vocative formula for Achilles after the feminine caesura (5 x *Iliad*, 1 x *Odyssey*)." Shive 1987, 111–114 suggests that the formula "is not used automatically, but only when effective." De Jong correctly provides an explanation in this sense for the passage XXII. 279.

[5] It is difficult to decide: if the expression ἀεικέα μήδετο ἔργα means "disfiguring actions," it does not really condemn Achilles but rather characterizes the effect of the actions on Hector's body; yet these actions are shameful if they characterize Achilles in his intention to wrong a man like Hector, a "divine" man in the sense of "beautiful, great, shining, mighty, close to Zeus, dear to Zeus," etc.

The manifold aura of the "divine" and the rich porousness between human and divine traits also affect the image and notion of "human" in the Homeric text. For these two different, even contrasting, beings permeate each other. Gods are immortal and superhuman and are identifiable with natural phenomena, yet they can resemble men both physically and mentally. Heroes too, though mortal, are marked by divine aspects: like gods, they are handsome, splendid, and shining, and, through an enormous crop of synecdoches and similes, they are also marked by similarity with natural phenomena: they are shining like stars, their tears run like streams, they fight like lions, etc. A generalized transparence and permeability unifies the whole of Being in this theological poem.[6]

The cosmographic and transparent writing of the myth of the *Iliad*, however, neither gives any comfort nor warrants any optimism. For this writing constantly insinuates the difference, the disjunction, and the asymmetry in the permeability: the blessed gods' embrace of human nature is always provisional, and potentially murderous, since it brings about the unhappy destiny of man. It is precisely their destiny about which the heroes —however similar to the gods, and even if descending from Zeus— are worried; although they live nearly godlike, through a total commitment to their people and to their tasks, wanting to be the best in their deeds.[7]

---

6 This transparence is produced by a spectacular rhetoric. The epithets are constant synecdoches which, through a selected part, evoke the semantic whole of each thing or person; they project into semantic space innumerable identifications of the same person or object, attaching them to a whole universe of meaning. Thus, an army of men is compared to a deep cloud in the sky or to the tumultuous waves of the sea, or to the various winds like Notos or Euros, or to the streams of rivers: this process is systematic and endless and little by little it transforms singular and temporal events, things, and persons into a general and constant natural phenomenon. This process that is brought about by the constant flowing of epithets, similes, and tropes grants the consistency and the order of the natural world to the countless, transient, disjointed fragments that make up the human world. Nothing is suspended in the void, nothing is deprived of its semantic context. Iliadic poetic energy encapsulates every particle of the world into a complete and absolutely meaningful totality. This orderly and transparent network of relationships is the readable writing that the *Iliad* imprints upon the real world's illegible scrawl.

7 Snell 1960 vigorously upholds this view. See a famous passage often quoted: "When Homer says that a man is good (*agathos*), he does not mean thereby that he is morally unobjectionable, much less good-hearted, but rather that he is useful, proficient and capable of vigorous action" (p. 158).

# Appendix 2

## The Muses and the Poet

As I add here a few remarks on the relationship between the Muses and the Poet, and in general between myth and the nature of the hypertext, I leave aside and take for granted the panorama that recent scholarship has opened up on the Greek and Near Eastern-Aegean gods. Burkert has drawn astonishing parallels in the religious *koine* of anthropomorphic gods; he has underlined the peculiar feature that the Greek names of gods are not significant, while the Summerian, Hittite, and Ugaritic names are, so that, in contrast, "the names of the Greek gods cannot be immediately identified with the functions, ideas, abstractions their names would designate, but can be identified only as named entities, therefore as 'persons'" (Burkert 1985, 182–83). The Greek gods are persons with arbitrary names, as is often, for persons, the case.[8]

I also take for granted the assertions I have often made concerning the topics of the Greek anthropomorphic gods, the Muses, and poetry. I only recall Detienne's definition of the limited and ambivalent nature of Greek divine anthropomorphism; I do not stress the fact that Greek poetry is unique among those Near Eastern cultures in having conceived a special genre of gods, the Muses, as divine poets, singing in Olympus and inspiring poetry to men.

As I have argued in my 2002 paper and repeated here, it is anachronistic to introduce a genre distinction between religion and poetry in the text of the *Iliad*. The permeability between divine and human voices is a wishful ideological and metaphysical premise that the *Iliad* derives from the mythical hypertext and whose principle the *Iliad* celebrates in a famous passage (II. 484–87):

> Tell me now, you Muses, who have your homes in Olympus—
> for you are [*este*] goddesses, you are present [*pareste*] and you know [*iste*] everything—[9]

---

**8** For Cicero's and others' attempts to connect the names of the gods to their abstract functions, see Calame 2015, 44 ff.
**9** Ford 1992, 60–61 writes: "In a line of nearly incantatory assonance (*Il.* II. 485: ὑμεῖς γὰρ θεαί ἐστε πάρεστέ τε ἴστέ τε πάντα ["you are goddesses, you are present, and you know everything"]) Homer attributes three things to the Muses: first of all, they exist and they are goddesses; second, they are present to the poet as he calls them and also presumably present as spectators at the events of which he wishes to speak; finally they know these things in the special sense compressed in the Greek verb, by having seen them. [...] It is not only a philosopher who says, 'the eyes are more accurate witnesses than the ears.'" See also Pucci 1998, 36–39. Rarely the Poet confesses that he operates without the help of the Muses. On XII. 176, for

> but we [the poets] hear only the fame [*kleos*] and know nothing
> of who were then the chief men and the lords of the Danaans...

The poet leaves us, distant Narratees, in some doubt as to how to understand line 486: "but we [the poets] hear only the fame [*kleos*] and know nothing." The trouble lies in the word *kleos*, which has a vast range of connotations. In this context it can evoke two different series of "heard things": either human reputations, such as family traditions (*prokluta epea*, "stories heard from mortal men" XX. 204), rumors, transmitted stories gathered from the hypertext, etc.; or the divine reputations that the Muses transmit to poets. In the former connotation of *kleos*, the text would say: You Muses know everything, but we poets hear only human rumors and stories and accordingly we know nothing. In the latter connotation of *kleos*, the poet would say: You Muses know everything, but we poets hear the fame [of things] [you Muses tell us], otherwise, we know nothing. Both interpretations can be sustained, and even combined. For *kleos* implies a repetition of stories that, being merely human, is at once passive and a source of ignorance, and a repetition that is alive and creative as it repeats the voice of the Muses. Since the text leaves the two forms of repetition in an ambivalent relation, it in fact creates the situation that the Poet, according to his wishful thinking, envisages as ideal: to repeat human stories from the hypertext —which itself is not uninspired by the Muses— by repeating them according to the present voice of the Muses, and therefore to imprint in them the immediacy of a new, truthful perdormance. (See Pucci 1998, 31–48).

This ambivalence often takes recognizable forms and patterns, as we have seen: the Iliadic allusion to a previous text —even a quotation— appears not simply as a repetition, a reusing of a text, but a disapproval, or an amused or mocking rewriting of it. Unfortunately, the lack of the original model has made it impossible for us to decide. Analogously, by attributing to a "poetic voice" questions, disapproving comments, surprising apostrophes, invocations and similes, I suggest some sort of ambivalence: the text repeats the voice —the topic, etc.— of the Muses, but it melts into it human perspectives and interpreta-

---

instance, as the Poet is about to describe the confused battle around the wall, he declares: "Hard it is for me to say all this, as if I were a god." The Narrator identifies himself as the author of the description: his task is difficult since he is not a god, i.e. a Muse. Ford 1992, 78–9 illustrates the exact function of this line in its context: "The warriors rushing about indiscriminately are like the many traditions that crowd a poet's mind, seeking expression. A god might tell them all, but hard indeed is it for the mortal poet to say what was there to be seen. [...] The appearance of the Muses in the *Iliad*, book 2, is not simply a scene of instruction, but also one of selection."

tions. The Poet is handling two different voices. The Muses' inspiration is not unproblematic.

This point leads us to analyze the issue of "invention" (or "fiction") as a process by which the Poet(s) creates the plots and characters of the epic poems. The question is whether the Poet(s) of oral poetry were convinced that they were reciting the truth in the events they narrated, or were aware of inventing and imagining part or all of the narratives they produced before their public[10] (and whether the audiences were convinced of the narration's truth or were aware of its inventions).

The epic poets necessarily knew that they were narrating different versions of the same stories, and Hesiod confirms this when he asserts (*Theog.* 26–28) that the Muses are the sources of different versions. As he writes, the Muses — for inexplicable reasons— can "tell many lies that are similar [or even almost identical] to real things": such lies, because of their similarity to truth, could never be identified as lies by any poet or any audience.[11] Accordingly, a poet could always assert that his own version was exactly what the Muses saw and told him, and his assertion would receive the credit that the Narratees would accord to him also on other, general grounds: coherence in a longer narrative, persuasiveness, adherence to the central patterns of the myth, etc. In itself, his version would be correct and as basic as any other.[12] Divine things could appear

---

**10** See for instance a short treatment of this issue and a bibliography in Nünlist 1998, 13 ff., and the bibliography in Calame 2015, 632, n. 26.
**11** The Muses address Hesiod with the following words (*Theog.* 26–28):

ποιμένες ἄγραυλοι, κάκ' ἐλέγχεα, γαστέρες οἶον,
ἴδμεν ψεύδεα πολλὰ λέγειν ἐτύμοισιν ὁμοῖα,
ἴδμεν δ' εὖτ' ἐθέλωμεν ἀληθέα γηρύσασθαι.

"Field-dwelling shepherds, ignoble disgraces, mere bellies,
we know how to say many false things similar to real ones,
but we know, if we want, how to proclaim true things."

Christos Tsagalis (2006, 83 ff.) has amply reinterpreted this passage and has emphasized the connotation of "human truths" for *etuma* and "divine truths" for *alêthea*. In my view, the *etuma* become "false truths" and therefore "human truths" in contrast to the divine truths because they are "similar" (*homoia*) to the divine truths. The notions of "imitation," "invention" etc. are already perceived here as a difference that corrupts the identity of divine truths. Unfortunately, this difference cannot be read, since it is similar to the identity of the divine word. Thus, when the Muses speak that false language to the poets, they are giving them only a semblance of divine truth, something that, by contrast, can be called human truth.
**12** This theoretical and perhaps excessively dogmatic principle can be confirmed, though on different terms, by the practice of oral poetry as described by Nagy 1990, 130: "...in oral poetry,

in different lights to human eyes. Hesiod, for instance, lets his Narratee deduce, from the Muses' friendship with him, that the Muses inspire false stories — which nonetheless are similar to the truth— to other poets, but not to himself. But he cannot prove it, of course.[13] Since "invention" or "fiction" are perceived as modes of corruption, but cannot be detected in a text, they cannot be used to define the "nature" of an epic text: the "lies equal/similar to truth" are sung by the Muses themselves.

The *Iliad*, through the invocation to the Muses (II. 484–93), asserts the reality of the entire narrated event, but it remains unclear to what extent it asserts it depends on the Muses' inspiration.[14] I imagine that, as soon the Poet would begin to recite, the epic language would carry him out of the immediate coordinates of reality and the Poet might feel, or wishfully assume, that the inspiration was running through his mind and voice, whatever he would sing about. For the epic language itself had elaborated and lent crystallized brightness and stability to the very nature of gods and things. Yet the poet ought also to be aware of the complex construction he was composing through that language.

Poets learned the art through the training delivered to them by the Muses (the practicing *aoidoi*) and could see themselves as the artisans of the poetic construction (Calame 2015, pp. 79 ff.). They behaved in the contrary fashion to their characters, who forget or minimize divine help. Hector, as we have seen, feels he has been responsible for the death of Patroclos, even if he received such substantial help from Apollo, that we understand why the gods assert that Apollo killed Patroclos and gave the *kudos* to Hector. The Poet, on the contrary, minimizes his own responsibility and, through wishful thinking and a will to produce a divinely inspired image of himself for his audience, he enlarges his dependence on the divine. I recall here the point I made in the introduction: while the Poet is aware of the problematic imbalance that rattles the collaboration and permeability between humans and gods in the action of the Poem, he assumes that, in the case of the poetic production, divine inspiration is essential and unproblematic. Which, as we have seen, is not the case.

---

a given theme may have more than one version or variant, but such multiplicity of thematic variants does not mean that any one of them is somehow basic, while the others are derivative. In terms of any operating system of oral poetry, each thematic variant is but a multiform, and not one of any variants in a given isolated grouping may be treated as a sort of *Ur*-form. The same principle applies also to the study of myths in general." Other critics have also underscored the protection that the Poets' claim of repeating the words of the Muses granted them against the Narratee's criticism and abuse.

13 See Pucci 2007, 65–70 and Calame 2015, 632, n. 26.
14 The *Iliad* (II. 594–600) recalls Thamyris of Thracia who challenged the Muses, boasting that he would surpass even them in singing; and they in anger mutilated him, took away his power of song and his ability to play the lyre. On the meaning of the name Thamyris, see Nagy 1979, 311.

# Bibliography

Aceti, C./Leuzzi, D./Pagani, L. 2008. *Eroi dell'Iliade*. Rome.
Adkins, A.W.H. 1975. "Art, Beliefs and Values in the Later Books of the *Iliad*," in: *CPh* 70, 239–254.
Alden, M. 2000. *Homer Beside Himself*. Oxford.
Allan, W. 2006. "Divine Justice and Cosmic Order in Early Greek Epic," in: *JHS* 126, 1–35.
Allan, W. 2008. "Performing the Will of Zeus: the Dios *Boulê* and the Scope of Early Greek Epic," in: Revermann/Wilson 2008, 204–216.
Ameis, K.F./Hentze, C. 1913. *Homers* Ilias. Leipzig.
Andersen, O. 1987. "Myth Paradigm and Spatial Form in the *Iliad*," in: Bremer 1987, 1–12.
Arrighetti, G. 1998. *Esiodo*. Milano.
Auerbach, E. 1953. *Mimesis: The Representation of Reality in Western Literature* (trans. W.R. Trask). Princeton (German original 1946).
Austin, J.N.H. 1966. "The Function of Digressions in the *Iliad*," in: *GRBS* 7, 295–312.
Bakker, E. 1997. *Poetry in Speech. Orality and Homeric Discourse*. Ithaca.
Bakker, E. 2017. "Hector (and) the race horse: the telescopic vision of the *Iliad*," in: Chr. Tsagalis/A. Markantonatos (ed.), *The Winnowing Oar: New Perspectives on Homeric Studies*. Berlin, 57–74.
Bakker, E./Kahane, A. 1997. *Written Voices Spoken Signs*. Cambridge, MA.
Barmeyer, E. 1968. *Die Musen*. Munich.
Bassett, S.E. 2003 (1938). *The Poetry of Homer*. Lanham, MD.
Beck, D. 2012. *Speech Presentation in Homeric Epic*. Austin, Texas.
Bergson, L. 1956. *L'epithète ornamentale*. Lund.
Bespaloff, R. 1947. *On the* Iliad (trans. M. Mc Carthy). New York.
Borgeaud, Ph. 2004. *Exercices de mythologie*. Geneva.
Bonnet, C. 2016. "Gli dei in assemblea," in: Pironti/Bonnet, 113–146.
Bouvier, D. 2002. *Le sceptre et la lyre. L'Iliade ou les héros de la mémoire*, Grenoble.
Bouvier, D. 2016. "La scelta di Afrodite e le cause della Guerra," in: Pironti/Bonnet, 231–63.
Bowra, C.M. 1972. *Homer*. London.
Bremer, J.M./De Jong, I.J.F./Kalff, J. (eds.). 1987. *Homer: Beyond Oral Poetry. Recent Trends in Homeric Interpretation*. Amsterdam.
Bremmer, J.N. 1998. "'Religion', 'Ritual' and the Opposition 'Sacred' vs. 'Profane,'" in: F. Graf (ed.), *Ansichten griechischer Rituale*. Stuttgart/Leipzig, 9–32.
Brouillet, M. 2016. *Des chants en partage. L'epopée homerique comme expérience religieuse*. Paris.
Brügger, Cl. 2009. *Homers* Ilias *Gesammtkommentar*. Band VIII, 24. Gesang. Faszikel 2: Kommentar. Berlin.
Burgess, J.S. 2001. *The Tradition of the Trojan War in Homer and Epic Cycle*. Baltimore/London.
Burkert, W. 1955. *Zum altgriechischen Mitleidsbegriff*. Diss. Erlangen.
Burkert, W. 1985. *Griechische Religion der archaischen und klassischen Epoche*. Stuttgart 1977. [English Translation: *Greek Religion*. (trans. by J. Raffan)]. Cambridge, MA.
Cairns, D.L. 2001. *Oxford Readings in Homer's* Iliad. Oxford.
Calame, C. 2015. *Qu'est-ce que la mythologie grecque?* Paris.
Carastro, M. 2006. *La cité des mages*. Grenoble.
Cauer, P. 1921–23. *Grundfragen der Homerkritik*. 3rd. ed. Leipzig.
Cerri, G. 1999. *Omero. Iliade*. Intr. di W. Schadewalt. Trad. G. Cerri, Commento di A. Gostoli. Milan.
Chantraine, P. 1934. "Sur l'archaïsme des parties 'récentes' de l'Iliade. A propos de VIII, 1–52," in: *REG* 47, 282–96.

Chantraine, P. 1942. I. *Grammaire homerique*. 1953. vol. II. Paris.
Chantraine, P. 1952. "Le Divin et les Dieux chèz Homère," in: *La Notion du Divin d'Homère jusqu'à Platon*. Fondation Hardt pour l'Etude de l'Antiquité Classique, Entretiens sur l'antiquité classique 10, 47–94.
Clarke, M. 1999. *Flesh and Spirit in the Songs of Homer*. Oxford.
Clauss, J.J./Cuypers, M./Kahane, A. (eds.). 2016. *The Gods of Greek Hexameter Poetry*. Stuttgart.
Codino, F. 1965. *Introduzione a Omero*. Torino.
Collobert, C. 2011. *Parier sur le temps. La quête héroïque d'immortalité dans l'épopée homérique*. Paris.
Coray, M. 2009. *Homers Ilias Gesammtkommentar*. Band VI, 19. Gesang. Faszikel 2: Kommentar. Berlin.
Daraki, M. 1980. "Le héros à *menos* et le héros δαίμονι ἶσος. Une polarité homérique," in: *ASNP* 10, 1–24.
Dawe, R.D. 1967. "Some Reflections on *Atê* and *Hamartia*," in: *HSPh* 72, 96–97.
De Cristofaro, L. 2014. "L'episodio Iliadico di Glauco e Diomede," in: *Rivista di Cultura Classica e Medioevale* 56, 11–54.
De Jong, I.J.F. 2001. *A Narratological Commentary on the* Odyssey. Cambridge.
De Jong, I.J.F. 2004. *Narrators, Narratees, and Narratives in Ancient Greek Literature*. Leiden.
De Jong, I.J.F.[2] 2004. *Narrators and Focalizers. The Presentation of the Story in the* Iliad. Amsterdam (1st ed. 1987).
De Jong, I.J.F. 2012. *Iliad. Book XXII*. Cambridge.
De Man, P. 1979. *Allegories of Reading*. Yale.
De Romilly, J. 1983. *Perspectives actuelles sur l'épopée homérique*. Collège de France. Essais et Conférences. Paris.
De Romilly, J. 1997. *La mort d'Hector*. Paris.
Derrida, J. 1967. *De la grammatologie*. Paris.
Derrida, J. 2003. *Voyous*. Paris.
Detienne, M. 1967. *Les maîtres de vérité dans la Grèce archaïque*. Paris.
Diano, C. 1970. *Il concetto della storia nella filosofia dei Greci*. Florence.
Di Benedetto, V. 1994. *Nel laboratorio di Omero*. Turin.
Dietrich, B.C. 1967. *Death, Fate and the Gods*. London.
Dodds, E.R. 1951. *The Greeks and the Irrational*. Berkeley/Los Angeles.
Doherty, L.E. 1995. *Siren Songs. Gender, Audiences and Narrators in the* Odyssey. Ann Arbor.
Dubel, S. 2011. "Changement de voix: sur l'apostrophe dans *l'Iliade*," in: E. Raymond (ed.), *Vox Poetae*, Paris, 129–144.
Dué, C. 2010. "Agamemnon's Densely-Packed Sorrow in *Iliad* 10: A Hypertextual Reading of a Homeric Simile," in: C. Tsagalis, *Homeric Hypertextualily*, Trends in Classics 2.2.
Durante, M. 1976. *Sulla preistoria della tradizione poetica Greca*. Rome.
Edwards, M.W. 1987. *Homer. Poet of the* Iliad. Baltimore.
Edwards, M.W. 1991. *The Iliad: A Commentary*. Volume V: books 17–20. Cambridge.
Elmer, D.F. 2013. *The Poetics of Consent*. Baltimore.
Erbse, H. 1986. *Untersuchungen zur Funktion der Götter in homerischen Epos*. Berlin.
Fagles, R. 1990. *The Iliad*. (trans. by R.F.). New York.
Feeney, D. 1993. *The Gods in Epic. Poets and Critics of the Classical Tradition*. Oxford.
Fenik, B. 1968. *Typical Battle Scenes in the Iliad. Studies in the Narrative Tehnique of Homeric Battle Description*. Wiesbaden.
Finkelberg, M. 1995. "Patterns of Human Error in Homer," in: *JHS* 115, 15–28.
Foley, H.P. 1978. "Reverse Similes' and Sex Roles in the *Odyssey*," in: *Arethusa* 11, 7–26.

Foley, J.M. (ed.) 2005. *A Companion to Ancient Epic*. Oxford.
Ford, A. 1992. *Homer. The Poetry of the Past*. Ithaca/London.
Fränkel, H. 1921. *Die homerischen Gleichnisse*. Göttingen.
Gaskin, R. 2001. "Do Homeric Heroes Make Real Decisions?," in: Cairns 2001, 147–69.
Gernet L./Boulanger, A. 1932. *Le génie grec dans la religion*. Paris.
Gill, Ch. 1996. *Personality in Greek Epic, Tragedy and Philosophy. The Self in Dialogue*. Oxford.
Goldhill, S.D. 1991. *The Poet's Voice. Essays on Poetics and Greek Literature*. Cambridge.
Gostoli, A. 1999. *Omero. Iliade*. Traduzione di G. Cerri. Commento di A. Gostoli. Milan.
Griffin, J. 1980. *Homer on Life and Death*. Oxford.
Griffin, J. 1995. *Homer.* Iliad *Book Nine*. Oxford.
Hainsworth, B. 1993. *The Iliad. A Commentary*. Volume iii: books 9–12. Cambridge.
Havelock, E.A. 1978. *Dike*. Cambridge.
Heidegger, M. 1950. *Holzwege*. Frankfurt am Main.
Heiden, B. 1997. "The Ordeals of the Homeric Gods," in: *Arethusa* 30, 221–240.
Heiden, B. 2008. *Homer's Cosmic Fabrication. Choice and Design in the* Iliad. Oxford.
Heubeck, A. 1981. *Omero Odissea* vol. I. Libri I–IV. A cura di A. Heubeck e S. West. Traduzione di G.A. Pivitera. Milan.
Higbie, C. 1995. *Heroes' Names. Homeric Identities*. New York/London.
Hirvonen, K. 1968. *Matriarchal Survival and Certain Trends in Homer's Females Characters*. Helsinki.
Hoekstra, A. 1965. *Homeric Modification of Formulaic Prototypes*. Amsterdam.
Holoka, J. 1983. "Looking Darkly. Reflections on Status and Decorum in Homer," in: *TAPA* 113, 1–16.
Janko, R. 1992. *The Iliad: a Commentary*, vol. iv: books 13–16. Cambridge.
Jedrkiewicz, S. 2014. "Simile o uguale? Il contesto mitologico della formula δαίμονι ἶσος nell'*Iliade*," in: A. Pérez Jiménes (ed.). 2014. *Realidad, Fantasia, Interpretación, Functiones y Pervivencia del Mito Grieco*. Málaga.
Judet de la Combe, P. 2017. *Homère*. Paris.
Kahane, A. 1994. *The Interpretation of Order : a Study in the Homeric Poetics of Repetition*. Oxford.
Kahane, A. 2005. *Diachronic Dialogues. Authority and Continuity in Homer and the Homeric Tradition*. Lanham.
Kahane, A. 2018. "The complexity of Epic Diction," in: *YAGE* 2, 1–54.
Kakridis, J.Th. 1949. *Homeric Researches*. Lund.
Kelly, A. 2007. *A Referential Commentary and Lexicon to Homer. Iliad VIII*. Oxford.
Kirk, G.S. 1985. *The Iliad: A Commentary*. Vol. 1 (Books 1–4). Cambridge.
Kirk, G.S. 1990. *The Iliad: A Commentary*. Vol. 2, (Books 5–8). Cambridge.
Kullmann, W. 1956. *Das Wirken der Götter in der Ilias*. Berlin.
Kullmann, W. 2012. "Neoanalysis between Orality and Literacy," in: F. Montanari/A. Rengakos/Chr. Tsagalis (eds.). *Homeric Contexts*. Berlin, 13–25.
Lamberton, R.D. 1986. *Homer the Theologian*. Berkeley.
Lasserre, E. 1965. *Homère. L'Iliade*. Paris.
Latacz, J. 1999. *Homer. His Art and His World*. (trans. by J.P. Holoka). Ann Arbor, Michigan.
Latacz, J. 2000. *Homers Ilias Gesamtkommentar*. Band I, 1. Gesang. Faszikel 2: *Kommentar*. Munich.
Lattimore, R. 1951. *Iliad of Homer*. Chicago/London.
Leaf, W. 1902. *The Iliad*. 2 vols. London.
Lesky, A. 1961. "Göttliche und menschliche Motivierung im homerischen Epos." Heidelberg: SHAW 1961, Abh. 4.
Letoublon, F. 1983. "Défi et combat dans l'*Iliade*," in: *REG* 96, 27–48.

Letoublon, F. 1987. "Le messager fidèle," in: Bremer etc., 123–44.
Lloyd, G.E.R. 1996. *Polarity and Analogy. Two Types of Argumentation in Early Greek Thought.* Cambridge.
Lloyd-Jones, H. 1971. *The Justice of Zeus.* Sather Classical Lectures 41. Berkeley/Los Angeles/London.
Lohmann, D. 1970. *Die Komposition der Reden in der* Ilias. Berlin.
Loraux, N. 1986. *The Invention of Athens: The Funeral Oration in the Classical City.* Cambridge, MA.
Louden, B. 2005. "The Gods in Epic or the Divine Economy," in: Foley 2005, 90–104.
Lowell, E. 2005. "Epic and Myth," in: Foley 2005, 31–44.
Lowenstam, S. 1981. *The Death of Patroclos. A Study in Typology.* Königstein.
Lucci, C. 2011. *Le diverse percezioni del tempo nell'Epica Greca Arcaica.* Pisa.
Macleod, C.W. 1982. *Homer Iliad: Book XXIV.* Cambridge.
Mahaffy, J.P. 1881. *Über den Ursprung der homerischen Gedichte.* Hannover.
Maehler, H. 1963. *Die Auffassung des Dichterberufs im frühen Griechentum bis zur Zeit Pindars.* Hypomnemata 3. Göttingen.
Marks, J.R. 2001. *Divine Plan and Narrative Plan in Archaic Greek Epic.* Ph.D. Thesis, University of Texa, Austin.
Martin, R.P. 1983. *Healing, Sacrifice and Battle.* Innsbruck.
Martin, R.P. 1989. *The Language of Heroes.* Ithaca.
Martin, R.P. 2005. "Epic as Genre," in: Foley 2005, 9–19.
Mondolfo, R. 1958. *La comprensione del soggetto umano nell' antichità classica.* Florence.
Montanari, F. 1992. *Introduzione a Omero.* Florence.
Moulton, C. 1974. "Similes in the *Iliad*," in: *Hermes* 102, 381–397.
Moulton, C. 1977. *Similes in the Homeric Poems.* Göttingen.
Muellner, L. 1976. *The Meaning of the Verb EUXOMAI through its Formulas.* Innsbrücker Beiträge zur Sprachwissenschaft 13. Innsbrück.
Muellner, L. 1997. "The Alienation of Achilles: on the Artistic Control of the Traditional Poet," in: F. Létoublon (ed.), *Hommage à Milman Parry: le style formulaire de l'épopée et la théorie de l'oralité poétique.* Amsterdam, 147–157.
Mülder, D. 1910. *Die* Ilias *und ihre Quellen.* Berlin.
Murnaghan, S. 1997. "Equal Honor and Future Glory. The Plan of Zeus in the *Iliad*," in: D.H. Roberts/F.M. Dunn/D. Fowler (eds.). *Classical Closure.* Princeton.
Murray, G. 1924. *Rise of the Greek Epic.* Oxford.
Murray, A.T. 1995. *Homer. The Odyssey.* With an English Translation by A.T. Murray. Revised by G.E. Dimock. Cambridge, MA.
Naas, M. 1995. *Turning: From Persuasion to Philosophy: A Reading of Homer's* Iliad. New Jersey.
Nagy, G. 1979. *The Best of the Achaeans.* Baltimore/London.
Nagy, G. 1990. *Greek Mythology and Poetcs.* Ithaca/London.
Nagy, G. 2003. *Homeric Responses.* Austin.
Nagy, G. 2005. "The Epic Hero," in: Foley 2005, 71–89.
Nagy, G. 2013. *The Ancient Greek Hero in 24* Hours. Cambridge, MA.
Nannini, S. 1995. *Nuclei tematici nell'Iliade.* Florence.
Nannini, S. 2003. *Analogia e polarità in similitudine.* Amsterdam.
Nünlist, R. 1998. *Poetologische Bildersprache in der frühgriechischen Dichtung.* Stuttgart/Leipzig.
Otto, W. 1955. *The Homeric Gods.* London.
Pagliaro, A. 1956. *Nuovi saggi di critica semantica.* Messina/Florence.
Parker, R. 2011. *On Greek Religion.* Ithaca/London.

Pasquali, G. 1968. "La scoperta dei concetti etici nella Grecia antichissima," in: *Pagine meno stravaganti*. Florence, 288–303.
Peigney, J. 2011. "La voix de l'aède au chant 16 de l'Iliade et la colère de Patrocle," in: Raymond 2011, 145–56.
Pelliccia, H. 1995. *Mind, Body and Speech in Homer and Pindar*. Hypomnemata 107. Göttingen.
Pelloso, C. 2012. *Themis e dike in Omero. Ai primordi del diritto dei Greci*. Alessandria.
Perpillou, J.L. 1996. *Recherches lexicales en Grec ancien*. Louvain/Paris.
Perceau, S. 2011 "Voix auctoriale et interaction de *l'Iliade* à *l'Odyssée*: de l'engagement éthique à la figure d'autorité" in: Raymond 2011, 33–56.
Piettre, R. 1996. *Le corps des dieux dans les épiphanies divines en Grèce ancienne*. Paris. Thèse de doctorat. École Pratique des Hautes Études.
Pirenne-Delforge, V./Pironti, G. 2016. *L'Héra de Zeus. Ennemie intime, épouse definitive*. Paris.
Pironti, G. 2007. *Entre ciel et guerre. Figures d'Aphrodite en Grèce ancienne*. Liège.
Pironti, G. 2009. "Les dieux Grecs entre polyvalence et spécificité," in: *Europe* 87, n. 964–65, 289–304.
Pironti, G./Bonnet, C. 2016. *Gli dei di Omero. Politeismo e poesia nella Grecia antica*. Rome.
Pucci, P. 1977. *Hesiod and the Language of Poetry*. Baltimore/London.
Pucci, P. 1987. *Odysseus Polytropos: Intertextual Readings in the Odyssey and in the Iliad*. Ithaca.
Pucci, P. 1994. "Peitho nell' «Orestea» di Eschilo," in: *Museum Criticum* 29, 75–138.
Pucci, P. 1998. *The Song of the Sirens. Essays on Homer*. Lanham.
Pucci, P. 2002. "Theology and Poetics in the *Iliad*," in: *Arethusa* 35, 17–34.
Pucci, P. 2003. "Prosopopée d'Helène," in: M. Broze/L. Couloubaritsis/A. Hypsilanti/P. Mavromoustakos/D. Viviers (eds.), *Le mythe d'Hélène*. Brussels, 89–119.
Pucci, P. 2003a. Review of I.J.F. De Jong 2001. *A Narratological Commentary on the* Odyssey, in: *Classical Philology* 98, 81–87.
Pucci, P. 2007. *Inno alle Muse* (Esiodo Teogonia, 1–115). Testo, introduzone, traduzione e commento a cura di P. Pucci. Pisa/Roma.
Pucci, P. 2007. "Euripides and Aristophanes. What Does Tragedy Teach?," in: Chr. Kraus/S. Goldhill/H.P. Foley/J. Elsner (eds.), *Visualizing the Tragic*. Oxford, 105–126.
Pucci, P. 2010, "The Splendid Figure of *Kudos*," in: *Lexis* 28, 201–225.
Raymond, E. 2011. *Vox Poetae*. Paris.
Ready, J. 2011. *Character, Narrator, and Simile in the* Iliad. Cambridge.
Redfield, J.M. 1975. *Nature and Culture in the* Iliad. *The tragedy of Hector*. Chicago.
Renehan, R. 1987. "The Heldentod in Homer," in: *CPh* 82, 99–116.
Reinhardt, K. (1938) 1960. "Das Parisurteil," in: *Tradition und Geist. Gesammelte Essays zur Dichtung*. Göttingen 1960, 16–36.
Reinhardt, K. 1961. *Die Ilias und ihr Dichter*. Göttingen.
Rengakos, A. 2006. "Homer and the Historians: the Influence of Epic Narrative Technique on Herodotus and Thucydides," in: *La poésie épique grecque: Metamorphoses d'un genre littéraire*. Entretiens sur l'antiquité classique, vol. LII. Geneva, 183–214.
Revermann, M./Wilson, P. (eds). 2008. *Performance, Iconography, Reception. Studies in Honour of O. Taplin*. Oxford.
Richardson, N. 1993. *The Iliad: A Commentary*. Volume 6: books 21–24. Cambridge.
Rösler, W. 1980. "Die Entdeckung der Fiktionalität in der Antike," in: *Poetica* 12, 283–319.
Rossi, L.E. 1994. "L'epica greca fra oralità e scrittura," in: *Reges et Proelia. Orizzonti e atteggiamenti dell'epica antica*. Dipartimento di Scienze dell'Antichità dell'Università di Pavia. Como, 29–43.

Rousseau, P. 1995. Διὸς δ' ἐτελείετο βουλή. *Destin des héros et dessein de Zeus dans l'intrigue de l'Iliade*. Thèse d'état. Lille.
Rudhardt, J. 1992. "De l'attitude des Grecs à l'égard des religions étrangères," in: *RHR* 209, 1992, 219–238.
Rudhardt, J. 1999. *Themis et les Horai*. Geneva.
Ruijgh, C.J. 1971. *Autour de Te Épique: Études sur la syntaxe grecque*. Amsterdam.
Rutherford, R.B. 2001. "From the *Iliad* to the *Odyssey*," in: Cairns 2001, 117–146.
Sacks, R. 1987. *The Traditional Phrase in Homer*. Leiden.
Samoyault, T. 2015. *Roland Barthes*. Paris.
Schnapp-Gourbeillon, A. 1981. *Lions, héroes, masques: les répresentations de l'animal chez Homère*. Paris.
Scott, W.C. 2009. *The Artistry of the Homeric Simile*. Hanover/London.
Seaford, R. 1994. *Reciprocity and Ritual: Homer and Tragedy in the Developing City-State*. Oxford.
Schäfer, M. 1990. *Der Götterstreit in der Ilias*. Stuttgart.
Scodel, R. 2017. "Homeric fate, Homeric poetics", in: Chr. Tsagalis/A. Markantonatos (ed.), *The Winnowing Oar: New Perspectives on Homeric Studies*. Berlin, 75–93.
Shipp, G.P. 1972. *Studies in the Language of Homer*. 2nd ed. Cambridge.
Shive, D. 1987. *Naming Achilles*. Oxford.
Sinos, D. 1980. *Achilles, Patroklos, and the Meaning of Philos*. Innsbruck.
Slatkin, L. 1991. *The Power of Thetis*. Berkeley.
Snell, B. 1960. *The Discovery of the Mind*. (trans. T.G. Rosenmeyer). New York.
Steinrück, M. 2016. *Vers und Stimme*. Trieste.
Taplin, O. 1992. *Homeric Soundings*. Oxford.
Tarenzi, V. 2005. "Patroclos *therapôn*," in: *QUCC* 80, 23–38.
Thornton, A. 1984. *Homer' Iliad: its Composition and the Motif of Supplication*. Hypomnemata 81. Göttingen.
Tsagalis, C. 2008. *The Oral Palimpsest. Exploring Intertextuality in the Homeric Epic*. Washington DC.
Tsagalis, C. 2012. *Space in the Iliad*. Washington DC.
Tsagalis, C. 2016. "The Gods in Cyclic Epic," in: Clauss 2016, 95–117.
Van Hille, G.E.W. 1938. "Zu Homers *Ilias* IV 351–355," in: *Mnemosyne* 6, 252–260.
Vernant, J.-P. 1965. *Mythe et pensée chez les Grecs*, Paris.
Vernant, J.-P. 1979 "PANTA KALA. D'Homère à Simonide," in: *Annali della Scuola Normale Superiore di Pisa* 9, 1365–74.
Vernant, J.-P. 1982. "La Belle Mort et le cadavre outragé," in: G. Gnoli/J.P. Vernant (eds.). *La Mort, les morts dans les sociétés anciennes* Cambridge/Paris, 45–76. = "A Beautiful Death and the Disfigured Corpse in Homeric Epic," in: J.P. Vernant, *Mortals and Immortals: Collected Essays*. Princeton 1991 = Cairns 2001, 311–341.
Vivante, P. 1991. *The Iliad. Action as Poetry*. Boston.
Weiss, M. 1998. "Erotica: on the Prehistory of Greek Desire," in: *HSCPh* 98, 31–81.
West, M.L. 1997. *The East Face of Helicon. West Asiatic Elements in Greek Poetry and Myth*. Oxford.
West, M.L. 2001. *Studies in the Text and Transmission of the Iliad*. Munich/Leipzig.
West, M.L. 2007. *Indo-European Poetry and Myth*. Oxford.
West, M.L. 2011. *The Making of the Iliad*. Oxford.
West, S. 1981. *Omero Odissea*. Vol. I. Libri I–IV. A cura di A. Heubeck e S. West. Traduzione di G.A. Privitera. Milan.
Whitman, C. 1958. *Homer and the Heroic Tradition*. Cambridge.
Wilamowitz-Moellendorf, U. von. 1916. *Die Ilias und Homer*. Berlin.

Wildberg, Chr. 1999–2000. "Piety as Service, Epiphany as Reciprocity: Two Observations on the Religious Meaning of the Gods in Euripides," in: *ICS* 24–25, 235–256.
Willcock, M.M. 1978. *Homer. Iliad*. London.
Willcock, M.M. 2001. "Mythological Paradeigma in the *Iliad*," in: Cairns 2001, 435–455.
Wilson, D. 2002. *Ransom, Revenge, and Heroic Identity in the* Iliad. Cambridge.
Winkler, M. (ed.) 2007. *Troy. From Homer's* Iliad *to Hollywood Epic*. Malden, MA.
Zanker, G. 1996. *The Heart of Achilles. Characterization and Personal Ethic in the* Iliad. Ann Arbor.

# Index of Rhetorical and Critical Notions

allusion 4, 14, 28, 50, 58, 87, 124, 150, 158, 162, 163, 172, 175, 177f., 186, 188f., 207, 209, 236, 242, 247, 249, 266
ambiguity (see also polysemy) 2, 4 n. 5, 32 n. 2, 38, 56, 73, 78, 119 n. 90, 120, 131, 168, 206 n. 16, 218, 221, 251
ambivalence 2, 3, 37, 90, 121, 179, 222, 266
*andróphonos* 47 n. 39
anthropomorphy 2f., 5f., 11f., 16, 19, 53ff., 65, 70, 78, 89, 129, 131, 136, 151, 173, 179, 181, 185, 210, 212, 218f., 220f., 232, 242, 250, 253, 255f., 264
apostrophe 7, 61, 87, 108, 114, 117, 148, 226f., 266
assembly 1, 18, 21, 22–5, 30, 52, 54, 127, 139, 143, 149, 151f., 153–161, 167f., 175, 193ff., 234
assonance 10, 55, 88, 261, 265
asymmetry 205, 246, 253, 263
*atê* 42, 84, 109f., 119, 138–148
autocracy 21 n. 51, 170, 192, 253
autonomy 40, 46, 61, 92, 108ff., 199
authority 6, 9, 17, 18, 19, 23, 25, 34, 51, 62, 87, 93, 101, 128, 139, 149, 151, 158, 161, 163, 166, 171, 175, 180, 190, 194, 196f., 217, 225, 245, 248, 255
being of things 21, 67, 77f., 118 n. 83, 121, 128, 229, 262
beauty 24, 65–7, 115, 176, 179, 189, 237, 258, 260f.
belief 73, 84, 122, 127, 145, 147, 150, 229
brother (see also enemy brothers) 196f., 199
*boulê* 3, 5, 16, 42, 45, 53, 55, 61, 66, 68, 83, 86, 98, 99, 107, 112, 114, 119, 131, 142, 149, 153, 168, 170, 175, 177, 221, 251
Cartesian Principle 121
chiasmus 9, 21, 23, 47, 60, 89, 261
collaboration 3, 7, 36, 153, 163, 184, 193, 218, 230, 232, 239, 244, 247, 249, 252, 268
comedy 26, 173, 188, 201–222, 231
compensation 13, 70ff., 76, 78–81, 125, 138, 140, 219, 235, 248
conflict 2f., 6, 15, 17, 21, 28, 35, 45, 53f., 70, 86, 100f., 117, 146f., 157, 161, 184, 195, 199, 213f., 218, 221f., 230, 250, 253, 256, 259
conspiracy 41, 58, 68–75, 103–118, 164, 174
contradiction 2, 32, 35–38, 52, 99, 110, 129, 185, 213, 246
convergence 43, 45, 64, 83, 100, 110, 124
cosmos 67, 241
*dîos* 50 n. 48, 85, 203 n. 7, 259–262
deterrence 25, 154, 190
double truth 147
double voice 118–123
double truth 117, 147
edifying 22, 33, 37f., 63, 65, 77f., 96, 184, 238, 249, 253, 262
endurance 3, 27, 132, 234f.
enemy brothers 18
epiphany 2, 6, 43, 60, 65, 75f.
equal to a god 101, 111, 113f., 258
equal to Ares 83
etymology 139, 201, 259
Father of Men and Gods 23, 50, 55, 101, 149, 188, 192, 196, 245, 252, 254
focalization 49, 79, 174

forecast (see also prophecy) 34 n. 7, 39 n. 20, 83
free will 3, 34, 43, 63f., 110, 122, 140f., 147, 150
frivolity 173
Golden Scales 19, 32, 38, 47, 49, 55f., 66, 78, 128f., 136, 160, 182, 199, 213, 231, 256
grey-eyed Athena 158, 162, 164–66
heroic death 37, 45f., 62f., 72, 76f., 80, 125, 134
heroism 49, 57, 67, 79, 82, 97, 133, 228, 235f., 251f.
*hippodamos* 47 n. 39
honor (see also *time*) 13 n. 20, 14f., 23 n. 56, 34, 42, 54, 72f., 82, 84, 86 n. 11, 91, 93 n. 30, 97 n. 37, 98–101, 105f., 130, 158, 171, 196ff., 231f., 237 n. 76, 240f., 247 n. 99
human condition 3, 7, 54, 64, 79, 136, 235, 251
humor 173, 181, 205, 251
hybrid, hybridism (see also permeability) 2f., 7, 49, 110, 116, 120ff., 134, 148, 249f., 253
hymn 20, 31, 176f., 180, 241, 249
hypertext 3f., 9, 18, 25, 77, 79, 102, 122, 146, 156, 162, 173, 175, 190, 201, 209, 213, 249, 250f., 265f.
immortality 37, 40, 62, 72, 96, 201, 241, 251f., 258, 261
indifference 25, 38, 217, 234, 237, 241
instrument 33, 45, 55–7ff., 120, 241, 245
ipsocracy 154
invincible hands 24, 94f., 103, 128, 167, 176, 199
irony 23, 69, 101, 111, 113, 122, 136, 158, 169, 203, 218, 227–30, 247, 251
jealousy 4, 18, 173, 184, 188f., 191

justice 5, 12, 32, 38, 127f., 150, 152, 155, 209, 254
*kelainephês* 64
*kleos* 37, 45, 77, 80ff., 86, 102, 112, 117, 201, 266
*kudos* 45, 67, 73ff., 80ff., 103, 117, 119ff., 138, 167, 218, 239, 248, 268
laughter 29
madness (see *Atê*)
*mênis* 12, 153
metapoetic 54, 61, 114, 162, 166, 198
mimetic effects 38
might (French «Puissance») 2–5, 10, 33, 42, 53, 55, 78, 113, 138, 180, 182, 249, 256, 259
mockery 61, 79, 86ff., 156, 158, 163, 210
monologue 43f., 46, 60f., 123
*mêtieta Zeus* 15 n. 27 , 73
monotheism 5, 150, 174
motivation 1–5, 19, 26, 29, 36, 38, 43, 45, 51, 63, 87, 93, 100f., 108ff., 112, 117, 124, 127, 141, 148, 155, 164, 178, 186, 199, 208ff., 212, 217, 219ff., 229, 234, 237f., 251
Muses' inspiration 46, 76, 267f.
Muses' lies 6f. n. 8, 121f., 265ff.
*mysterium* 67, 112, 122, 214, 251
necessity 19, 133, 160, 197, 211, 214, 256f.
*nephelêgereta* 16 n. 31, 17, 20, 27 n. 65, 64
nodding 17, 19f., 35, 69, 74
orality 146
order of the world 6, 19, 66f.
oxymoron 101, 211f., 218f., 221
pairing 56, 91–103, 116, 123
parody 4, 29, 60, 123, 145, 205, 222, 228, 231, 251, 253
paradox 2f., 5, 7, 33, 38, 48f., 52, 57, 63, 69f., 72, 75, 77–82, 101, 108, 112, 123,

125, 130ff., 136ff., 146, 164f., 199, 227, 231ff., 247, 250, 252, 256
permeability (see porousness, hybridism) 2f., 6f., 33, 53, 76–9, 96, 122, 190, 218, 246, 252f., 256, 261–3, 265, 268
persecution 4, 189
perversion 22, 24, 65, 79, 110, 115, 120, 145, 156, 165, 178f., 182, 189, 201–222, 225–7, 230f.
pity 2, 32, 34–41, 50, 54, 56, 69, 78f., 85f., 90, 92, 111, 124, 126, 136f., 148, 161, 221, 233f., 238
piety 3, 6, 50f., 53f., 62, 150, 213f., 237, 251
plot 4, 9, 13, 19, 22, 50, 97, 105, 111, 143f., 156f., 175, 185, 191, 194, 201, 218, 248, 267
poetic voice or poet's voice 6, 48, 54, 61–3, 65–8, 77–82, 84, 92, 108f., 111, 123, 146, 148, 151, 157, 166, 179, 198, 220, 225, 227f., 243, 262, 266–8
polysemy (see also ambivalence) 174 n. 56
polyvalence 54, 65, 89
porousness 2, 33, 53, 235, 263
prophecy (see Forecast) 26, 76f., 81f., 118, 169 n. 43, 193
provocation 22, 25, 31, 175, 206, 208
psychology 1, 9, 18, 27, 44, 46, 52f., 78, 85ff., 101, 129, 131, 146, 162, 169, 213ff., 218, 221, 249f.
quotation 58, 89, 143ff., 163, 166, 169, 255f.
regret 78, 131ff., 135ff., 172, 211, 214, 218, 221
religion 39, 265
repetition 10, 17, 26, 32, 57f., 66, 70, 79, 84, 87, 108, 113, 124f., 146, 159, 165, 167, 169, 176, 179, 183, 186f., 195, 223f., 226, 236, 244, 266

revolution 4, 54, 146, 192, 253
reticence 5f., 8, 39, 208, 217, 222
ritual 2f., 10ff., 39, 48, 51, 53, 56ff., 62, 83, 86, 91, 94, 103f., 125, 135ff., 204, 214, 218, 220, 222, 231–4, 238, 242f., 246, 249
script 34
succession myth (see also enemy brothers) 25, 56 n. 61, 154, 163 n. 30, 174f.
simile 7, 30, 47–50, 64–8, 78, 80, 83–9, 116–120, 127f., 136, 178, 222f., 226, 228, 231, 236, 240f., 261, 263, 266
sky god 17
soliloquy 7, 43–46, 60f., 68f., 79, 122
song for men of the future 132
supplement 91, 95–103, 123, 261
teaching 147
temporal module 55, 111, 113
theology 1, 5, 8, 63, 65, 7f., 149, 151f., 210, 214, 253
*timè* (see also honor) 15, 237 n. 73, 237f., 247
tradition 4, 11f., 16, 18, 25, 28, 31f., 34, 59, 77, 82, 89, 125f., 128, 139, 146, 153, 156, 158, 162–4, 171, 174f., 179f., 183f., 188f., 204, 209f., 215, 249ff., 253, 255, 265
Troy 1, 4f., 16, 32, 36–39, 42–47, 50, 52–4, 57, 73, 82, 87, 94, 98–103, 107, 109–112, 123, 128, 130–3, 161f., 189, 193f., 198f., 204, 206–221, 225, 227–34, 237, 240, 250f., 253f.
trick 37, 45, 52, 54, 58, 60, 74, 110, 140–7, 161, 183, 190, 205, 218, 228, 250
theography 9
theriomorphic epithet, image 24, 26, 37, 176

violence 3ff., 13, 21, 24f., 28, 67, 113, 114, 117, 122, 133, 151, 168, 190, 195ff., 240, 249, 256, 260
world order 6, 19, 35, 66f.

wrath of Achilles 12, 15f., 76, 83–91, 93, 102, 107, 131, 140, 142, 146, 201, 230, 260
writing 137, 146, 263

# Index Locorum

*Amos*
3–7  155

Archil.
fr. 13, 5–7  234 n. 68

Aristotle
*Poetics* 1460a11–17  54 n. 54

*Cypria*
fr. 1  209 n. 25

Herodotus
2.53  255f.

Hesiod
*Theogony*
26–9  6f. n. 8, 267f.
211–12  185 n. 78
217–9  234 n. 68
36ff.  31
103  127 n. 13
318  162 n. 24
383ff.  185
842  167 n. 35
904–06  234 n. 68

*Catalogue of Women*
fr. 155  209 n. 25

*Erga*
90–104  128
252–62  254f.
718  127 n. 13

[Hesiod]
*Scutum*
1225–7  162 n. 24

Homer
*Iliad*
I. 1
I. 3–5  107, 210 n. 28
I. 5–7  259f.

I. 55  24 n. 59
I. 70  67
I. 74  56 n. 63
I. 141  258
I. 152–62  209 n. 25
I. 169ff.  124 n. 1
I. 171  16 n. 28
I. 175  14f.
I. 186ff.  195 n. 97
I. 195  24 n. 59
I. 202–18  12 n. 16
I. 208  24 n. 59
I. 231–2  13 n. 22
I. 244  16 n. 28
I. 247ff.  200
I. 332–3  167
I. 341  88 n. 18
I. 348ff.  86f.
I. 352  13 n. 19
I. 357–9  89 n. 22
I. 363  87
I. 396–406  13, 20, 56 n. 61, 163f., 175
I. 408–9  13 n. 22
I. 410  191 n. 89
I. 414  137 n.43
I. 417  136
I. 421–2  10, 142
I. 449–50  154
I. 469–74  30 n. 73, 31
I. 488  10
I. 493–530  9 n.1
I. 494–5  9
I. 498–9  9f.
I. 500–01  10, 12, 16 n. 31, 57 n. 68
I. 503–10  12ff.
I. 505  13 n. 19
I. 505–06  16 n. 28
I. 507  14
I. 508  13 n. 21, 15
I. 511–12  16f.
I. 512–16  17
I. 515–16  16 n. 28
I. 517  16 n. 31, 17
I. 517–25  17

I. 518ff.  26, 157 n. 11
I. 522  18
I. 524–30  18ff., 35, 69 n. 100, 78, 105, 151f.
I. 528  10
I. 531–5  21
I. 533–69  18 n. 39
I. 533–604  22
I. 536–7  22
I. 540–3  22
I. 545–50  22f., 180
I. 551  24 n. 59, 26 n. 62
I. 552  168 n. 42
I. 555–9  17 n. 37, 23f., 57 n. 68
I. 560ff.  37 n. 17
I. 561–7  23, 180
I. 567  24 n. 58
I. 568  26 n. 62
I. 570–6  26f.
I. 572  24 n. 59
I. 578–83  26f.
I. 580  26f. n. 64
I. 587–94  27f., 190
I. 595  24 n. 59
I. 596–600  28f.
I. 601-04  30 with n. 73
I. 609  26f. n. 64

II. 3–6  106 n. 52
II. 102  10 n. 9
II. 111  140 n. 52
II. 112  17 n. 33
II. 118–19  13 n. 18
II. 196–7  15
II. 205  32 n. 2
II. 299–332  121
II. 319  32 n. 2
II. 419  220 n. 38
II. 484–7  264f.
II. 484–93  6f.
II. 594–600  268 n. 14
II. 669  13 n. 18

III. 36  66
III. 100  230 n. 56
III. 112  137
III. 139–40  167 n. 34
III. 142  85 n. 8

III. 156–60  204 n. 11, 209 n. 25
III. 164–5  132 n. 27, 149 n. 71
III. 171–180  209 n. 25
III. 276–80  220
III. 300–01  220
III. 302  205 n. 14
III. 330–8  202
III. 351–4  203f., 229
III. 354–60  209 n. 25
III. 365–7  204f.
III. 373–82  205
III. 379–80  35 n. 10
III. 441–42  187

IV. 1–4  201f.
IV. 1–72  25 n. 60
IV. 5–6  206f.
IV. 7–14  207
IV. 10–11  238 n. 77
IV. 17–19  207f.
IV. 24–9  208
IV. 25  36 n. 14, 168 n. 42
IV. 30  16 n. 31
IV. 30–5  208f., 217
IV. 34–6  209
IV. 40–9  50 n. 47, 211ff.
IV. 51–6  214ff.
IV. 56  37 n. 17
IV. 57–67  17, 180 n. 68, 216
IV. 58–9  180 n. 67
IV. 66–7  228
IV. 68–72  223, 225 n. 46
IV. 70–2  216, 220, 228
IV. 74–80  222f.
IV. 81–4  224
IV. 84  13 n. 18
IV. 89–91  226
IV. 93–103  224f.
IV. 104  225 n. 46
IV. 105–11  226
IV. 127–31  30, 227f.
IV. 158–68  228f.
IV. 163–8  204 n. 11
IV. 165  229 n. 56
IV. 169–75  225f., 229
IV. 268–71  228 n. 53
IV. 409  148 n. 68

V. 1–8   81
V. 382–400   235
V. 392–4   189 n. 85
V. 437–44   111 n. 61
V. 445   35 n. 10
V. 588   16 n. 31
V. 662   35 n. 10
V. 670   236 n. 70
V. 721   11 n. 10, 180
V. 733–7   164f.
V. 738ff.   182
V. 745–7   164f.
V. 747   165
V. 906   217 n. 36

VI. 128ff.   40 n. 22
VI. 142–9   136 n. 40
VI. 156   40 n. 22
VI. 198–99   188 n. 84
VI. 353   191 n. 89
VI. 357–8   132 n. 27
VI. 476–81   60 n. 74
VI. 526–9   60 n. 74

VII. 38   47
VII. 178   66
VII. 200   10 n. 9
VII. 202   66
VII. 320
VII. 454   16 n. 31
VII. 478   15 n. 27
VII. 478–9   153 n. 2

VIII. 1–40   18 n. 40
VIII. 1–52   153
VIII. 2–4   153f.
VIII. 5–6   143 n. 59
VIII. 5–27   21, 37 n. 17
VIII. 10ff.   156, 171
VIII. 11   153
VIII. 17   154f.
VIII. 13–14   185
VIII. 17   154
VIII. 19–27   155f., 156 n. 8
VIII. 23–6   157, 192
VIII. 28–9   158, 195
VIII. 30   166 n. 33

VIII. 30–4   158f.
VIII. 31ff.   158 n. 13, 168f.
VIII. 35–7   159
VIII. 38–40   16 n. 31, 32, 159f., 164
VIII. 69   38 n. 19
VIII. 72   198 n. 103
VIII. 130–6   252 n. 103, 254
VIII. 169–83   70 n. 104
VIII. 170   15 n. 27
VIII. 185–97   171
VIII. 199   167 n. 35
VIII. 199–207   177
VIII. 204   171 n. 50
VIII. 205–7   171
VIII. 209–11   172, 195
VIII. 218–19   159 n. 15, 160
VIII. 245   73
VIII. 247   64 n. 86
VIII. 358–61   162
VIII. 360–73   161f.
VIII. 362–9   189 n. 85
VIII. 367–9   163
VIII. 370–4   159 n. 17, 162
VIII. 373   164, 166
VIII. 383   11 n. 10, 179
VIII. 384–91   164f.
VIII. 389–91   164f.
VIII. 391   165
VIII. 401–05   168
VIII. 406   164
VIII. 406–8   165ff., 192f.
VIII. 420–5   164 n. 32
VIII. 423–4   166
VIII. 438–83   18 n. 40
VIII. 442–3   167
VIII. 446   167
VIII. 447–56   167f.
VIII. 456   192
VIII. 462   36 n. 14, 168 n. 42
VIII. 462–7   168
VIII. 462–8   160 n. 21, 169
VIII. 470–7   34 n. 7
VIII. 470–82   169f.
VIII. 471–7   159 n. 18
VIII. 477b–83   170
VIII. 478–81   11

VIII. 484  237
VIII. 530  24 n. 58

IX. 14–15  84
IX. 18  141 n. 52
IX. 19  17 n. 33
IX. 25  13 n. 18
IX. 37  32 n. 2
IX. 115ff.  84
IX 115–19  139 n. 49, 140 n. 52
IX. 240  258
IX. 300–02  90
IX. 337–40  209 n. 25
IX. 358–61  169 n. 43
IX. 410–16  124, 131
IX. 412–15  81
IX. 427–9  124 n. 1
IX. 495  88 n. 18
IX. 496–7  90
IX. 501ff.  142
IX. 511–12  148 n. 69
IX. 524–99  102
IX. 571  139 n. 46
IX. 624–42  90
IX. 650–5  93 n. 31, 97

X. 104  15 n. 27
X. 231  236 n. 70
X. 498  236 n. 70

XI. 16–48  177
XI. 44–5  179
XI. 52ff.  107
XI. 62  223
XI. 182–209  159 n. 15
XI. 200  53 n. 52
XI. 278  15 n. 27
XI. 604  83 n. 2
XI. 611  56 n. 63
XI. 631–7  104, 235
XI. 659–62  88 n. 15
XI. 690  189 n. 85
XI. 785–8  87f.
XI. 794ff.  91
XI. 794–803  88 n. 15

XII. 90  73
XII. 175
XII. 200ff.  73
XII. 201  64 n.65
XII. 236  17 n. 33
XII. 241–42  13 n. 18
XII. 275  26f n. 64
XII. 292  15 and n. 27
XII. 308  15
XII. 310ff.  15
XII. 319  32 n. 2
XII. 402–03  35 n. 10
XII. 450  32 n. 2

XIII. 1–10  174
XIII. 345  11 n. 10, 172 n. 52
XIII. 352  174, 195
XIII. 353–7  195f.
XIII. 355  197 n. 99
XIII. 357  174
XIII. 362  17 n. 33
XIII. 454–6  218
XIII. 458  106
XIII. 516–20  194 n. 94
XIII. 569  136 n. 38
XIII. 620–5  229 n. 56
XIII. 796–7  20
XIII. 822  64 n. 86

XIV. 23  106
XIV. 60  178
XIV. 85–7  80 n. 16
XIV. 153ff.  174
XIV. 153–353  176
XIV. 153–XV. 77  173ff.
XIV. 159  24 n. 59
XIV. 159–62  175f.
XIV. 167–9  177
XIV. 169–72  171
XIV. 173–4  178
XIV. 178  178
XIV. 181  177
XIV. 184–5  178f.
XIV. 194  11 n. 10, 179
XIV. 197ff.  22 n. 53, 144 n. 63, 174, 180
XIV. 215–17  181f.
XIV. 217  187 n. 82

XIV. 222   24 n. 59
XIV. 231–37   182f.
XIV. 243   11 n. 10, 179
XIV. 249–56   183
XIV. 250–5   162, 184, 188
XIV. 256ff.   190
XIV. 263   24 n. 59
XIV. 270–9   185, 193
XIV. 293–6   186f.
XIV. 300   22 n. 53, 144 n. 63
XIV. 313–16   186f.
XIV. 314–28   143 n. 58, 187f.
XIV. 323–34   189 n. 85
XIV. 329   22 n. 53, 144 n. 63
XIV. 330   36 n. 14, 168 n. 42
XIV. 346   190
XIV. 347   258

XV. 4–270   190
XV. 4–77   34 n. 7
XV. 16–17   191
XV. 16–32   25 n. 60, 37 n. 17, 162
XV. 18–20   191
XV. 24–300   191
XV. 25–6   189 n. 85
XV. 31–3   192
XV. 36–46   192
XV. 39   193
XV. 49–55   193f.
XV. 62–77   198
XV. 64–7   34f., 83, 101 n. 46, 118 n. 86, 204 n. 10, 213 n. 33
XV. 64–77   98f., 194
XV. 68   42 n. 25, 53 n. 51
XV. 69–77   34 n. 7
XV. 70–1   42, 100, 161 n. 23, 194, 212f., 219, 228
XV. 72–7   199
XV. 87–112   194 n. 94
XV. 152   10 n. 8, 244 n. 90
XV. 153   20
XV. 163–5   195 n. 96
XV. 176–83   194f.
XV. 184–6   196
XV. 187–8   11 n. 10
XV. 194–9   196f.
XV. 201–4   197

XV. 206–7   197f.
XV. 208–17   198f.
XV. 221–35   198
XV. 224–5   195 n. 98
XV. 226–8   195 n. 98, 199
XV. 234–5   198f.
XV. 370–1   66
XV. 374   17 n. 33
XV. 377   15 n. 27
XV. 390–6   87
XV. 597   9ff., 16, 100
XV. 598   72f.
XV. 598–9   16 n. 29
XV. 610–14   72, 110
XV. 612   72
XV. 639–40   189 n. 85
XV. 690–5   64f., 68
XV. 718–25   70 n. 104

XVI. 2–4   2ff., 83f.
XVI. 7–19   85f.
XVI. 11   85 n. 8
XVI. 19   87
XVI. 21   87
XVI. 22   88
XVI. 31–5   88f.
XVI. 36–43   90f.
XVI. 40–1   97
XVI. 46–7   92, 114 n. 70
XVI. 58–61   107
XVI.60–3   93
XVI. 64–7   94, 97 n. 38
XVI. 74–5   98
XVI. 80–2   97 n. 38
XVI. 82   97
XVI. 83–6   91
XVI. 89–90   99
XVI. 95–6   97 n. 38
XVI. 97–100   100
XVI. 99–100   112
XVI. 101–24   100
XVI. 119–25   101
XVI. 126–9   100ff.
XVI. 140–4   95 n. 34
XVI. 179–81   51
XVI. 207   90
XVI. 203–04   90

XVI. 221–4   104
XVI. 225–48   103
XVI. 225–7   104
XVI. 233   203f.
XVI. 236–7   98 n. 41
XVI. 237   15
XVI. 241–5   94f., 103
XVI. 249   15 n. 27
XVI. 249–52   103ff., 204
XVI. 273–4   94
XVI. 349   15
XVI. 365   258
XVI. 381   129 n. 17
XVI. 384–8   127 n. 15
XVI. 421ff.   51
XVI. 431–2   32 n. 3, 50 n. 46, 180 n. 67
XVI. 433–8   32ff.
XVI. 434   34
XVI. 440–4   36f., 168 n. 42, 208 n. 24
XVI. 443   208 n. 24
XVI. 454–5   40
XVI. 458–61   39, 105, 107f.
XVI. 492–501   39 n. 20
XVI. 521–2   40
XVI. 563–8   105, 138 n. 44
XVI. 638   34 n. 8
XVI. 644–55   138 n. 44
XVI. 652–5   106
XVI. 658   38 n. 19
XVI. 670   39
XVI. 671–3   40
XVI. 678   34 n. 8
XVI. 680   39
XVI. 684–93   108f.
XVI. 685ff.   140 n. 53
XVI. 686–91   114 n. 70, 138 n. 44
XVI. 688   139 n. 48, 141
XVI. 693   61
XVI. 698–709   111f.
XVI. 701ff.   113
XVI. 707–11   101 n. 45, 109, 113
XVI. 717   47
XVI. 730   103
XVI. 752–61   117f.
XVI. 779–85   105
XVI. 783–93   112f.
XVI. 786–9   114f.

XVI. 793–800   68 n. 97, 69 n. 99
XVI. 796–9   115
XVI. 799-800   115f.
XVI. 804–5   119
XVI. 823–8   116ff.
XVI. 833–6   119
XVI. 844–5   74 n. 108, 113 n. 66
XVI. 844–50   109 n. 60, 118f.
XVI. 847–8   122
XVI. 849–50   41 n. 24, 120
XVI. 867   129 n. 17

XVII. 177–8   108 n. 56
XVII. 200–10   68ff.
XVII. 204   135 n. 34
XVII. 206–8   110
XVII. 207   71
XVII. 210ff.   68, 73f.
XVII. 401–11   94 n. 33, 106
XVII. 426–54   134f.
XVII. 434   137
XVII. 441   37f.
XVII. 441–3   137
XVII. 443–7   135f.
XVII. 448ff.   137
XVII. 454–5   138
XVII. 459ff.   138
XVII. 514   149 n. 71
XVII. 545   106
XVII. 669   135 n. 34

XVIII. 35ff.   242
XVIII. 39   89 n. 19
XVIII. 54–64   137 n. 43
XVIII. 58–9   37 n. 18
XVIII. 93   71
XVIII. 94   128 n. 17
XVIII. 95   13 n. 19
XVIII. 95–100   124f.
XVIII. 115–16   76f.
XVIII. 117–21   77, 162
XVIII. 121–5   70
XVIII. 172   169 n. 44
XVIII. 254–83   43 n. 30
XVIII. 293   32 n. 2
XVIII. 293–5   45
XVIII. 305–91   60 n. 74

XVIII. 361   36 n. 14, 168 n. 42
XVIII. 364–6   17
XVIII. 394–405   28
XVIII. 450ff.   119
XVIII. 451–2   101 n. 46

XIX. 18   129 n. 17
XIX. 85–90   84, 149 n. 71
XIX. 86–90   139f.
XIX. 95–133   140 n. 51, 189 n. 85
XIX. 96–7   22 n. 53, 144
XIX. 100   145 n. 65
XIX. 100–105   143f., 188 n. 84
XIX. 105–7   22 n. 53, 144 n. 63, 145 n. 65
XIX. 137–8   139f.
XIX. 216   87
XIX. 219   196 n. 99
XIX. 223   38 n. 19
XIX. 224   13 n. 18
XIX. 257   66
XIX. 259–60   197 n. 102
XIX. 270–4   140ff.
XIX. 282ff.   135 n. 34
XIX. 315–37   94 n. 33
XIX. 323   85 n. 8
XIX. 369–91   177
XIX. 387–91   95 n. 34
XIX. 409–10   140 n. 50, 149 n. 71
XIX. 443–7   213
XIX. 490–94

XX. 4–12   154
XX. 30   152 n. 76
XX. 127–8   234 n. 68
XX. 145–9   189 n. 85
XX. 183   164
XX. 201   244 n. 93
XX. 204   265
XX. 321ff.   35 n. 10
XX. 336   151 n. 76
XX. 432   244 n. 93
XX. 435   149 n. 71
XX. 443–4   57

XXI. 83–4   41 n. 24
XXI. 272   66
XXI. 388–90   156 n. 10

XXI. 406   74 n. 107
XXI. 440   196 n. 99
XXI. 461ff.   136
XXI. 517   151 n. 76
XXI. 526   259
XXI. 597   35 n. 10

XXII. 3   50 n. 45
XXII. 5   53 n. 51, 63, 74, 83, 128, 141, 235 n. 68
XXII. 5–6   41
XXII. 7–20   57
XXII. 15   204 n. 13
XXII. 20   57 n. 68
XXII. 25–32   43 n. 29, 65 n. 88, 223
XXII. 94   209 n. 26
XXII. 99–110   43f.
XXII. 110   45
XXII. 116   204 n. 11
XXII. 123–4   234 n. 67
XXII. 129–30   60 n. 74
XXII. 130   63
XXII. 131–5   65 n. 88
XXII. 133   66 n. 92
XXII. 147–56   47
XXII. 158–60   47
XXII. 162–6   48ff.
XXII. 167   149 n. 70
XXII. 167–76   50f.
XXII. 182–5   52ff.
XXII. 183ff.   60 n. 76, 160
XXII. 205–7   120
XXII. 208–13   38 n. 19, 55f., 129
XXII. 211   47
XXII. 213   136 n. 40
XXII. 216   56 n. 63
XXII. 216–17   80
XXII. 216–223   56ff.
XXII. 217   81
XXII. 217–18   120 n. 91
XXII. 247   226
XXII. 261–72   59f., 79
XXII. 270–1   75
XXII. 276–7   59f.
XXII. 279   60, 261
XXII. 295   60 n. 75
XXII. 297–305   60f., 134

XXII. 300–3  122
XXII. 308–11  64
XXII. 312  67
XXII. 317–20  65f., 179
XXII. 319–27  67 n. 95
XXII. 330  74
XXII. 347ff.  210 n. 27
XXII. 365–6  76
XXII. 391–4  74f., 261
XXII. 392  80
XXII. 393  81
XXII. 822  119

XXIII. 56
XXIII. 272  135 n. 34
XXIII. 279ff.  135 n. 34
XXIII. 281  135 n. 34
XXIII. 283–4  135 n. 34
XXIII. 312  198 n. 99
XXIII. 367  20

XXIV. 2–18  233 n. 63
XXIV. 3ff.  232
XXIV. 18–22  233
XXIV. 22  234
XXIV. 27–30  234
XXIV. 33ff.  233 n. 64
XXIV. 44–54  234f., 238
XXIV. 49  132 n. 26
XXIV. 66–70  50 n. 47, 211f. n. 31, 237
XXIV. 71–6  238f.
XXIV. 77–88  239f.
XXIV. 82–4  238, 244
XXIV. 83–6  135 n. 32, 232, 242
XXIV. 90–2  239, 241
XXIV. 93–6  242f.
XXIV. 98–100  10 n. 8, 244
XXIV. 103  149 n. 70
XXIV. 104–05  244f.
XXIV. 106–19  245ff.
XXIV. 113–14  237
XXIV. 131–3  246
XXIV. 209–10  127 n. 11
XXIV. 210  82
XXIV. 212ff.  210 n. 27
XXIV. 314  15 n. 27
XXIV. 315  64 n. 86

XXIV. 408–09  233
XXIV. 449–51  234 n. 68
XXIV. 465–7  126 n. 9
XXIV. 478–9  126 n. 9
XXIV. 493  130 n. 19
XXIV. 503–6  126 n. 9, 236
XXIV. 507–55  112
XXIV. 527–33  13 n. 18, 126f., 149
XXIV. 534  129 n. 17
XXIV. 534–8  127 n. 11
XXIV. 534–42  129f.
XXIV. 538–40  126
XXIV. 532  259
XXIV. 541–2  131
XXIV. 547–9  128
XXIV. 547–51  131f.
XXIV. 720–2  243
XXIV. 804  47

*Odyssey*
i. 5–8  148f.
i. 26–40  149ff.
i. 34  151
i. 45  158 n. 13
i. 65–7  53 n. 52
i. 66  150 n. 74
i. 81  158 n. 13
i. 267  149 n. 71
i. 347–9  149 n. 71

v. 82–4  189 n. 86
v. 105  136
v. 221–4  236 n. 70
v. 456  151 n. 76

vi. 188–90  149 n. 71

vii. 197

viii. 314–18  28
viii. 579  127 n. 11

xi. 319  127 n. 11
xi. 478  87
xi. 558–60  149 n. 71
xi. 626  162 n. 24

xiii. 291ff.  53 n. 52

xvi. 64  127 n. 11
xvi. 129  149 n. 71
xvi. 332  85 n. 8

xx. 196  127 n. 11

xxii. 403  209 n. 26

xxiv. 473  158 n. 13
xxiv. 482–6  254
xxiv. 516ff.  254
xxiv. 539–40  254

[Homer]
*Hymn to Aphrodite*
33–44  180
58–65  177

*Hymn to Dionysos*
13–150  20f. n. 48

Pisander
*Heracles and Theseus*
fr. 7  162 n. 24

Plato
*Apology*
28  62 n. 83
*Euthyphron*
14d–15a  147
*Rep.*
380b6–7  129 n. 16
579d1ff.  129 n. 16

Psalms
82  155
89. 35 [34]  19

www.ingramcontent.com/pod-product-compliance
Lightning Source LLC
Chambersburg PA
CBHW020327240426

43665CB00044B/788